Mafia M.
The Judith Exner Story
The Life of the Mistress of
John F. Kennedy

by Sam Sloan

Plus excerpts by
Judith Campbell Exner

ISHI PRESS
INTERNATIONAL

Mafia Moll: The Judith Exner Story
The Life of the Mistress of John F. Kennedy

Copyright © February, 2008 by
Sam Sloan
and Ishi Press International

Excerpts © 1977 by
Judith Campbell Exner

All rights reserved according to International Law. No part
of this book may be reproduced by any mechanical,
photographic or electronic process nor may it be stored in a
retrieval system, transmitted or otherwise copied for public
or private use without the written permission of the
publisher.

ISBN 0-923891-90-0

Ishi Press International
1664 Davidson Avenue, Suite 1B
Bronx NY 10453
USA
917-507-7226

Printed in the United States of America

Table of Contents

This book was created in separate sections and then was assembled together. As a result, the pages in each section are individually numbered. What follows are the actual page numbers, with the current page being page number 3.

There are six text sections and six photographic and graphics sections. The six sections of photographs and graphics are labeled "Sisters", "Evidence", "Rivals", "Rogues", "News" and "Jewels". These labels are only somewhat explanatory. The Rogues include Mafia wise guys. The Rivals include a few of other women who slept with Kennedy or Sinatra. This is just in general. There are many exceptions:

Exner Prologue

The name of Judith Immoor Campbell Exner (1934-1999) would probably never be known today had it not been for the investigations of the *Church Committee*, named after Senator Frank Church, a United States Senator from Idaho who was running for president. The Church Committee is the common term referring to the *"United States Senate Select Committee to Study Governmental Operations with Respect to Intelligence Activities"* chaired by Senator Frank Church in 1975. The Church Committee was investigating reports that the CIA had tried to assassinate Cuban President Fidel Castro and Congo President Patrice Lumumba. Both assassination attempts had been unsuccessful. Lumumba had been killed on January 17, 1961, three days before Kennedy took office as president, but not by the CIA, rather by other Congolese. Fidel Castro is, of course, still alive.

In hindsight, the investigations by the Church Committee must be considered one of the bright and shining moments of US History. Nowadays, such an investigation would be unthinkable. Everything would be covered up. If there were an investigation at all, it would be why the assassination attempts failed. What kind of incompetents do we have at the CIA anyway? An additional factor is that the investigation was bi-partisan. Nowadays, you have only the Democrats investigating the Republicans or the Republicans investigating the Democrats. However, the Church Committee was investigating both the Republican Administration of President Eisenhower and the Democratic Administration of President Kennedy. It was clear that both assassination plans originated under Eisenhower. By the time Kennedy took office on January 20, 1961, Lumumba was already dead, and the attempts to kill Castro involving a wide variety of devices including poison pills and exploding cigars, had all failed. The plan to kill Castro was said to have been abandoned after the Bay of Pigs fiasco on April 17-20, 1961. However, Kennedy continued to attempt to overthrow Castro, but not necessarily to kill him, until Kennedy himself was killed on November 22, 1963. For this reason, one of the leading theories as to why Kennedy was killed continues to be retaliation by Castro.

The Mafia had their own reasons for wanting to kill Castro. The Mafia had controlled casino operations in Cuba. John Roselli, who later became involved with Judith Immoor Campbell Exner, was for many years the manager of a casino in Cuba. Casino operations were closed down and Roselli was thrown out when Castro took over the Government of Cuba on January 8, 1959.

Thus, the idea that the CIA would hire and pay the Mafia to kill Castro is not as ridiculous as it might seem today. It was a natural fit. The Mafia wanted to get their casinos back, and the CIA of course wanted to restore Democracy plus Truth, Justice and the American Way by killing Castro.

The Church Committee found that Sam "Momo" Giancana and John Roselli had been offered $150,000 by the CIA to kill Castro. But how did the CIA and the Mafia communicate with each other ? Does the CIA just pick up a telephone, dial a number, and call the Mafia? "Hello, Mr. Mafia. This is the CIA calling. We would like for you to kill Castro and for this service we will pay you $150,000." Did it work like that?

No. It could not have been like that. There must have been an intermediary. Perhaps a woman. Yes, that's the ticket! Some completely undistinguished woman, an unknown person, a high school dropout, a person nobody would ever suspect.

But who was that woman? Who was the mystery woman?

That was indeed the question being asked all around the world, when the story finally broke: WHO WAS THE MYSTERY WOMAN?

I know this because I was staying in Reykjavik, Iceland at the time with my lady friend Inga Brandsdottir, who was a long-distance telephone operator. She came home one night with a newspaper with a big headline saying in Icelandic *"Who Is the Mystery Woman?"*. The entire world wanted to know.

JFK'S MYSTERY WOMAN

Los Angeles Times Dec 16, 1975; pg. A1

Kennedy Friend Denies Role in Plot to Kill Castro

𝕿𝖍𝖊 𝕹𝖊𝖜 𝖄𝖔𝖗𝖐 𝕿𝖎𝖒𝖊𝖘   December 18, 1975

The first mention of her name came in an article in the Washington Post on November 16, 1975 on page 6A entitled *"Probers Doubt Kennedy Knew of Poison Plot Against Castro"*. However, this story got the sequence of events backwards, suggesting that the Mystery Woman might have told Kennedy about the Mafia's plans to kill Castro. The real situation proved to be the other way around.

This article attracted little attention until one month later when on December 16, 1975 William Safire in *The New York Times* accused the Church Committee of covering up the true nature of the relationship between President Kennedy and the Mystery Woman.

Two days later, on December 18, 1975, headlines in the Los Angeles Times blared, *"John Kennedy's Mystery Woman Tells Her Story"*. The Story of Judith Immoor Campbell Exner, a previously unknown person, a person whose name had never appeared in any major print publication, nor in any radio, TV or news broadcast, was suddenly the focus of the attention of the entire world.

Considering that everyone who saw her remembers her as a spectacular beauty, there are surprisingly few pictures of Judith that survive.

We can best get an idea of how beautiful Judith Immoor was by looking at pictures of her sister, Jacqueline, who was a minor movie star under her screen name of "Susan Morrow".

A picture of Jacqueline is in the upper left. The other three pictures are of Judith. The picture in the lower left seems to be the earliest picture that can be found off Judith. It was taken while she was a teenager.

Judy Loves Billy

Every description of the marriage between Judith Immoor and William Campbell describes it from her point of view, saying that he was a womanizer, a drunkard and so on. The movie "Power and Beauty" depicts him inquiring about Doris Day at a party and then Judith catches him making out with a Doris Day-lookalike.

However, to his credit, William Campbell has never said a bad word about Judith. Not one word. When the "Mafia Moll" Scandal broke, William Campbell said only that he could not understand how Judith got involved in this, since she is completely non-political.

William Campbell is, like Judith, a Catholic, and after Judith divorced him he never remarried. Divorce is, of course, prohibited by the Catholic Church. Other than the claims and statements by Judith, there is no record of him being a drunkard. The gossip columns make no mention of him dating other women. William Campbell is still to this day alive and is active in the film industry as a studio executive and sometimes still appears as an actor, especially in the Star Trek Series. One suspects that William Campbell is not as bad a guy as Judith made him out to be.

This and the following two pages are photos from the August 1955 issue of *Movie Stars Parade* magazine, page 42. This picture, taken three years after they were married, shows them to be the epitome of marital bliss. Obviously they did not have a lot of money, as it says that they live in a "cozy home".

Bill and Judy live in a cozy Early American-style home, high in the Hollywood Hills. They're looking for something bigger, hope to start a family soon. No nightlifers, the Campbells prefer quiet evenings playing Scrabble, looking at home movies or planning motor trips.

Here is a picture of Judith playing SCRABBLE with her husband, William Campbell. We always just knew that she must be a scrabble player! Who would have imagined the sexy siren that she was known to have become a few years later.

■ **BILL CAMPBELL** really hit his stride when he starred in Caryl Chessman's own story, *Cell 2455, Death Row*. Any actor who could make so brutal a character both believable and sympathetic must be stardom-bound. Bill, who's tall, dark and 28, has been acting since he was a high-school senior in Newark, N. J. He got a thorough training in summer stock and road companies before being tapped for Hollywood. Almost the first person he met there was Judy Inmore, a pretty, black-haired model. She was a blind date but she sure looked good to Bill. And vice versa. They were married on October 25, 1952, honeymooned at Del Coronado. They still like to return there for golfing weekends, but they don't manage it often. Bill's schedule is too full. His latest starrer: *The Lock and the Key* for Batjac.

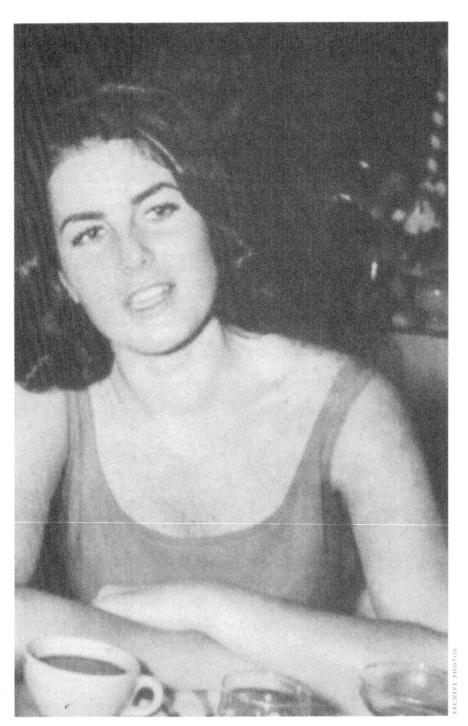

Judith Campbell Exner

ARCHIVE PHOTOS

Judith with her husband Daniel Exner on her way to testify before a Senate Committee. Dan Exner looks like a low-lifer compared to the President, Movie Stars and Mafia Dons with whom Judith had been sleeping previously. Note that Judith is wearing large, dark glasses to hide her appearance. This demonstrates that she was not seeking publicity.

Right photo: Dan and Judith Exner waiting with her assigned counsel, right in the photo, preparing to answer questions from the Church Committee of the United States Senate.

William Campbell singing with Elvis Presley in the 1956 movie "*Love Me Tender*". This is one of the few and perhaps the only time that any other singer shared center stage with Elvis. There were several other first-and-lasts in this movie. It was the only movie where Elvis did not have top billing. The star was Richard Egan. It was also the only Elvis movie where the leading lady, Debra Paget, left, was beautiful. It has been theorized that Col. Tom Parker, his manager, did not want beautiful women in Elvis movies, because that would distract the audience away from Elvis. Debra Paget was one of the very few women who ever got to kiss Elvis in a movie. Elvis almost never kissed or did anything else with women in the movies or in real life.

As to what made Elvis great, when Frank Sinatra sang, he had a full orchestra to accompany him. However, Elvis went on stage alone, just strumming his guitar and sometimes in *Love Me Tender* sang without even his guitar. Elvis was perhaps the only singer who could hold an audience without instrumental backup.

Judith Campbell was still an attractive woman at age 41 when she testified before the Church Committee of the United States Senate in 1975. She wore large, dark glasses to hide her appearance and to make identification difficult.

This is strong evidence that she did not want publicity.

The other two pictures are from her interviews late in life.

Copyright 1955 COLUMBIA PICTURES CORP. Property of Columbia Pictures Corporation. Printed in U.S.A.

Permission is hereby granted to newspapers, magazines and other periodicals to reproduce this photograph for other than advertising purposes, shall not be sold, resold or given away.

Here is a publicity photo of William Campbell for the 1955 movie *Cell 2455, Death Row*. In this movie he played Caryl Whittier Chessman, "the Red Light Bandit", who raped women by flashing a red light at them pretending to be a police officer and getting them into his car. The woman in the picture is Marian Carr. Notice that while kissing the woman here he is also holding a pistol.

One can easily imagine that Judith would suspect her husband of sleeping with his leading lady here, especially since she was divorced at the time, but there is no evidence or even rumors linking them together.

Publicity photo of William Campbell for the 1955 movie *Cell 2455, Death Row.*

Introduction

I have been debating the case of Judith Campbell Exner on the Internet since the mid-1990s. I have been the main one to defend her, often the only one to defend her. I feel that there is nothing wrong with what she did. Many women would like to have lived her life, if only they had the beauty and the charm that were her native attributes. The most common remark about her was that she looked like Elizabeth Taylor, only more beautiful.

There have consistently been those who attack her generally, stating that she was in this for the money, trashing the Kennedy name for her own financial benefit. She has been compared to the riding master or the butler of Princess Diana, men got to sleep with a beautiful woman and then got paid huge amounts of money writing for the British tabloids about it.

There have been those who even claimed that Judith Exner was malingering, faking her illness with lung cancer in order to justify getting paid for allowing herself to be interviewed about her relationship with President Kennedy.

I disagree. The record clearly shows that Judith Campbell never tried to exploit her relationship with the president. She never spoke about it except to her close friends. Nobody knew about it except for FBI Agent Dodge and other FBI and CIA agents who followed her for years. It was only through secret FBI documents that the Church Committee learned of her existence and of her relationship with the president.

She was subpoenaed and compelled to testify. It is often suggested that somebody in the Republican Party leaked the information about her existence to the press, so as to embarrass the Democrats due to her relationship with Kennedy, a Democratic President. There is no known basis for this claim. The leak could have come from many sources. Any of the Congressmen or Senators, their aids, office staffs or even stenographers, pages, maids and other

Congressional workers could have been the source of the leaks.

Once the news was out, Judith Exner did the right thing. It has been suggested that she feared being killed. If she did feel this way, it was not an irrational belief. Almost everybody who is mentioned in her story had been killed or died under mysterious circumstances. This includes John F. Kennedy and Robert F. Kennedy plus Mafia wiseguys Sam Giancana, John Roselli and Manny Skar, plus other Kennedy mistresses Marilyn Monroe and Mary Pinchot Meyer, plus the list of mysterious deaths of all of the people associated with the Kennedy Assassination.

If those people were killed to keep them quiet and to prevent them from testifying, her best strategy, once being exposed, was to tell all she knew right away. Once everything she knew had been published, she would have no secrets to hide and thus there would be no reason to kill her. I do not know if that was the reason behind her "tell all" book but, if it was, it was a good reason.

Judith Exner complained that she never got paid anything for her book "*My Story*". She had been promised $100,000. She believed that the IRS had taken it for a tax lien on her husband's golf winnings. It seems unlikely that this was the case. She was apparently not aware that Grove Press was essentially bankrupt and out of business at the time it agreed to publish her book. No other publisher would touch her book for fear of being sued. It was fortunate that Ovid Demaris was available, probably agreeing to be her collaborator on speculation.

History must thank her for telling us what she knew.

I have included in this book a number of the key newspaper articles and CIA reports, not for their factual content, but to show how the story broke, which explains what happened in what order. First, there was a mention in the *Washington Post* that President Kennedy had a "friend" who was also a friend of Mafia personalities. This report was not considered a big deal. Lots of people have friends. The initial 349-page Church Committee report did not state the gender of the friend nor did it explain the nature of the "friendship". As a result, there was nothing further for the next month about this friendship.

It was only when one month later William Safire revealed that the "friend" was a woman and accused the Church Committee of covering up the true nature of the relationship, that a world-wide frenzy developed that within two days forced Judith Campbell to come out of hiding.

In short, the claim that she was trying to exploit her relationship with the president is totally untrue.

Many statements often seen about her are inaccurate. For example, it is said that she was a "failed movie actress" or that she was trying to get into the movies. It seems unlikely that this was true. If she had wanted to be in the movies, she easily could have been. Her sister Jackie was a successful actress who appeared in 28 films. Judith often accompanied her sister to movie parties and events. This is how she came to meet many famous movie stars. Judith did interview once for Joe Pasternak, a well known movie producer. He said that she had some talent and told her to come back in six months. However, she never returned. It seems that Judith did not have the desire, the drive, the ambition or the willingness work hard that is necessary to become a movie star.

Never mind the casting couch issue. It is believed that during that era it was virtually a requirement for a female actress to sleep with the producer in order to get a part in a movie. Natalie Wood, age 16, is believed to have slept with the director and the producer and at least one of the stars to get her breakthrough role in *"Rebel Without a Cause"*. Perhaps Judith was not willing to make the supreme sacrifice. However, in the case of Sinatra movies, Judith had met the required criteria, because she had slept with Sinatra. It seems that every or almost every leading lady in any Sinatra movie had spent at least one night with Frank Sinatra.

Introduction

Those who knew Judith best paint an entirely different picture of her. Her ex-husband, William Campbell, said that she was "a bit introverted" and was not outgoing. Columnist Liz Smith describes her as "soft spoken".

Her renowned great beauty did not come about by accident. She slept late and then spent hours every day bathing and preparing her hair and clothing, although she did not put anything on her face, which was good enough. Sadly, few pictures survive of her except for pictures taken when she was testifying before the Church Senate Committee, when she was wearing large, dark glasses to hide her appearance.

There are only four pictures from the time when she was young and her beauty was at its peak that are used over and over again. One of these was from a photo machine booth where you put in a quarter and after one minute a strip of four pictures comes out. This is regrettable, as everybody who reads about her wants to see a good picture of her to see if she was really as beautiful as everybody who saw her says that she was.

Sam Sloan

Introduction Page No. 4

Starting in 1977, Judith Campbell Exner produced several items of evidence to prove that she did indeed have a close personal relationship with President Kennedy. Here is some of that evidence.

Judith often rejected or returned gifts that she received. However in August 1961, Judith accepted a gift from Kennedy of a large diamond and ruby broach. She describes the broach on page 239-240 of "*My Story*" as similar in design to a daisy. Each pedal is 18 carot gold and each has a cluster of nine or ten rubies in the center. It has about thirty full cut diamonds set in platinum on the edge.

Here is a picture of that broach.

After Kennedy was elected president, Judith was invited to the White House to attend the Inaugural Ball. At first, Judith was going to go but finally she decided not to go for fear of embarrassing Jackie Kennedy.

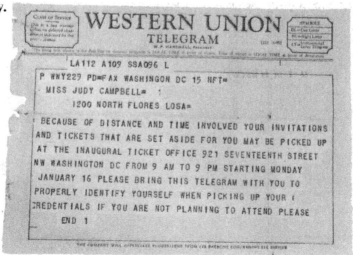

In August 1961, Judith accepted a gift from Kennedy of a large diamond and ruby broach. Here is a 1977 picture of Judith wearing that broach.

Right is a strip of four photos that was obviously made in a machine where you put in a quarter and four photos come out. Since so few photos survive of her, these four photos are often used.

On November 16, 1961, Judith gave JFK a pencil sketch she had made of him. She says that he liked the sketch. Here is that sketch. However, one minor mystery is that she implies that he kept the sketch. If he had kept it, why would she have it now?

Bottom is a photo of the autographed book that Kennedy gave her.

The Assassination of JFK

It is Perfectly Obvious How Kennedy was Really Shot!

by Sam Sloan

Judith Campbell Exner and the Assassination of JFK

Any discussion of anything about JFK invariably reaches the question of the Kennedy Assassination.

No, Judith Campbell did not kill him. She was in Los Angeles at the time, in her room at the Beverly Crest Hotel.

Now that we have gotten that out of the way, who did??

It is simple and obvious and indeed almost everybody who has considered the question has come to the same conclusion, which is that the fatal shot came from the *"Grassy Knoll"*.

It can be proven that Oswald did not fire the fatal shot, as follows:

The Kennedy motorcade came down Main Street. It turned right on the corner of Houston. Now it was coming up Houston street, but very slowly as Kennedy waved to the crowds.

Oswald, who is believed to have been on the sixth floor of the Texas School Book Depository building, was now looking directly into the face of Kennedy who was coming towards him, but very slowly.

This was the perfect time to shoot. He could not have missed. A direct easy shot into the face of the president.

Why would Oswald not shoot him at that moment, if he was going to shoot him at all?

Then, the motorcade reached the corner of Elm and Houston Streets. Now, Kennedy was directly below Oswald. This was a somewhat more difficult shot, as it required the rifle to be pointed almost straight down. Still, the shot would not have been difficult. Rather, it would have been difficult to miss at such a close range.

Again, Oswald did not shoot. Why not?

Now, the motorcade turned left and started down Elm Street. This is a curved street. It is the entrance to the Expressway. This was a slight downward incline. Then the car passed from Oswald's view behind the branches of a tree. A shot from here would have required the bullet to pass through the branches of the tree, a shot made difficult by the possibility that it might hit one of the branches. By the time the car emerged from the other side of the branches, the car was starting to accelerate because at that point it was at the entrance to the expressway. The crowds had greatly thinned out, so there was nothing else to do but to proceed onward to the next destination.

It was at this point where the shots rang out and the president was shot and killed.

For Oswald, shooting from the six floor window of the Texas School Book Depository Building to have hit the president would have been extremely difficult. It would not have been impossible because sharpshooters have been tested and have proven that it can be done. However, those tests by sharpshooters were not performed on the actual conditions that existed on the day in question. In those tests, the sharpshooters shot a stationary non-moving target from a position standing on level ground. Why would Oswald shoot, when the President's car was moving away and accelerating? Why risk shooting when the probability of missing was high? Why not shoot when the president was coming towards him on Houston Street and would have been much easier to hit and almost impossible to miss?

This is a question that many have pondered and everybody has reached the same answer. There were two shooters and possibly even three. They had agreed in advance to shoot when Kennedy reached a particular spot on the highway. This is the reason why three shots were heard to ring out almost simultaneously. It is obvious.

This means that, assuming Oswald was involved, Oswald knew who the other shooter or shooters were or that they were going to shoot at that instant of time. In one of the few statements Oswald made before he himself was shot, Oswald said that he did not shoot anybody and that he was a "patsy".

The exact quotes are, "I didn't shoot anyone," and "They're taking me in because I lived in the Soviet Union. I'm just a patsy!"

The exact spot from which Oswald would have been perched when he shot is closed to the public but, by public demand, a webcam has recently been stationed there so you can see day and night what Oswald would have seen had he been there today. The webcam is at: http://earthcam.com/jfk/

In October, 1997, I was staying with my girlfriend, Passion Julinsey, in her sister's apartment Dallas. Passion had a job working in the Dallas Recorder's Office, which is right next to where the motorcade carried President John F. Kennedy, just before he was assassinated, and is across the street from the Texas School Book Depository, from which Lee Harvey Oswald is said to have assassinated JFK.

One day, while I was waiting for Passion to finish working, I took the six dollar tour of the Texas School Book Depository, where conditions have been almost perfectly preserved in a glass case of the situation in which Oswald shot Kennedy on November 22, 1963.

After that, I went in search of the famed *"grassy knoll"*. This was difficult to find. I searched and searched and still I could not find it. I was convinced that as part of the conspiracy it had been dug out. Then, suddenly I found it. The Problem: It was too close. I had imagined a hillside some far distance from the road from which a man with a telescopic sight could have shot the president. However, the real grassy knoll is right next to the entrance to the expressway, only about 60 yards from the road where Kennedy's car went. I paced it off myself. A kid with a slingshot could have hit Kennedy from such a close distance.

More than that, there was a picket fence along the grassy knoll and a parking lot behind the fence. What a perfect place to shoot! Just put your rifle over one of the notches in the picket fence, which provides a perfect rest for the rifle plus a hiding place for the shooter, fire and then jump into a car conveniently parked in the parking lot and take off.

What could be easier? A more ideal place to assassinate the president could not be imagined.

The famed Zapruder film, which was on display, provided more evidence than I had previously imagined. Because the film is so clear, it is possible to figure out the exact spot where Zapruder was standing when he took the film. Again, he was remarkably close to the president. More importantly, he was directly between the grassy knoll and the motorcade. In fact, it is almost as though Zapruder himself could have shot the president. What clearly happened was the gunman was standing almost directly behind Zapruder. The shot came over Zapruder's right shoulder.

The next important "discovery" on my part (I use quotation marks because it is obvious that millions have previously made the same discoveries that I have made) is that the same parking lot behind the grassy knoll was also the parking lot which served the Texas School Book Depository building.

Thus, a picture of what really happened formed. There were three gunmen, one of whom was a driver. The plan was that Kennedy would be shot simultaneously from two directions. Oswald would shoot him from the sixth floor of the Texas School Book Depository, while the other two would shoot him from the grassy knoll.

After the shooting, Oswald would come downstairs and wait to be picked up. The other two would get into their car and drive over a few hundred yards to where Oswald would be waiting, and then all three would take off in the car.

What went wrong was that, having just shot the president, the other two were not willing to idle their car next to the entrance of the Texas School Book Depository, while waiting for Oswald to walk down six flights of stairs. They probably came by but, when Oswald was not there, they took off. As Oswald was coming down the stairs, on the second floor, he encountered Dallas police officer Marion Baker who had driven his motorcycle to the door of the Depository and sprinted up the stairs in search of the shooter. With Baker was Oswald's supervisor Roy Truly, who identified Oswald as an employee, which caused Baker to let Oswald pass. The few seconds that Oswald was detained on the second floor was probably what caused him to miss his ride.

Oswald's subsequent actions seem to confirm this. For the next few hours, Oswald aimlessly wandered back and forth on the streets of Dallas, clearly trying to figure out what to do next. He was as if lost at sea. He had missed his ride and could not come up with a plan. He went back to his room in his rooming house, then left again after a few minutes. Finally, he entered a movie theater, a strange thing to do for a man who had just shot the president, and watched a movie until he was captured.

Further evidence that Oswald did not act alone is from the setup within the School Book Depository. Again, seeing it with my own eyes made the picture more clear. The Kennedy motorcade came slowly down Houston Street going directly towards the School Book Depository. This gave Oswald a clear downward shot at the president, at point blank range. Again, a kid with a sling shot could have hit the president from that direction.

Yet, Oswald did not shoot there. Instead, he waited. The motorcade made a sharp left turn onto Elm Street and then proceeded onto the main highway. The car accelerated, going down hill past a tree. It was at this point that Oswald shot at the president. It was a difficult shot, requiring an expert marksman. Oswald had to shoot between the branches of a tree at a target which was accelerating. Only an expert marksman could have hit such a target.

Why would Oswald not shoot when he had the target at point blank range and could not have missed, only to shoot later when the target had become much more difficult?

The obvious answer is that Oswald had two accomplices. From the point where he was standing almost directly above the slow-moving presidential car, only a person in Oswald's position could have shot him. However, at the point where the president was actually shot, he could have been hit simultaneously from the grassy knoll and from the Texas School Book Depository and possibly from a third direction.

Using boxes of school books, Oswald had constructed a blind for himself. He had stacked a ring of boxes of books around the spot where he would be shooting. Thus, if any other worker had happened in at that point in time, he would not have seen Oswald, who was behind those stacks of books.

There is a report, unconfirmed, that somebody actually saw him perched there with a rifle and just assumed that he was a security officer there to protect the president, not imagining that he was really there to kill the president.

On the other hand, had Oswald shot Kennedy while Kennedy was coming down Houston Street, Oswald would have had to come directly to the window, where someone in the Dallas Recorder's

Office or even from the street might have seen him briefly. However, at the point where Kennedy was actually shot, Oswald would have been crouched around the corner, at a spot from which nobody outside the building could have seen him.

It is often said that Oswald was a "patsy". It seems that this was literally true. The other two men involved in the assassination probably realized that the shot from the Texas School Book Depository was so difficult that the chance for a successful assassination from there was slim. However, from the point blank range provided by the grassy knoll, the success of the operation was virtually guaranteed. Therefore, the other two probably wanted Oswald involved so that he would be given full blame for the assassination and they would escape scott free, which is exactly what happened.

Nothing I have just said is new. Thousands of other writers and observers have said the same thing before me. What is remarkable is that this conclusion is so obvious and still there are those who believe that "Oswald Acted Alone".

Now that we have established that the fatal shots almost certainly did not come from the School Book Depository Building, let us consider the Dal-Tex Building across the street. The Dal-Tex Building is a red building with a white roof that has been until recently ignored.

Consider the same scenario: The Kennedy motorcade came down Main Street and turned right on Houston Street. As it came down Houston Street, a shooter in the Dal-Tex Building would not have had a clear shot at Kennedy because his view would have been partially blocked by the Dallas Recorders Office, the same building where my beloved girlfriend, Passion Julinsey (the one who says that she was never my girlfriend) worked.

Next, the motorcade turned left onto Elm Street. Now, as the motorcade went down Elm Street, a shooter in the Dal -Tex

Building would have had his view partially blocked by both the School Book Depository Building and more importantly by the row of trees.

However, just before the underpass, the road curves to the left. At that point, for the first time, a shooter in the Dal-Tex Building would have an unobstructed direct line of fire at the President. That would have been his first clear chance to shoot the President and that in fact is where the president was shot.

The only slightly negative factor is that the Dal-Tex Building was slightly further away by the distance of the width of Houston Street. However, that extra distance is more than offset by the fact that the shooter would have had a clearer and more direct view of the spot where Kennedy was shot.

This is only the beginning of the inquiry of course. Now that we have established how it was done, we need to figure out who did it.

One immediate question concerns the Warren Commission. If it was so completely obvious that the fatal shots came from the grassy knoll, why did the Warren Commission find that the shots came from the School Book Depository Building?

The Warren Commission consisted of Chief Justice Earl Warren, Richard B. Russell, John Sherman Cooper, Hale Boggs, Gerald R. Ford, Allen Welsh Dulles and John Jay McCloy.

The Commission was initially announced as a highly qualified group, but in reality none of them were suited to the task. They were primarily a bunch of political hacks.

Chief Justice Earl Warren had by far the greatest reputation. He is considered to have been one of the most distinguished judges of our time. His majority decisions on the Supreme Court deeply affect our society today, even though they were substantially rolled back by the Rehnquist Court.

However, he was primarily a politician, not a judge, a lawyer or a prosecutor. Thus, he had no real experience or qualifications to investigate the Kennedy Assassination. Prior to being nominated to the US Supreme Court, he had been Governor of California for ten years.

The other six members of the Warren Commission were primarily politicians, Congressmen or Senators, with no real qualifications, such as for example, that well-known political hack, Gerald R. Ford.

What many people do not realize is that Lee Harvey Oswald was announced on TV as having been the lone assassin even before he was arrested in the Texas Theatre. I know this because I was sitting in my apartment in Berkeley California where I was attending the University of California at Berkeley, watching all of this unfold. It was announced on TV that Oswald had been the shooter only a few minutes after Kennedy had been shot at 12:30 PM. Presumably the reason they knew that Oswald had done it was he was the only employee who had left the building after the shooting and he had left his rifle behind on the sixth floor of the School Book Depository. This was strong evidence but it was still surprising that they would make the announcement that he was the shooter so soon after the shooting had taken place.

His picture was put on TV. This explains why Officer Tippit in a patrol car was able to recognize him walking down the street. Officer Tippit called Oswald over and got out of his patrol car, whereupon Oswald shot and killed him.

Oswald then walked into the Texas Theatre without buying a ticket, again strange behavior. By now the entire world had seen Oswald's photograph on TV, but Oswald probably did not realize that. The Theatre Manager notified the police that Oswald was in the theater. A hoard of more than 20 police officers converged on the theater, and surrounded and arrested Oswald at 1:40 PM after a brief struggle.

Assuming that all this is true, it seems to provide convincing proof that Oswald was involved. However, it fails to prove that Oswald acted alone.

Perhaps the biggest single problem with the Warren Commission's finding that Lee Harvey Oswald acted alone is the "magic bullet theory". This theory holds that one bullet fired from the Texas School Book Depository Building passed through President Kennedy's neck, Governor Connally's chest and wrist and embedded itself in the Governor's thigh. Yet, there were no marks or damage to the bullet that was found.

That was not the bullet that killed the president. Another bullet that hit Kennedy in the head was what killed him.

The magic bullet theory is central to the findings of the Warren Commission because Oswald, who had a bolt action rifle, would clearly not have had enough time to fire three bullets at the president considering that the car was moving. Thus, if there were three bullets fired, there must have been at least two and possibly three shooters.

Now, in the space of less than two pages, I have just proven convincingly that Oswald could not have been the only shooter. I have done nothing new or unique. Thousands and perhaps millions of others have reached the same conclusion for much the same reasons. For years, Mark Lane and others went around the country making speeches about this to interested audiences. Even today, the Kennedy Assassination holds nearly as much interest as it did the day that these events occurred.

Judith Campbell Exner was not in Dallas on the fateful day. She was in her home in Los Angeles. However, several people involved in her story were there.

Among these were David Powers. He is the person who came down to greet Judith when she first came to the White House to visit the President. In the movie, "*Power and Beauty*", his character is given the name "Weston". In the movie, he tells Judith not to get into a lovers quarrel with the President in front of the White House staff. This reflects a real life quarrel that took place between Judith and the President on August 8, 1961. In real life, Powers was also sitting in the presidential motorcade in the car immediately behind the President. He had a personal movie camera with him but it ran out of film at 12:17, just 13 minutes before the president was shot.

Regarding Judith Campbell, Powers later made the infamous quote, "The only Campbell I know is chunky vegetable soup".

By the time of the "Campbell soup" quote, Powers was serving as Museum Curator of the John F. Kennedy Library and Museum. He retired in 1994 and died in 1998. One would hardly imagine that a person in his position would admit that his boss, the president, had been sleeping around.

Powers testified before the Warren Commission that he had heard three shots coming from the School Book Depository. However, he later admitted that the FBI told him to say that and that he had actually heard the shots coming from the grassy knoll.

This admission that he had fudged the testimony before the Warren Commission destroyed any credibility that might be attributed to his "chunky vegetable soup" remark.

Kenneth P. O'Donnell, another close aid to president Kennedy, was seated next to David Powers immediately behind the Presidential limousine. Like Powers, he was told to say that he heard the shots coming from the Texas School Book Depository but later admitted that they actually came from the grassy knoll.

When the Judith Campbell Scandal broke in December 1975, O'Donnell told the Boston Harold-American that all reports of extra-marital affairs by Kennedy are lies. "They are all lies", said O'Donnell.

According to "*My Story*", Kenneth P. O'Donnell was in the room with Kennedy and the "tall thin woman" with whom JFK wanted Judith to make a threesome. O'Donnell left the room but waited in the next room. The "tall, thin woman" was given the name "Amy" in the movie "*Power and Beauty*".

The Warren Commission Report was ruinous to the reputation of Chief Justice Earl Warren because of the obvious cover-ups it contains. In addition, it was highly inappropriate for a Chief Justice of the United States Supreme Court to take time off from his important official duties to engage in an investigatory inquiry. Since then, in the many scandals that have since erupted, such as the Watergate Affair, the Iran-Contra Affair and the Lewinsky Scandal, no Chief Justice has followed this example. The question is: Why did the Chief Justice, who had nothing to gain, involve himself in this dubious plot?

The answer may lie in considering the alternatives. From the beginning, it was widely believed that Fidel Castro and the Government of Cuba had something to do with the Kennedy Assassination. The motivation is obvious. Castro has reported that there have been so far 40 attempts by the American CIA to assassinate him. It is just due to our bungling and incompetence that we cannot seem to get the job done right. Therefore, Castro had good reasons to want to kill JFK, and RFK too, since, as we now know, RFK was personally directing the plans to kill Castro.

I personally believe, and have long believed, that when Castro dies, which is likely to happen soon as he is ill, news and information will start coming out of Cuba regarding the Kennedy Assassination.

President Lyndon B. Johnson has been quoted as saying privately that the reason Kennedy was assassinated was in retaliation for Kennedy's attempts to assassinate Castro. Johnson is believed to have shut down CIA Operations to kill foreign leaders for that reason. Henceforth, the USA would only kill the little guys, not the top leadership.

Some years ago, Barbara Walters personally interviewed Fidel Castro about this subject, asking Castro directly whether he had killed Kennedy. Castro answered that he did not kill Kennedy, direct or order anybody to kill Kennedy, encourage anybody to kill Kennedy, did not know who killed Kennedy and did not have anything to do with the Kennedy Assassination.

Perhaps that will turn out to be the truth, or perhaps not.

The fact that Oswald had been applying for a visa to travel to Cuba and was handing out "Fair Play For Cuba" leaflets shortly before the Kennedy Assassination, provides some indication that Cuba might have been directly or indirectly involved.

A remarkable new development is James E. Files, an inmate of Joliet State Penitentiary in Illinois, has confessed to being one of two assassins firing at JFK in Dallas on November 22, 1963. The other was Charles Nicoletti, who was firing from the Dal-Tex Building. Nicoletti is now deceased. According to James Files, Oswald was only involved to the extent of planting false evidence to throw off any investigation.

The Dal-Tex Building is across Houston Street from the School Book Depository. It is slightly further away from the spot where Kennedy was when he was shot. On the other hand, it is in a direct line of sight. If the real shooter were there he would probably not have been able to shoot Kennedy as he came down Houston Street. He would have had to lean out the window and shoot from an angle, which would have been not only difficult but would have put him in danger of being spotted.

Files claims that Nicoletti shot from the Dal-Tex Building but did not succeed in killing Kennedy. This left it to Files to fire the fatal shot. Files says that he fired with a 1962 prototype bolt-action Remington XP-100 "Fireball" pistol, not a rifle, that had been given to him by CIA agent David Atlee Phillips.

What is truly remarkable is that in view of his detailed and credible confession, it has been virtually ignored by the press and the prosecutor's offices. Why is that? Here is a man who has confessed to the Crime of the Century, yet his confession is ignored.

On the other hand, E. Howard Hunt, the infamous Watergate Burglar, recently gave a deathbed confession on tape. In the tape, Hunt named Cord Meyer, Frank Sturgis, David Sánchez Morales and David Atlee Phillips as participants in the assassination, with Vice-President Lyndon Johnson apparently approving the assassination for political gain.

Many of these names are familiar. Cord Meyer hated Kennedy because his wife had been a mistress of John F. Kennedy. His wife, Mary Pichot Meyer, was subsequently murdered. Frank Sturgis was the well known Watergate Burglar. David Sánchez Morales and David Atlee Phillips are former CIA agents whose names have long been on every list of suspects in the Kennedy assassination.

It is especially noteworthy that all of the above people are now dead, except for James E. Files, who is alive and healthy but in prison.

It must be mentioned that there are weaknesses in his story. The biggest is that he says that he parked his car in the parking lot of the Dal-Tex Building and, after he had shot Kennedy, he went back to the car where Roselli and Nicoletti were already waiting. He then drove away and, after leaving them off, drove back to Chicago.

However, the DAL-TEX BUILDING DOES NOT HAVE A PARKING LOT.

Also, James Files says that he drove his car five or six blocks before turning onto the expressway for the drive back to Chicago. However, the expressway was then several blocks further than that.

Another discrepancy is that he says that he helped train some of the Bay of Pigs Invaders in the Florida Everglades. However, the Bay of Pigs Invaders were trained in Guatemala.

Finally, it is said that he would not have confessed to the Kennedy Assassination, even though he is already serving a life sentence, because TEXAS HAS A DEATH PENALTY.

None of these objections are dispositive. Although the Dal-Tex Building does not have its own parking lot, there is a large parking lot across the street that serves many surrounding buildings including the School Book Depository. The first time Files confessed to the Kennedy Assassination was in 1994. By then, 31 years had passed and it is entirely likely that his recollection would have faded about exactly where he parked his car. The same can be said about discrepancies about how many blocks he drove his car before turning right onto the Expressway and the other details about the events of 31 years earlier. There is still a lot of top secrecy about the training of the Bay of Pigs Invaders. Guatemala was given as the training place in order to make it appear that the US Government was not involved, plus some of the invaders were not legal US residents. It is entirely possible that some training took place in the Florida Everglades. Finally, the last argument is ridiculous, because the US Supreme Court abolished the death penalty in the famous case of Furman vs. Georgia, 408 U.S. 238 (1972). The death penalty was reinstated in 1976 but not retroactively, so there is no possibility that James Files could be now executed for the Kennedy Assassination.

The main objection to the "Confession" of James Files is that he could feel that he has nothing to lose since he is already serving a 50-year sentence for the attempted murder of two police officers and he may believe that he will be paid some money for a book or story about the JFK Assassination. These are legitimate concerns, but there could still be about a 50-50 chance that what James Files says is true.

The last word has not been written on this subject. Some day, perhaps some day very soon, we will know for sure who really did Assassinate President John F. Kennedy.

Sam Sloan

Here are three photos of Dealey Plaza where JFK was assassinated. The small photo to the left shows the route his motorcade followed. Although the Warren Commission found that all of the shots came from the School Book Depository, top center, the current view was that there were two or three shooters, none of whom were in the School Book Depository and one of whom was in the Dal Tex Building which is the red building with the white top in the far corner.

Here are photos of Dealey Plaza from Google Earth.

Now that we have established how JFK was assassinated, all that remains is to figure out who did it.

Fortunately, we have a man who has confessed to the act. His name is James Files and his original name was James Sutton. He has provided specific and credible details as to how and why JFK was shot. Files says that there were actually three shooters, but that he fired the fatal bullet.

Files, whose mug shots are above, says that he shot JFK from the "Grassy Knoll" using a Remington XP-100 "Fireball" pistol (not a rifle). The second shooter was Charles Nicoletti, whose photo is on the upper left, who shot from the Dal-Tex Building. The third shooter would have been John Roselli who had hired Files and Nicoletti, but he did not shoot.

Lee Harvey Oswald was just a patsy. He was involved just to leave fake evidence, to lead investigators astray.

Johnny Rosselli

Here are two versions of the Remington "Fireball" XP-100 pistol that James E. Files says that he used to assassinate President John F. Kennedy. What is especially interesting is that this weapon had just come out in 1963 and thus was new, yet it had never previously been associated with the Kennedy Assassination.

Thus, if it can be proven that this was or even could have been the weapon used to assassinate the President, that would add great credibility to Files' story.

A satellite view of the "Grassy Knoll" and a photo of the wooden fence behind which the shooter undoubtedly fired.

What is remarkable is how the Warren Commission was so insistent that all of the shots in the JFK Assassination came from the School Book Depository, when that was a difficult shot through the branches of a tree some distance away, whereas the "Grassy Knoll" was at point blank range only 65 years away. (I paced it off myself.)

The "grassy knoll" is really just an embankment of the type often found on the sides of a freeway. In this case, at the top of the grassy knoll is a wooden fence. The shooter was easily able to stand behind the wooden fence and use it as a gun-rest to hold the gun steady while taking a shot at the president. Then, since a parking lot is behind the wooden fence, the shooter was able just to get in his car and drive away, before anybody realized what had happened.

Senator Frank Church holding up the infamous Church Committee Report. Although the report was 349 pages long, only slightly more than one page was devoted to the matter that made the report famous, namely that President John F. Kennedy had a "friend" who had also been a friend of a Mafia Don. The gender of the "friend" was not

mentioned. The world was shocked when one month later it was revealed that the "friend" had been a woman who was said to have been having sexual intercourse with both the President and the Mafia Don at the same time, mixing up their semen.

The famous photo seen live around the world of Jack Ruby shooting and killing Lee Harvey Oswald two days after the Kennedy Assassination. It was later discovered that the real name of Jack Ruby was Jacob Rubinstein and he had been born in Chicago and had been associated with Al Capone's mob.

Jack Ruby said that he had shot Oswald because he was a public spirited citizen who wanted to avenge the death of President Kennedy. Almost every conspiracy theorist maintains that Ruby was involved in the plot to kill Kennedy. There has been no proof or evidence developed to support these theories, and the majority view is still that Ruby was merely a publicity seeker.

Controversy Linking the F-111 to the Kennedy Assassination

The General Dynamics F-111 is a medium-range strategic bomber, reconnaissance, and tactical strike aircraft designed in the 1960s. It is no longer in service except that it is flown by the Australian Air Force. Virtually every recent book about the Kennedy Assassination has advanced the theory that Kennedy was assassinated because of the TFX contract, under which the F-111 was developed. Essentially, the conspiracy theorist say that the CIA was opposed to the development of the F-111, favoring a competing aircraft by Boeing instead. When, after many warnings, Kennedy insisted on proceeding with the development of the F-111 anyway, he was shot, they say.

Seymour Hersh in his book "The Dark Side of Camelot" states that General Dynamics got the contract by blackmailing President Kennedy. Hersh states that Bobby and Billy Hale, twin sons of the General Dynamics security chief I. B. Hale, broke into the apartment of Kennedy's mistress Judith Campbell and placed bugs and wiretaps on her telephone. With these bugs, they were able to establish proof that Kennedy was sleeping with Campbell. When presented with the evidence, Kennedy agreed to award the $6.5 billion contract to General Dynamics. It was the largest defense contract ever awarded.

Antoinette Giancana

Photograph by Sam Manno

Antoinette Giancana, daughter of Chicago Mafia Don Sam "Momo" Giancana, has written two books about her famous father.

The first was *"Mafia Princess: Growing Up in Sam Giancana's Family"* ISBN 0688026206. In it, she discusses mostly her personal life. She acknowledges having met Judith Campbell and cites her book, "My Story", with favor. Antoinette makes an interesting observation that her father never carried a gun and was afraid of them. This confirms the report of Robert Maheu that when he offered to hire Giancana to kill Castro, Giancana advised that guns not be used and recommended poisoning Castro's food instead.

In the second book, *"JFK And Sam: The Connection Between the Giancana And Kennedy Assassinations"*, ISBN 1581824874, she states that she believes that her father, Sam Giancana, ordered the Kennedy Assassination. She explains how and why it was done. Basically, she supports the account by James E. Files, who said that he killed Kennedy, having been hired by Roselli who in turn had been instructed by Sam Giancana to do so.

President John F. Kennedy on Crutches

While Kennedy was President, photos like this were never published. Had they known the truth, the Kennedy Assassins possibly need not have bothered. It was not revealed until after he had died that President Kennedy was very seriously ill and might not have survived his presidency even if he had not been shot.

Kennedy had a variety of ailments. He had Addison's Disease, a withering of the adrenal glands. He also had severe injuries to his spinal column. He had to take several shots every day. When he traveled to Europe on presidential business, he took a doctor with him to administer the shots. Yet, none of this was mentioned in the newspapers while he was alive.

Chief Justice Earl Warren who squandered his reputation as a great chief justice on the "Warren Report" which purported to establish that President John F. Kennedy was assassinated by a lone gunman named Lee Harvey Oswald.

Even in its time, the "lone gunman" theory was dismissed as absurd and ridiculous. An interesting question is why would the chief justice espouse such a ridiculous idea.

The answer seems to be to insure the stability of the country. Naturally, the top suspect from day one was President Johnson because it was he who benefited most from the Kennedy Assassination, plus the fact that the Assassination occurred in Dallas, Texas which was Johnson's Home State. Nowadays, few Americans believe that Johnson was involved but that view is widely held in other countries.

Another factor is that the other members of the Warren Commission were incompetent politicos such as future President Gerald Ford, or those with conflicts or with something to hide, such as Allen W. Douglas, Director of the CIA, who was conflicted because from the beginning the CIA was suspected of being involved.

Earl Warren did not deserve the great reputation he had a chief justice. Most of the great decisions supposedly written by him were actually written by his great associate justices including Black, Douglas, Harlan and Frankfurter.

Warren had little prior experience as a lawyer, judge or prosecutor. He had limited qualifications for the work required of the Warren Commission. Prior to being appointed to the US Supreme Court, Warren had been the Governor of California for ten years.

Judith Campbell Exner, her place in history

Judith Immoor Campbell Exner and her place in history

When I think of Judith Immoor Campbell Exner, in my mind I compare her to *Forest Gump*. This may seem unlikely but I will explain. Forest Gump is an entirely fictional character who was a mildly retarded man who just happened to be there at every important junction of history. At every event of major significance involving Kennedy, Johnson or Nixon, Forest Gump was there.

Forest Gump was not the only one who was there. Judith Immoor Campbell Exner was there too. There was just one difference. Judith Immoor Campbell Exner was a real person. She was like an extra in a movie who appears in every scene, yet has no lines to speak. Every important event of the 1960s and 1970s seems to have involved Judith Immoor Campbell Exner in some way. She dated, was seen with or was on the arm of many of the important men of that generation. She dated or at least knew almost the entire A-list of Hollywood Movie Stars, yet she never appeared in a movie. Everyone who ever saw her reported that she was a spectacular beauty, one of the most beautiful women of all time, yet few photographs survive of her. The most frequent remark made about her was that she looked like Elizabeth Taylor, only she was more beautiful.

She is also one of the most reviled and hated women. She has been called every bad word in the book, "a common street slut", "a whore", "a high-class hooker", "a party girl", yet if you believe her biography, she was a deeply conservative, prudish, Catholic woman who never slept with more than one man at a time. How many women can say that nowadays?

Judith Immoor Campbell Exner is still in the news constantly. Turn on CNN news almost every night and there will likely be something involving Judith Immoor Campbell Exner. Every news story involving President John F. Kennedy, the Bay of Pigs Invasion or covert operations by the CIA against Fidel Castro of

Judith Campbell Exner, her place in history

Cuba will probably in some way involve Judith Campbell Exner.

However, two allegations involving Judith Immoor Campbell Exner must be dealt with.

The first is that she was involved with the delivery of a huge satchel of cash from John F. Kennedy to Mafia Don Sam Giancana to insure that Kennedy would defeat Hubert Humphrey in the 1960 West Virginia Presidential Primary.

According to biographer Kitty Kelly, *"while JFK's lover, she had served as a courier between the President and Giancana. According to Exner, JFK wanted the mobster's help in nailing down votes in the 1960 West Virginia primary."*

JFK was not the President at the time of the West Virginia Primary. He was just a candidate for the nomination, one of many.

Seymour Hersh in his book *"The Dark Side of Camelot"*, page 303, says that Kennedy had Exner carry a bag containing $250,000 in cash to Sam Giancana.

Sam Giancana was the Don of the Chicago Mafia, a successor to Al Capone. It was known in 1960 that the Mafia controlled most Las Vegas Casino operations and had infiltrated into labor unions, including especially the United Mine Workers in West Virginia. Kennedy wanted to be president. West Virginia, a relatively minor state, was of utmost importance in the 1960 campaign because it was an anti-Catholic state. Kennedy was a Catholic and the Catholic-Issue was a big albatross for Kennedy in 1960.

I will give a personal example. My father was a liberal and always voted Democratic. (This was back in the old days when the Democrats were the tax-and-spend liberals and the Republicans were the fiscal conservatives, unlike today when the opposite is the case.) There was only one time in his life that my father ever voted

Republican. That was in 1960, and the reason was that my father feared that if Kennedy was elected, he would fly over to the Vatican where the Pope would tell him what to do.

Many voters felt that way. Therefore, Kennedy needed to win in West Virginia to demonstrate that he could be elected president even in an anti-Catholic jurisdiction.

Politics makes strange bedfellows. No doubt Kennedy legitimately believed that mob influence was needed to win the West Virginia primary. It became even more critical in the 1960 Presidential general election, when most observers believe that mob influence was critical in delivering to Kennedy the Illinois electoral votes by a razor-thin margin of only 8,858 votes. Thus, sending money to Chicago mob boss Sam Giancana was a reasonable decision.

Life is like that. If you want to win an election, whether it be to the Presidency of the United States or to the Executive Board of the United States Chess Federation, you may have to pay off the right people. The question often asked during the Kennedy-Nixon Presidential Campaign was, "Would he rather be right, or be President?"

On the other hand, no evidence has emerged that Giancana actually did anything to help Kennedy win in West Virginia or to carry Illinois in the subsequent general election. Giancana probably just pocketed the money. More pertinent to the issue here, it is difficult to see how Judith Immoor Campbell Exner played a role in this. She had been introduced to Senator Kennedy by her former lover Frank Sinatra on February 7, 1960. Then, Sinatra had introduced her to "Sam Flood" during a party at Hotel Fontainebleau in Miami, Florida on March 26, 1960. The West Virginia primary was held on May 10, 1960. So, by the time of the West Virginia Primary, Judith had only known Senator Kennedy for three months. She writes that she first made love to the future President Kennedy in the Plaza Hotel in New York City on March 7, 1960. More than that, she did not find out that the real name of "Sam Flood" was actually Sam Giancana until four days before Kennedy had actually been elected President, when the FBI informed her of this.

What Judith Immoor Campbell Exner almost certainly did not know was that Joseph Kennedy, the father of John F. Kennedy, had connections with the Chicago Mafia dating back to the Roaring Twenties. It was Joseph Kennedy, not John F. Kennedy, who frequently met with Sam Giancana during the 1960 election campaign. The Kennedy family is nowadays often thought of as one of the old-line Blue Blood Families. Not true. It is now well established that the Kennedy wealth comes from a bootlegging operation in the 1920s. The grandfather of Joseph Kennedy had been Patrick Kennedy, who had died at an early age, leaving his wife, Bridget Murphy, destitute with four small children. She had survived by working as a domestic servant in private homes. Her son, Patrick Joseph Kennedy (1858-1929), who had been less than one year old when his father had died, grew up in poverty. However, he and his son, Joseph Patrick Kennedy (1888-1969), became rich through illegal activities, including bootlegging.

Even the marriage of John F. Kennedy to Jacqueline Bouvier was part of a long-range plan to raise the social status and wealth of the Kennedy clan. Jacqueline was of the upper crust. Her step-father was Hugh Auchincloss, a wealthy man and principal of a Wall Street securities firm, who gave away Jacqueline as a bride. His uncle was the son-in-law of Sam Sloan (1817-1907), the railroad tycoon, one of the richest men in America, who built the railroad system that now services New York City. The marriage of John F. Kennedy to Jacqueline Bouvier had been part of a plan to gain control of the fabulous wealth of the Sloan-Auchincloss Family. The mother of Jacqueline, Janet Lee, had been concerned that her daughter was marrying into a family of low social status like the Kennedys, but was unable to dissuade her daughter from taking this fateful step.

Judith Campbell Exner, her place in history

When President Franklin D. Roosevelt appointed Joseph Kennedy as the First Chairman of the Securities and Exchange Commission, and somebody asked Roosevelt why he had chosen Kennedy, Roosevelt replied, "It Takes a Crook to Catch a Crook!"

When John F. Kennedy was in the final stages of his election campaign, President Truman said, "It's not the Pope I'm afraid of, it's the Pop. Old Joe Kennedy is as big a crook as we've got anywhere in this country."

Sam Giancana, Don of the Chicago Mafia and a successor to Al Capone, is quoted as saying, "Joe Kennedy was one of the biggest crooks that ever lived".

Originally, Joseph Kennedy had planned to run for President of the United States himself. He was appointed ambassador to Great Britain by President Roosevelt. There, he sought a compromise with Nazi Germany and supported Prime Minister Neville Chamberlain's policy of appeasement. In September 1940, after the war had started, Joseph Kennedy sought a personal meeting with Hitler, without State Department approval, *"to bring about a better understanding between the United States and Germany."* As a result, when the United States finally entered World War II in December 1941, it became unthinkable for Joseph Kennedy to run for president himself, so he started grooming his sons so that at least one of them would become president.

Joseph Kennedy Senior had decided that the crowning achievement in raising the status of his family from poverty to wealth would be to get his son elected President of the United States. It has been suggested that when his eldest son, Joseph Kennedy Jr., volunteered for an extremely dangerous aircraft mission to drop explosives over Nazi Germany and then bail out, this was part of a plan to become a war hero, thereby paving the way to the presidency. However, the explosives detonated prematurely and Joseph Kennedy Junior was killed, so the mantle fell upon his younger brothers to run for president.

On December 19, 1961, Joseph Kennedy, the father of by-then President John F. Kennedy, suffered a major debilitating stroke. After that, the father was out of the picture and, for the first time in his life, John F. Kennedy had to start making decisions on his own without parental guidance. In hindsight, several bad decisions that President Kennedy made occurred after that date.

A allegation that must be addressed is that Judith Immoor Campbell Exner carried documents between JFK and Sam Giancana, regarding a decision by the CIA to hire the Chicago mob to kill Fidel Castro, President of Cuba. However, this observation usually ignores the fact that the mob operation to kill Castro started in 1960. In 1960, KENNEDY WAS NOT YET PRESIDENT!!!! Kennedy did not become president until January, 1961. In 1960, Eisenhower was president. Obviously, there is politics here. The Republicans want to blame the Democrats for it. The Democrats want to blame the Republicans for it.

This is what is meant by writing that Judith Immoor Campbell Exner seems to be like a movie extra who appears in every scene yet has no lines to speak. Here she was, a little 120 pound 26-year-old girl taking the train back and forth between Chicago and Washington DC or New York, receiving and delivering documents. What did these documents contain? Did they concern the Plot to Assassinate Castro, the Cuban Missile Crisis, the Bay of Pigs Invasion and the eventual Assassination of JFK? The world would like to know.

But there is more:

Antoinette Giancana, daughter of Mafia Don Sam Giancana, has a written a book about this. In her book, she names the actual killer of President Kennedy and the motive, never previously suggested.

The motive concerns the Controversy Linking the F-111 to the Kennedy Assassination.

The General Dynamics F-111 was a medium-range strategic bomber, reconnaissance, and tactical strike aircraft designed in the 1960s. Virtually every recent book about the Kennedy Assassination has advanced the theory that Kennedy was assassinated because of the F-111 contract. Essentially, the conspiracy theorist say that the CIA and the military were opposed to the development of the F-111, favoring a competing aircraft by Boeing instead. When, after many warnings, Kennedy insisted on proceeding with the development of the F-111 anyway, he was shot, they say. The shooters justified the assassination of the President on the belief that Kennedy had been bribed or blackmailed into developing the inferior F-111, and therefore the assassination of the president was justified as a matter of patriotism and as a national security measure.

If that was the reason, the assassination was a failure, because the development of the F-111 went ahead anyway. After Kennedy was assassinated, it became unthinkable to change or abandon any of the initiatives the President had started. Had Kennedy lived, the pressure on the President to abandon the F-111 project in favor of the superior aircraft designed and to be built by Boeing might have been unbearable. On the other hand, General Dynamics was tottering on the brink of bankruptcy. Had the F-111 project been abandoned, General Dynamics might have gone out of business. As things turned out, President Kennedy, a weak and ineffective president in life, became an icon after his death. Nothing that he started could be stopped, including the trip to the moon.

The development of the F-111 has since been linked to numerous Kennedy Assassination Theories. General Dynamics was not favored to win the contract under which the F-111 was ultimately built. Another aircraft designed by Boeing was favored. It was a controversial last-minute decision by Secretary of Defense Robert

McNamara to overrule the military and to build the F-111 instead. Assassination Theorists state that actually President John F. Kennedy ordered that the contract be awarded to General Dynamics. As this was the largest defense contract ever awarded, this attracted the attention of the press. Kennedy was asked about this repeatedly in press conferences. The United States Senate started an investigation. However, the investigation was shut down after Kennedy was Assassinated.

Seymour Hersh in his book *"The Dark Side of Camelot"* suggests that General Dynamics got the contract by blackmailing President Kennedy. Hersh states that on August 7, 1962, Bobby and Billy Hale, twin sons of the General Dynamics security chief I. B. Hale, broke into the apartment of Kennedy's mistress Judith Campbell Exner at 1200 North Flores Street, Apartment 201, in Los Angeles and placed bugs and wiretaps on her telephone. With these bugs, they were able to establish proof that Kennedy was sleeping with Exner. When presented with the evidence, Kennedy agreed to award the $6.5 billion contract to General Dynamics, or so goes this theory.

The major problem with this theory is that Kennedy did not seem to be concerned about the fact that many people knew that he had numerous mistresses, some of whom were even on the White House staff and had no other duties than to sleep with him. Two of those women whose only duties were to have sex with the president were known to the Secret Service by their code names of "Fiddle" and "Faddle". An article in *Time* magazine for December 29, 1975 entitled *"Jack Kennedy's Other Women"* states that the revelation that Judith Campbell had been his mistress only "confirmed what had long been a matter of open speculation" concerning "a legend of prodigious sexual activity" involving naked girls running around the White House or swimming nude in the White House pool. (The White House indoor pool was covered over and sealed by subsequent presidents because of this scandal, but it is still there, underneath the new Press Briefing Room.)

Judith Campbell Exner, her place in history

Antoinette Giancana in her book "JFK and Sam" expresses the belief that Kennedy was assassinated because of the F-111 contract. The CIA favored Boeing over General Dynamics and, dissatisfied with the decision to build the F-111, hired her father, Sam Giancana, to carry out the hit. The actual shooter was James Files, also known as James Sutton, who worked for Charles Nicoletti, who worked for Sam Giancana, according to Antoinette Giancana.

The 2002 made for television movie *"Power and Beauty"* starring Natasha Henstridge as Judy Exner, Kevin Anderson as John F. Kennedy, Peter Friedman as Sam Giancana and John Ralston as Frank Sinatra recreates many of the scenes from the Kitty Kelly interview and the book by Seymour Hersh. The most controversial, and indeed the only really controversial, remaining question is whether Exner actually arranged face-to-face meetings between John F. Kennedy and Mafia Don Sam Giancana while Kennedy was president.

The term *"Camelot"* that is so often applied to the Kennedy Administration comes from the Lerner and Loewe Musical *"Camelot"*. This musical opened on Broadway on December 3, 1960, just after Kennedy was elected president but before he took office, and closed on January 3, 1963. It was President Kennedy's favorite. He played the music over and over again. Thus, it will always be associated forever with the Kennedy Term of Office.

The musical speaks of the mythical country of Camelot, where life was so perfect that:

> *"It never rains till after sundown.*
> *"By eight the morning fog must disappear*
> *"In short, there's simply not*
> *"A more congenial spot*
> *"For happ'ly-ever-aftering than here*
> *"In Camelot."*

Her place in History, Page No. 9

However, in the musical, this all disappears and is destroyed when Queen Guenevere, the wife of King Arthur, commits adultery and runs off with Sir Lancelot. King Arthur chases after them. They fight to the death and Camelot is destroyed.

This turned out to be almost what happened in the real-life John F. Kennedy version of Camelot.

Credibility Issues

The biggest issue and the issue with which must always be dealt is the issue of credibility. Was Judith Immoor Campbell Exner really the mistress of President John F. Kennedy? Or, was she just a high class $200 hooker, as detractors say she was, who tried to make the big score, become famous and get paid a lot of money by claiming to have had an affair with the president?

Was she the American version of the Riding Instructor, or the Telephone Partner or the Bodyguard of Princess Diana, who got the benefit of the full enjoyment of good sex by sleeping with a beautiful woman, plus on top of that received millions of pounds and became celebrities by writing about their experiences in bed with the princess?

George Jacobs, Frank Sinatra's personal valet, who met Judith many times when she was sleeping with or just visiting Sinatra, clearly is among those who not believe her story that she was a "volunteer". Jacobs constantly refers to her as a "*hooker*", yet he offers no real proof of this such as a request from her for payment.

In "*Mr. S My Life with Frank Sinatra*" by George Jacobs, he writes on page 133:

> "*In her memoirs, Judy Campbell was one lady who did protest too much. She insisted that she never took a penny*

from either JFK or Mr. Sam, that she traveled to Washington, Chicago, Vegas, Miami, wherever they were, planes, trains, luxury hotels, all at her own expense, because she cared so much about them. Barbara Hutton or Doris Duke could barely afford Judy's travel bills. No, Judy was a major player. What made her so special is that she was a brilliant actress in not seeming in any way like what she really was."

A second issue concerns differences between Judith's 1977 book and the 1988 interview with Kitty Kelly published in the February 29, 1988 issue of *People* magazine and the interview published in the January 1997 issue of *Vanity Fair* magazine.

On this last point, I fail to see the issue. Although the 1988 interview starts with the words "I lied", it can be seen that this was part of a plan by interviewer Kitty Kelly to make the story new and sensational and to sell more magazines. I have not found any actual significant discrepancies between the 1977 book *"My Story"* and the 1988 interview published in *"People"* magazine. Rather, the 1988 interview added some more details. There was a good reason for these additional details. In 1975, Judith Immoor Campbell Exner married Professional Golfer Daniel Exner. Judith became the devoted wife she had always dreamed of becoming, accompanying her husband down to the golf course every morning and watching him practice and play golf all day long, while she was sipping tea. Her affair with the late President had been all but forgotten. The FBI was no longer trailing her, stopping her at embarrassing moments to ask her questions. It was all in the past, or so she hoped, UNTIL THE HEADLINES BROKE.

However, by 1988, she no longer feared being assassinated. Most of the people who might have wanted to kill her were dead. She was separated from Dan Exner, who could no longer play golf because he had had a brain tumor removed. A curious fact about Daniel Exner is that no biographical information is available about him. One website states that his birth date has been suppressed. He is known to have been born in about 1946 and to have been 12 years younger than his wife, Judith. Since he had a brain tumor removed in 1988, it would seem likely that he in no longer alive, yet there is no record of his death or of his existence after 1988. He is not listed in the Social Security Death Index.

Actually, the FBI had lost track of Judith by 1975 because she was then living under her married name of Exner and living in a mobile home, which she and her husband drove to golf tournaments. The FBI could not find her until her sister Jackie, upon being questioned by the FBI, gave her up.

It was then that Judith was subpoenaed to testify before a Senate Committee, the Church Committee. The Church Committee is the common term referring to the *United States Senate Select Committee to Study Governmental Operations with Respect to Intelligence Activities*, a U.S. Senate committee chaired by Senator Frank Church, a Democrat from Idaho, who had also been running for president.

The Church Committee subsequently decided, correctly of course, that the question of with whom the President was sleeping was none of its concern.

In November, 1975, Church Committee issued a report. Although the report was 349 pages long, only slightly more than one page of that report was devoted to the matter that made the report famous, namely the fact that President John F. Kennedy had had a "friend" who had also been a friend of a Mafia Don. The gender of the "friend" was not mentioned. The world was shocked when, one month later, it was revealed that the "friend" had been a woman who was said to have been having sexual intercourse with both the President of the United States and the Mafia Don at the same time, mixing together their semen in her vagina.

As they say, THE REST IS HISTORY.

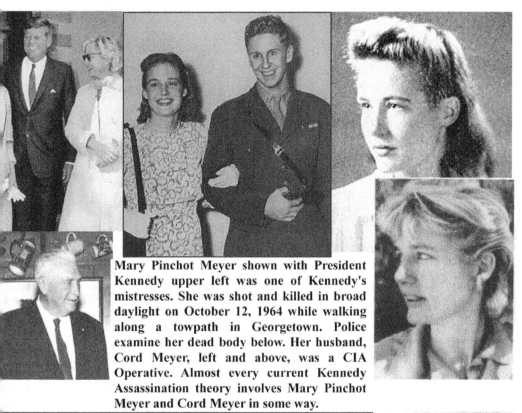

Mary Pinchot Meyer shown with President Kennedy upper left was one of Kennedy's mistresses. She was shot and killed in broad daylight on October 12, 1964 while walking along a towpath in Georgetown. Police examine her dead body below. Her husband, Cord Meyer, left and above, was a CIA Operative. Almost every current Kennedy Assassination theory involves Mary Pinchot Meyer and Cord Meyer in some way.

Ellen Rometsch was at the center of a great controversy during the Kennedy administration. She was born in Kleinitz, Germany, in 1936 in what became East Germany after the war. She came to America as the wife of a West German diplomat. She was apparently one of the girls who was seen lounging naked around the White House swimming pool. She was known to have had sexual intercourse with President Kennedy frequently. She was often described as a "prostitute" but there are no recollections of her actually asking for money for sex.

J. Edgar Hoover was concerned that she might be an East German or Soviet spy since she was born in East Germany. Hoover alerted Robert F. Kennedy to this and on August 21, 1963 RFK immediately had her deported to Germany on a U.S. Air Force transport plane.

Nothing further was heard of her, except that in 1963 she was living in Germany, possibly in Bonn. In 2007, documents were released under the Freedom of Information Act detailing concerns that she might be a spy. These documents are summarized on the FBI Internet site at http://foia.fbi.gov/foiaindex/rometsch_e.htm

ALL INFORMATION CONTAINED
HEREIN IS UNCLASSIFIED
DATE 5-29-91 BY
317 022-001

October 25, 1963

MEMORANDUM TO MR. TOLSON
MR. BELMONT
MR. MOHR
MR. DE LOACH
MR. EVANS
MR. SULLIVAN

O
Ellen Rometsch

I called Kenneth O'Donnell, Special Assistant to the President, and told him about my meeting with Senators Mansfield and Dirksen and that everything is well in hand. I advised Mr. O'Donnell that the Senators assured me that they would say nothing; that statement by Senator Williams of Delaware seemed to pull the rug from under Mollenhoff's story.

I advised Mr. O'Donnell that I had briefed Senators Mansfield and Dirksen on the material which we had sent to the President and that Senator Mansfield was suprised as to the activities which had been going on.

I informed Mr. O'Donnell that we had made a thorough investigation and no security element was involved and that we had in writing that no contact with the White House was made by the woman in Germany.

REC-24 105-122316 2

I told Mr. O'Donnell that both Senators assured me that they would not talk or say anything to the press and that all they would say was what they had seen in the papers.

Mr. O'Donnell extended an invitation from the President for me to have luncheon with the President on Thursday, October 31, 1963, at 1:00 p.m., which I accepted.

Very truly yours,

J E H

John Edgar Hoover
Director

SENT FROM D. O.
TIME 5:30PM
DATE 10-30-63
BY

Here are three pages of FBI documents concerning the Ellen Rometsch scandal. According to these documents, the scandal was about to be or had already been publicized in the *New York Daily News* and the *Associated Press News Wire*. President Kennedy wanted the story killed. FBI Director J. Edgar Hoover had spoken to Senators Mansfield and Dirksen and assured them that there was nothing to these stories. They had agreed to keep quiet.

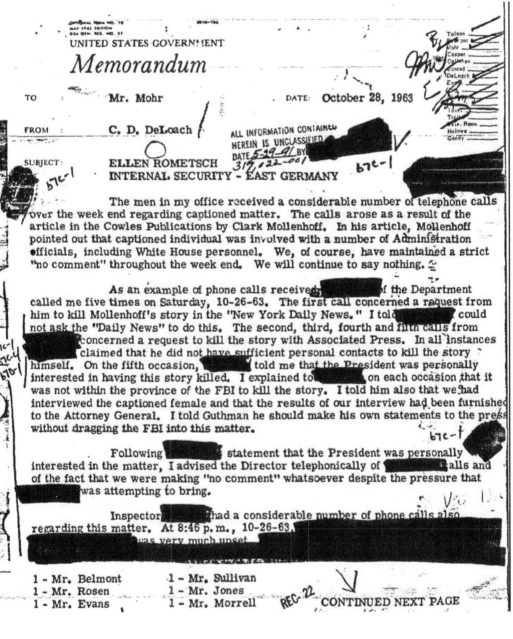

ALL INFORMATION CONTAINED
HEREIN IS UNCLASSIFIED
DATE 5-29-91 BY
319,122-061

Memorandum

UNITED STATES GOVERNMENT

TO : Mr. Mohr

DATE: October 28, 1963

FROM : C. D. DeLoach

SUBJECT: ELLEN ROMETSCH
INTERNAL SECURITY - EAST GERMANY

The men in my office received a considerable number of telephone calls over the week end regarding captioned matter. The calls arose as a result of the article in the Cowles Publications by Clark Mollenhoff. In his article, Mollenhoff pointed out that captioned individual was involved with a number of Administration officials, including White House personnel. We, of course, have maintained a strict "no comment" throughout the week end. We will continue to say nothing.

As an example of phone calls received, ████████ of the Department called me five times on Saturday, 10-26-63. The first call concerned a request from him to kill Mollenhoff's story in the "New York Daily News." I told ████ could not ask the "Daily News" to do this. The second, third, fourth and fifth calls from ████████ concerned a request to kill the story with Associated Press. In all instances ████ claimed that he did not have sufficient personal contacts to kill the story himself. On the fifth occasion, ████ told me that the President was personally interested in having this story killed. I explained to ████ on each occasion that it was not within the province of the FBI to kill the story. I told him also that we had interviewed the captioned female and that the results of our interview had been furnished to the Attorney General. I told Guthman he should make his own statements to the press without dragging the FBI into this matter.

Following ████████ statement that the President was personally interested in the matter, I advised the Director telephonically of ████████ calls and of the fact that we were making "no comment" whatsoever despite the pressure that ████ was attempting to bring.

Inspector ████████ had a considerable number of phone calls also regarding this matter. At 8:46 p.m., 10-26-63, ████████ was very much upset

1 - Mr. Belmont
1 - Mr. Rosen
1 - Mr. Evans

1 - Mr. Sullivan
1 - Mr. Jones
1 - Mr. Morrell

REC-22

CONTINUED NEXT PAGE

However, according to Seymour Hersh in *"The Dark Side of Camelot"*, page 388, Ellen Rometsch really was a prostitute who had slept with 50 men, including the president, for money. Also, she had left East Germany in 1961, the same year she had arrived in the USA, and she had been a member of the Communist Party in East Germany. Thus, there was a real possibility that she might be a spy.

Mr. Tolson

        The Director spoke once again of false allegations
regarding Ellen Romesch and other prostitutes of wide publicity.
The Director indicated that there had, of course, been some
truth to the fact that a small number of senators had involved
themselves with prostitutes and that the late President Kennedy
had on one occasion asked the Director to see Senators Dirksen
and Mansfield relative to this matter.

        Vinson stated that the Attorney General, on the
morning of 3/16/66, had requested him to summarize all matters
relative to the Canadian hoodlum and forward this information
to the FBI so that we, in turn, could give it to the RCMP.
The Director stated we would handle this matter.

        The Director referred to the investigation by two
Royal Commissions which had been set in motion by the Canadian
Parliament. He stated it was wrong to have one commission,
much less the confusion of two at the same time.

        Vinson stated his letter to the Director concerning
the Canadian matter, mentioned above, would also contain a
request that the FBI maintain a "loose watch" on

                                The Director made no commitment
in this regard.

                          8

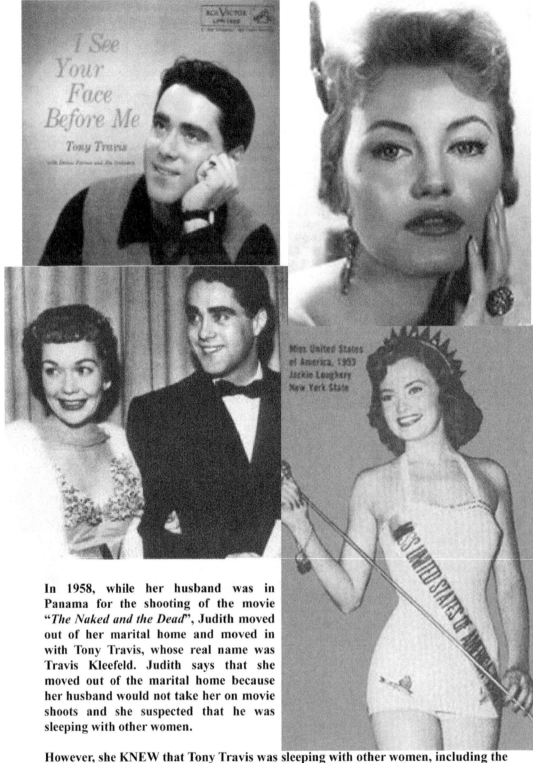

I See Your Face Before Me

Tony Travis

Miss United States of America, 1953
Jackie Loughery
New York State

In 1958, while her husband was in Panama for the shooting of the movie *"The Naked and the Dead"*, Judith moved out of her marital home and moved in with Tony Travis, whose real name was Travis Kleefeld. Judith says that she moved out of the marital home because her husband would not take her on movie shoots and she suspected that he was sleeping with other women.

However, she KNEW that Tony Travis was sleeping with other women, including the Miss USA 1952 Jackie Loughery, upper right, and Jane Wyman, the first wife of Ronald Reagan, above left. Why would she leave her husband for a man whom she knew was a notorious womanizer?

20th Century-Fox presents COLE PORTER'S
CAN-CAN
starring FRANK SINATRA • SHIRLEY MacLAINE • MAURICE CHEVALIER
and LOUIS JOURDAN • COLOR by DE LUXE • a Jack Cummings production
Directed by Walter Lang • Screenplay by Dorothy Kingsley and
Charles Lederer • Associate Producer Saul Chaplin
Produced by Suffolk Cumming Productions
and released through 20th Century-Fox Film Corporation

After Judith Campbell refused to sleep with Frank Sinatra any more, after he had tried to include her in a threesome, Frank took up with dancer Juliet Prowse as his "number one girl". This made Judith feel "liberated". However, Frank did not stay with Juliet long. "It was just one of those things", as Frank sang to Juliet in the movie "*Can-Can*".

Juliet Prowse became famous for her performance in the 1960 movie "Can-Can" starring Shirley McClain and Frank Sinatra, when Nikita Khrushchev, in a rare visit by a Soviet leader to America, was invited to the movie set and, after seeing her performance, labeled her dancing "immoral".

This did not have the result Khrushchev intended, because everybody went to see the movie.

Dan Rowan of the Comedy show "*Rowan & Martin's Laugh-In*". However, it was no laughing matter when Mafia Don Sam Giancana suspected Rowan of sleeping with his girlfriend Phyllis McGuire. This can get a man killed. In a prudent and appropriate use of federal taxpayer's money, the CIA agreed to Giancana's request to bug Rowan's hotel room to see if he was sleeping with McGuire, in return for which Giancana agreed to help the CIA to kill Castro. This would all be funny if it were not serious.

Angie Dickinson as she appeared in the movie "*Ocean's Eleven*". She had a minor part in the movie, was not involved in the central plot, but delivered a great speech about why she wanted Sinatra to come back and be her husband, rather than making his living by betting on horses or playing cards.

Little did she realize that the Sinatra character had reformed and decided to give that all up and secure a comfortable retirement for himself and his wife Angie by ROBBING FIVE CASINOS simultaneously!!!

When the "*Judith Campbell, Mobsters' Moll*" story broke in the newspapers in December 1975, Angie denied knowing Judith. She has also never admitted to knowing John F. Kennedy either. However, her name comes up all the time and everybody realizes that she did know them.

Gloria Swanson (1899-1983), sultry star of the silent screen, was the mistress of Joseph P. Kennedy, father of John, Robert and Teddy Kennedy. An often forgotten fact is that Joseph Kennedy took time off from his bootlegging, stock market swindling and other illegal activities to become a Hollywood Movie Producer for four years from 1926 to 1930. He was involved in the production of and sometimes even appeared in 72 movies and was listed in the producer of eight movies, most of which starred Gloria Swanson.

The famous "lost movie" of this era was "What a Widow" starring Gloria Swanson, produced by Joseph P. Kennedy. Although widely shown in the theaters of that time, no copies of it are known to exist. It seems possible that Joseph Kennedy bought them all up and had them destroyed after he decided to leave the movie business.

Gloria Swanson was no slouch in the adultery department. Her third husband, a movie producer, divorced her in 1925 alleging that she had committed adultery with 13 men. Most of those men were movie producers. Joseph Kennedy was not on the list. When she took up with Joseph Kennedy the following year, she already had a new husband, but that did not slow her down. She certainly knew which side her bread was buttered on. The long list of men she is said to have slept with included most of the prominent movie producers of her era.

When John F. and Robert F. Kennedy allegedly took up with Marilyn Monroe, they were just following in the grand tradition established by their father, Joseph Kennedy. Joseph Kennedy even took Gloria Swanson to his home in Massachusetts and introduced her to his wife, Rose, even though all the gossip columnists had been writing that Kennedy and Swanson had been sleeping together.

A United Artists Picture.   *What A Widow!*

TAM BROOKS, WIDOW OF GRANT BROOKS,
LEAVES BEDFORD, MASS , FOR NEW YORK.

"*What a Widow*" starring Gloria Swanson as Tam Brooks and produced by Joseph P. Kennedy is famous as a lost movie. No copies are known to exist. You may be wondering where I got this photo.

Joseph P. Kennedy (1888-1969), right, in 1914. Joseph Kennedy became Chairman of the Securities and Exchange Commission (1934-1937), Chairman, Maritime Commission (1937), and Ambassador to Great Britain (1938-1940). It was he who made the Kennedy Fortune and he was the one who had the capabilities of being a good president, not his worthless sons.

The picture below right is believed to be a picture of Joseph P. Kennedy with Gloria Swanson. She was known as "The Queen of the Screen". He was running three movie studios at the same time. One became Warner Brothers. The other two became RKO. Gloria Swanson was the first Hollywood movie star to make one million dollars.

Older than Jerry, Dean wants to slow down, be home more with Jeanne, his kids

Dean Martin called Judith Campbell frequently, but not for the reason other men called. Unlike the others, he did not want to sleep with Judy. Rather, he had a strange request. He wanted to find out if his wife, Jeanne, was sleeping with his agent, Mort Viner, lower left.

How strange! Why would his lovely wife, Jeanne, want to sleep with an ugly man like Mort Viner when she could sleep with Dean Martin?

Unlike Frank Sinatra, who could and often did sleep with a different Hollywood movie star every night, Dean Martin was a sleep-at-home-with-his-own-wife kind of guy, a rarely in Hollywood. His wife Jeanne said he was "home every night for dinner with his children".

On May 19 1962, Marilyn Monroe sang "Happy Birthday to You" to President Kennedy at Madison Square Garden in New York City for a live TV Nationwide Audience. Her gown was so tight it had to be sewn onto her body, and then cut off her after her performance. In 1999, her gown was auctioned for $1.5 million at Christie's.

In this picture, a cameraman surprised John F. Kennedy and Robert F. Kennedy while they were speaking to Marilyn in private quarters while she was still wearing the gown. Both John and Robert Kennedy are rumored to have slept with Marilyn Monroe.

Jacqueline Kennedy, below far right, with Gianni Agnelli, left, principal shareholder of Fiat, in Ravello, Italy in 1962. The other men are Benno Graziani and Stanislas Radziwill Not to be outdone in the adultery department, Jacqueline Kennedy spent several nights aboard Gianni's yacht in the Mediterranean. President Kennedy was annoyed, not because his wife was sleeping with other men, but because it was becoming publicly obvious. Kennedy wrote to her, "A little more Carolyn and less Agnelli".

Benjamin C. Bradlee, Executive Editor of the Washington Post, was a close personal friend of Jacqueline Kennedy and her husband, President Kennedy. Here, Bradley, left sits next to Jacqueline, Bradley's wife, and President Kennedy.

This looks like a wife-swapping couple in a scene out of the movie "Bob & Carol & Ted & Alice", especially when you take a close look at Jacqueline's dress.

That is not really a dress. That is black ink. The actual dress she was wearing was so short her panties were showing, so they covered her legs in the photo with black ink to make her look respectable.

Jacqueline Kennedy with John Kenneth Galbraith, US Ambassador to India. Jacqueline is suspected of having committed adultery with Galbraith as well. It is said that when she went to India in 1963 supposedly on a diplomatic mission, it was actually to visit her lover Galbraith. According to *Dog Days in the White House* by Traphes Bryant, Kennedy was so fearful that Jacqueline was sleeping with Galbraith in India that he called her back to the White House.

Galbraith advised President Kennedy to make a deal with the Soviets to pull out of Vietnam. His recommendations were opposed by McNamara. Had the advice of Galbraith been followed, the Vietnam War would have not happened.

Evelyn Lincoln (1909 – 1995) was the personal secretary to John F. Kennedy from his election to the United States Senate in 1953 until his assassination in Dallas. Mrs. Lincoln was in the motorcade when Kennedy was assassinated.

It was Mrs. Lincoln who made reservations for Judith Campbell to stay at the Mayflower Hotel in Washington DC when she came to visit President Kennedy. It was Mrs. Lincoln who sent a White House car to pick Judith up and who gave her a train ticket back to New York City when Judith was preparing to leave.

One question does come up: It has been reported from several sources that President Kennedy was known to have had sexual relations with female members of the White House staff. Traphes Bryant in *"Dog Days in the White House"* wrote "half the secretaries and other women around him would gladly have stood in line outside his bedroom door. Some would kiddingly tell me what they would give for only one night with that man."

One must suspect that Evelyn Lincoln was one of those women. She was not very beautiful, but Kennedy did not seem to care much whether the woman was beautiful or not.

The Entire Kennedy Clan

This picture of the Kennedy Klan was taken on the morning of Wednesday, November 9, 1960, right after it had been officially announced that John F. Kennedy had been elected president.

Standing from left are: Ethel Skakel Kennedy, Stephen E. Smith, Jean Kennedy Smith, JFK, Robert F. Kennedy, Patricia Kennedy Lawford, Joan Bennett Kenndy, Peter Lawford. Sitting from left: Eunice Kennedy Shriver, Rose Fitzgerald Kennedy, Joseph P. Kennedy, Jacqueline Bouvier Kennedy, Edward Moore Kennedy, and Sargent Shriver.

This is probably the only picture of the entire clan ever taken. (Of course, there is one Kennedy missing, but that is a story for another day.)

Ted Kennedy in 1960

On the night of February 7, 1960, Teddy Kennedy escorted Judith Campbell to her hotel room door, then entered the room uninvited and sat on her bed, obviously hoping to sleep with her.

However, Judith did not enter the room. She stayed in the alcove, pointing him out the door, indicating that she did not wish to sleep with him. Finally, Teddy gave up and left.

The following day Judith spent time with his elder brother, John F. Kennedy. That was a different story.

Although she claims that she did not sleep with John Kennedy on that occasion (this is disputed), she did start a relationship with him one month later.

An interesting question is why was Judith willing to sleep with John but not with Edward Kennedy. A likely reason was simply age. Teddy was 15 years younger. John was 42. Teddy was 27. Many women prefer a more mature man.

There is another, more interesting, question: Why did John F. Kennedy immediately take an interest in Judith? Judith says in her book that she suspects that the reason was precisely because she had turned Teddy down. John F. Kennedy was playing a game of one-upsmanship, making Teddy jealous that he got something his younger brother could not get.

Prime Minister Nehru of India with President Kennedy. David Powers is behind them, center. David Powers (1912-1988) was Special Assistant to President Kennedy. He was also a personal friend of John F. Kennedy. He was seated in the limousine directly behind the President at the time of the Kennedy Assassination.

After the Assassination, Powers served as Museum Curator of the John F. Kennedy Library and Museum from 1964 until 1994. When The Judith Campbell Exner Scandal broke, Powers said, "The only Campbell I know is chunky vegetable soup". However, one could hardly expect the curator of John F. Kennedy Library and Museum to admit that the man he was supposed to honor was a philanderer.

Prime Minister Nehru (1889-1964) was vehemently anti-American and pro-Soviet. Under Nehru, India became virtually a Soviet client state. Nehru's daughter Indira Gandhi (1917-1984) was a little better from the point of view of America, but not much. Indira Gandhi's rule was brought to an end in 1984 through the efforts of Satwant Singh. Her son Rajiv (1944-1991) then ruled, but his re-election campaign was concluded in 1991 by the Sri Lankan patriot Thenmuli Rajaratnam.

The end of the Nehru-Gandhi Rule plus the fall of the Soviet Union has brought great benefits of the people of India. The economy and the standard of living have vastly improved. The Indian people are happier, healthier and better off in every way. They are even catching up with us in chess. (Some say they have passed us.)

Frank Sinatra with new president John F. Kennedy at the Kennedy Inaugural Ball on January 20, 1961. This is one of the last times that Sinatra and Kennedy would be seen in public together. In spite of the help the "Rat Pack" provided in getting Kennedy elected, JFK proceeds to distance himself from them. A Kennedy aid calls Sammy Davis Jr. and informs him that JFK requests that Davis NOT attend the inaugural ball. He is sure Davis will understand, the aid says. Davis does understand and becomes a staunch supporter of Richard Nixon and the Republican Party after this snub. Dean Martin also provides a lame excuse as to why he is otherwise engaged and is too busy to attend the Kennedy inauguration.

According to her book, Desi Arnaz tried to sleep with Judith Campbell but she fled his hotel room as soon as she realized that she had been tricked into being left alone with him. After that, she was fearful that others suspected that she had gone through with it.

How could Desi do this, when he was the world's most famously married man?

Judith says that it was because he had broken up with Lucille Ball after their show "*I Love Lucy*" had been canceled.

However, this was not exactly what happened. Lucy was still married to Desi at that time but they had broken up because of his notorious womanizing.

As to "I Love Lucy" being canceled, it is still being shown on TV to this day. Just turn the knob and it will be there. Some works of genius cannot be replaced by modern technology.

Robert Wagner and Natalie Wood

Robert Wagner was the first movie star who dated Judith Campbell (except that he was not a movie star yet). It was Robert Wagner who first introduced Judith to many Hollywood movie stars including Billy Campbell, whom she married.

Robert Wagner starred with Natalie Wood, then married her, then divorced her, then got back with her.

Robert Wagner is still in the movies. He stars as *"Mr. Wilson"* in *"Dennis the Menace"*. Natalie Wood's greatest performance was as part of a wife-swapping couple in *"Bob & Carol & Ted & Alice"* (forget *"West Side Story"*).

On November 29, 1981, Natalie Wood drowned after falling off their yacht. Natalie did not know how to swim and Robert Wagner forgot to call the life saving crew or the police.

The moral to this story is:

BE SURE TO TEACH YOUR KIDS HOW TO SWIM

MGM motion picture producer Joe Pasternak presents Connie Francis with MGM gold record for selling one million records.

Joe Pasternak produced one hundred motion pictures. (Few of his pictures were really famous, though.) He interviewed Judith Campbell, told her she had some talent and to return in six months.

She never went back. It seems that she did not have much interest in appearing in movies. It would not have been difficult. All she would have had to do was look beautiful.

Brad Dexter was a tough guy in the movies, who was one of the many Hollywood Movie Stars that Judith met. Brad Dexter was friends with Frank Sinatra and with some of his Mafia wiseguy friends.

Dexter is most famous for saving Sinatra's life. Sinatra was swimming off the coast of Hawaii when the tide swept him out to sea. Dexter swam out and saved him. When they later had disagreements and broke up, Dexter claimed that he was the only man who ever fired Frank Sinatra.

Here are a few of the famous people Judith Campbell mentions in her book as having met:

On March 10, 1960, Judith flew to Miami with Toni Carroll to see the Frank Sinatra Show at the Hotel Fontainebleau. Toni Carroll was a singer who sung "I'm Just Wild About Harry".

Judith Campbell writes that she danced at a party with Senator Abraham Ribicoff (1910 – 1998). Ribicoff was President Kennedy's Secretary of Health, Education, and Welfare and was later Governor of Connecticut and a United States Senator.

Alain Delon bottom was a French movie star Judith met in Hollywood.

Judith was escorted around Miami by Bob Neal. She reports that Bob Neal was the most gentlemanly of all the men who ever escorted her. This means, of course, that Bob Neal was the only man who never tried to sleep with her.

Bob Neal is best known for being the first manager of Elvis Presley. First picture is of Bob Neal with Elvis in 1955.

Second is Bob Neal, Elvis and Sam Phillips. However, this picture seems to have been reversed, as it shows Elvis signing with his left hand. Other versions of the same picture are flipped, showing Elvis signing with his right hand.

Third picture is of Colonel Tom Parker, Elvis, Bob Neal and Hank Snow. Colonel Tom Parker was much later revealed to be an illegal alien who had reached America by jumping ship. His real name was Andreas Cornelis van Kuijk. He was constantly afraid of being arrested and deported and for that reason Elvis never toured internationally because Tom Parker, who always accompanied him, was afraid to leave the country for fear that he would not be able to get back in. Even when Elvis performed in Canada, Tom Parker remained on the USA side of the border.

Jimmy Van Heusen, the famous song writer who wrote many if not most of the songs that made Frank Sinatra and Bing Crosby famous, including "All the Way", "High Hopes", "Call Me Irresponsible", "Love and Marriage", "Come Fly with Me" and "Only the Lonely". Judith met Van Heusen at Sinatra's home in Palm Springs.

Barbara Rush was a Hollywood Movie Star that Judith met at a party when Judith was about 17.

Jane Wyman (1917-2007) was the first wife of President Ronald Reagan and the mother of Maureen and Michael Reagan.

When Judith Campbell moved out of the marital home of William Campbell, she moved in with Tony Travis, even though she knew that he was romantically linked to Jane Wyman.

Walter Winchell (1897–1972), an American newspaper and radio commentator, was the inventor of the modern gossip column. He broke the journalistic taboo against exposing the private lives of public figures. Soon, they discovered that they liked it as it increased their popularity and got them jobs in the movies and night clubs. One person who did not like it was Judith Campbell. If she found out that any journalist was considering publishing her name, she would call that journalist and tell him not to do it. On May 8, 1962, Walter Winchell published in the Los Angeles Herald Examiner, "Judy Campbell of Palm Springs and Bevhills is topic no. 1 in Romantic Political circles." Judith was upset about this. Nobody knew where Winchell had received this news item or what it was all about.

Walter Winchell
OF NEW YORK AND HOLLYWOOD

Judy Campbell of Palm Springs and Bevhills is Topic No. 1 in Romantic Political Circles . . . Quip sweeping the nation:

Inga Brandsdottir, Sam's friend in Iceland.

Above: Sam holding up Inga's friend Solveig, who was a bit drunk. Solveig was also a long distance telephone operator and they put her picture on the cover of the Icelandic telephone book

Sam Sloan first learned of the relationship between John F. Kennedy and Judith Campbell Exner in January 1976, from Inga Brandsdottir, a long

distance telephone operator in Reykjavik, Iceland. Previously, Inga had worked for Sam in New York in his Wall Street broker-dealership, Samuel H. Sloan & Co. By 1976, Sam was staying with Inga in her apartment in Reykjavik. Inga came

home from work one day with this news. Within a matter of days, the whole world including China and Russia had heard about it.

Right: Inga plays the piano. Left: Inga's daughter Tinna, who now works as a high fashion model on the runways of London and Paris.

Eddie Fisher with his two wives, Elizabeth Taylor and Debbie Reynolds. Fisher really had it good. Just imagine being able to sleep with these women any time he wanted.

Eddie Fisher, not satisfied with Liz and Debbie, also dated Judith Campbell. Judith does not reveal whether she slept with him or not.

The most frequent comment made by those who saw Judith Campbell was that she looked like Elizabeth Taylor, only more beautiful.

Elizabeth Taylor looks really good in this photo. One wonders how anyone could look more beautiful than this.

Traphes Bryant and Friends

Traphes Bryant worked at the White House for 21 years from 1951 to 1972. His main job was White House Kennel Keeper, taking care of the dogs. He wrote that he kept his job by keeping his eyes and ears open and his mouth shut. He kept a diary and wrote down many questionable goings-on. His book about this, "Dog Days at the White House", came out in July, 1975 and was the first to reveal the true situation of President Kennedy.

Traphes Bryant and "Dog Days in the White House"

Even while Kennedy was President, there were reports in the press that JFK sometimes swam naked in this White House indoor swimming pool. Nobody paid much attention to this, or cared much about this, because every man has a right to be naked in the privacy of his own home.

What these news reports did not mention was that when the President was swimming naked in the White House pool, he often had a few naked females in the pool with him. Seymour Hersh reports that there was one nude party in the White House with five men and twelve women present, all naked.

This would certainly have upset the sensitivities of the religiously conservative General Public, because it implies that adulterous relationships occurred while Jacqueline Kennedy was not present.

A common, often asked question is how could Jacqueline have tolerated this, since she must have known about it.

The answer may lie in the fact that Jacqueline's father, John "Black Jack" Bouvier (1891-1957), was the same way, a notorious womanizer, who slept with many women while married to Jackie's mother, Janet Norton. Similarly, JFK's father, Joseph Kennedy, was the same way too, sleeping with numerous Hollywood Movie Stars while married to Rose. Thus, both Jack and Jacqueline had been raised in similar circumstances.

The most notorious or often repeated story about this is that one time Jacqueline Kennedy discovered a woman's panties in the presidential bed in the White House. She held them up to JFK and said, "Would you please shop around and see who these belong to? They're not my size."

This story is found in the *Time* magazine article for December 29, 1975 and in the Seymour Hersh book, *"The Dark Side of Camelot"*,

Traphes Bryant and "Dog Days in the White House"

published in 1997, but without attribution to the original source.

The original source to this story was unlikely. It comes from a book about the pet dogs in the White House.

The first time the news started to come out about the JFK sexual romps in the White House was from an unlikely source, a book about the dogs of the presidents. The book, *"Dog Days at the White House"* by the White House official Kennel Keeper Traphes Bryant is a book about the presidential dogs, with a few words in between about the people too.

In that era, all the presidents kept dogs in the White House, if only to get the dog-lover's votes. President Johnson, the only president who sincerely loved his dogs, became infamous by picking up one of his pet beagles by the ears.

Traphes Bryant worked at the White House for 21 years from 1951 to 1972. His initial job was night shift electrician, primarily changing burnt out light bulbs. When it was noticed that he devoted a lot of attention to the dogs, he was given the added duties of White House Kennel Keeper.

Every time a new president comes in, he brings his own aids. However, the maintenance workers at the White House generally stay the same. Thus, the cooks, maids, cleaners, sweepers and gardeners often have extended stays of employment there.

The best known example of this was Lillian Rogers Parks, who was a maid and seamstress in the White House from 1931 to 1961. She was preceded by her mother, who was head housemaid at the White House from 1909 to 1939, Parks, who died in 1997 at age 100, published *"My Thirty Years Backstairs at the White House"* with journalist Frances Spatz Leighton. The book was on the New York Times bestseller list for 26 weeks and has since been made into a made for television movie, "Backstairs at the Whitehouse".

Traphes Bryant and "Dog Days in the White House"

Frances Spatz Leighton wrote more than 30 books and countless articles on subjects such as the White House chef during the Eisenhower years, Jacqueline Kennedy's dressmaker and personal secretary, the man who ran the Senate restaurant, the man who worked as the House of Representatives doorkeeper for 42 years and the dogs who have occupied the White House.

This last book, however, will never be made into a made-for-television movie, unless they greatly relax the censorship laws or play it as a late night X-rated video, because it casually mentions sex orgies and nude romps at JFK's White House. The author, Traphes Bryant, says that he kept his job at the White House by keeping his ears and eyes open and his mouth shut. He never told anybody what was really going on at the White House, not even his wife, but he wrote it all down and his diary forms the basis for his book.

Here are some excerpts from pages 22-40 of the hard cover edition:

> *President Kennedy certainly seemed to enjoy his women. I don't know for sure about Marilyn Monroe, but I did hear backstairs talk, after he was dead, that during his visits to California he had enjoyed a few discreet meetings with her at a private home.*
>
> *I never saw her around the White House and I never heard talk of her being either an official or "O.R." - off the record-guest there in his administration, even though she once sang "Happy birthday, Mr. President, happy birthday to you" to him in New York's Madison Square Garden.*
>
> *But this much I can tell you: he did enjoy having beautiful women around him at the White House and he did entertain them when Jackie was away. There was a conspiracy of silence to protect his secrets from Jacqueline and to keep her from finding out. The newspapers would tell how First*

Traphes Bryant and "Dog Days in the White House"

Lady Jacqueline was off on another trip, but what they didn't report was how anxious the President sometimes was to see her go. And what consternation there sometimes was when she returned unexpectedly.

I remember one time it was a beautiful tall blond girl skinny -dipping in the pool with him. JFK liked to swim nude and so did some of the girls who popped in to visit him. But this particular girl must have been just waiting for the First Lady to be on her way. She came in the South West Gate and straight to the South Portico, and a trusted aide met her there. He walked her through the Diplomatic Room and along the Colonnade, as if he were taking her to the President's office, but instead he took her to the gymnasium, where she shed her clothes and went to the pool.

Jack Kennedy was already there, lounging naked beside the pool and sipping a daiquiri. Sometimes one or two from a group of trusted staff aides and friends would join Kennedy in the pool, and often there would be just one other male and female to make up a foursome. This time there were several girls and several male friends.

I was there that night because the tall girl had taken a notion she wanted to pet the famous space dog, Pushinka. So I brought the little Russian mongrel to the aide who had escorted her in. The aide kept hurrying the girl along, saying, "The President is waiting for You. He's getting impatient. You can't keep a President waiting, you know." But she insisted on playing with the dog, saying, "Jack won't mind waiting."

While all this was going on, Mrs. Kennedy was supposed to have gone to Atoka, Virginia. But the First Lady circled back because she had forgotten something-or maybe she just had a hunch. Bobby Kennedy was also there. Well, suddenly the ushers were sounding the alarm, and first thing I knew naked bodies were scurrying every which way.

It was easy to get rid of bodies, but gathering up the drinks was another matter and the help had a time clearing away the evidence - like highball glasses. Only the President remained in the pool.

As I remember it, Jacqueline seemed not to notice anything amiss. Soon word came that she was getting back into her car, and then that it had driven off. But just in case, the President swam alone in the pool for a while.

Thinking of this incident reminds me that Jackie wasn't the only one who influenced the decor of the White House-I helped bring about one small alteration myself. When the President noticed that some of us male workers were standing outside the glass door watching him swimming nude with mixed company, he ordered the door to the pool changed to frosted glass. The President always did try to be discreet. He tried to have as few household people as possible know whom he was entertaining. The way he would work it was this. After Jacqueline would leave on one of her numerous outings, he would tell the kitchen help to prepare some food and drinks and just leave them. Then he would tell the waiters they could go home. "I can take care of it," he'd say. What he liked on these occasions was little wiener sausages with bacon wrapped around them. They were kept in a portable warmer. And a pitcher of daiquiris was kept in the refrigerator. JFK liked them.

And usually when he wanted to be alone with his female company, JFK passed the word that the private family quarters on the second floor were off-limits. One night I got word not to go upstairs after the First Lady left. But somehow, thinking of an electrical appliance I had to fix, it slipped my mind and I accidentally went up. I was headed for the third floor anyway, the floor above the living quarters, but the elevator stopped by itself at 2. I could hear lovey-dovey talk. Another man went to the second floor to see if the gas was off in the kitchen - it had been a problem and a bit of a danger. When he stepped out of the back elevator he saw a naked woman walking from the kitchen.

When Jackie was away, riding the elevator was hazardous duty, as this diary entry shows:

> *"Just as the elevator door opened, a naked blond office girl ran through the hall between the second-floor kitchen and the door leading to the West Hall. Her breasts were swinging as she ran by. There was nothing to do but to get out fast and push the basement buttons."*

It was natural for us to exchange information backstairs so that we would know how to handle ourselves. But while the Kennedys were in the White House I told no one outside the White House - not even my wife.

The way I heard it, the shots in the arm or hip that the President took every day for his health had the side effect of making him feel very sexy. I don't know how he felt, but I do know how the women of the White House reacted to him - half the secretaries and other women around him would gladly have stood in line outside his bedroom door. Some would kiddingly tell me what they would give "for only one night with that man."

They may not have gotten anywhere near his bedroom but they were delighted to help him relax as best they could in the office. Kennedy had an unusual way of relaxing at the end of the day. I found out because my hours officially were three-thirty to eleven-thirty at night, and frequently ended up at midnight or later. Here's the way I described it in my diary, when I was writing down some of my memories after Kennedy had been assassinated.

I'd be out at the C-9 Post* (*Every station at which a White house policeman stands guard is designated by a letter-number combination. Policemen are rotated so that the same policeman may stand guard at several posts or stations on the same day.) with the dogs and I'd tell the policeman, "Well, I see the President is getting his brush job." The policeman would laugh and say, "I wish she'd come out and fix my hair that way." The girl, a pretty office girl, would take her time, brush Jack Kennedy's hair very slow, back and forth, back and forth, brush the sides, brush the back. He'd be sitting at his desk in the office. Maybe working. It relaxed him to have his hair brushed.

I liked Kennedy. I didn't set myself up as his judge. I figured he had his reasons for whatever he did. Also, I liked Jacqueline Kennedy. I liked her a lot. I don't want to give the impression she was some kind of angel. I remember one particular White House party. Mrs. K. was loaded on champagne and flung her shoes off. I looked through the ushers' window, which guests don't know is a one-way mirror, and saw her kick her shoes off while dancing under the chandelier in the main lobby, officially called the Grand Entrance Hall. That's where the good dance floor is, and the Marine Band plays out there. The Usher's Office adjoins the main lobby, just inside the North Portico - what you would call a front porch.

Getting back to that party, Jacqueline seemed to flirt with every guy she danced with - making eyes, throwing her head back lovey-dovey. All the men danced with her. I could see that some of the female guests were plenty jealous. I'll bet their husbands had some explaining to do that night.

She didn't flirt with me, but she did make me feel like a man and someone especially important to her.

For some reason she chose me to help her with various chores, maybe because I understood her-or tried to-and sympathized with her need to feel that she was doing things for herself. I remember Mrs. K. had me help her move a gigantic dollhouse from one side of Caroline's room to the other. I wanted to do it alone but the First Lady pushed right along with me, tugging and huffing and puffing and enjoying the effort.

Once she had the dogs out in the station wagon. She liked to take her big German shepherd to one of the parks and run and hike with him. This time she was waiting for a Secret Service man who would accompany her. She asked me for a cigarette and I didn't have one. I was smoking cigars. I jokingly held one out to her and she giggled. Then I said I'd go get her a cigarette. She said, "No, please, let me." She jumped out and went to the Usher's Office and got her own cigarettes.

I think as marriages go, her marriage to the President wasn't too bad. They had a lot going for them. They both loved their kids and, I think, each other, very much. They were always looking out for each other, sometimes protectively, sometimes trying to think up little surprises. And they did not air their problems in front of the household staff.

When they had anything to say to each other they took walks together inside and outside the White House grounds, no matter what the weather. Sometimes I brought them a dog or two to walk with them. I could tell when they were squabbling with each other, or were just sullen.

Even in the rain or snow I'd find them making their late-night rounds. No umbrella. She with a scarf over her head.

He bareheaded. No tourist would take a second look and the Secret Service men kept a discreet distance, usually in a car. It would be dark and rainy. Either Clipper or Charlie would be on a leash. Or both.

What tourist would dream that a President and First Lady were walking a dog? When the Kennedys were happy and playful they didn't want to use a leash, but I would insist, sometimes not so gently, saying I was sure the dog would run into traffic and be run over. Jacqueline would be slightly annoyed with me. She prided herself on her control over dogs. She personally had taken her dogs to the U.S. Park Service's Dog Obedience School, watching the trainers and participating, and now she felt she could make any dog heel and obey. But when I acted tough, she would look resignedly at the President and say, "Oh, all right, Bryant" - pronouncing my name in her appealing little-girl voice - "give it here."

The President never interfered. I felt he enjoyed the little byplay.

I was sure that the Kennedys' dogs were somehow helpful in their marriage, a means they had of communicating with each other in a close and affectionate way.

Did Kennedy play around much at the White House? Yes, he did. Every time one of his feminine guests left, the help would scour the rooms for hairpins and bobby pins. Kennedy was following a tradition established by a lot of earlier Presidents.

More than once I heard talk in the White House of how Woodrow Wilson had played around after his first wife died. According to the story, the President's doctor, Cary Grayson, was so worried that rumors would sweep the country about a "playboy in the White House" that he introduced him to a widow he considered suitable for marriage, Edith Rolling Galt. Luckily the meeting "took."

President Wilson proposed. Nevertheless, he had such a wild reputation that a joke went the rounds of Washington, and even today people occasionally resurrect it at the White House while reviewing the love lives of the Presidents.

Question: What did Mrs. Galt say when President Wilson proposed to her?

Answer: Nothing. She was so surprised she fell out of bed.

There's still talk about a packet of love letters that Wilson is supposed to have exchanged with some other woman before Edith Galt entered his life. At the time people thought the letters had damaging material that might keep him from being reelected. But the best letters weren't revealed and never have been. The lady in question clammed up, She was rumored to have received a gift of money from a close friend of the President. One of the President's daughters sought to counteract the bad publicity by gathering and publishing his love letters to her mother, his first wife.

And what about the shocking White House romance of another very sexy President in the 1880's, Grover Cleveland? That story has it that President Cleveland was romancing his ward, Frances Folsom, daughter of his old law partner and his responsibility since she was eleven.

The President tried hard to keep his feelings about the pretty girl a secret, but as every President learns, no secrets survive for long in the White House. On the night of June 2, 1886, President Cleveland, who was pushing fifty, filled the Blue Room with flowers and made Frances, who was twenty-one or twenty-two years old - versions differ - his bride, with only a few close friends and his Cabinet present.

Traphes Bryant and "Dog Days in the White House"

When Eisenhower moved into the White House, backstairs talk began immediately about his wartime relations with his W.A.A.F driver and how he gifted her with pretty gowns from Paris. The story told was that five-star General Ike really cared deeply about his chauffeur, Kay Summersby, and that he wanted to divorce Mamie to marry her. At Mamie's request, people said, General Marshall, the Chief of Staff, sent Ike's son John to be his father's aide, in order to help save the marriage. The strategy worked.

Scratch almost any President and you will find a bit of a lady's man. Even McKinley, with his reputation as a stiffneck, had a fine eye for the ladies. When he was President, he supposedly taught a parrot to tell the difference between men and women. Every time a female approached the parrot would shriek, "Look at the pretty girl!" But McKinley didn't need a parrot to tell him.

LBJ loved women, too. Within my sight he confined himself to grabbing an occasional kiss, but the talk backstairs and among his aides was that he didn't stop just there a few times when he'd gone driving off into the night with some charmer - usually on his way to the presidential yacht. He was even said to have "inherited" two very pretty girl reporters from Kennedy. At least, they were LBJ's favorites and he would mention one or the other to me as "all woman" or "a lot of woman" and even accord them the ultimate compliment he ordinarily reserved for his favorite dog, Yuki, telling me they were "pretty as a polecat."

At a party, LBJ would back a pretty girl off in a corner and sweep her off her feet by telling her, "You're the prettiest thing I've ever seen." What he didn't add was "since yesterday." Sometimes he'd tell the gal who caught his eye to step into the next room away from the noise, where they could hold a "serious discussion."

She may have been serious. He wasn't. If ever there was a kissing President, it was he. When he got into the party spirit at a White House dance, someone had to get the lipstick off him. Lady Bird would be on the alert to break it up. She'd say kind of plaintively, "You're wanted over there, Lyndon. You're neglecting some of your friends." She found safety in numbers. As long as the President was kidding all the girls, she was safe.

Once Lyndon Johnson actually got jealous of me! I'll tell you about it later. The point I want to make now is that LBJ was a sexy man. He told me so and I'm willing to take his word for it. Lady Bird frequently slept in LBJ's bed. I would go up to deliver the dogs and she would be tucked under the covers.

After Johnson died, I read somewhere that Lady Bird was interviewed about her husband's playful way with the girls and you could tell that she had understood him all the time. Asked about her husband's flirtations, Lady Bird said, "He got a lot of solace and happiness and inspiration from women," and admitted Lyndon was "a flirt and a ladies' man."

Then she said something that showed her true humility. "I hope that I was reasonable. And if all those ladies had some good points that I didn't have, I hope that I had the good sense to try to learn by it."

When it comes to the Nixons, what can I say? Pat Nixon herself admitted she could not sleep in the same bed with the President because he was too fretful - kept waking up, dictating into a Dictaphone, turning lights off and on. But more on that later.

Traphes Bryant and "Dog Days in the White House"

There was nothing fretful about Kennedy and his sleep habits. He enjoyed his bed - day or night.

And he certainly enjoyed women, as I can attest by my own eyes. He would often kid with his male staff about women. An item from my diary shows his style of banter:

Dave Powers once asked the President what he would like to have for his birthday. He named a TV actress from California. His wish was granted.

Even President Ford commented on Jack Kennedy's obsession with girls. They used to have offices across the hall from each other when Kennedy was a congressman. After Ford became President and was still in his "honeymoon stage" with the press, I read that he had reminisced with a newspaperman about those days. Congressman Kennedy would come in, he said, prop his feet up on Ford's desk, and sit around talking about his favorite theme. As Ford put it, "he always talked about one subject - girls."

One of Kennedy's girlfriends commented that he was the only man she knew who could make love with one eye on his watch.

Even so, there were sudden exits and Jackie once found a woman's undergarment tucked in a pillowcase. She delicately held it out to her husband between thumb and forefinger-about the way you hold a worm-saying, "Would you please shop around and see who these belong to? They're not my size."

Some newspaper and magazine articles say Marilyn Monroe was smuggled into the White House. If so, I'm sorry I missed her. But the gals I did see were not bad. Not bad at all. Even though his wife was brunette, his girls all seemed to be blonde - and one was a near redhead. The backstairs help used to mutter, "Why can't he make it easier for us? Why do we always have to be searching for blond hairs and blond bobby pins? Why can't he get himself a steady brunette?"

With Kennedy, the story was that in spite of his marriage to Jacqueline, he had never given up his bachelorhood. Many people have heard the rumor that Joseph Kennedy, the President's father, gave Jackie one million dollars in return for her promise not to divorce his son while he was running for the Presidency, or if he made it, as long as he was in the White House.

Less widely known was the theory of just what the straw might have been that broke the camel's back and prompted the gift in the first place. After all, Jack had been the playboy of the Western world for some time before the campaign began, and Jackie hadn't made waves.

The story around the White House was that the blow she finally could not forgive had come when a fifteen-year-old babysitter accused the senator of making her pregnant. That, Jackie was quoted to have said, was the limit beyond the limit. It was also, supposedly, what the ambassador was trying to soothe her for.

Despite all the stories I've heard about other past Presidents, I doubt we will ever have another one like Kennedy. I even heard him say to one of his buddies, "I'm not through with a girl till I've had her three ways."

There was something else interesting about Kennedy's pre-White House escapades. When he and a congressional buddy used to get a hotel room in another city, they would get two girls and trade around. Nowadays he would be called a "swinger". Then he was called just plain wild.

Traphes Bryant and "Dog Days in the White House"

Even Jackie realized that her husband wouldn't be satisfied with just one woman. I used to think how amazed the country would be to find out that Jacqueline Kennedy, supposedly the most desirable and exciting woman in the whole world, couldn't keep her husband content. It really wasn't her fault. Another man would have desired nothing more than the opportunity to stay close to her in the White House or wherever she was. But Kennedy's way, or his previous training, simply made him different. As every dogkeeper says, "You cant teach an old dog new tricks."

Jackie sought a little solace herself - a close friend she could talk to and let her hair down with. One such comforter was the famous economist and ambassador to India, John Kenneth Galbraith.

Once when Jackie was traveling with Galbraith on an official visit, the word was Jack became afraid he would lose ground with her himself, and she would get too much sympathy, so he called her to come back to the White House.

And he did that again, insiders knew, when she was on the luxury yacht of Aristotle Onassis, with her sister, Princess Lee Radziwill.

Some people may have mentioned it, but I never saw anybody point out the full significance of the fact that when President Kennedy died, one of the men at the White House comforting Jacqueline was Aristotle Onassis, whose yacht she had been on not too long before.

So when she later married him, she was marrying an old, old friend, not someone who had just entered her life. Backstairs at the White House, though we were amazed she had married a foreigner, once we got used to that thought we were not surprised that it was Onassis.

And I'll tell you another thing that seemed without significance at the time, but important looking back. My wife, Doris, reminded me after the news of the Onassis marriage exploded in the headlines that we had seen Onassis at the commissioning of the aircraft carrier John F. Kennedy when Robert McNamara had been the speaker. "Don't you remember," Doris said, "when Jackie Kennedy came up and talked to you, she suddenly swung around and said rather excitedly to a strange-looking, rather short, gray-haired man, `Oh, Ari, I didn't know you were here!"' So evidently the friendship had been going on for quite some time before anyone paid any attention.

One might ask, "How come Kennedy got away with his romantic escapades, and few stories ever came out?" The answer is simple. Politics on a high level is a club. You protect the club member. Henry Cabot Lodge, for example, who was a close friend of LBJ, once ran against Kennedy. That was when Kennedy was a congressman, running for senator. During the campaign, so the story goes, Lodge's people came across a picture showing Jack Kennedy and a blond, both naked, lying on a beach. Lodge could have worked the picture for a lot of mileage, but when it was shown to Congressman Kennedy, he just laughed and said, "Oh, yes, I remember her. Naw, Henry won't use that." And he didn't. As I said, politics is a club.

For some reason Kennedy liked soft romantic music coming from under him when he was in bed. The Army Signal Corps installed stereo speakers under his bed and the President also had a stereo speaker mounted on the second-floor balcony. One day someone switched the balcony speaker on loud and German martial music suddenly blared out over the South Lawn. I'm not sure what the tourists thought, but Pushinka, Clipper, and Charlie figured it was a

> *carnival and started barking loudly. I called the usher and someone quickly cut the speakers off.*
>
> *After Kennedy died, LBJ ordered the stereo ripped out. He liked the sound of telephones and his own voice better. I'd come into his bedroom at any hour, bringing or picking up a dog, and he'd be talking and laughing on the phone or cussing someone out. I'd wonder how the guy on the other end could take so much abuse.*

One would imagine that this book created a great sensation. It did not. The reason was nobody believed it. Reviewer Richard R Lingeman published the following in the New York Times:

> *The Washington gossip mills provide the city's most lucrative literary export. Despite competition from such massive, direct-from-the-source revelations*
>
> *Gossip and Innuendo*
>
> *Unfortunately, Mr. Bryant-or rather his collaborator, I suspect-sees fit to fatten his story with rather stale gossip and innuendo, presumably to give the book an R-rating, thus making it more salable. So we have stories about Mr. Kennedy's nude swimming parties while Mrs. Kennedy was away, some catty stuff about White House children and the like. Questions of taste aside, this tends to spoil the tone f Mr. Bryant's otherwise workaday confessions of an honest white House workingman, who did share the limelight frequently with the Presidential pets.*

Note that Richard Lingeman writes that, except for the "gossip", Bryant's book was "otherwise . . . . honest". In short, Lingeman does not believe the "gossip" which, he believes, was inserted by the collaborator to make the book more salable. Never mind that the collaborator, Frances Spatz Leighton, had written several other well-regarded biographies of White House maids and similar personnel and had never previously been accused of "improving" their stories.

Please note that the Traphes Bryant book was not "gossip". Bryant did not write that he heard about naked women running around the White House. Rather, he wrote that he personally saw them with his own eyes running nude or swimming naked in the White House pool with a naked President Kennedy. This is not gossip. It is testimony.

The end result was that the "Dog Days" book was immediately discounted and almost completely forgotten. It is rarely cited and almost never included in the bibliography of any subsequent book. It is not mentioned at all in the Seymour Hersh book, *"The Dark Side of Camelot"*, even though Hersh used material that obviously originated from the Traphes Bryant book, such as the story of Jacqueline Kennedy finding another woman's panties in the presidential bed. It would take the FBI reports and the revelations of the Church Committee five months later to make this into a national news story.

Barney Rosset was the publisher of "My Story". A known risk-taker, who made publishing history by publishing "Tropic of Cancer" by Henry Miller and an uncensored version of D. H. Lawrence's novel "Lady Chatterley's Lover". Both cases wound up in the United States Supreme Court because they violated the censorship laws at that time.

However, Rosset took the biggest risk of all in 1977 by publishing "My Story", not a financial risk that he might be sued because he was broke anyway, but a physical risk that the FBI, the CIA, the Mafia or some pro-Kennedy nut might bump him off. Even his advertising agency dropped him as a client. Fortunately, he survived and is still publishing today.

Kitty Kelley published an interview of Judith Campbell Exner in the February 29, 1988 issue of People magazine. Judith accuses her of trying to make her story even more sensational than it already was, for example by saying that John F. Kennedy was the father of her son, even though the son was born 18 months after JFK was killed.

This is a serious accusation, because Kitty Kelley has written several scandalous biographies and all of her targets have claimed that she falsified facts.

Liz Smith, who now writes for a scandal sheet called the New York Post, interviewed Judith for the January 1977 issue of Vanity Fair and did a commendable job of correcting the facts.

Seymour Hersh, investigative reporter for the New York Times, wrote a pot boiler called "The Dark Side of Camelot" that contains many shocking revelations, none of which have yet been refuted.

Significantly, there is no photo available of Ovid Demaris, perhaps because he usually wrote about organized crime and preferred to live a long life.

Ben Bradlee can claim to be the World's Most distinguished Journalist. As Executive Editor of the *Washington Post*, he stood up to the Nixon Administration in the *"Pentagon Papers"* case. He supervised the work of Woodward and Bernstein in the Watergate Affair and he was the only one outside of them who knew the true identity of *"Deep Throat"*. He was a personal friend of Jacqueline Kennedy and lives today at the former Bouvier Family Estate.

When the Judith Exner Scandal broke, he verified all of the personal top secret telephone numbers of President Kennedy on page 128 of her book which provided strong corroborating evidence that all of her allegations were true.

Tina Sinatra wrote, *"My Father's Daughter: A Memoir"*, a sympathetic biography of her famous father. She recognizes her father's weaknesses, a womanizer, a friend of the Mafia, a man who divorced her mother without a good reason, but credits him with being a good and devoted father. She says that his friendship with gangsters was because they had given him jobs in the clubs and had kept him alive through the bad years in the 1940s, so he owed it to him.

However, she reserves a special place in HELL for his last wife, Barbara Marx who she says forced him to work to make more money for her when he was old, tired and did not want to perform any more.

Frankie and the Boys in 1976 in Westchester County. All of the characters in this infamous photo are Mafia wise guys, except for Frank Sinatra. - Left to right: Paul Castellano, Gregory DePalma, Frank Sinatra, Tommy Marson, Carlo Gambino, Aladena Fratianno, Salvatore Spatola, Seated: Joseph Gambino, Richard Fusco

Sinatra's open association with Mafia characters has raised a lot of eyebrows. It has been pointed out that he gained legitimate benefits from this association. As a short skinny guy, he needed protection, and nobody would mess with him if he was seen as protected by the Mafia. Because of mob control of the Las Vegas Casinos, the Mafia gave him jobs earning as much as $100,000 per week. No entertainer could perform in Las Vegas without mob approval.

Sinatra also became the front man for the mob, gaining a stake in the Cal-Neva Lodge on Lake Tahoe and in the Sands Casino in Las Vegas without having to put up his own money.

The bottom line is that Frank Sinatra was born in poverty. He did not have much talent. He could not sing, dance or act very well. He was a short, skinny guy, and was not good looking. Yet, when he died he was one of the richest and most influential men in America and still today his estate had earned more than $10 million per year from his royalties and residuals. Other famous performers died in poverty. Was Sinatra's success due to his association with the Mafia?

Mug shot of Frank Sinatra when he was arrested on November 27, 1938 in Hoboken, Bergen County, New Jersey, for "seduction" in connection with "breach of promise to marry". This was an archaic charge usually brought on behalf of a young virgin who had surrendered her virginity because of believing that her paramour would marry her.

The charge read, "being then and there a single man over the age of 18, under the promise of marriage, did then and there have sexual intercourse with the said complainant who was then and there a single female of good repute for chastity whereby she became pregnant."

In this case, when it was discovered that the "victim", Toni Della Penta, was already married, the charge was dropped but three weeks later she brought a new charge for adultery. That charge was soon dropped too. As it turned out, Toni Della Penta suffered a miscarriage so that baby was never born. At about the same time, Sinatra got another girl pregnant, so he married her instead. That girl, Nancy Barbato, gave birth to Nancy Sinatra on June 8, 1940, produced two more children for him, and remained devoted to him even after he divorced her.

Sinatra should have learned something from this, but did not.

Phyllis McGuire sitting on the lap of Mafia Don Sam Giancana. Phyllis was the lead singer of the famous group "The McGuire Sisters" whose most famous song was "*Sugartime*" that went "Sugar in the morning. Sugar in the evening. Sugar at supper time."

Sam Giancana dumped Judith Cambpell in favor of Phyllis McGuire immediately after the Kennedy Assassination. Judith did not understand this. It took a decade before somebody explained to her that Giancana's interest in her was based on her relationship with Kennedy and, with Kennedy dead, he no longer had any interest in her. Giancana got in trouble because of his relationship with Phyllis McGuire. In July, 1963, he got in a fight with Victor LaCroix Collins, road manager for the McGuire Sisters, at the Cal-Neva Lodge on the North Shore of Lake Tahoe, concerning Phyllis McGuire. In 1967, he was ousted as Mafia Don of the Chicago Outfit because of the publicity that his relationship with Phyllis McGuire brought.

Sam Giancana and Phyllis McGuire

Fidel Castro. On January 8, 1959 Castro's Army rolled into Havana and took power. His government was officially recognized by the United States within a few hours. The United States had no idea that Castro was a hard-line Communist. Within days, Castro started conducting show trials of members of the Batista Government. They were tried, found guilty and taken before a firing squad and shot usually the same day or the next day. After several hundred of these executions by firing squad, the US started to pull back its support of Castro. By October, 1959, the US under President Eisenhower had started planning the overthrow of Castro.

On September 14, 1960, CIA Undercover Agent Robert Maheu (lower right) met with Mafia Wiseguy John Roselli at the Plaza Hotel in New York City. Maheu claimed to represent businessmen who were thrown out of Cuba by Castro. He offered to pay Roselli $150,000 to kill Castro. In all likelihood, Roselli realized that Maheu was a Government spook and not a businessman almost from the beginning. However, Maheu agreed to introduce Maheu to "Sam Gold", whose real name was Momo Giancana.

E. Howard Hunt (1918-2007), who organized the infamous Watergate Burglary, was a spy who was worked for the Central Intelligence Agency (CIA) and later the White House under President Richard Nixon doing dirty tricks and creating forged documents to discredit the Democrats.

In a deathbed statement, Hunt named Cord Meyer, Frank Sturgis, David Sánchez Morales, and David Atlee Phillips as participants in the Kennedy Assassination, with Vice-President Lyndon Johnson apparently approving the assassination for political gain.

Frank Sturgis (1924–1993) was one of the Watergate burglars. He served in Fidel Castro's revolutionary army as a soldier of fortune and later trained Cuban exiles for the Bay of Pigs Invasion. Sturgis has long been one of the leading suspects in the Kennedy Assassination. In 1959 he conspired with Castro's mistress Marita Lorenz to poison Castro. However, this assassination attempt failed.

President Kennedy's two most trusted aids, David Powers and Kenneth O'Donnell. They were sitting next to each other in the limousine directly behind Kennedy's car in the Motorcade when Kennedy was Assassinated.

They both had extensive direct dealings with Judith Campbell when she was seeing President Kennedy. They both denied knowing her when the scandal first broke. (At least Evelyn Lincoln admitted knowing her from the start, saying that she was a "campaign volunteer".)

David Powers, above, said, "The only Campbell I know is chunky vegetable soup".

Kenneth O'Donnell, below, said, "They are all lies".

However, that was only at the beginning. As the evidence mounted including FBI reports and other secret documents, they could no longer deny it, so they wisely kept silent.

Neither Powers nor O'Donnell ever had a paying job other than taking care of Kennedy's stuff after Kennedy left office.

Dr. Max Jacobson

Dr. Max "Feelgood" Jacobson. Dr. Jacobson regularly gave shots to both President John F. Kennedy and his wife Jacqueline Kennedy to make them feel better. He also gave the same shots to Judith Campbell and to several Hollywood personalities.

These shots are believed to have contained amphetamines.

I have not been able to find the name of Dr. Max Jacobson in any medical directory. If it is there, it should be right next to my own mother's name. My mother was Dr. Marjorie Jacobson.

Bill Thompson, Railroad Lobbyist and future President of Florida East Coast Railways. Thompson was present on April 6, 1960 when President Kennedy gave Judith Campbell a satchel containing $250,000 for delivery to Sam Giancana. Judith could not understand why Thompson was there. Probably the reason why he was there was he had provided the $250,000.

This fuzzy picture is a result of the fact that it is difficult to obtain good pictures of Thompson.

Sidney Korshak, lawyer for the Mafia, was another Mafia guy that Judith
Campbell met through Sam Giancana. This photo is of Korshak testifying
before a Senate Committee. Although thoroughly investigated, the FBI was
never able to pin anything on Korshak. The worst that could be proven was
that he was overzealous in his representation of his Mafia clients.

As one Mafia wise guy said to another, "If you tell something to Korshak,
you are it to telling us. If you hear something from Korshak, you are hearing
it from us."

There is a new 2007 book out about Korshak by Gus Russo entitled,
*"Supermob: How Sidney Korshak and His Criminal Associates Became
America's Hidden Power Brokers"*.

David Atlee Phillips (1922–1988) was a CIA officer for 25 years. Most currently popular Kennedy assassination theories claim involvement by Phillips. The "confession" by James Files to the Kennedy Assassination states that Phillips gave him the murder weapon, which was a Remington XP-100 Fireball. The deathbed confession by E. Howard Hunt also stated that Phillips played an important, but different, role in the Kennedy Assassination.

David Sánchez Morales (1925 - 1978) was a CIA operative who worked in Cuba. Kennedy Assassination buffs give Morales credit for double duty, stating that he killed both John F. Kennedy and Robert F. Kennedy.

Señor Morales had a few other exploits as well. He was allegedly involved in the plot to assassinate Fidel Castro, the Bay of Pigs operation, the CIA's secret war in Laos, the capture of Che Guevara, and the overthrow of Salvador Allende of Chile.

Morales also overthrew the democratically elected government of Guatemala in his spare time.

UPI/CORBIS-BETTMANN

Robert F. Kennedy, John F. Kennedy, and Joseph P. Kennedy

Robert F. Kennedy, John F. Kennedy and Joseph P. Kennedy standing in front of the airplane "*The Caroline*" that Joseph had given to his son Jack to enable him to fly around the country campaigning for president.

After Sam Giancana had been instrumental in helping John F. Kennedy be elected president, first by helping him win the 1960 West Virginia primary even though the United Mine Workers had officially supported Hubert Humphrey for President and secondly by helping Kennedy win Illinois by only 8,858 votes due to mob influence on Chicago's West Side, Giancana felt that Kennedy owed Giancana and should pay him back by lightening up on the mob.

When the opposite proved to be the case and the Department of Justice under Attorney General Robert Kennedy turned the screws on the Mafia, Giancana was inclined to retaliate. However, it was not Kennedy but rather Sinatra who had made promises to the Mafia. Therefore, the debt was owed by Sinatra, not by Kennedy.

This put Sinatra in serious danger of being killed. As a result, Sinatra agreed that the Rat Pack would perform free of charge for eight nights at *Villa Venice*, a new club built just north of Chicago owned by Giancana.

Under threat of death, the *"Rat Pack"* gave one of their most memorable performances which is now available on audio DVD.

The "*Copa Room*" at the Sands Hotel in Las Vegas. Named after the Copacabana Club in New York City which in turn was named after Copacabana Beach in Rio de Janeiro, Brazil, all the biggest stars performed in the Copa Room. It was here on February 7, 1960 that Judith Campbell sat between Frank Sinatra and Senator John F. Kennedy, who was running for President. The press corps that was there following the Kennedy campaign for president and everyone else was shocked when a completely unknown woman came and sat down next to the future president. Judith told the other people at the table that she had been told by Frank Sinatra to sit there. Judith later "went upstairs" with Senator Kennedy. This event will someday be featured on "*Great Events of History*".

DVDs and audios of the performances by Frank Sinatra, Sammy Davis Jr., Dean Martin and other members of the "Rat Pack" in the Copa Room are now available.

Sam Giancana arriving to give testimony. The two men behind him are presumably FBI agents who have been watching and following him.

Below, Sam Giancana handcuffed to a chair after he has been arrested for contempt of court for refusing to testify after being given a grant immunity. Giancana spent nearly one year in Cook County Jail on the contempt charge until the Grant Jury expires. Coincidentally, the judge who locked him up was named Judge Campbell.

(Under the Fifth Amendment to the constitution a person cannot be compelled to testify against himself. However, a loophole to this rule was established in the Giancana Case. If a person is granted immunity then the government cannot use his testimony against him and thus he can be compelled to testify.)

Jack Entratter (1913-1971) worked for the Copacabana Club in New York. He was sent to Las Vegas to handle entertainment at the new Sands Hotel. There he established the Copa Room where the biggest performers in Las Vegas appeared, including Frank Sinatra and "The Rat Pack" plus Eddie Fisher and others.

Miami Mafia Don Santos Trafficante (1913-1987). On September 25, 1960, John Roselli introduced CIA Undercover Agent Robert Maheu to "Joe" at the Fontainebleau Hotel in Miami. "Joe" was operating a courier service to Cuba using high speed boats to evade the Cuban Navy. "Joe" was actually Miami Mafia Don Santos Trafficante.

Tony Accardo (1906-1992) was one of the many mobsters that Judith Campbell met while she was spending time with Sam Giancana. On April 27, 1961, Sam Giancana took Judith Campbell to a wedding reception for the daughter of Tony Accardo. Accardo was The Outfit's *"consigliere"*, or advisor. He was the boss of the Chicago Outfit from 1945 to 1992. There is a difference of opinion as to who was the actual boss. Sam Giancana was publicly known as the boss. However, in 1967, when Accardo was unhappy with the flashy and attention gathering lifestyle of Giancana, Accardo replaced Giancana with Joseph *"Joey Doves"* Aiuppa. This indicates that Accardo, not Giancana, was the real boss.

Accardo often bragged to other mobsters that the St. Valentine's Massacre was his operation. Mafia watchers feel that this claim was not true. However, it seems likely that the assassination of Sam Giancana in the basement of his Oak Park Illinois home in 1975 was ordered by Accardo.

The movie *"Sugartime"* (1995) starring John Turturro and Mary-Louise Parker about the relationship between Phyllis McGuire and Sam Giancana depicts Giancana being murdered on orders of Accardo.

Movies depicting Sam Giancana always show him wearing dark glasses. However, he rarely wore dark glasses in real life. He just wore them when he was being forced to testify in court or before a Congressional committee.

Here, Sam Giancana is testifying in 1959 before Bobby Kennedy, who was serving as chief counsel to the Senate Labor Rackets Committee, better known as the McClellan Committee. Giancana took the Fifth.

In order to humiliate Giancana and try to provoke an outburst, when Giancana said: *"I decline to answer because I honestly believe my answer might tend to incriminate me."* Kennedy replied: *"I thought only little girls giggled, Mr. Giancana."*

This scene is depicted in the movie, *"Sugartime"*.

Moe Dalitz, manager of the Desert Inn, a lavish Las Vegas hotel and gambling casino. On December 31, 1963, during a New Year's Eve Party at the Desert Inn, Judith Campbell slapped him when he tried to kiss her. Everybody was shocked, not only because of his Mafia connections, but also because Judith had apparently forgotten than on New Years Eve everybody is supposed to kiss whatever man or woman is standing next to you, as depicted in the movie *"Ocean's Eleven"*.

Al Capone (1899-1947), a "used furniture dealer", was the Boss of the Chicago Outfit from 1925 until 1931, when he was sent to prison for income tax evasion. A flamboyant showman, he was the most famous Mafia mobster ever. His criminal career has been greatly exaggerated. Capone was NOT the biggest crook in America. We know this because two US presidents and one of Capone's successors stated there was a bigger crook in America: When President Franklin D. Roosevelt appointed Joseph Kennedy as the First Chairman of the Securities and Exchange Commission, and somebody asked Roosevelt why he had chosen Kennedy, Roosevelt replied, "*It Takes a Crook to Catch a Crook!*" When John F. Kennedy was in the final stages of his election campaign, President Truman said, "*It's not the Pope I'm afraid of, it's the Pop. Old Joe Kennedy is as big a crook as we've got anywhere in this country.*" Sam Giancana, Don of the Chicago Mafia and a successor to Al Capone, is quoted as saying, "*Joe Kennedy was one of the biggest crooks that ever lived*".

Time Line
Main events in the Life of Judith Eileen Katherine Immoor

January 11, 1934 Judith Eileen Katherine Immoor born in New York City. Her father was an architect with the firm of Daniel, Mann, Johnson and Mendenhall. http://www.dmjm.com/

May 25, 1931 Sister Jackie, a movie actress with the screen name "Susan Morrow", previously born in Teaneck, New Jersey.

1942 brother Allen Immoor born.

Judith attends Santa Monica's Catholic School. Later, her parents move to New Jersey. Her parents separated briefly and during that time she lives with an uncle and aunt in Chicago. When she rejoins her parents in West End, Long Branch, New Jersey, she is held back a year because of time she missed at Star of the Sea Academy. She lives at 720 Ocean Avenue, West End, Long Branch for four years.

1948 When she is in the eighth grade, the family returns to Hollywood, California. There she attends Immaculate Heart School.

1949 Judith dates her first love, Tom Branigan.

1950 Judith Immoor drops out of high school and receives lessons from a tutor after this. She never graduates from high school but passes the tests required of a home schooled student. She feels that not going to school caused her not to develop emotionally, which caused her to be married at too early an age.

Dates Robert Wagner who later became a movie star. He takes her to a party where she meets Billy Campbell.

1951 Her parents do not like Billy Campbell. One night they throw him out of the house. Judith is so upset that she decides to jump out of her bedroom window and run away with him. Judith tries to jump out of her bedroom window to meet Billy Campbell and is injured. She is injured in the fall and has to be taken to Midway Hospital.

1951   Judith is dating Billy Campbell. Her sister Jackie has just had her name changed to "Susan Morrow" by Paramount Pictures. Dean Martin and Jerry Lewis say that the studio wants Jackie to go to San Diego to do a layout for a movie magazine for the movie *Sailor Beware* (1952). They invite Judith to come along, too. Later, Jackie finds out that this is not a studio project but is just a little scam by Dean and Jerry. The sisters are angry and refuse to go. (Judith writes about this incident several times. Apparently she feels that it was all a scam just to get the two of them into bed. It is not clear why she finds this incident so upsetting. Perhaps she has a "dirty mind".)

October 26, 1952   Judith marries William Campbell in St. Ambrose Church in West Hollywood. She has such bad memories of this marriage that she later says she cannot remember the exact date or month.

William Campbell, born October 30, 1926, was eight years older than Judith was, but she did not find out his real age until after they were married. William Campbell is a well known actor who appears in 82 movies and numerous TV episodes. He is perhaps best known for singing along with Elvis Presley in the movie "*Love Me Tender*" (1956). He is still active in 2007 in the motion picture industry, appearing several times in the *Star Trek* series, most recently as Klingon Captain Koloth. To his credit, he has never said anything bad about his ex-wife, Judith Campbell, although she has had many bad things to say about him. He has said that he is surprised at her involvement in the Kennedy affairs, as she is "completely apolitical". As a result of her marriage to William Campbell, Judith socializes with movie stars such as Steve Forrest, Hugh O'Brien, Charlton and Lydia Heston and Lloyd and Dottie Bridges.

August 1955 One page of "Movie Stars Parade" magazine is devoted to photos of William Campbell and his wife Judith. The article is entitled "*New Men in Town*" and says that Bill and Judy are planning on moving to a bigger house and starting a family soon. (The "family" never materializes. One wonders what went wrong.)

1956 Comedy Team of Dean Martin and Jerry Lewis break up. Dean was considered the weak member of the team, but by the 1960s, Dean Martin had become more popular than Jerry Lewis.

1958 Judith is aware that William Campbell is dating other women while married to her. Whenever he goes on location, he never takes Judith with him but instead spends time with other women, she believes. (There is reason to doubt whether he was actually seeing other women while out on location. Perhaps he was just leaving his wife at home so as to not be bothered while he was working. William Campbell has never been romantically linked to any other woman except for Judith's elder sister Jackie, who William Campbell had been dating before he met Judith.) Finally, while William Campbell is in the Republic of Panama acting in the movie "*The Naked and the Dead*", Judith moves out and moves in with another actor named Tony Travis, whose real name is Travis Kleefeld. William Campbell is angry when he comes back from Panama and discovers that his wife has left him.

April 2, 1958 Judith files for divorce with William Campbell and lives with Tony Travis for the next two years. Tony Travis is a notorious womanizer who dated and slept with many movie stars, but Judith makes no mention of this fact in her book. An odd fact is that there have never been any rumors linking William Campbell romantically to any woman other than Judith and her sister. He never remarries. On the other hand, Tony Travis is a notorious womanizer. At the time Judith moves in with him, he is living with Miss USA 1952 Jackie Loughery. He has been linked to a Sinatra-esque list of famous movie stars including Jane Wyman, wife of Ronald Reagan. Judith knows about this, but it does not seem to bother her.

January 8, 1959   Fidel Castro enters Havana and takes power in Cuba.

April 24, 1959   Divorce with William Campbell is final. (There is a difference of opinion as to the date of her actual divorce.) The divorce calls for him to pay her $500 per month alimony. After two years, she accepts a lump sum settlement of $6,000. She uses the $6,000 to buy the mink coat shown in the cover photo here.

August 1959   Judith goes to New York on a trial separation from Tony Travis. Upon her return, she moves out and moves in with her sister, Jackie, who is now a movie actress with the screen name "Susan Morrow". Judith remains close friends with Tony Travis for many years thereafter, although they are no longer lovers.

November 1 or 2, 1959   According to *"Sinatra: The Life"* by Anthony Summers and Robbyn Swan, Judith Campbell and Angie Dickinson were in Puccini's restaurant in Beverly Hills when John F. Kennedy and Frank Sinatra spotted them and picked them up. This scene is depicted in the movie *"The Rat Pack"*. However, Judith does not remember it that way. She says that neither John F. Kennedy nor Angie Dickinson were there. She was seen by Frank Sinatra, who was with Nick Sevano. Both accounts place Nick Sevano as being there.

November 9, 1959   Judith flies to Honolulu with Frank Sinatra, although they take separate airplanes because it does not look good for her to be traveling with a man. (Judith is still a prude at this time. Later, she becomes the opposite, as she will not go out unless she has a man with her. She finds it embarrassing to be seen in public without a man on her arm.) Judith had met

Sinatra several times previously, but this time a mutual friend, Nick Sevano, had told her that Sinatra wants to date her. Judith agrees. Upon arriving in Hawaii, Judith is given a room in the Surfrider Hotel. Peter and Patricia Lawford are in the next room. Pat Kennedy Lawford is the sister of John and Robert Kennedy. Dr. Leone Krohn and his wife Ester are in another nearby room.

November 11, 1959   Judith is nervous as she walks into Frank Sinatra's suite for the first time. It is filled with all of these people plus several others. Eventually, the others are all cleared out and Sinatra steers her towards the bedroom, where they make love several times that night.

November 14, 1959 Judith, Frank, and Pat and Peter Lawford are sitting in Frank Sinatra's bedroom when two tiny Japanese girls arrive. Frank says that it is time for their message. Peter Lawford and Frank Sinatra go off to a private room for their massage. Judith figures out what is really going on. Patricia Lawford seems not to care that her husband is obviously philandering in front of her. (The opening scene of the movie *"Ocean's 11"* that was being made at this time shows Lawford and Sinatra being massaged by two women, but not by Japanese women.)

Later that evening, Pat goes back to her room. All the others leave and Judith is left alone with Peter Lawford. Lawford comes over and sits next to her and suggests that they take a walk on the beach. Judith realizes that Peter wants to sleep with her and she has no intention of doing this, so she tells him to go down to the hotel lobby and wait for her. She will come down soon, she says. She then goes to her own room and goes to bed. He calls many times but she does not answer the telephone. The next morning, Lawford is angry and complains to Frank Sinatra about this. Frank is angry too because Judith did not sleep with Frank that night. This seemingly minor incident has reverberations for years to come. Judith writes, "Frank is a tiny man with a big man complex". Judith does not sleep with Frank Sinatra for the second night in a row, although Frank is waiting in bed for her. The next day, Judith departs Hawaii for California.

November 16, 1959 Judith arrives back at her sister Jackie's apartment in Los Angeles and learns that Frank Sinatra has been calling several times. Judith is thrilled that Frank wants to see her again. "Life had become so good", she writes.

Now that she is living with her sister Jackie and is not living with a man, the telephone never stops ringing with men calling Judith and asking her for a date. She goes out on a date with a man every night for months. She sleeps late and then spends several hours every day bathing, fixing her hair, putting on makeup and then dressing to perfection. She never goes out alone or with another woman. If there is no man calling to take her out, she just stays home. (Regarding these dates, she never broaches the subject of sex. The reader is not told whether she winds up in bed with of all these men that she is dating.)

December 7, 1959   Judith has a date with Frank Sinatra. Goes to his home in Palm Desert, California where she finds it filled with people including Peter and Pat Lawford, Jimmy Van Heusen, the famous song writer, Jack Entratter and Johnny Formosa. They are working on a song for the movie "*Oceans 11*". Frank Sinatra asks Judith to spend the night with him and she agrees. They make love and sleep in each other's arms.

December 8, 1959   The entire group goes to dinner at Romanoff's in Beverly Hills. During the dinner conversation, the name of Jack Kennedy comes up for the first time. At first, Judith does not know who he is. Then, she finds out that he is Pat Lawford's brother and is also a candidate for President of the United States. That night, Judith sleeps with Frank Sinatra again and they make love. The next morning, Frank is sullen. Judith does not know the reason but decides to go back to her sister's apartment in Beverly Hills.

December 12, 1959 Judith returns to Palm Springs with her former lover Tony Travis but they do not meet Frank Sinatra. They spend most of the next month attending parties in Palm Springs.

Gossip Columnist Harrison Carroll writes in the *"Herald Express"*, "Judy Campbell says she wasn't dating Frank Sinatra as such but that they did get around together in Hawaii since they were in a group and saw a lot of each other". Judith tells Harrison Carroll that she does not like to see her name in the newspapers like this. He stops writing about her in his gossip column.

January 5, 1960 Judith has date with actor Richard Ney. He takes her to his house in the Hollywood Hills, turns on romantic music and the works, but she does not agree to sleep with him so finally he returns her to her home.

January 1960 Judith becomes friends with Marty Tannenbaum and Sy Devore. Marty and Judith have dinner with Dean Martin and his wife Jeanne Biegger. Jeanne is typical of Hollywood wives who "Are not threatened by Hollywood starlets who will sleep with anybody just to get a movie part" but are threatened by single, attractive women. Jeanne can not figure out Judith, who did not fit into the first category. From then on, Dean Martin calls Judith regularly. Judith feels that Dean Martin does not want to date her. Rather, he is trying to find out if his wife Jeanne is sleeping with Mort Viner, his agent. Judith basically feels that not only are all the Hollywood men trying to sleep with other men's wives, but all of the women are trying to sleep with other women's husbands too.

Judith's next date with Frank Sinatra is a disaster. They start with dinner at Romanoff's in Beverly Hills. After they arrive at Frank's home, Frank tells Judith to go to bed, as he has to make a phone call. Judith goes to bed and wakes up when Sinatra is crawling into bed with her. Then, a black girl without a stitch on climbs into bed with them and makes love to Frank. Judith is shocked and freezes up. When the black girl has finished having sex with Frank, Frank gets up and walks her out the door. Judith does not know what to do, so she goes to sleep. The next morning Judith tells Frank how angry she is. Frank sends his driver to take her home. The next day Frank invites her to the set of *"Oceans 11"* which is being filmed in Las Vegas. Judith accepts and Frank feels that this means that she has forgiven him. Judith has not forgiven him and never sleeps with Frank Sinatra again after this incident.

January 12, 1960   During a party at the home of Joe Perrin, he tells the story of how he tried to fix up Jackie Immoor with Aly Khan. As the story goes, when they were about to arrive at the home of Jackie and her mother, Jackie said to her mother, "Tell Joe I had to go somewhere". When they had arrived, Jackie was gone. They had a hot dog and finally they gave up and left. At that time, Aly Khan had just broken up with his second wife, movie actress Rita Hayworth, and Jackie has red hair just like Rita Hayworth had, so Joe had figured that they would make a good match.

This story has religious implications. The Aly Aga Khan (1911-1960) was not merely one of the world's richest men. He was also a direct descendant from the Prophet Muhammed 46 generations back and his father was the prophet to 12 million members of the Ismaili branch of Islam, all of whom donated 10% of their annual income to him, which is the reason why he was rich. Due to his involvement with fast racehorses and even faster women, Aly Khan was passed over when his turn came to become Imam. His son became the Imam. Aly Khan was killed shortly thereafter in an automobile accident on May 12, 1960.

January 23, 1960   Frank Sinatra invites Judith to see a performance in Las Vegas of the *"Rat Pack"*. starring Frank Sinatra, Dean Martin, Joey Bishop, Sammy Davis Jr. and Peter Lawford. Judith flies to Las Vegas with Richard and Marilyn Ellwood. After the show, they go out to dinner with Frank Sinatra and Dean Martin. After the dinner, Judith goes to her hotel room and goes to sleep by herself. Frank calls. He had been expecting to sleep with Judith again. Judith refuses, reminding him of the night when he had brought in an extra woman, trying to make it a threesome. Two days later, Judith flies back to Los Angeles without ever having spent any time alone with Frank Sinatra.

February 5, 1960   Judith flies to Las Vegas at the request of Dean Martin. Has dinner with Dean and the gang. Judith suspects that Dean's wife Jeanne suspects that Dean is sleeping with Judith. That is not what is going on. What is really going on is Dean Martin suspects that Jeanne is sleeping with Mort Viner and keeps calling Judith to find out. Sinatra introduces his new number-one girl, Juliet Prowse, the dancer. This makes Judith feel liberated.

February 7, 1960   Judith introduced by Frank Sinatra to John F. Kennedy and Teddy Kennedy at the Sands Hotel in Las Vegas. They all have dinner together with Peter Lawford and Gloria Cahn. Then, they all go to the Copa Room for the late show. Judith spends her time studying John F. Kennedy and is favorably impressed. He is "The World's Greatest Listener". (Judith has often complained that most Hollywood movie stars are only interested in themselves and do not listen to what anybody says about anything else.) After that, they go casino hopping. At the end of the night, which was really early the next morning, they arrive back at Judith's room in the Flamingo. Teddy Kennedy goes in the room first and sits on the bed. Judith stands out in the alcove outside the room and points Teddy out the door. Finally, Teddy gives up and leaves.

February 8, 1960   The next morning, Jack Kennedy calls and asks for a date. Judith agrees. When Judith arrives to meet Jack, he is in the middle of a press conference. Judith is surprised. Jack breaks away from the press conference and spends three hours alone talking to Judith about the Catholic religion. When they go back, Gloria Cahn and Pat Newcombe appear and drag Kennedy off. Judith is upset and goes back to her room at the Flamingo. At midnight, Kennedy calls and asks Judith to come back. Judith agrees, and when she goes to meet Jack, he is waiting for her, but Gloria Cahn and Pat Newcombe are there too. They finally see him off to the airport. Judith goes back to her room, but then Dean Martin calls and asks her out again. She agrees. Finally, she goes to bed (alone). She wakes up the next morning "feeling like Scarlett O'Hara the morning after the night when Rhett Butler carried her up the stairs", even though she had not slept with anybody that night. She returns to Beverly Hills the next day.

February 12, 1960   Jack Kennedy calls Judith from Fresno.

February 24, 1960   Judith and her sister Jackie go to see Frank Sinatra on the set of *Oceans 11* in Los Angeles. Frank invites them to come to the Hotel Fontainebleau in Miami, where he will be doing another show. Judith does not say yes, but she does not say no either. Good thing, because later that evening Jack Kennedy calls and wants to meet her in New York on March 7. She agrees.

March 7, 1960   John F. Kennedy comes to the hotel room that Judith has taken at the Plaza Hotel in New York City. Judith sleeps with John F Kennedy for first time. At first she says "no", but then, as JFK is leaving, she changes her mind and says "yes".

March 8, 1960   Kennedy wins New Hampshire Primary

March 10, 1960   Judith flies to Miami with Toni Carroll to see the Frank Sinatra Show.

March 11, 1960   Frank Sinatra introduces Judith to her first Mafia character, Joseph Fischetti a/k/a "Joe Fish", a cousin of Al Capone.

March 23, 1960   Judith goes with Bob Neal to a party at Frank's. Bob Neal was "as docile an escort as I ever had", meaning that he did not try to sleep with her.

March 24, 1960   Judith goes with Bill Orr and Hugh Benson to a Cuban show at one of the hotels. Desi Arnaz is there. (Desi Arnaz had just broken up with Lucile Ball after their show *"I Love Lucy"* had been canceled.) Bill Orr tells Judith that there will be a party in Desi Arnaz's hotel suite. Judith arrives at the supposed party with an escort but suddenly the escort disappears, leaving Judith alone in the hotel room with Desi. Judith quickly excuses herself and leaves. This is another incident that has reverberations later on, as Judith believes that a rumor has spread that she slept with Desi Arnaz. (Actually, Judith need not have worried about this, because the real rumor was that she had slept with just about everybody.)

March 26, 1960   Dean Martin and Jack Entratter take Judith to a party in the Poodle Bar at the Hotel Fontainebleau. Frank is sitting there with Juliet Prowse. Frank Sinatra dresses Judith down for what he believes happened the previous night with Desi Arnaz.

March 27, 1960   Judith introduced by Frank Sinatra to "Sam Flood", whose real name is Sam Giancana, at Fontainebleau Hotel in Miami. She also meets John Matassa, who is a bodyguard and chauffeur for "Sam Flood".

When Judith goes to check out of the Fontainebleau Hotel after staying there for two weeks, she looks for one of the managers to guarantee her check. San Giancana finds out about this and picks up the check himself. (Due to his position with the Mafia, it is unclear whether Sam is even required to pay his hotel bills.) Judith insists on giving Giancana a check for $2,000 to cover the bill. Giancana finally agrees to take the check. Later, Judith tells Giancana that she will refuse to see him again until he deposits the check in the bank. Giancana finally deposits the checks. Judith later shows the canceled check to her biographers to prove that this really happened.

April 6, 1960   Judith sleeps with John F. Kennedy in the Kennedy home in Georgetown while Jacqueline Kennedy is away.

With railroad lobbyist William B. Thompson, who later becomes President of Florida East Coast Railroad, present, Kennedy asks Judith to carry a bag containing $250,000 cash to Sam Giancana in Chicago. Judith agrees and does so. Martin Underwood, a former political operative for Mayor Richard Daley and a Kennedy campaign worker in 1960, is said to have followed Judith on the train and to have watched her deliver the package containing the cash to Giancana. (However, in an appearance before the "Assassination Records Review Board" Martin Underwood later denies having done this.)

May 7, 1960   Judith moves in with her parents in Laurel Canyon, California. She finds an envelope that Kennedy has placed in her purse that contains two one thousand dollar bills. She deposits the two one thousand dollar bills in her checking account. (The Treasury Department now no longer prints one thousand dollar bills.)

May 10, 1960   John F. Kennedy wins West Virginia Primary

May 24, 1960   Judith has operation in Cedars of Lebanon by Dr. Krohn to remove one of her ovaries.

May 31, 1960   The day after she checks out of the hospital, John F. Kennedy comes to visit Judith and gives her a dozen red roses.

July 11, 1960   Democratic National Convention begins.

July 12, 1960   After the conclusion of a campaign party at the Biltmore Hotel in Los Angeles in room 8315, John F. Kennedy tries to get Judith into a sexual threesome with a "tall, thin lady". Judith refuses and is angry. (Kenneth O'Donnell, a Kennedy Aid, who is waiting alone in the next room, later says that he has no recollection of Judith.)

July 13, 1960   Kennedy receives the Democratic Presidential

Nomination.

July 20, 1960   Judith flies to New York to meet Marty Tannenbaum. Judith stays in Tannenbaun's apartment in The Navarro Hotel, 112 Central Park South, because Tannenbaum is in the hospital with a heart condition. (The Navarro is now called the Central Park Inter-Continental.)

July 25, 1960   Frank Sinatra sends a limo to The Navarro to pick up Judith and bring her to the Claridge Hotel in Atlantic City to meet Mafia wise guys Joe Fish and Skinny D'Amato.

August 4, 1960   Kennedy visits Judith at The Navarro and they make love.

August 19, 1960   Judith flies to Washington DC. Evelyn Lincoln makes room reservation for Judith at the Mayflower Hotel. Judith takes a cab to Kennedy's Georgetown home. Kennedy sleeps all night with Judith (a rare occurrence) and the next morning she takes a taxi back to the hotel. The next day, Judith goes to Evelyn Lincoln to pick up her train ticket back to New York, as Kennedy has already departed for Independence, Missouri to campaign for election.

August 1960   Judith carries a second bag of cash from Kennedy to Giancana.

August 10, 1960   Movie *Ocean's Eleven* released starring Frank Sinatra, Dean Martin, Sammy Davis, Peter Lawford, Joey Bishop, Angie Dickinson, Shirley MacLaine and Cesar Romero.

August 23, 1960   Marty Tannenbaun re-introduces Judith to Jerry Lewis, who starts talking about a movie named *"Ladies Man"* he is thinking of producing with Judith in it. In *"My Story"* Judith expresses the belief that the movie is never produced. However, in reality, the movie was produced and released on June 28, 1961.

September 4, 1960   Judith flies to California with Jerry Lewis.

September 14, 1960 According to the CIA "Family Jewels" documents, on this day CIA Undercover Agent Robert Maheu met with Mafia Wiseguy John Roselli at the Plaza Hotel in New York City. Maheu claims to represent businessmen who were thrown out of Cuba by Castro. He offers to pay Roselli $150,000 to kill Castro. Roselli offers to introduce Maheu to "Sam Gold" who, he says, has connections in Cuba.

September 14, 1960 After having breakfast with her mother, Judith flies to Chicago where she is picked up at O'Hare Airport by Sam Giancana and Joe Fish. Sam Giancana takes Judith to dinner at The Singapore. Judith sees all the bowing and scraping of the waiters and restaurant personnel towards Sam. Judith is surprised at this. In "*My Story*", Judith claims that she did not yet know that Sam Giancana was a Mafia don. She still thought that his name was Sam Flood.

September 25, 1960 As promised, John Roselli introduces Maheu to "Sam Gold" and "Joe" at the Fontainebleau Hotel in Miami. "Joe" is operating a courier service to Cuba. Maheu later realizes that "Sam Gold" is Chicago Mafia Don Sam Giancana and "Joe" is actually Miami Mafia Don Santos Trafficante.

September 26, 1960 First presidential debate between Kennedy and Nixon. 66 million people watch, a record for television at that time. Most authorities believe that it was this debate that made Kennedy president.

October 18, 1960   Memorandum linking Giancana to Castro Assassination plot.

November 3, 1960   Judith moves into an apartment on 1200 North Flores in Los Angeles.

November 4, 1960   The FBI comes to see Judith for the first time. FBI Agent Dodge informs Judith that the real name of "Sam Flood" is Sam "Momo" Giancana and that he is in the Mafia. Agent Dodge is accompanied by IRS Agent Vern Lynch.

November 8, 1960   Kennedy elected president.

November 13, 1960 Rat Pack member Sammy Davis Jr. marries Swedish actress May Britt. This marriage had been postponed until after the election at Kennedy's request because it was an inter-racial marriage and might cost Kennedy votes in the South. May Britt never makes another movie after this marriage.

November 25, 1960 John F. Kennedy Junior, "John-John", born to Jacqueline Kennedy. (Note that JFK has been sleeping with Judith during the time that Jacqueline Kennedy is pregnant.)

December 1960   Jerry Lewis gives Judith a job at $100 per week to work on the "*Ladies Man*" project. Later, Jerry Lewis asks Judith to place a call to Sam Giancana and put him on the line as soon as she reaches Sam.

January 20, 1961   John F. Kennedy takes office as President

January 20, 1961   Judith invited to the Kennedy Inaugural Ball but does not attend for fear of embarrassing Jacqueline Kennedy. Kennedy aid calls Sammy Davis Jr. and informs him that JFK requests that Davis NOT attend the inaugural ball. Frank Sinatra does attend but Joseph Kennedy has all of the pictures of Sinatra at the inaugural ball removed. These are the first signs that now that Kennedy is president, he wants nothing to do with Sinatra and his friends. From this time forward, Kennedy increasingly distances himself from Frank Sinatra and the "Rat Pack".

March 1961 Judith fired from her $100 a week job with Jerry Lewis, apparently because Jerry's wife, Doris, objects. (Judith does not claim to have ever slept with Jerry Lewis.)

April 4, 1961 Carlos Marcello, boss of the New Orleans crime family, deported to Guatemala. One of the most popular Kennedy Assassination theories is that Marcello had JFK killed in retaliation for this deportation.

April 17, 1961 Bay of Pigs invasion. After this fiasco, plots to assassinate Fidel Castro are said to have been abandoned. However, information suggests that under Attorney General Robert F. Kennedy, there were further attempts to assassinate Castro until RFK resigned as Attorney General in 1964.

April 27, 1961 Sam "Momo" Giancana takes Judith to a wedding reception for the daughter of Tony Accardo, another Mafia Don, at the "*Villa Venice*". a club owned by Sam. Sam and Judith sit at the same table with Sam's daughters, Antoinette and Bonnie Giancana. Sam shows them a ring he has given to Judith. That ring had actually belonged to the late mother of Antoinette and Bonnie, who had died in 1954. Sam had obviously done this to make the daughters angry, as they had wanted this ring.

April 28, 1961 Kennedy, now president, comes to visit Judith in her hotel room in the Ambassador East in Chicago. They have quickie sex and he leaves after only 20 minutes.

April 28, 1961 Different version in the article by Kitty Kelley: Kennedy and Giancana meet in Judith's hotel room in the Ambassador East. Judith sits in the restroom on the edge of the tub during the meeting because she does not want to know what they are talking about.

April 29, 1961 At Kennedy's request, Judith flies to Florida where she has drinks with Giancana and Roselli, who are there for a gangland meeting. She picks up another envelope from them for delivery to JFK.

May 4, 1961 Judith flies from Florida to Washington to deliver the envelope to JFK in the White House. Kennedy makes love to Judith. This is the first time that they make love in the White House. Just prior to going to the White House, Judith has dinner in Washington DC with an old friend, Richard Ellwood, owner of a small electronics firm in Culver City, California, who just happened by coincidence to be in Washington DC. (In the book, "*The Dark Side of Camelot*", pages 315-316, Seymour Hersh says that Ellwood and several other defense contractors were paying cash bribes to JFK and were using Judith to deliver the cash to Kennedy. Here, there is a small discrepancy. Judith spells his name Elwood. Seymour Hersh spells his name Ellwood. I cannot find any references to this man under either spelling in any other source. His name is not listed in the Social Security Death Index.)

May 6, 1961 A White House car picks up Judith at the Mayflower Hotel and brings her to the East Gate of the White House. David Powers comes to greet her in the reception room, introduces himself, and takes her to the Oval Office to see the president. After making love, Kennedy realizes that it is late. He has a White House car take Judith back to the Mayflower Hotel, where she collects her bags and races to Washington National Airport. An airplane, ready to take off, is called back to the departure gate so that Judith can board. She arrives in Chicago at 6:40 PM, where she is met by Sam Giancana. (The interesting question here is why was Kennedy so concerned about her being late for her meeting with Sam Giancana.)

May 7, 1961 Judith flies to Las Vegas where she meets Johnny Roselli, whom she had met for the first time a few days earlier. Judith and Joe Pignatello, another Mafia guy, go to see the performance of Jerry Lewis at the Copa Room. They sit in the front row and stare at Jerry the entire time, making him nervous. The purpose of this was to get her revenge on Jerry Lewis for firing her from her job working for Lewis. (Although her autobiography says that she met Johnny Roselli for the first time on May 7, 1961, other sources say that she met Roselli years earlier. The movie "*Power and Beauty*" has Roselli arranging the introductions of her to Sinatra, Kennedy and Giancana. It shows Exner and Roselli together as early as 1952. However, this movie is just plain rubbish, filled with scenes for which there is no known historical basis. For example, it depicts Roselli offering Judith to have her husband, William Campbell, killed. *The New York Times* later quotes Mafia sources as saying that Roselli first met Judith in 1951 when she was 17 years old. However, this is easily explained. Judith often attended parties with her movie star sister Jackie. She would not have known who these people were or remembered them. However, they would have remembered a spectacularly beautiful teenage girl in their midst. Exner is later insistent that she never slept with Roselli, although she admits to having slept with Sinatra, Kennedy and Giancana.)

May 8, 1961   Judith flies to Los Angeles to meet Richard Ellwood, with whom she had met only four days earlier in Washington DC. (Notice how within a few days she is flying all around the country, meeting all the major players. Are these just coincidences? Who is paying for her air tickets? Is she delivering money or messages or what?)

May 22, 1961   Date of memorandum linking Giancana to "dirty business" involving CIA operation against Cuba.

June 6, 1961   Judith flies to New York with Richard Ellwood. Judith has trouble finding a hotel room so Sam has Joe DiMaggio get her a hotel room at the Plaza, even though the hotel is booked solid. (Everybody was just wondering when Joe DiMaggio was going to get into this.) Judith lives for some time in the Plaza Hotel in New York City. This is one of the most expensive hotels and is located on Central Park South at Fifth Avenue. Judith has never explained who paid her hotel bill.

June 8, 1961   Richard Ellwood has a heart attack and is hospitalized.

Summer 1961   Judith, who had previously rented a house in

Malibu, Southern California, returns to California. Among her neighbors are Albert and Joyce Lennick, Paul and Renon Ross, Lionel and Louise Steinberg and Diane Gussman and her husband. Among this small group, there are two divorces and one suicide attempt that summer, as everybody is trying to sleep with the other guy's wife and sometimes succeeding. Judith meets with John Roselli and Frank Sinatra there. John Roselli asks to sleep at Judith's place one night and then, in the middle of the night, sneaks off to sleep with Diane Gussman.

August, 1961   Kennedy gives Judith a large diamond and ruby broach. The broach is similar in design to a daisy. Each pedal is 18 carot gold and each has a cluster of nine or ten rubies in the center. It has about thirty full cut diamonds set in platinum on the edge.

August 8, 1961   Judith flies to Washington. The White House has made a reservation for her at the Mayflower Hotel. The White House sends a car to pick up Judith. Evelyn Lincoln meets her in the reception area of the White House and takes her to meet Kennedy and David Powers who are standing by the pool area. Later, upstairs, in the presence of David Powers, Kennedy asks if it is true that Judith has been telling people that JFK was trying to include her in a threesome. Judith is upset that Kennedy would bring this up with Powers present. Powers leaves the room so Judith is left alone with Kennedy. However, Judith is so upset that she refuses to make love to Kennedy. Kennedy has Powers take Judith on a tour of the White House. Judith then leaves the White House without going back to say goodbye to Kennedy. (Powers later makes the infamous quote, "The only Campbell I know is chunky vegetable soup".)

August 9, 1961   Kennedy calls Judith in her hotel room at the Mayflower and tries to make it up to her by inviting her to dinner the following night. To the surprise of Judith, Sam Giancana and his son-in-law, Anthony Tisci, come to her hotel room. She wonders how Giancana knew that she was there.

Here there is a minor discrepancy in dates: In *"My Story"* Judith wrote that on August 10, 1961, she flew back to California again. However, in subsequent interviews she said that she set up a meeting between Kennedy and Giancana at this time. This was to be the last meeting between Kennedy and Giancana. (August 8, 1961: Last meeting between JFK and Giancana, according to Judith.)

August 14, 1961   Judith flies to Chicago. After arriving, she learns that her sister Jackie is seriously ill in the hospital. As Jackie is pregnant, there is grave danger that there will be a miscarriage. Jackie has previously suffered five miscarriages. As it turns out, both Jackie and the baby survive.

August 24, 1961   Judith flies to Washington DC. As before, Evelyn Lincoln books a room for her at the Mayflower and then sends a White House car to pick her up. Kennedy meets her near the Oval Office. Powers is not present this time. Kennedy gives her a large diamond and ruby broach. (The article in *People* magazine by Kitty Kelley published February 29, 1988 has a picture of Judith wearing this broach.) Judith is very happy with this gift. Kennedy and Judith lay in bed in the White House for a long time making love.

Later the same day, Judith has dinner with Richard Ellwood and General Lou Meyers, concerning a company Ellwood has just formed called Magnatronics. Ellwood has some papers he wants Judith to take to Kennedy. Judith does not like the idea. Ellwood says, "it would be quite a sum of money to me" if Kennedy signs the papers. Finally, Judith agrees to give the papers to Evelyn Lincoln to give to Kennedy. This entire incident seems to indicate that Ellwood is trying to bribe the President of the United States, possibly succeeding. After delivering the envelope, Judith returns to New York where she is staying at the Plaza Hotel.

Throughout the fall of 1961 and winter and spring of 1962, Judith continues to see Kennedy regularly at the White House. Always, the routine is the same. She comes down from New York, has a room waiting at the Mayflower. The White House sends a car to pick her up and brings her to the East Gate of the White House. Kennedy greets her, they go to bed. However, Judith is becoming annoyed by the routine. Among other things, Kennedy always assumes the same position, lying on his back. Judith feels she is just there to service him. Judith believes that the man should make love to her, meaning Man on Top, Girl on Bottom. Judith realizes that Kennedy is suffering serious back problems, and this may almost require him to lay on his back during sex. However, she still does not like it. (After his death, it was revealed that Kennedy had serious injuries to his spinal column and he might not have survived his presidency even if he had not been assassinated.)

Although she is not happy about the meetings with Kennedy in the White House, where she feels that she is just coming to service him for sex, it is much better when she meets him elsewhere.

Mid-October, 1961 Judith rents a house in Palm Springs for three months, while keeping her apartment at 1200 North Flores in Los Angeles. (One wonders where she is getting all the money to do this.)

November 16, 1961 House Speaker Sam Rayburn dies. Kennedy flies to Texas for the funeral and then flies to Los Angeles a few days later to see Judith and to speak at a dinner in North Hollywood. Judith sits in the front row next to Jerry Nathanson and Evelyn Lincoln. Judith is now living at 1200 North Flores. After the speech, Kennedy comes to Judith's home where she gives him a pencil sketch she has made of him. After giving Jack a tour of her apartment, they make love. There is nothing wrong with his back this time.

December 19, 1961 Joseph Kennedy, father of JFK, suffers major debilitating stroke. Up until this date, JFK had "lived in a tight paternal grasp". After this, with his father incapacitated, JFK must think on his own for the first time in his life.

February 7, 1962   Attorney General Robert Kennedy briefed on the case of a technician that had been hired by the CIA to bug the hotel room of Dan Rowan in Las Vegas to find out if Rowan had been sleeping with singer Phyllis McGuire. The technician had been arrested by the sheriff's department and had called Maheu to bail him out of jail, thus blowing his cover. The Department of Justice had announced its intention to prosecute Maheu along with the technician. Upon being informed that all these people were all working for the CIA, RFK agrees to drop the prosecution.

February 27, 1962 FBI Director J. Edgar Hoover sends memorandum to Bobby Kennedy notifying him that the "President's Friend" (Judith) is in contact with Mafia characters Giancana and Roselli and has been calling JFK.

March 1962   Judith moves into a new apartment on 8401 Fountain Avenue in Los Angeles. Soon thereafter, she comes home at an unexpected time and finds two FBI agents standing in her apartment. They show her their IDs. She screams at them to leave, which they do. She apparently does not think to write down their names. Ever since, she and others have been trying to find out who they were.

March 22, 1962   J. Edgar Hoover has lunch meeting with John F. Kennedy, presumably confronts him regarding Judith's relationship with the Mafia. FBI Director J. Edgar Hoover meets with JFK and informs him that he knows that Kennedy has been sleeping with Judith.

Several sources claim that after the March 22, 1962 meeting with J. Edgar Hoover, Kennedy had only one further phone call with Judith and broke off relations with her. However, Judith claims that this is not true. She met Kennedy several times after that and they made love. This continued for another nine months. The last time they made love was December, 1962, according to an interview of Judith in *Vanity Fair* magazine published January 1997. Probably, what really happened is they found a way to exchange telephone calls that would not be recorded in the White House logs. However, by March, 1962, they were both beginning to tire of the relationship and had many little arguments. Kennedy wanted her to move to Washington DC. Judith did not really like being "the other woman". Kennedy was otherwise occupied (with other women) and called her less frequently.

March 24, 1962 Kennedy's and Sinatra's friendship officially end after President Kennedy chooses to stay at Bing Crosby's house instead of Frank's house. Kennedy had previously offered to stay at Frank Sinatra's home in Palm Springs and Frank had spent several hundred thousand dollars building extensions to his house, including five bungalows for Secret Service agents and a helicopter landing pad for the presidential helicopter. Sinatra had announced to the press that his home would become the "*Western White House*". After Kennedy backed out of this deal, they were no longer friends and Sinatra became a strong supporter of Richard Nixon. Also, Sinatra kicked Peter Lawford out of the "Rat Pack", because Lawford was the brother-in-law of President Kennedy. Sinatra did use the helicopter landing pad occasionally.

May 8, 1962 Walter Winchell, newspaper gossip columnist in the *Los Angeles Herald Examiner*, writes, "Judy Campbell of Palm Springs and Bevhills is topic no. 1 in Romantic Political circles." No mention is made of Kennedy but a number of people seem to know that Judith is Kennedy's girlfriend.

May 19 1962 Marilyn Monroe sings "Happy Birthday to You" to President Kennedy at Madison Square Garden in New York City.

August 1962 Break-in at Judith's home by sons of a General Dynamics security official during a period when the FBI was staking out her house. Bobby and Billy Hale, twin sons of the General Dynamics security chief I. B. Hale, break into the apartment of Kennedy's mistress and place bugs on her telephone.

Seymour Hersh later suggests in *"The Dark Side of Camelot"* that the purpose of this break-in is to gather information to be used to blackmail President Kennedy.

August, 1962 Jacqueline Kennedy almost certainly conducts a sexual affair with Gianni Agnelli, an Italian industrialist and principal shareholder of Fiat, aboard Gianni's yacht in Italy where Jacqueline stays with him for several nights. Gianni is a notorious womanizer who conducts affairs with many famous women. Jacqueline may have taken up with Gianni in retaliation for JFK's affair with Marilyn Monroe, which had become public knowledge.

August 5, 1962   Marilyn Monroe dies. Officially ruled a suicide but many believe that she was murdered. Had a presumed affair with JFK. It was rumored that she was depressed because JFK had dumped her. Another rumor (that this author heard at the time) was that when she killed herself, she was pregnant with John F. Kennedy's baby (or possibly with Robert F. Kennedy's baby).

October 10, 1962   Judith enters Billings Hospital at University of Chicago and the doctors discover that she has a chronic kidney condition. After being released from the hospital, Judith takes an apartment at the Oak Park Arms in Chicago to be closer to Sam Giancana and the hospital. However, things were never the same with Sam, she says. Soon, Judith learns from the newspapers that Sam is seeing singer Phyllis McGuire of the famous McGuire Sisters and has dropped Judith.

October 14-28, 1962 Cuban Missile Crisis

November 1962 $5.6 billion contract to build TFX jet fighter (later renamed F-111) awarded to General Dynamics by Kennedy's Secretary of Defense, Robert McNamara. This contract becomes subject of a Senate investigation. Seymour Hersh suggests that Kennedy was blackmailed into awarding this contract.

November 16, 1962 Sam takes Judith to the *"Villa Venice"* in

Wheeling, Illinois just north of Chicago where many famous performers are appearing, including Eddie Fisher and Sammy Davis Jr. The Villa Venice is apparently owned by Sam Giancana. Their performances were arranged by Frank Sinatra. Giancana is angry because Kennedy, whom Sam had helped elect, is now tightening the screws on the Mafia, so these performers appear free of charge for two weeks to pay back Sam Giancana. Sinatra and other members of the Rat Pack perform at the "Villa Venice" owned by Sam Giancana in Wheeling, Illinois to pay him back for his help in getting Kennedy elected.

November 28, 1962 Judith goes to New York and checks into the Essex House at the suggestion of Eddie Fisher. Eddie introduces Judith to Dr. Max Jacobson. Dr. Jacobson immediately tells Judith that he knows all about the fact that she has been sleeping with Kennedy. Later, as Eddie Fisher is taking Judith back to the Essex House, Judith feels faint so Fisher takes her to see Dr. Jacobson. Dr. Jacobson gives her a shot, and she feels better. Dr. Jacobson has also been giving these same shots to President Kennedy and even accompanies the president on some trips to Europe for that purpose. Later, Judith finds out that the shots contain amphetamines and that he is known as "Dr. Feelgood Jacobson". Judith starts going to Dr. Jacobson regularly to receive the shots. It has been suggested that JFK, who has been getting the same shots, was really a "junkie" during this period.

December 8, 1962   Judith goes to Chicago where Sam Giancana gets her a room at the Sahara, a new hotel on Mannheim Road. Judith wants a smaller room because all of the shots she has been getting from Dr. Max Jacobson are making her nervous and jumpy. Judith stays at the hotel for two months. The owner is Manny Skar. Later, Manny Skar is killed in a gangland rubout. Judith is still sleeping with Sam, but he never stays the entire night with her any more.

December 1962   Judith has intercourse with Kennedy for the last time.

January 1963 Judith informs JFK that she is pregnant. JFK says that if she wants to have the baby, she can. Judith says that she cannot do that. JFK then tells her that Sam Giancana will take care of it. When Judith informs Sam that she is pregnant, she has intercourse with Giancana and then he offers to marry her to give the baby a father. She declines. Sam Giancana offers to marry the pregnant Judith so that the baby will have a father. Judith turns down the offer and has an abortion instead.

In an article in January, 1997 issue of *Vanity Fair* magazine, Judith claims that Kennedy had to be the father because she had made love only to Kennedy during the period when she could have become pregnant. However, this seems to be contradicted by her 1977 book where she states that she had been sleeping with Sam Giancana. Both claims could still be true if she is stating that she only slept with Kennedy during the interval of time around 14 days after the start of her last period. However, sometimes women have light false periods when they are pregnant, so it seems that Giancana could possibly have been the father, which explains his offer to marry her. Also, if JFK had turned out to be the father, Giancana could have used that to blackmail JFK.

January 27, 1963 Judith finds out she is pregnant, agrees with JFK to get rid of the baby. Judith has abortion of JFK's baby at Chicago's Grant Hospital, according to an interview she gave to syndicated columnist Liz Smith that appeared in January 1997 issue of *Vanity Fair* magazine. Note that at this time, abortions were highly illegal and birth control pills were not yet readily available.

February 4, 1963 Judith leaves for California. By this time, the FBI is all over Sam Giancana, following him everywhere he goes. Giancana derisively refers to the FBI Agents trailing him as "The Boy Scouts". Sam takes Judith to O'Hare Airport. To make fun of the FBI agents trailing him, Sam runs on to the airplane at almost the last minute. A bunch of FBI agents run on right after him, flashing their credentials to the stewardess. Then, just as the stewardess is about to close the aircraft door, Sam runs off the airplane again and all the agents all run off the aircraft after him. Sam is making fun of them.

February 27, 1963   Sister Jackie Immoor has second baby after nearly suffering a miscarriage, goes on to have two more babies.

March 6, 1963   Judith needs the shots again, so she goes to see Dr. Tommy Jacobson, son of Dr. Max Jacobson, in Los Angeles. FBI agent Dodge is there to greet her. Judith concludes that her parent's telephone must be bugged. Otherwise, how would Dodge know where she was going to be? (On the other hand, it is possible that the FBI was bugging the telephone of Dr. Jacobson.)

March 1963   Judith starts sleeping with Bo Bolinsky, the famous baseball pitcher with the Los Angeles As. Sam apparently finds out about it and is angry. (Bo Bolinsky was known for dating Ann-Margaret, Connie Stevens, Tina Louise and Mamie Van Doren, as well as for marrying Playboy centerfold Jo Collins.) A few days later, Judith flies to Las Vegas where she dates Eddie Fisher.

April 15, 1963   Eddie Fisher gives a cocktail party at Au Petit John in Beverly Hills. Judith takes a limo with Angie Dickinson and Alain Delon. Angie says, "You're Judy Campbell. John has said so much about you." (Angie Dickinson later suggests that she never even met John F. Kennedy. However, there are many accounts of Angie Dickinson and JFK being seen together.)

April 19, 1963   Judith has cocktails with Sidney Korshak, lawyer for the Mafia, in Beverly Hills.

June 6, 1963   Judith has D&C. The next day, two FBI agents enter her hospital room, accuse her of having had an abortion (which was illegal at that time) and demand to know who the father and the doctor was.

July 27, 1963   Sam Giancana, while having dinner with Frank Sinatra at the Cal-Neva Lodge on the North Shore of Lake Tahoe, gets into fight with Victor LaCroix Collins, road manager for the McGuire Sisters, concerning Phyllis McGuire, who is now Sam Giancana's girlfriend. The Cal-Neva Lodge is a hotel-casino that straddles the border between California and Nevada. Sam Giancana is in the Nevada State Gaming Commission's "Black Book", which means that he is not allowed to enter any casino in the State of Nevada. This means that Sam Giancana is okay as long as he stays in the California end of the Cal-Neva Lodge. However, during the fight, Sam Giancana strays across the border and is observed by the FBI to be on the Nevada side of the hotel. The Nevada State Gaming Commission starts an investigation. As a result, Frank Sinatra, who is part owner of the Cal-Neva Lodge and of the Sands Hotel in Las Vegas, loses his license and is forced to sell his interest in both hotels. (To this day, the Cal-Neva Lodge advertises that it was owned by Frank Sinatra.)

August 7, 1963   Patrick Bouvier Kennedy is born to Jacqueline Kennedy, but tragically the infant dies only two days later. Jacqueline had been swimming in the Atlantic Ocean only two days before this premature birth. (Note that JFK tends to sleep with Judith during times when Jacqueline Kennedy is pregnant.)

August 1963   Ellen Rometsch, suspected of being an East German spy who was sleeping with Kennedy, deported to Germany. (Rometsch is often referred to in FBI memorandums as a "prostitute". She was the wife of a German diplomat. It is unproven that she was actually a common prostitute.)

November 19, 1963 JFK tells Evelyn Lincoln that he plans to replace Vice-President Johnson when he runs for re-election.

November 20, 1963 Judith checks into the Beverly Crest Hotel in Los Angeles, where her mother had reserved a room.

November 22, 1963 Kennedy Assassinated in Dallas. Judith

Campbell learns about this when her mother calls her room in the Beverly Crest Hotel in Los Angeles and tells her about it.

November 24, 1963 Lee Harvey Oswald shot and killed by Jack Ruby.

December 8, 1963 Frank Sinatra Jr. kidnapped at Harrah's Lake Tahoe. He is released two days later after his father pays out the $240,000 ransom demanded by the kidnappers, who are later captured, prosecuted, convicted, and sentenced to long prison terms. It has been suggested that Sinatra believes that the Chicago Mafia was behind this kidnapping, to warn Sinatra not to reveal what he knew about Mafia involvement in the JFK Assassination.

December 31, 1963 During a New Year's Eve Party at the Desert Inn in Las Vegas, Judith slaps Moe Dalitz, manager of the Desert Inn, when he tries to kiss her.

October 12, 1964 Mary Pinchot Meyer, another mistress of JFK, shot dead as she walks along a towpath in Georgetown, Washington DC. Mary Pinchot Meyer had been mistress of President John F. Kennedy and had taken LDS with him. Her ex-husband, Cord Meyer, had been a CIA Operative in charge of "Project Mockingbird". He had also been an exceptionally close friend of Jacqueline Kennedy. Watergate burglar E. Howard Hunt subsequently claims on this deathbed that Cord Meyer had JFK shot in retaliation for the affair between JFK and his wife. Cord Meyer in contrast claims that the same people had killed his former wife as had killed JFK. There are many JFK assassination theories surrounding Cord Meyer and Mary Pinchot Meyer. The murder of Mary Pinchot Meyer remains unsolved today.

January 1965 Judith discovers that she is pregnant again and considers having an abortion.

May 28, 1965 Baby boy born to Judith two months prematurely. Judith refuses to reveal the identity of the father. The baby is later given away for adoption, with Judith saying, with good reason, that with the FBI on her tail all the time, there is no way that the baby can have a happy, healthy, normal life if he stays with her. (Judith later reveals the name of the child. However, since the adopted child, who is now a prominent White House journalist, has never identified himself, that name is not provided in this book.)

June 1, 1965   Sam Giancana jailed in Cook County Jail for contempt for refusing to testify before federal grand jury. Giancana appeals to the US Court of Appeals and then to the US Supreme Court, where Justice Tom Clarke denies his application for interim relief. Ultimately, certiorari is denied. *Giancana v. United States*, 352 F.2d 921 (C. A. 7th Cir.), *cert. denied*, 382 US 959 (1965), cited in *Shillitani v. United States*, 384 U.S. 364 (1966).

Giancana was released from jail one year later by Judge William Campbell when the grand jury had expired. Soon thereafter, Sam Giancana was removed as Don of the Chicago Outfit, so he moved to Mexico where he resided for the next seven years, from 1967 to 1974, in exile in Cuernavaca, Mexico, until he was extradited back to the US by the Department of Justice.

1966   Richard Ellwood, director of a small electronics company in Culver City, dies. (According to Seymour Hersh in *"The Dark Side of Camelot"*, Ellwood was one of several defense contractors who had been paying cash bribes to JFK.)

June 6, 1968   Robert F. Kennedy assassinated in Los Angeles minutes after winning the California Primary.

October 20, 1968   Jacqueline Kennedy marries Aristotle Onassis, a Greek shipping tycoon, on Skorpios, Greece. American public greets this marriage with the same level of enthusiasm that the British Royal Family greeted the prospect of a marriage of Princess Diana to Dodi Fayed.

January 18, 1969   Joseph P. Kennedy, father of John F. Kennedy, dies.

April 7, 1971   Katherine Shea Immoor, mother of Judith, dies at age 65.

May, 1971   I.B. Hale, who was born on September 9, 1915, dies in Texas. He and his sons Billy and Robert Allen "Bobby" Hale have been implicated in a break-in to Judith's apartment, which has been associated with the Kennedy Assassination. Robert Hale takes up religion, has 15 children, and is still unavailable for comment today.

May 2, 1972 FBI Director J. Edgar Hoover suddenly dies unexpectedly. Investigators almost immediately try to seize the secret files in his office he is believed to have used to blackmail presidents, only to find that they were destroyed illegally by his two loyal secretaries in the hours after his death.

June 17, 1972   Burglars attested during the Watergate break-in. Several of the burglars were involved in the Bay of Pigs Invasion and have also been implicated in the Kennedy Assassination.

Spring 1973   Judith meets professional golfer Daniel Exner.

August 9, 1974   President Nixon resigns amid Watergate Scandal.

November 1974   Joseph Immoor, father of Judith, dies at age 70.

March 15, 1975   Aristotle Onassis dies at age 69 in Neuilly-sur-Seine, France.

May 20, 1975   Judith marries Dan Exner, after living with him for two years.

June 19, 1975   Sam Giancana murdered in the basement of his Oak Park, Illinois home just five days before he was scheduled to testify before a Senate Committee. As Giancana was under constant surveillance at the time of his murder, one wonders how the killer was able to get in and out of his house without the FBI noticing it. Investigators noted that the execution bullet had been fired into the back of his head and six others into his mouth and throat. The six additional shots were said to indicate that the Mafia knew that Giancana could no longer be trusted to remain silent. Senate Intelligence Committee staff members had that day arrived in Chicago to make arrangements for Giancana to testify.

July 1975 *"Dog Days at the White House"* by Traphes Bryant published. The author was the White House kennel keeper and night time electrician from 1951 to 1972. This book, on pages 22-40, provides eye-witness accounts, revealing for the first time Kennedy's huge appetite for sexual romps, with naked girls swimming together in the White House Swimming Pool and running naked through the second floor private family area of the White House, while Jacqueline was away, which was most of the time. The book is discounted and disbelieved, until the Judith Campbell story breaks in the world press five months later.

September 12, 1975 Judith subpoenaed to testify before a Senate Committee. She is now living in a mobile home which she and Dan Exner drive to the professional golf tournaments in which he is competing. She has a new name and no fixed address, which has made it difficult for the FBI to locate her.

September 19, 1975 Judith appears before a Senate committee for the first time. After arriving in Washington DC the previous day, Judith is taken to a Senate Office Building, were she is first interviewed by Chief Counsel FAO Schwartz, Jr. and Minority Counsel Curtis R. Smothers. She is then taken to Senator John Tower's office. Tower is not present. Judith is questioned by eight members of the US Senate Staff. The main questions concern whether she was involved in any Castro Assassination Plots, which she denies. She never personally meets a senator.

November 16, 1975 First *Washington Post* article revealing that Kennedy and Mafia Characters shared the same mistress. Article is entitled *"Probers Doubt Kennedy Knew of Poison Plot against Castro"*. (The probers would be proven wrong.)

November 20, 1975 Church Committee 349-page report released, mentions "friend" of JFK but does not provide the name or even the sex of the "friend". The report states:

> *"Evidence before the committee indicates that a close friend of President Kennedy had frequent contact with the president from the end of 1960 through mid-1962. F.B.I. reports and testimony indicate the president's friend was also a close friend of John Roselli and Sam Giancana and saw them often during this same period."*

December 15, 1975 William Safire of *The New York Times* in article entitled *"The President's Friend"*, accuses Church Committee of a cover-up.

December 17, 1975 Judith holds press conference in San Diego where she is living in a mobile home. Next day, newspapers around the world dub her *"Mobsters' Moll"*.

December 18-19, 1975 Every major newspaper in the world carries news reports that Judith Campbell had been sleeping with both John F. Kennedy and members of the Chicago Mafia at the same time.

December 23, 1975 Kenneth O'Donnell, former Kennedy Aid, tells *Boston Harold-American* that all reports of extra-marital affairs by Kennedy are lies. "They are all lies", says O'Donnell.

December 29, 1975 *Time* Magazine publishes article entitled *"Scandals: J.F.K. And the Mobsters' Moll"*. Companion article entitled *"Jack Kennedy's Other Women"* details many other sexual escapades by JFK in White House. *Newsweek* refuses to publish anything about this. Evelyn Lincoln refers to Judith as a volunteer "campaign worker". (Nothing wrong with that. She was a volunteer, she was on the campaign, and she worked very hard.)

August 9, 1976   John Roselli's decomposing body found in a 55-gallon steel fuel drum floating in Dumfounding Bay near Miami, Florida. His body had been chained to heavy weights intended to keep it on the bottom, but gases from the decomposing body had caused it to float to the top.

1977   Series of articles about Exner, Kennedy and Mafia relationships appear in the *National Enquirer*.

March 29, 1977   Charles Nicoletti murdered in Chicago. Nicoletti was due to appear before the Select House Committee on Assassinations where he was to be asked about his involvement in the assassination of John F. Kennedy. According to James E. Files, Nicoletti was one of two shooters in the Kennedy Assassination.

June 24, 1977   Sussman and Sugar Advertising Agency resigns *Grove Press* account, citing fears that it will be sued when the book by Judith Exner "*My Story*" is published.

June 25, 1977   "*My Story*" by Judith Exner as told to Ovid Demaris published by Grove Press.

May 8, 1985   Judith's sister Jacqueline Immoor, movie actress under the name of "*Susan Morrow*", dies at age 54.

1988   Judith separates from Daniel Exner after he has had a brain tumor removed. They apparently never divorced. Since then, there has been no trace of Dan Exner. It is not known whether he is dead or alive.

February 29, 1988   Kitty Kelley article in *People* magazine says that Judith carried cash from John F. Kennedy to Sam Giancana.

Kitty Kelley later says that she believes that Judith was paid "about $50,000" for this interview. (Kitty Kelley is the author of sensationalized and completely unauthorized biographies of Frank Sinatra, Jackie Kennedy Onassis, Nancy Reagan, Elizabeth Taylor, the Bush Family and the British Royal Family.)

October 2, 1991   *"Harlot's Ghost"*, a Historical Novel by Norman Mailer, is first published. Mailer explains that a character in this 1282 page novel named "Modene Murphy" is based loosely on Judith Exner. In the Mailer novel, "Modene Murphy" is an Eastern Airlines stewardess.

May 19, 1994   Jacqueline Kennedy Onassis dies.

November 25, 1995 Movie *"Sugartime"* starring John Turturro and Mary-Louise Parker released about the affair between Sam Giancana and singer Phyllis McGuire. The title is the same as the name of the famous hit song by the McGuire Sisters.

September 29, 1996 Book *"The Kennedy Women"* by Laurence Leamer published. The hard cover edition came out in 1994. Judith later tells columnist Liz Smith that she is upset by the book and is considering filing a lawsuit, because on page 486 it says, "Judith Campbell, a young woman who looked like an erotic voluptuous version of Jackie" and quotes Milton Ebbins as saying that Judith was a $200 hooker. It seems unlikely that the author, Laurence Leamer, ever met Judith. Nobody who saw Judith has ever referred to her as "voluptuous" which usually means "big breasted". The statement that she was "voluptuous" is probably not true. Her main attribute was a beautiful face. She was embarrassed to wear a bikini. The book contains some other mild inaccuracies, but probably not enough to sustain a libel suit.

January 1997   In article by Liz Smith in *Vanity Fair* magazine, Judith reveals that she had been pregnant with John F. Kennedy's baby, but aborted the baby. Liz Smith writes, Judith *"is by nature one of the most soft-spoken and gentle people I have ever known".*

March 12, 1998   Ovid Demaris dies.

May 14, 1998   Frank Sinatra dies.

August 22, 1998   Movie *"The Rat Pack"* starring Ray Liotta, Joe Mantegna, Don Cheadle, Angus Macfadyen and William Petersen is released. This movie is a serious attempt to be historically accurate. There are some inaccuracies in the movie such as, for example, Kennedy receives the president nomination before the event at the Sands where he meets Judy Campbell. However, the major events are described as accurately as could be expected from any movie. *"Judy Campbell"* is played by actress Michelle Grace. Judith considers filing a lawsuit because she does not like the way she is portrayed. This movie would probably have resulted in several lawsuits, were it not for the fact that Sinatra and almost everybody else depicted in the movie EXCEPT FOR Judy Campbell was already dead.

Here is one sample scene:

> SCENE: Puccini's Restaurant in Beverly Hills. John F. Kennedy, Robert Kennedy, Marilyn Monroe, Joe DiMaggio, Frank Sinatra, Dean Martin, Sammy Davis Jr. and May Britt are all having dinner together. The FBI is there too, having bugged the conversation, they are tape recording it.

> Mobsters Mickey Cohen and John Roselli enter the restaurant. Almost every gets upset because they do not want to be associated with mobsters, so they all get up and leave, except for Sinatra and JFK. Now, the restaurant is empty except for two "broads" who just arrived and are seated at the bar. Those two broads are none other than Angie Dickinson and Judith Campbell. The Sinatra character says to JFK, "Which one do you want?"

This scene depicts events said to have occurred on the night of November 2, 1959. However, Judith denies that this happened like that. The movie does depict the events of the night of February 8, 1960 reasonably accurately, except that the night ends showing Judy Campbell in bed having sexual intercourse with JFK. (Judith claims in her book that this did not happen then.)

This perhaps forms the basis for Judith Campbell's threat to sue, since she claims that the first time she ever had intercourse with JFK was one month later on March 7, 1960. The reader will have already noticed several other inaccuracies. Judith probably could have won a court judgment over these misrepresentations but the damages would probably have been minimal.

The movie does poorly probably because few viewers can follow the complex relationships and realize that the events depicted are actually history.

September 1, 1998   Seymour M. Hersh book *"The Dark Side of Camelot"* published.

September 25, 1999 Judith Immoor Campbell Exner dies of lung cancer at age 65 in the City of Hope Cancer Center, a cancer hospice, in Duarte, California, a suburb of Los Angeles.

Aug. 12, 2000   Frederick Immoor Junior, brother of Judith, dies at South Lake Tahoe, Nevada.

July 21, 2002   *"Power and Beauty"*, the Judith Exner Story, starring Natasha Henstridge, Kevin Anderson and Peter Friedman, released in a made for television movie. Unfortunately, this movie like most movies plays fast and loose with the facts. Although some of the facts are historically accurate, much of it is rubbish. Too bad, the real story is more interesting than the made up story. The movie is painful to watch because of its inaccuracies, especially at the beginning, although it has many good points.

May 17, 2005 "*Sinatra: The Life*" by Anthony Summers and Robbyn Swan is published. A chapter in this book entitled "*The Candidate and the Courtesan*" deals with the relationships between Kennedy, Sinatra and Judith Campbell Exner. (Anthony Summers is the author of sensationalized biographies of J. Edgar Hoover, Marilyn Monroe, Richard Nixon, Czar Nicholas II and a study on the Assassination of JFK.)

October 2005 Book by Antoinette Giancana, "*JFK And Sam: The Connection Between the Giancana And Kennedy Assassinations*" released. In this book, Antoinette Giancana states that her father had JFK assassinated. However, she offers no real evidence to prove this. She says that the actual shooter was James Files a/k/a James Sutton, who had been hired by John Roselli. The plan had not been for Files to shoot JFK. Another man had been assigned that task. Files, a former stock car race driver, had been assigned to drive the getaway car. However, when the other man had not been able to perform, Files had stepped in to "help out" by shooting JFK with a pistol he had just happened to bring along. JFK was shot from two directions, but the fatal shot came from James Files on the "*grassy knoll*". The other shot came from the Dal-Tex Building, a red colored building across Houston Street from the School Book Depository. Oswald had nothing to do with the shooting. Oswald had just been a patsy. Later, Sam Giancana had said that it had been a mistake to shoot JFK. They should have shot RFK instead.

January 23, 2007 Watergate burglar E. Howard Hunt dies. In a taped deathbed confession, Hunt names Cord Meyer, Frank Sturgis, David Sánchez Morales and David Atlee Phillips as participants in the assassination of John F. Kennedy.

June 25, 2007 CIA "*Family Jewels*" made available

February 2, 2008 Sam Sloan publishes this book.

To Be Continued. Be sure to tune in for the sequel.

Exner Sources

A time line has been created using a wide variety of sources. With many sources being used, one would expect that there would be many disagreements as to who did what and where and when. There are surprisingly few of these.

The main reason for this seems to be that Exner herself was a "Pack Rat". She tended to keep everything. Columnist Liz Smith reports that Exner showed her canceled checks for hotel bills, plane tickets and train tickets as well as newspaper items, date books, photographs and even cleaning bills.

The investigations by the Church Committee on CIA Assassination Plots is how Judith was found out. The FBI had been tracking her for years and this was brought to the attention of the Church Committee. The Church Committee, after finding out that Judith had been sleeping with JFK, voted unanimously to leave that out of its report, feeling that the President's personal sex life was irrelevant to its investigations. Since the Church Committee had failed to uncover any evidence that Judith was involved in the plot to kill Castro, it just devoted one paragraph to her on page 129 of the report. That paragraph stated:

> *"Evidence before the committee indicates that a close friend of President Kennedy had frequent contact with the president from the end of 1960 through mid-1962. F.B.I. reports and testimony indicate the president's friend was also a close friend of John Roselli and Sam Giancana and saw them often during this same period."*

The *Washington Post* found out about it and published mention of it on page 6A of the Post on November 16, 1975. This article attracted little attention until the following month when William Safire wrote a column in *The New York Times* accusing the Church Committee of a cover-up.

Exner Sources

It is important to note that this came shortly after the Watergate Cover-ups that led President Nixon to resign in 1974 and sent more than 30 high administration officials to prison. The public was interested in learning about other cover-ups. At any other time, the Kennedy-Campbell-Mafia Connection might never have become publicly known. FBI Records, White House logs and other documents and records establish that there was a relationship between Campbell and Kennedy, although the president's secretary Evelyn Lincoln stated that Judith was merely a volunteer "campaign worker".

The most complete record comes from Exner's book, *"My Story"* as told to Ovid Demaris. Ovid Demaris was the ideal choice to write this biography because he had already written several books on the Mafia, so he knew who those people were. For example, when Judith briefly met Mafia characters "Joe Fish" and Sidney Korshak, Judith would not have known who those people were, but Ovid Demaris certainly knew because he was an authority on this subject.

Among the other books by Ovid Demaris were *"The Last Mafioso"*, a biography of Jimmy "The Weasel" Fratianno, *"The Green Felt Jungle"*, his expose on Mafia operations in Las Vegas, *"The Director"*, a biography of J. Edgar Hoover, *"Jack Ruby"*, a biography of Jack Ruby, *"Brothers in Blood: The International Terrorist Network"* about international organized crime, and *"Captive City"*, the story of Chicago and the Mafia which has a photo of Sam Giancana on the cover. The knowledge that writing these books gave Ovid Demaris about Mafia operations was invaluable. Judith Campbell Exner herself never graduated from high school, so it is not likely that she could have written this book or even have pieced together the parts of this complex story without the help of Ovid Demaris.

As an aside, I personally met Barney Rosset, the owner of Grove

Exner Sources

Press and the publisher of *"My Story"*, in 1971 on a business matter. In the 1950s, Grove Press had become famous by publishing *"Lady Chatterley's Lover"* and *"Tropic of Cancer"*. Both books resulted in court cases after they were banned under the censorship laws. Grove Press won the court cases in the United States Supreme Court and the works became accepted as great literature. In 1968, I met an editor for Grove Press at the Grove Press booth at the American Orthopsychiatric Association Convention in Chicago, to which my mother, a child psychiatrist and a member of that association, had taken me. I tried to get the Grove Press representative interested in publishing my book about the *History of the Sexual Freedom League*, of which I had been the president. He took part of my manuscript home for the night, but returned it the next day and said that he was not interested. (It still has not been published.)

By 1971, the situation had reversed. By then, I was the principal of a registered securities Broker-Dealer, Samuel H. Sloan & Co. I was a market-maker in over-the-counter securities. Grove Press was a public company and I had been trading the stock. By then, I had lots of money. Barney Rosset was by this time broke, busted. Grove Press was essentially bankrupt, its offices had been closed and all employees had been laid off.

So, my plan was to buy or take over Grove Press, which was a public company, which would then publish my book. I made an appointment to meet Barney Rosset in the office of my attorney, Roy L. Weiss. We met with Barney Rosset for about two hours, but nothing came of the conversation, as he still had big plans and dreams of making millions. I felt that Barney Rosset was finished, but there was nothing I could offer him that would interest him.

Thus, I was surprised to read that in 1977, six years later, Grove Press had put up big money to buy the rights to the Judith Campbell Exner story. I still suspect that this was not what really happened. Probably the $100,000 offer was just a publicity stunt.

Ovid Demaris likely wrote it on the fly. Grove Press was certainly the right choice for a publisher. Being bankrupt, it could not be sued or, if it was sued, no money would be forthcoming.

In her interview by Liz Smith in 1997, Judith Exner said that she never got the $100,000 that had been promised her because the IRS had taken it for a tax lien on the golf winnings of her husband, Dan Exner, a professional golfer. However, this does not seem right either. Although Dan Exner was a professional golfer, he never won a major tournament and the best he ever did was being accepted on the Florida Mini-Tour. He never made much money. I doubt he owed the IRS $100,000. Also, would the IRS take the proceeds from his wife's sale of her book, even if he did? I do not know. I do know something that few in the outside world knew, which was that Barney Rosset was flat-on-his-ass broke and had no way to pay $100,000.

In her interview with gossip columnist Liz Smith, Judith Campbell said that the best part of her 1977 book was the first page, because it was blank. She said that although she was given a draft of the book prior to publication and offered the chance to make any changes she deemed necessary, she had just bothered to read the first section. She never read the rest. She complains about misrepresentations in the book. However, one suspects that her complaints are not valid because things she seems to think are in the book are not there. It seems likely that she never read the book and just relied on what others told her it contained. For example, she seems to think that the book implies that she was a "party girl" and was promiscuous. In reality, the book contains no such implication. It characterizes her behavior as rather prudish. The book mentions sexual relationships with eight men: William Cambpell, Tony Travis, Frank Sinatra, John F. Kennedy, Sam Giancana, Bo Bolinsky, the unnamed father of her son who was born in 1965, and Daniel Exner whom she married. This is over a period of 25 years from 1952 when she married for the first time with William Campbell until 1977 when the book was published.

Any unmarried woman who has slept with only eight men over a period of 25 years is certainly not promiscuous. Rather, she has led a dull life. (Of course, one suspects that there may have been a few more lovers whom she forgot to mention to her biographers. It is hard to believe that she only slept with eight men in her life.)

Judith Campbell Exner had less kind words for Kitty Kelley, who interviewed her for an article in the February 29, 1988 issue of *People* magazine. She says that Kitty Kelley tried to get her to agree to make the article more sensational by changing some of the facts and adding some new, false facts.

Kitty Kelley does her best by starting with a quote from Exner stating "*I lied*" [in her 1977 book]. However, the facts presented are hardly convincing that she really lied. It is more like she evaded or that she told the truth but not the whole truth. For example, one of the questions asked of her by the Church Committee was whether Sam Giancana or John Roselli had ever asked her to carry messages to President Kennedy. Her answer was "no". That was the correct answer. They had never done that. However, the truth was the other way, because the President had asked her to carry messages to Sam Giancana. The Church Committee had never asked her that question.

Another source must be the movie "*Power and Beauty*" starring Natasha Henstridge, Kevin Anderson and Peter Friedman. I have just played that movie through several times on video. The movie has so many mistakes that it is virtually worthless as a historical document, although it does have a few good points. Nevertheless, anybody writing a book on any subject must read or view all of the literature on that subject before picking up a pen. The most annoying misrepresentation in "*Power and Beauty*" comes at the very beginning when it depicts Judith being close friends with John Roselli at a party in 1952 where she meets William Campbell, Frank Sinatra, and Peter and Patricia Lawford. Later there is a fight between William Campbell and Peter Lawford. In reality, none of these things happened. Judith says that she first met Roselli in May 1961, after she had met Sinatra, Kennedy and Giancana, and that she never slept with Roselli. No credible evidence has emerged disputing this fact. It is true that The New York Times reported that *"Mafia Sources"* said that Roselli had met Judith in 1951. Also, Judith says on page 215 of her book that she had been reminded that she had met John Roselli years earlier at a party at Warner's but she had forgotten about it. John Roselli recalled telling Bryan Foy that Judith was more beautiful than Elizabeth Taylor (This was one of the most frequent statements people made about Judith.) (Many people have seen the 1955 movie *"The Seven Little Foys"* starring Bob Hope about a vaudeville family. What most do not realize is that this is actually a true story. They became Hollywood producers and Bryan Foy was one of them.)

It was almost certainly true that John Roselli met Judith Campbell in her early years because Roselli was in with the Hollywood Set and was involved in the affairs of many Hollywood movie stars. Judith Immoor often attended parties with those stars with her elder sister Jackie, who was herself a minor Hollywood star. So, it could be that Roselli met Judith. However, there is no evidence supporting the claim depicted in the movie *"Power and Beauty"* that Roselli was such a close friend of Judith that he would offer to kill her husband, William Campbell, as a favor.

Many people seem to believe that Judith made up her entire story. However, it can be readily observed from reading through her 304 page book filled with checkable facts on every page that if it were not all true there would be complaints from people whose names are mentioned in the book. For example, the book on page 128 provides the private telephone numbers of President Kennedy and numerous other government officials. Most of those telephone numbers were non-public. The Washington Post Editor Ben Bradlee, who was a close personal friend of both President Kennedy and his wife Jacqueline, checked all of those telephone numbers and every one of them was proven to be correct.

There are other completely independent sources. Jimmy "The Weasel" Fratianno, a Mafia wise guy and a killer, while in the *Federal Witness Protection Plan*, reported being told that Judith was none other than the girlfriend of the President of the United States. Fratianno said, *"Beautiful. Looks like Liz Taylor, but nicer, a real sweet kid, comes from a good family, lots of class, ... And this broad is none other than Jack Kennedy's mistress."*

Another book, *"Sinatra: The Life"* by Anthony Summers and Robbyn Swan, has a 14-page chapter devoted to Judith Campbell entitled *"The Candidate and the Courtesan"*. This book tells an entirely different story, quoting Peter Lawford, brother-in-law of President Kennedy, as saying that Judith was a *"hooker"*. However, it hardly matters. It was extremely important to Judith Campbell that she be portrayed as a non-hooker who never took money for sex and who paid her own way. However, to the rest of the world, it does not matter much whether money changed hands or not. The important question is whether she had intercourse with the President. Everybody agrees that she did. Whether she did so on a paid or a volunteer basis is not that important.

The Summers and Swan book adds a new story. It says on page 260 that Kennedy and Campbell actually first met one month earlier, on November 1-2, 1959, before Kennedy had declared for President. The meeting took place in Puccini's restaurant in Beverly Hills. Sinatra and Kennedy were dining together and noticed two beautiful broads at another table. They sent Nick Sevano over to the table with a note asking them to join them. The two broads came over and turned out to be Angie Dickinson and Judith Campbell. The four of them went out to see movies together. However, the girls did not sleep with the boys. They just went home after the movies.

There is no mention of this incident in *"My Story"*. However, it is possible that Judith had forgotten about it. After all, *"My Story"* was written 18 years after the event in question. Also, nothing significant had happened. In addition, the story lacks credibility for a number of reasons. By November 1959, Angie Dickinson was a well established actress, who had appeared in 37 movies. Most were minor roles but she had been the leading lady in the box office hit *"Rio Bravo"* starring John Wayne, Dean Martin, Ricky Nelson and Angie Dickinson. *Rio Bravo* had been released on April 4, 1959. It is thus impossible that Frank Sinatra did not know who Angie Dickinson was. Also, the book by Judith Exner on page 49 recounts a similar incident also at Puccini's, also in the first week of November 1959 and also involving herself and Frank Sinatra and Nick Sevano. However, she says that she was having dinner with "friends". Neither Angie Dickinson nor John F. Kennedy are mentioned as being present on that occasion.

As to the first meeting with JFK as described by Judith in "My Story", there are lots of witnesses to that, because it took place in the middle of the election campaign and an entire press corps was following around Kennedy, making every stop he made. Kennedy had his own airplane, the *"Caroline"*, purchased for him by his father a few months earlier. When he stopped in Las Vegas on February 7, 1960, the press corps was wondering why he was stopping there as he had nothing to do there. According to Summers and Swan, page 263, Kennedy stopped there to meet Sinatra. They give as sources CBS Reporter Blaire Clark and Mary McGrory of the *Washington Star*, who saw Judith Campbell sitting between Sinatra and Kennedy at the Sands. Later, Judith "went upstairs" with Kennedy. Another witness who saw them together on that occasion was Milt Ebbins.

It also says on page 263 that Giancana knew that Kennedy had a weakness for women. *"Throw him a broad and he will do anything"*, Giancana said in 1959, according to the book. However, there are serious problems with this quote. Not only is no date, place or source given but he seems to be talking about Joseph

Exner Sources

Kennedy, the father of John F. Kennedy. The father was also known for philandering. He openly conducted an affair with movie actress Gloria Swanson (1899-1983) and even brought her to his home when his wife Rose was there. Summers and Swan suggest that arrangements had been made for Judith Campbell to sleep with Joseph Kennedy, the father, not with his son, John, the future president. The source given for this statement is a Las Vegas card dealer, Count Guido Deiro. Not the greatest source, however.

Summers and Swan state that JFK had sex with *"a hooker"* on February 7, 1960. They imply that Judith Campbell was that hooker. However, as everybody knows, Las Vegas is filled with fantastically beautiful hookers. Also, Summers and Swan state that there was a sex party involving Kennedy that night at the El Rancho Vegas where there was *"some sort of indiscreet party"* with *"showgirls running in and out of Kennedy's suite"* where there occurred *"certain sex activities by Kennedy that he hopes are never publicized"*.

All this creates the impression that Judith Campbell was one of the "showgirls" and that she was the "hooker" who had sex with Kennedy that night. However, Campbell does not appear to have been at the El Rancho Vegas that night. She was staying at the Sands. The El Rancho Vegas is nowhere mentioned in her book. (It burned down later the same year.) Also, Judith was not a *"showgirl"*. She often states that she refused to wear a bikini because her body did not measure up to that of the other girls. (There is perhaps another reason why Judith rarely wore a bikini. She obviously viewed all other women as competition. She had something that they did not have: A beautiful face. Why should she reduce herself to showing her body, when her body was no better than their's.) Thus, it seems likely that the showgirls and the hooker were other women of which there are a multitude available in Las Vegas, and that Judith Campbell was not there.

Summers and Swan also quote Peter Lawford as saying that Campbell was a "*hooker*" who had been paid $200 by Sinatra to sleep with Kennedy. The source for this quote is Milt Ebbins. However, this quote is suspicious because another source quotes Lawford as saying that he never met Campbell at all. Also, just because Lawford thought that Campbell was a hooker does not mean that she actually was. (Milt Ebbins was also said to be one of the first persons to learn that Marilyn Monroe had committed suicide. Not the best source.)

Summers and Swan claim that Sinatra did not want to use any of the local talent, so he placed a phone call to Los Angeles and had the most beautiful hooker anybody had ever seen flown in to sleep with John F. Kennedy. The name of that hooker was, you guessed it, Judith Campbell. This is the story as told by Summers and Swan.

Unfortunately, the book "*Sinatra: The Life*" is unacceptable as a source for anything. It slurs events and sources together so that one often cannot determine which is which. I have been going through the book looking for independent verification of the events described in the book, "*My Story*", and the interviews of Judith Campbell. Since "*My Story*" is one of their sources, whenever they are simultaneously using *My Story* and the recollection of somebody else as a source they need to be specific about what part comes from "*My Story*" and what part comes from someone else. Summers and Swan do provide three sources not found in "*My Story*" for the fact that JFK and Judith Campbell were in the audience watching the Rat Pack performance at the Sands on February 7, 1960, and that Kennedy and Campbell "went upstairs" together. These are good sources, including two reputable and well known newspaper reporters. This however fails to prove that Kennedy and Campbell had sex with each other on that night. Just because they went upstairs together does not necessarily mean that they had sex, especially since lots of other people were with them. The other sources in the book by Summers and Swan are unacceptably vague, such as *"hotel staff, such as those involved in cleaning the senator's rooms"* and *"the phone operators who knew who was calling and who heard things"*.

This problem does not arise in any of the writings by Ovid Demaris, Kitty Kelly or Liz Smith. Reading them, you know exactly what their source is. Another problem is that for example Summers and Swan say that Sinatra was in Las Vegas on February 7, 1960, Kennedy flew there to see him, Sinatra then picked up the phone and called a broad (Judith Campbell) to come to sleep with him. However, Judith says that she did not sleep with Kennedy that weekend. She did not sleep with anybody. Sinatra wanted her for himself that night, not for John Kennedy. She refused to sleep with Sinatra then or ever again because of the incident in January 1960 when he had tried to include her in a threesome with another girl. She slept in her own hotel room, by herself. She first slept with Kennedy later on March 7, 1960 at the Plaza Hotel in New York City, she says.

Anybody reading about Judith Campbell starts to wonder whether she ever in her entire life slept in her own hotel room by herself without a man. If Summers and Swan have any source for their statements that Judith slept with Kennedy on the night of February 7, 1960, they should include that in their book. Unfortunately, no exact source is provided. Thus, much of their book must be dismissed as rumor and speculation.

It is a good thing that *"Sinatra: The Life"* by Summers and Swan was not published until after her death, because Judith Campbell would certainly have sued. Judith Campbell did in fact sue Laurence Leamer over his 1996 book *"The Kennedy Women"*, because it suggested on page 489 that she had been a hooker. The suit was dismissed after she walked out of a deposition. She was trying to get the suit reinstated when she died in 1999. She would probably have lost the case anyway, as the book clearly does NOT state that she was a hooker.

I personally believe that Judith Campbell was not a hooker and that she was telling the truth when she said that she never hooked and never took money for sex. There are several reasons for my belief. One is that hookers are used only for one night stands. A man sleeps with a hooker, pays her in the morning, and the next night he sleeps with a different hooker. Why would a man pay each night to sleep with the same woman two nights in a row, when there are so many hundreds of other equally beautiful women available? Judith Campbell maintained relationships with Sinatra, Kennedy and finally Giancana for more than two years. Hookers never do that.

As to why several witnesses have referred to her as a hooker, that is not difficult to explain. Here was this stunningly beautiful woman constantly hanging around Sinatra and other famous movie stars. However, she was not an actress, an extra or the wife or the girlfriend of anybody. Yet, she was always there. What else could she be? Ergo, she must be a hooker.

As to why they always enjoyed her company, this too has a simple explanation. Every man likes to be accompanied by a beautiful woman. Movie stars especially need beautiful women around to get publicity for themselves and get their names in the gossip columns. Nowadays it is common knowledge that publicists even today assign movie stars to sleep with each other for just one night so the movie magazines will have a new scandal to write about next month. It is their bread and butter. The great thing about Judith Campbell is she never demanded money. She never asked to be paid. Thus, she was always in high demand.

One question Judith never answers satisfactorily in her book and her interviews is where did she get the money to do all the things she did. She says that her father lived beyond his means. She lived in beautiful homes while she was growing up, but her father was often broke and real estate records show that her father never owned any of the houses they lived in. She often writes that she got money from an inheritance and from Grandmother Immoor. She received $500 per month in alimony from William Campbell for two years after their divorce until she accepted $6,000 in a lump sum final payment. She used that money to buy a mink stole. The movie "*Power and Beauty*" shows her constantly wearing that mink coat and often being asked where she got it. The movie "*The Rat Pack*" also shows her character wearing a mink stole when she arrives to meet "Momo" Giancana and Johnny Roselli. Basically, the Mink Stole was her signature. Whenever there is a movie about these events, one can be sure that the woman wearing the mink stole is depicting Judith Campbell and the man wearing dark glasses is depicting Sam Giancana. Judith Campbell did briefly have a job earning $100 a week working for Jerry Lewis. That was the only time she ever had a regular job. She never graduated from high school, so her typing and secretarial skills were probably limited.

Yet, look at her lifestyle. She lived for months in the Plaza Hotel in New York City. When in Miami, she always stayed at the Fontainebleau Hotel. In Washington DC, she always stayed at the Mayflower. When in Los Angeles, she often had two apartments, although sometimes she moved in with her sister or her parents.

Judith describes how she slept late and then spent hours every day bathing, fixing her hair, putting on make up and dressing so that she was absolutely stunningly perfect when she went out on dates. Every woman would like to be able to enjoy that lifestyle. How was she able to do it? Naturally, one suspects that she was hooking, especially since she states that her telephone was constantly ringing with men asking her out and that she went out on dates every night for months on end.

Another book with negative commentary is "*John F. Kennedy, A Biography*", by Michael O'Brien, a retired Professor of History at the University of Wisconsin-Fox Valley. In an article entitled "*The Exner File*", he expresses doubt that Kennedy would use a mere girl as courier to deliver money and important documents to the Mafia, saying that Kennedy would have sent one of his top aids instead. However, I cannot accept this criticism. It seems obvious that a girl whom nobody would notice and who herself would never question the propriety of what she was doing and nobody would (and did) believe her anyway, was far preferable for this task than a top aid. When I was in the securities business, I always used Icelandic girls as my couriers to deliver securities and pick up checks (which is how I met Inga Brandsdottir previously mentioned). None could be better. Also, Michael O'Brien is almost slavish in his admiration for John F. Kennedy and seems unwilling to believe anything negative about his hero. The contentions by Michael O'Brien have been strongly disputed if not refuted in articles by Jim Lesar, a Washington DC attorney.

Another source is the 1998 movie "*The Rat Pack*" starring Ray Liotta, Joe Mantegna, Don Cheadle, Angus Macfadyen and William Petersen. This can be considered a source because it makes a serious effort to be as historically accurate as possible and still be an entertaining movie. The movie contains some great scenes and great acting. I liked best the parts that featured Judy Campbell. "*Judy Campbell*" is played by actress Michelle Grace. Her character speaks only two lines and is there to look beautiful, as in real life. The best part is where Judy gets out of a car "Va-Va-Voom" wearing her stunning mink stole and delivers a briefcase (containing cash) to Sam Giancana and Johnny Roselli. Earlier scenes show her "*going upstairs*" with Senator Kennedy and then having sexual intercourse with the Senator, with Judy on top, although we know from her book that she preferred to be on the bottom. Someone should complain about this.

Two scenes in the movie are not mentioned in any book. Both take place at Puccini's Restaurant in Beverly Hills.

Exner Sources

SCENE: Puccini's Restaurant in Beverly Hills. John F. Kennedy, Robert Kennedy, Marilyn Monroe, Joe DiMaggio, Frank Sinatra, Dean Martin, Sammy Davis Jr. and May Britt are all having dinner together. The FBI is there too, the *"Untouchables"* having bugged the conversation, and they are tape recording it.

Mafia Mobsters Mickey Cohen and John Roselli enter the restaurant. Almost every gets upset because they do not want to be associated with mobsters, so one-by-one they all get up and leave, except for Sinatra and JFK. Now, the restaurant is empty except for two "broads" who just arrived as the others were leaving and are seated at the bar. Those two broads are none other than Angie Dickinson and Judith Campbell. The Sinatra character says to JFK. *"Which one do you want? I will take the other one, unless you want both of them."*

Kennedy replies, *"Who is the one who looks like Elizabeth Taylor?"*

Sinatra says, *"Judy Campbell. She looks like Elizabeth Taylor, only better. You don't have to marry her to sleep with her."*

In a later scene, Judy comes out to the swimming pool in the morning after having slept with JFK. She is asked, *"Is he up yet?"* Judy replies, *"Yes, he's up alright."* (This is a double entendre that I hope everybody catches.)

Still later, "Momo" Giancana asks the Sinatra character, *"Who's the doll that looks like Elizabeth Taylor?"* Sinatra replies, *"She looks like Liz Taylor. You don't have to marry her to f___ her."* (Elizabeth Taylor was married eight times.)

The other questionable scene also takes place at Puccini's. The entire Rat Pack plus May Britt who is with Sammy Davis Junior is having dinner. Everything is going fine until Sinatra spots a journalist having a drink whom he recognizes as having referred to Sinatra as a "gangster" in a gossip column. Sinatra grabs the journalist and beats him up. Journalist is chased out the door by the bouncers in Puccini's. (We know from other sources that Sinatra was a small man who never got into a fight unless there were others present to back him up.)

Sinatra is highly sensitive about anybody who calls him a gangster, because of the infamous 1976 photograph of Sinatra with eight Mafia characters. This photograph is mentioned twice in the movie. However, this was a major blunder in the movie as it depicts a party held in 1960, 16 years before the picture was taken.

In view of the fact that the movie is otherwise historically accurate except that the order the events occurred in real life is mixed up, I am willing to bet that those events did occur substantially as shown in the movie. There are some inaccuracies in the movie concerning the order in which the events occurred, such as, for example, Kennedy receives the Presidential Nomination before the event at the Sands on February 7, 1960 where he meets Judy Campbell.

The main problem I find with this movie is that the plot is so complex (being based on real life which is more complex than any movie) that the average viewer will not be able to follow what is going on. As it happened, I did not see the movie until I had substantially completed this book, so I knew who all the characters were and their roles in the actual events in real life. I doubt that anybody else who has not read this book and is not a serious student of history of that era will be able to follow the scenes and the issues.

The movie depicts the events of the night of February 8, 1960 reasonably accurately, but the night ends showing Judy Campbell in bed having sexual intercourse with JFK. Judith, of course, maintains that she slept alone that night. However, several other biographers have suggested that she slept with Kennedy that night, so it is reasonable to put that scene in the movie.

This perhaps forms the basis for Judith Campbell's threat to sue, since she claims that the first time she ever had sexual intercourse with JFK was one month later on March 7, 1960. The reader will have already noticed several other inaccuracies. Judith probably could have won a court judgment over these misrepresentations but the damages would probably have been minimal.

A dramatic scene in the movie occurs when President Kennedy first offers to stay at the home of Frank Sinatra. JFK is later pressured by Robert Kennedy not to stay there because Robert Kennedy, as Attorney General, is investigating all of Sinatra's Mafia friends. As a result, JFK decides to stay at Bing Crosby's house instead of Frank's. Frank had spent several hundred thousand dollars building extensions to his house, including five bungalows for Secret Service agents and a helicopter landing pad for the presidential helicopter. Sinatra had announced to the press that his home would become the *"Western White House"*. After Peter Lawford, the brother-in-law of President Kennedy, delivers the bad news that JFK is not coming after all, Sinatra forcibly throws Lawford out of the house, then fires all of the construction workers, then takes a sledge hammer and starts knocking down all the construction work that has taken place.

According to biographer Kitty Kelley, this is exactly what happened, but in her book, *My Story*, Judith Campbell states that eventually the construction work was completed and Sinatra even used the helicopter landing pad occasionally. In real life, Sinatra did break relations with Peter Lawford after this.

The movie deals with many other issues. One is the brave stand Sinatra took on the Albert Maltz issue. Albert Maltz was a screenwriter who was one of the *Hollywood Ten* who were blacklisted by the Hollywood movie studios during the era of McCarthyism because of their left leaning views. Prior to being blacklisted, Maltz had been nominated for the Academy Awards. After being blacklisted, Maltz had been required to use front men to keep his identity hidden in order to get his screenplays produced. This era forms the basis for the 1976 Woody Allen movie *"The Front"*. In 1960, Frank Sinatra bravely hired Maltz openly to write a screenplay for a movie Sinatra wanted to produce. As Sinatra was the most visible supporter of Kennedy for President, the Kennedy Family pressured Sinatra to drop Maltz because Maltz, and thereby Sinatra, and thereby Kennedy was being labeled as a Communist. As a result of intensive pressure, Sinatra finally did drop Maltz. All this is accurately depicted in the movie *"The Rat Pack"*.

Similarly, another crisis occurred when Sammy Davis Junior, an African American singer, dancer and musician, announced that he was going to marry the whiter-than-white Swedish actress May Britt. It may seem unbelievable now, but in 1960 most states had laws against inter-racial marriage. Even in 1967, The Virginia Supreme Court in a decision by the racist Chief Justice Harry L. Carrico ruled that the states had a right under the constitution to prohibit a Black Man from marrying a White Woman. Fortunately, this decision was overturned by the United States Supreme Court in the case of *Loving vs. Virginia*, 388 U.S. 1 (1967).

In the 1960 Presidential election, inter-racial anything was a sensitive issue. Therefore, the Kennedy Family put pressure on Sinatra and on Sammy Davis Jr. to abandon his plan to marry May Britt. Finally, the marriage was postponed until five days after the presidential election. Frank Sinatra was the best man. May Britt never appeared again in a movie (although she continued to take chess lessons from teachers at the chess clubs). Also, Sammy Davis Junior, who had sung at the Kennedy nomination, was dis-invited to the Kennedy inauguration. He thereafter became a non-person as far as Kennedy was concerned. Sammy Davis Jr. became a staunch Republican. May Britt and Sammy Davis Junior thereafter had one black-and-white baby.

All this is accurately depicted in the movie.

In another scene, Johnny Roselli is shown suggesting to Sam Giancana that they kill Frank Sinatra and the rest of the Rat Pack as a warning to JFK. This suggestion probably did happen. Giancana had felt that they had a deal, get Kennedy elected and in return the Kennedy Administration would curtail the FBI investigations of the Mafia. The Mafia did perform their end of the bargain. Authorities agree that it was due to Mafia influence in Chicago that Kennedy was able to carry Illinois by only 8,858 votes. However, that would not have been enough. Nixon needed to win both Illinois and one other state such as Texas to win the election. The 1960 election was close, but not as close as the 2000 and 2004 elections.

By their logic and reasoning, after the Mafia had gotten Kennedy elected, thereafter Kennedy was owned by the Mafia. It is well known that this is the way that the Mafia works. For example, if a businessman asks the Mafia to kill a rival businessman and the Mafia carries out the hit, then that businessman who made the request is "owned" by the Mafia and he had better do what they say or he will be killed.

In the Kennedy election in 1960, it is now well established that Joseph Kennedy, the father, and to a lesser extent John F. Kennedy did ask the Mafia to help him win the election.

However, Kennedy himself did not make the request. Rather, it was Frank Sinatra who spoke to Sam Giancana and made the request. When the Mafia was double-crossed after Robert Kennedy was made Attorney General and turned the screws on the Mafia, the Teamsters Union under Jimmy Hoffa, and the

Exner Sources

United Mine Workers that had helped Kennedy win the West Virginia Primary, Giancana had a right, under this reasoning, to kill Sinatra.

However, in the movie, and in real life, Giancana decided not to do that but rather decided to make Sinatra sing for him. This is why Sinatra and the rest of the Rat Pack performed for two weeks free of charge at "*Villa Venice*", a nightclub north of Chicago owned by Giancana. The audio of their performances there are now available on DVD.

The "*Villa Venice*" affair is also the subject of another movie entitled "*Sugartime*" starring John Turturro and Mary-Louise Parker. This movie depicts Sam Giancana romancing singer Phyllis McGuire while meanwhile ordering the murders of several other Mafia wiseguys who had been caught skimming the profits from Las Vegas gambling casinos. In the movie, Giancana builds the Villa Venice because Phyllis McGuire says that she wants to visit Venice, Italy. However, when he shows her the Villa Venice he has built for her, she rejects it, saying that she wants to go to the real Venice in Italy. She hops a plane to Italy. Giancana catches up with her and as a result the famous photograph is taken of Phyllis McGuire sitting on Giancana's lap in Italy.

The movie "*Sugartime*", which is apparently based on some other book and does not include Judy Campbell as one of the characters, has so many things wrong with it that it does not merit consideration. For example, it depicts Robert Maheu meeting Sam Giancana out in the open desert near Las Vegas, where Maheu offers to hire Giancana to kill Castro. In reality, the first meeting between Maheu and Giancana took place at the Plaza Hotel in New York City.

These movie do poorly at HBO probably because few viewers can follow the complex relationships and can realize that the events depicted are actually more-or-less an approximation of history.

Probers Doubt Kennedy Knew of Poison Plot Against Castro

By Laurence Stern Washington Post Staff Writer

The Washington Post (1974-Current file); Nov 16, 1975; ProQuest Historical Newspapers The Washington Post (1877 - 1991)
pg. 6

Probers Doubt Kennedy Knew of Poison Plot Against Castro

By Laurence Stern
Washington Post Staff Writer

Senate intelligence investigators pursued a bizarre White House episode which raised the possibility — now fully discounted — that President Kennedy may have learned of CIA plans to poison Fidel Castro from a woman friend of top underworld figures.

The highly sensitive investigation by the Senate intelligence committee will be alluded to briefly in the report on the CIA's involvement in plans to assassinate foreign leaders, scheduled for release Thursday.

The investigation centered on a 1960 Kennedy campaign volunteer, then known as

Judith Campbell, who became the subject of top-priority concern to the late FBI Director J. Edgar Hoover because of her association with crime figures John Roselli and the late Sam Giancana. Both men were involved in the CIA's plot to poison Castro.

Campbell's role in the episode was heightened by the fact that she frequently telephoned the Kennedy White House. Investigators found evidence of some 70 phone calls from her during an 11-month period in the log of former presidential secretary Evelyn Lincoln on file in the Kennedy Library.

Lincoln told the Senate intelligence committee that Campbell was a volunteer in the California campaign and

had met the President there. She said she could not recall that the former campaign worker ever visited the President in the White House or elsewhere after the 1960 election.

Campbell gave the committee a deposition saying that she never knew of the poison plot from Giancana, Roselli or anyone else. From the standpoint of the investigation into assassination schemes directed against foreign leaders this meant the entire Campbell episode was irrelevant to the committee's inquiry.

"We were not investigating President Kennedy's personal associations," said one ranking member of the investigating panel.

Campbell's calls to the

White House — usually logged into Lincoln's office — began on March 29, 1961, from the caller's Los Angeles residence. Many were described in the investigative files of the staff as "Campbell-JFK calls."

The files indicate that several of Campbell's calls to the White House were made from the Oak Park, Ill., residence of Giancana. At times, however, she would call from the Mayflower Hotel in Washington.

FBI Director Hoover, who was aware of the CIA's involvement with Giancana in anti-Castro operations, sent memos in February, 1962, to Attorney General Robert F. Kennedy and White House chief of staff Kenneth O'Donnell alerting them to the

potentially embarrassing range of Campbell's social acquaintances.

Hoover then submitted a memo on Campbell directly to President Kennedy and met with him for lunch on March 22, 1962. There is no record of the discussion. Close former aides to the President recall no mention of it.

Lincoln said she also received a copy of the first memo and at that point Campbell's calls were no longer accepted at the White House.

The committee decided unanimously to take a low-key approach to the Campbell episode, some members feeling that it would be more appropriate to ignore it as irrelevant to presidential awareness of the Castro

assassination schemes.

"We decided to allude to it in order to avoid any suggestion that we were playing favorites with some administrations," said one well-informed committee source.

Senate intelligence committee staff logs which came into the possession of The Washington Post indicate that Hoover sent a memo to then CIA Deputy Director for Plans (covert operations) Richard Bissell on Oct. 18, 1960, recording his awareness of Giancana's involvement in the Castro poison plot.

By January, 1961, Bissell was discussing an "executive action" — believed to be the Castro assassination plan — with two other high-level CIA officials. They were Sidney Gottlieb, who became chief of

the technical services division in charge of the agency's drug experimentation program, and William Harvey, a senior case officer for underworld recruits.

The same month Bissell is recorded as having briefed McGeorge Bundy, then the President's national security affairs adviser, on the executive action.

Also in January, 1961, the new President began receiving intensive briefings from then CIA Director Allen Dulles on the Bay of Pigs invasion plan.

That month of the Kennedy inauguration the new Attorney General undertook a coordinated investigation by federal and local agencies into the affairs of Giancana, who the CIA had recruited for the

attempt on Castro's life.

It could not be determined when Attorney General Kennedy first became aware of Giancana's dual role as a target of domestic criminal prosecution and an espionage agent in the pay of the U.S.

But by April, 1961 — days prior to the Bay of Pigs fiasco — there is evidence in the committee's files that the transmission of the poison materials toward its intended political target had begun.

Nonetheless, the committee could not determine whether President Kennedy ever learned of the CIA's recruitment of underworld figures, who were interested in re-establishing their bases in Havana, for the assassination attempt against Castro.

Probers Doubt Kennedy Knew of Poison Plot Against Castro

By Laurence Stern

Washington Post Staff Writer

Senate intelligence investigators pursued a bizarre White House episode which raised the possibility — now fully discounted — that President Kennedy may have learned of CIA plans to poison Fidel Castro from a woman friend of top underworld figures.

The highly sensitive investigation by the Senate intelligence committee will be alluded to briefly in the report on the CIA's involvement in plans to assassinate foreign leaders. The report is scheduled for release Thursday.

The investigation centered on a 1960 Kennedy campaign volunteer, then known as Judith Campbell, who became the subject of top-priority concern to the late FBI Director J. Edgar Hoover because of her association with crime figures John Roselli and the late Sam Giancana. Both men were involved in the CIA's plot to poison Castro.

Campbell's role in the episode was heightened by the fact that she frequently telephoned the Kennedy White House. Investigators found evidence of some 70 phone calls from her during an 11-month period in the log of former presidential secretary Evelyn Lincoln on file in the Kennedy Library.

Lincoln told the Senate intelligence committee that Campbell was a volunteer in the California campaign and had met the President there. She said she could not recall that the former campaign worker ever visited the President in the White House or elsewhere after the 1960 election.

Campbell gave the committee a deposition saying that she never know of the poison plot from Giancana, Roselli or anyone else. From the standpoint of the investigation into assassination schemes directed against foreign leaders this meant the entire Campbell episode was irrelevant to the committee's inquiry.

"We were not investigating President Kennedy's personal associations," said one ranking member of the investigating panel.

Campbell's calls to the White House — usually logged into Lincoln's office — began on March 29, 1961, from the caller's Los Angeles residence. Many were described in the investigative files of the staff as "Campbell-JFK calls."

The files indicate that several of Campbell's calls to the White House were made from the Oak Park, Ill., residence of Giancana. At times, however, she would call from the Mayflower Hotel in Washington.

FBI Director Hoover, who was aware of the CIA's involvement with Giancana in anti-Castro operations, sent memos in February, 1962, to Attorney General Robert F. potentially embarrassing range of Campbell's social acquaintances.

Hoover then submitted a memo on Campbell directly to President Kennedy and met with him for lunch on March 22, 1962. There is no record of the discussion. Close former aides to the President recall no mention of it.

Lincoln said she also received a copy of the first memo and at that point Campbell's calls were no longer accepted at the White House.

The committee decided unanimously to take a low-key approach to the Campbell episode, some members feeling that it would be more appropriate to ignore it as irrelevant to presidential awareness of the Castro assassination schemes.

"We decided to allude to it in order to avoid any suggestion that we were playing favorites with some administrations," said one well-informed committee source.

Senate intelligence committee staff logs which came into the possession of The Washington Post indicate that Hoover sent a memo to then CIA Deputy Director for Plans (covert operations) Richard Bissell on Oct. 18, 1960, recording his awareness of Giancana's involvement in the Castro poison plot.

By January, 1961, Bissell was discussing an "executive action" — believed to be the Castro assassination plan — with two other high-level CIA officials. They were Sidney Gottlieb, who became chief of the technical services division in charge of the agency's drug experimentation program, and William Harvey, a senior case officer for underworld recruits.

The same month Bissell is recorded as having briefed McGeorge Bundy, then the President's national security affairs adviser, on the executive action.

Also in January, 1961, the new President began receiving intensive briefings from then CIA Director Allen Dulles on the Bay of Pigs invasion plan.

That month of the Kennedy inauguration the new Attorney General undertook a coordinated investigation by federal and local agencies into the affairs of Giancana, who the CIA had recruited for the attempt on Castro's life.

It could not be determined when Attorney General Kennedy first became aware of Giancana's dual role as a target of domestic criminal prosecution and an espionage agent in the pay of the U.S.

But by April, 1961 — days prior to the Bay of Pigs fiasco — there is evidence in the committee's files that the transmission of the poison materials toward its intended political target had begun.

Nonetheless, the committee could not determine whether President Kennedy ever learned of the CIA's recruitment of underworld figures, who were interested in re-establishing their bases in Havana, for the assassination attempt against Castro.

Probers Doubt Kennedy Knew of Poison Plot Against Castro

By Laurence SternWashington Post Staff Writer
The Washington Post (1974-Current file); Nov 16, 1975;
pg. 6

The President's Friend

By William Safire

WASHINGTON — Senators Frank Church and Gary Hart, acting like a couple of frightened men, have been forcing intelligence committee staff members to sign affidavits swearing the staffers were not the source of leaks of the committee's most closely guarded secret.

The secret was hinted at on Page 129 of the committee report on C.I.A. assassination attempts. While straining to show that President Kennedy did not know that the C.I.A. had hired Mafia chiefs John Roselli and Sam Giancana to arrange the assassination of Fidel Castro, the committee report reluctantly and guardedly revealed a Kennedy-Mafia connection.

"Evidence before the committee," the report reads, "indicates that a close friend of President Kennedy had frequent contact with the President from the end of 1960 through mid-1962. F.B.I. reports and testimony indicate the President's friend was also a close friend of John Roselli and Sam Giancana and saw them often during this same period."

The report footnotes that "White House telephone logs show seventy instances of phone contact between the White House and the President's friend whose testimony confirms frequent phone contact with the President himself. Both the President's friend and Roselli testified that the friend did not know about either the assassination operation or the wire tap case. Giancana was killed before he was available for questioning."

There the Church committee hoped the matter would rest. But the reason for the plumbers' operation—complete with threats of perjury and warnings of lie detector tests—was the investigative reporting of Dan Thomasson and Tim Wyngaard of the Scripps-Howard Washington bureau.

According to their sources, which they say include F.B.I. documents, "the President's friend" was a beautiful girl who divided her time between the Chicago underworld leadership and the President of the United States. The President's secretary, Mrs. Evelyn Lincoln, is reported to have testified that the purpose of the almost twice-weekly calls over a year's time was to set up meetings between the President and his friend.

The private life of any public figure is nobody's business but his own, and salacious gossip of White House kennelkeepers and self-described intimates can be dismissed as offensive. But when the nation's Chief Executive receives even a few calls from the *home telephone* of the leader of the Mafia in Chicago, that crosses the line into the public's business.

That is particularly the case when —of all Mafia leaders around—the one with whom the President shared a close friend turns out to be the one whom the C.I.A. selects to handle the arrangements for the assassination of Fidel Castro, and the one who is murdered just before testifying.

F.B.I. documents show that J. Edgar Hoover, whose agents were watching "Momo" Giancana and John Roselli as part of Attorney General Robert Kennedy's war on organized crime, discovered the link between the President and the Mafia leaders. On Feb. 27, 1962, Mr. Hoover alerted Robert Kennedy and aide Kenneth O'Donnell to the associations of the President's friend, and on March 22, the F.B.I. director took another memo on this subject to a luncheon meeting with President Kennedy. After that, the relationship was abruptly broken off. That must have been some lunch.

But substantive questions remain: (1) Since gangland figures are concerned about the liaisons of their girl friends, did the Mafia figures encourage the girl's White House relationship, and if so, to what end? (2) Did Director Hoover's obvious concern with Mr. Giancana's White House connection suddenly cut off just short of knowledge of the Giancana-C.I.A. plot to get Castro? (3) Why did Mr. Hoover check in with the C.I.A. and then tell a Las Vegas sheriff to stop prosecuting Giancana for wiretapping an unfaithful girl friend—right after his luncheon showdown with President Kennedy?

Too many coincidences here. When Mafia leaders and a President share the same girl's attentions; when those two Mafiosi are chosen to make the hit on a foreign leader by our C.I.A.; when the delivery of poison pellets is made to one of them on the weekend the President is with the girl in Florida; when the F.B.I. is listening in, and cautioning the President—and when the President winds up murdered by a supporter of Castro, target of the aborted C.I.A. assassination plot, the matter is worth a thorough public examination.

The Church committee has attempted a cover-up from the Government's end; the Mafia, by silencing Giancana forever, has clamped down the lid from its end.

Thanks to the Thomasson-Wyngaard reporting, however, the story of the President's friend gives us a useful clue to a related mystery: why the Kennedy men were so ready to acquiesce in the wiretapping and bugging of Dr. Martin Luther King.

The clue: After that luncheon in March 1962, when the F.B.I. director laid out the evidence of the Mafia connections of the President's friend, the Kennedys must have been prepared to do anything and everything J. Edgar Hoover wanted.

Published: December 15, 1975
Copyright © The New York Times

Church Denies Cover-Up Of a Kennedy Friendship

By JOHN M. CREWDSON
Special to The New York Times

WASHINGTON, Dec. 15— Senator Frank Church acknowledged today that the Senate Select Committee on Intelligence Operations had uncovered evidence that President Kennedy and two reputed organized crime leaders had a close friendship with the same woman in 1961 and 1962. But he denied published suggestions that the committee had tried

---

Text of section of report is printed on Page 45.

---

to cover up information about the matter.

Mr. Church, an Idaho Democrat who heads the Senate panel, noted today that Mr. Kennedy's relationship with the woman had been discovered during the committee's inquiry into Mafia involvement in Central Intelligence Agency plots to kill Prime Minister Fidel Castro of Cuba during that same period.

But the Senator said that details of the relationship, mentioned in a segment of the committee's 349-page report on C.I.A. assassination plots released last month, had been withheld by unanimous agreement of the panel's 11 Senators on the ground that they were irrelevant to the subject at hand.

The brief reference in the panel's report did not identify the person even by sex. It referred to her only as a "close friend" of Mr. Kennedy, to whom she allegedly made some 70 telephone calls over a 54-week period, and of the two Mafia figures, Sam Giancana and John Rosselli.

Some of the calls, the report said, originated from Mr. Giancana's home. The panel reported that on Feb. 27, 1962, J. Edgar Hoover, director of the Federal Bureau of Investigation, sent a memorandum to the Attorney General and the White House stating that the President's friend had been associated with both Mr. Rosselli and Mr. Giancana. On March 22, 1962, President Kennedy and Mr. Hoover had lunch together, the report said, adding:

"According to White House logs, the last telephone contact between the White House and the President's friend oc-

Continued on Page 45, Column 1

𝕿𝖍𝖊 𝕹𝖊𝖜 𝖄𝖔𝖗𝖐 𝕿𝖎𝖒𝖊𝖘
Published: December 16, 1975
Copyright © The New York Times

KENNEDY COVER-UP DENIED BY CHURCH

Continued From Page 1, Col. 7

curred a few hours after the luncheon."

The Senate report asserted that Mr. Giancana, alleged one-time head of a large Chicago crime syndicate who was found murdered in his home there several months ago, acted with Mr. Rosselli in late 1960 and early 1961 on behalf of the C.I.A. in recruiting Cuban agents who might be persuaded to poison Mr. Castro's food.

A primary issue before the Senate Committee was the degree of knowledge of such plots possessed by Mr. Kennedy and others in his Administration, and the panel's interest in the woman was piqued by the possibility that she might have gained some knowledge of them from the two reputed members of the Mafia, which she then passed on to Mr. Kennedy.

'She Had No Knowledge'

Mr. Church said today, however, that "the committee looked very carefully into this matter," and "the evidence showed that she had no knowledge of assassination activities on the part of the Mafia leaders."

For that reason, he continued, the Senate panel agreed unanimously that it would not be "appropriate to wade into the personal life of the President" in its investigation or to add detail to the assassination report that went "beyond the subject matter."

Mr. Church said that the woman, who has been identified by other sources as Judith Campbell, was "extensively interviewed" by committee staff members, as were "others who knew her," and that there was no evidence to suggest that her relationship with Mr. Kennedy had been encouraged by the Mafia.

"Had we had such evidence," the chairman said, "we certainly would have included it in the report."

Mr. Church's discussion of the Campbell matter, which was first reported last Nov. 18 by the Scripps-Howard newspaper chain, was prompted by a charge today by William Safire, a columnist for The New York Times, that the Church committee had "attempted a cover-up" of Mr. Kennedy's relationship with Miss Campbell.

Charges Are Rejected

Mr. Church said today that Mr. Safire's charges were "preposterous," and he reiterated that "the committee has in every case agreed unanimously on the actions taken," and that "we included everything relevant to assassination in the assassination report."

None of the C.I.A.'s attempts to kill Mr. Castro or Patrice Lumumba, the late Congolese Prime Minister, were successful, the Senate committee said, and it found no evidence that either President Kennedy or his successor, Lyndon B. Johnson, had been informed of any of the anti-Castro plots until after the plots were terminated.

Brian Monaghan, a lawyer for Miss Campbell, said in a telephone interview today that she had married and was living under another name in the San Diego area.

Mr. Monaghan said that he had not yet spoken with the woman at length about her involvement with Mr. Kennedy, Mr. Giancana and Mr. Rosselli, but that he expected her to make a statement to reporters within a few days.

Reports Are Varied

None of the Senators who sit on the select committee reportedly was present when Miss Campbell was interviewed by F. A. O. Schwarz 3d, the panel's majority counsel, and Curtis Smothers, the Republican counsel, and reports of her testimony there vary.

Committee officials, who were described today as "very upset" by the leak of the Campbell matter last month to the Scripps-Howard organization, declined repeatedly today to discuss any aspect of her appearance.

Other committee sources said today that every member of the panel's staff had been askd to sign a statement to the effect that he or she had not been the source of the leak, and that some, but not all, of the panel's members had produced similar statements voluntarily.

A committee spokesman would say only that, thus far, the source of the initial leak regarding Miss Campbell had not been discovered, and the spokesman denied reports that polygraph, or lie-detector tests would be administered in the event that no one confessed.

According to two well-placed individuals who say they are familiar with Miss Campbell's tightly held testimony, the woman told committee investigators that she had indeed spoken with Mr. Kennedy by telephone on numerous occasions during the period in question.

Report Is Denied

One of the individuals denied emphatically, however, a report circulating in Washington today that she had admitted to intimacies with the late President.

According to evidence gathered by the Senate committee Miss Campbell's relationship with Mr. Rosselli, and subsequently with Mr. Giancana, was discovered by the Federal Bureau of Investigation in the course of an organized crime investigation.

The F.B.I. also uncovered the fact that some 70 long-distance calls had been placed from a telephone used by Miss Campbell to the White House, and on Feb. 27, 1962, a memorandum outlining the apparent relationship of Mr. Kennedy's "friend" with the two Mafia figures was sent by the F.B.I. to the White House.

The memorandum, signed by Mr. Hoover, was addressed to Kenneth O'Donnell, the special assistant to Mr. Kennedy, with a copy to Robert F. Kennedy, then the Attorney General and the late President's brother.

Evelyn Lincoln, the President's personal secretary, reportedly told the Senate committee that she had received the Hoover memorandum and thought she had passed it on to Mr. Kennedy, but a former high official of the Kennedy Administration said today he believed that the President had not seen it.

The former official, who asked not to be named, telephoned The Times after the appearance of Mr. Safire's column and said that while he recalled that Mr. Kennedy, while a Senator, met Miss Campbell in 1958, he believed that she never saw the President once he entered the White House.

The question of whether the F.B.I. tried a second time to bring Miss Campbell's connection with Mr. Giancana and Mr. Roselli to Mr. Kennedy's attention was addressed in the Senate committee's report in a reference to a luncheon meeting between the President and Mr. Hoover on March 22, 1962.

Mr. Hoover, the report said, was briefed about the affair by aides in advance of the meeting, and although there was no record of what was discussed over lunch, "the last telephone contact between the White House and the President's friend occurred a few hours after the luncheon."

The former Kennedy aide said today, however, that he was present for all but five minutes of the hour-long meeting, and that the Campbell matter was not discussed while he was in attendance.

Published: December 16, 1975
Copyright © The New York Times

JFK'S MYSTERY WOMAN

70 Calls to Friend of Mafiosi Told

From Times Wire Services

WASHINGTON—The Senate Intelligence Committee has uncovered a relationship between President John F. Kennedy and Judith Campbell, a California woman whose name also has been linked with Mafia figures. The committee came across the information in the course of its investigation of whether Kennedy knew of CIA plots to assassinate Cuban Premier Fidel Castro.

The committee said, however, it has no evidence that the woman served as a link between Kennedy and the Mafia in the plots.

"There is no evidence to suggest she was a conduit of any kind," committee chairman Frank Church (D-Ida.) told reporters.

Campbell now lives in San Diego under another name.

There was no evidence that Campbell knew of the assassination plot or that she was used by the Mafia in an effort to compromise Kennedy, Church said Monday.

According to records, there were 70 phone calls between the Kennedy White House and Campbell, whom the committee's report described as "a close friend" of the late President and also "a close friend" of Sam Giancana and John Rosselli, the two underworld figures used by the CIA in its unsuccessful attempts to kill Castro.

Campbell was interviewed extensively by the staff, Church said, but the relationship was outlined only briefly in the assassination report because "we did not think it appropriate to wade into the personal life of the President."

An attorney said in San Diego that Campbell now is married and has lived in San Diego for a year. The attorney, Brian Monaghan, said that she knew Kennedy, Giancana and Rosselli at the same time "but there was no connection there.

"She had only a personal relationship in those cases," Monaghan said. "She has nothing to hide and is not in hiding."

Monaghan refused to disclose the woman's present name but said she is living in a motor home and "she is hard to contact."

A news conference is planned with the woman for Wednesday.

According to the committee report, the late FBI Director J. Edgar Hoover first warned the White House about Campbell's links to Giancana and Rosselli in February, 1962.

In March, Hoover had a private luncheon with Kennedy, "presumably" to warn him personally about Campbell, the report said.

"There is no record of what transpired at that luncheon," the report added, but White House logs show that "the last telephone contact between the White House and the President's friend occurred a few hours after the luncheon."

The day after the luncheon with Kennedy, Hoover wrote a memo to CIA officials asking if they would object to federal prosecution of certain individuals, a prosecution that could have resulted in public exposure of Giancana's and Rosselli's involvement in assassination plots with the CIA. The CIA did object and exposure was avoided.

The committee report notes that FBI files on Giancana contained information at the time showing his connection with the CIA. The report says that could have led a reader to conclude that Castro's murder was being planned.

'Close Friend' of Kennedy Linked to Mafia Figures
JACK NELSON; RONALD J OSTROW
Los Angeles Times   Dec 17, 1975;
pg. 1

'Close Friend' of Kennedy Linked to Mafia Figures

BY JACK NELSON
and RONALD J. OSTROW
Times Staff Writers

WASHINGTON—The Senate Intelligence Committee's report on CIA assassination plots disclosed that President John F. Kennedy had a "close friend" who also associated with two underworld figures that were principals in one death plot.

But the report concealed that the friend was a California woman, Judith Campbell Exner, who in response to recent reports of her relationship with Kennedy has called a press conference for today in San Diego.

Officials of the Senate committee Tuesday confirmed published reports that the friend was a woman who met Kennedy—then a senator—at the 1960 Democratic convention in Los Angeles, which nominated him for the Presidency.

She was in contact with him frequently thereafter, according to the Senate committee reports. It said that records showed a total of 70 telephone calls between her and the White House over 54 weeks in 1961 and 1962.

The woman was identified by a committee source Tuesday as Mrs. Exner, a dark-haired artist who, according to her attorney, has been living in San Diego for the past year.

The committee discovered Mrs. Exner's relationship with Kennedy while investigating a Central Intel-

Judith Campbell Exner in 1960.

Times photo

ligence Agency plot to assassinate Cuban Premier Fidel Castro. The plot involved two underworld figures, Sam Giancana and John Rosselli, who the FBI learned were friends of Mrs. Exner.

Giancana, a Chicago Mafia leader, was murdered last June shortly before he was scheduled to testify before the Senate committee. Rosselli, once a protege of Giancana, testified in secret session about a week after Giancana's slaying.

Please Turn to Page 7, Col. 1

CLOSE FRIEND OF KENNEDY

Continued from First Page

Both Committee Chairman Frank Church (D-Ida.) and Vice Chairman John G. Tower (R-Tex.) denied Tuesday that there had been any effort to cover up any information pertinent to the committee's assassination enquiry.

Church said that there was no evidence that the woman knew anything about the plot against Castro and that "no one on the committee thought that the President's personal relationships with her, whatever they were, were the proper business of the committee.

"We would have been accused of being salacious and sensational and rumor-mongering if we had tried to go into personal relationships and it would have been highly improper," Church said. "Any attempt to characterize the report as a coverup is really outrageous."

The Senate committee's two-page reference to Kennedy's "close friend" in its 347-page assassination report went largely unnoticed when the report was issued Nov. 20. Attention focused on the committee's central findings that the CIA under four American Presidents had plotted the death or overthrow of five foreign leaders.

Kennedy's telephone contacts with Mrs. Exner were cited in a section of the report entitled, "Did President Kennedy learn anything about assassination plots as a result of the FBI investigation of Giancana and Rosselli?"

The report concluded that there was no way to know for sure, but said that Kennedy could have learned about

---

Church's committee was charged with attempting a government coverup.

---

the Castro plot from the FBI investigation.

Shortly before the committee's report was released last month the Washington Post and Scripps-Howard newspapers reported that the committee had established a link between Kennedy and a Judith Campbell. The news accounts also mentioned her relationship with Giancana and Rosselli and said that the committee was attempting to determine whether Kennedy could have learned from her about a CIA plot to kill Castro.

The committee's report, however, gave few clues to the identity of Kennedy's "close friend," mentioning neither sex nor age.

That prompted New York Times columnist William Safire to charge Monday that the committee "has attempted a coverup from the government's end; the Mafia, by silencing Giancana forever, has clamped down the lid from its end."

Safire, who served in the White House under former President Richard M. Nixon, said it was "the public's business" when a President shares a close friend with a Mafia figure selected by the CIA to arrange the assassination of Castro.

Church denied Safire's charge of coverup.

Mrs. Exner, who was in her mid-twenties when she first met Kennedy, testified in closed session that she had no knowledge of any assassination plot against Castro. Rosselli also testified that the woman had no knowledge of the plot.

Rosselli could not be reached for comment Tuesday, but a source close to him said, "Rosselli became very annoyed at the committee for trying to defame American womanhood and the reputation of a past President."

The source said that Rosselli refused to answer some questions about the Kennedy-Exner relationship.

The committee report noted that all living CIA officials who were involved in the underworld assassination attempt or who were in a position to have known of the attempt had testified that they never discussed the assassination plot with the President.

By May, 1961, however, the President's brother, Atty. Gen. Robert F. Kennedy and FBI Director J. Edgar Hoover had reason to know that Giancana was involved in the plot, the committee reported.

Although there was no evidence to indicate that anyone in the FBI had concluded that Giancana was involved, the report continued, the committee uncovered "a chain of events . . . which would have given Hoover an opportunity to have assembled the entire picture and to have reported the information to the President."

The committee reported that it had evidence indicating "that a close friend of President Kennedy had frequent contact with the President from the end of 1960 through mid-1962. FBI reports and testimony indicated that the President's friend was also a close friend of John Rosselli and Sam Giancana and saw them often during this same period."

Mention of the telephone calls between Kennedy and his friend was made in a footnote:

"White House telephone logs show 70 instances of phone contact between the White House and the President's friend whose testimony confirms frequent phone contact with the President himself."

On Feb. 27, 1962, the report continued, Hoover sent identical copies of a memorandum to the attorney general and Kenneth O'Donnell, special assistant to the President, stating that an FBI investigation of Rosselli had shown that Rosselli had been in contact with the President's friend.

"The memorandum also reported that the individual was maintaining an association with Sam Giancana, described as 'a prominent Chicago underworld figure,'" the report said.

"Hoover's memorandum also stated that a review of the telephone calls from the President's friend's residence revealed calls to the White House. The President's secretary (Mrs. Evelyn Lincoln) ultimately received a copy of the memorandum and said she believed she would have shown it to the President."

(Mrs. Lincoln, interviewed Tuesday by The Times, said she received a copy of the memo from O'Donnell, but could not recall sending it to the President and so testified before the Senate committee. O'Donnell told The Times that he never sent a copy of the memo to Mrs. Lincoln and did not believe the President ever knew about it).

The committee reported that the association of the President's friend with the "hoodlums" and "that person's connections with the President was again brought to Hoover's attention in a memorandum preparing him for a meeting with the President planned for March 22, 1962."

By that time, the FBI's files on Giancana contained information disclosing Giancana's connection with the CIA as well as his involvement in the Castro assassination plot, the committee reported.

Hoover and President Kennedy had a private luncheon on March 22, but there is no record of what happened at the luncheon, the committee said. According to White House logs, the last telephone contact between the White House and the woman occurred a few hours after the Kennedy-Hoover luncheon.

Although what actually happened at the luncheon may never be known because both principals are dead, the committee said that one topic presumably was that the President's friend was also a friend of Giancana and Rosselli and that this "raises several possibilities."

"The first is, assuming that Hoover did in fact receive a summary of FBI information relating to Giancana prior to his luncheon with the President, whether that summary reminded the director that Giancana had been involved in a CIA operation against Cuba that included 'dirty business' and further indicated that Giancana had balked about an assassination attempt against Castro.

"A second is whether Hoover would then have taken the luncheon as an opportunity to fulfill his duty to bring this information to the President's attention."

Still theorizing, the committee mentioned in a footnote that if Hoover had so notified Kennedy, the President "might then have inquired further of the CIA. The Presidential calendar indicates that the President had meet-

Please Turn to Page 8, Col. 1

FRIEND OF TWO MAFIA FIGURES

Continued from 7th Page

ings at which most CIA officials witting (sic) of the assassination plot were present during the period from February 27 through April 2, 1962. All of those persons, however, have testified that the President never asked them about the assassination plot."

Mrs. Lincoln told the Times that when the President's friend (Judith Campbell, now Mrs. Exner) telephoned the White House, "I never put any of her calls through to the President."

She said she so testified before the Senate committee.

"She was a campaign volunteer and she called many times, but I don't think there are records that the President ever talked to her at the White House, although I did put through calls from her to him when he was in the Senate."

"I have no way of knowing what she did or how she came to know him," Mrs. Lincoln said. "She was just one of many, many workers in the campaign. He was a very attractive man, you know, and there were a lot of girls who wanted to work for him."

Mrs. Lincoln said the woman "called so many times she became a pest," but that she always accepted her calls and talked to her until receiving the FBI memorandum following the Hoover luncheon with President Kennedy on March 22.

"I've never seen the girl, you know." Mrs. Lincoln said. "She would just call in and want to know how the campaign was going."

However, a committee source said that the relationshi between Kennedy and the woman was much closer tha that and that there was ample evidence they had been i frequent contact. The source indicated that the committe thought Mrs. Lincoln's testimony was somewhat colore by her close association and deep loyalty to Kennedy.

Some other former aides to Kennedy questioned wheth er Campbell's calls were put through to the President an said they could not recall Hoover's memorandum o Campbell and the underworld pair.

"I never would have given that memo to the Presiden of the United States." said O'Donnell, who was a speci assistant to Kennedy and the man who controlled th flow of persons into the oval office.

"The Russians were stopping our convoys, there wer problems in Cuba, in the Congo and all over the world O'Donnell said. "I really thought the FBI director and th attorney general could handle organized crime."

While O'Donnell said he had no recollection of any Ju dith Campbell, he added that he thought Dave Power another longtime Kennedy aide, had met the woman.

Powers, now curator at the Kennedy library in Wa tham, Mass., said O'Donnell was wrong.

"I've always been a name man, and I never, ever me her." Powers said, "The only Campbell I ever met was o a soup label."

Powers said that when Senate committee investigator examined White House logs of telephone calls, now store at the library, he saw no indication the calls went beyond Mrs. Lincoln and into the President's office.

John Stewart, chief archivist at the library, studied some of the logs Tuesday and said: "We have no way of telling (from the logs) whether the calls went through directly or indirectly to the President.

"It's our impression that Judith Campbell's name only appeared on Evelyn Lincoln's logs," and not on Kennedy's, he said. He added, however, that this did not take into account any calls Mrs. Lincoln decided to pass through to Kennedy, an act that would not have resulted in a log entry.

KENNEDY'S FRIEND –Judith Campbell Exner telling news conference in San Diego of her relationship with the late President.
Times photo by Joe Kennedy

John Kennedy's Mystery Woman Tells Her Story

Had 'Close, Personal' Ties and Visited White House; Says She Never Met Jacqueline but Knew Mafia Men

BY BILL HAZLETT
Times Staff Writer

SAN DIEGO—An attractive dark-haired mystery woman linked to John F. Kennedy and two Mafia figures said Wednesday her relationship with the late President was "of a close, personal nature."

Under intensive questioning during a 35-minute press conference, Judith Campbell Exner, 41, refused to comment when asked if she had been Kennedy's lover.

She did say she had visited the White House more than 20 times and met Kennedy at other locations during a 54-week relationship which developed after they met in Las Vegas in February, 1960.

However, she said she never met Jacqueline Kennedy.

Mrs. Exner said she also had personal relationships with underworld figures Sam (Momo) Giancana and John Rosselli, but she denied she was a link between them and Kennedy in plots to assassinate Fidel Castro.

She promised that full facts on her relationships have been transcribed, documented and stored for release at a later time.

"However," she said, reading from a prepared statement, "I can at this time emphatically state that my relationship with Jack Kennedy was of a close, personal nature and did not involve conspiratorial shenanigans of any kind.

"I will not allow the committee to implicate me in these absurd plots nor will I allow Evelyn Lincoln (Kennedy's secretary) or Kenny O'Donnell (special assistant to the late President) to sully or distort my personal relationship with Jack Kennedy.

The Senate Intelligence Committee said in a 347-page report on CIA assassination plots that during 1961 and 1962 there were 70 telephone contacts between Kennedy and Mrs. Exner.

The report identified Mrs. Exner only as a "close friend," but after her identity became known she called a press conference to explain her relationship.

She wore dark glasses, a blue and green checked jacket and blue slacks and was accompanied by her new husband, Dan Exner, a professional golfer, as she discussed her past.

She claimed that Evelyn Lincoln and O'Donnell were fully aware of the nature of her relationship with the late President and described as "entirely contrived" statements by Mrs. Lincoln that she was simply a "campaign worker."

O'Donnell had said he had no recollection of any Judith Campbell. He said he thought Dave Powers, now curator of the Kennedy library in Waltham, Mass., may have met her. Powers said he did not know her.

Mrs. Exner told newsmen she was introduced to Kennedy in February, 1960, by a friend, who also introduced her and Giancana the next month in Miami Beach.

She refused to identify the friend and replied "no comment" to questions whether that friend was singer Frank Sinatra or actor Peter Lawford, Kennedy's brother-in-law.

She met Rosselli through Giancana sometime after March, 1960, Mrs. Exner said.

"My relationship with Sam Giancana and my relationship with Johnny Rosselli were of a personal nature and in no way related to or affected my relationship with Jack Kennedy, nor did I discuss either of them with the other," she said.

Mrs. Exner admitted, however, that Giancana was aware of her relationship with Kennedy, although he never questioned her about it.

"He knew about it, but I didn't tell him," she said.

Kennedy, on the other hand, apparently was completely unaware of her friendship with the two reputed Mafia figures, she said, until he learned about the links from FBI reports.

She accused the Senate Intelligence Committee, headed by Sen. Frank Church (D-Ida.) of leaking details of her closed-session testimony before the senators.

The leaks, Mrs. Exner said, "have been distorted so as to implicate me in these bizarre assassination conspiracies between the underworld and the government."

The committee discovered her relationship with Kennedy while investigating CIA links with Giancana and Rosselli in a plan to kill Castro.

Giancana, a Chicago Mafia leader, was scheduled to testify before the committee last June, but he was murdered before he could appear.

Rosselli, once Giancana's protege, testified in a secret session about a week after Giancana's death.

"I imagine I probably knew they were part of the underworld," Mrs. Exner said.

Her attorney, Brian Monaghan, said that his client felt her life is in danger because of reports incorrectly describing her as an intermediary between the White House and the underworld.

"The inference put her in danger with those who think she might know something she doesn't," the attorney said.

Mrs. Exner disagreed with her attorney, saying she "wasn't disturbed"

John Kennedy Mystery Woman Tells Story

about the fact that Giancana and Rosselli were members of the underworld, "because of my lack of information about underworld activities, I don't feel I have anything to fear.

"It was only when statements were made that inferred (sic) I had such knowledge that I became concerned for my safety."

Church said there was no evidence that Mrs. Exner knew anything about the Castro plot and that no one in the committee thought Kennedy's relationship with her was "the proper business of the committee."

Mrs. Exner said Wednesday that it was "very difficult" to explain her relationship, but she said, "To me he was Jack Kennedy and not the President.

"It was close, but it was many years ago. Now I'm a happily married housewife."

In response to a question, she denied knowing top Teamsters officials but she said, "I've been to La Costa," a resort in north San Diego County

developed with Teamster pension funds," "but not for years."

Mrs. Exner denied making any telephone calls to Kennedy from Giancana's suburban Chicago home as indicated in an FBI memorandum.

She accused the FBI of conducting a "top-priority investigation" of her during her relationship with Kennedy "which resulted in substantial harrassment.

"The portions of the FBI file on me which were read during my session in the committee shocked me," she said.

"Their investigation was prying, insidious and sounded more like a scandal sheet than a governmental investigation. The information quoted was both incorrect and speculative."

Mrs. Exner is the former wife of actor William (Bill) Campbell, who described her as a "quiet, family kind of girl."

Campbell and the former Judith Katherine Imoor were married Oct. 25, 1952, when she was 18. They were divorced in Los Angeles April 2, 1958, after she testified her husband insisted on periodical leaves of

John Kennedy's Mystery Woman Tells Her Story

absence from matrimony.

Interviewed in his Woodland Hills home Wednesday night, Campbell, 49, a director of the Motion Picture and Television Fund, said he has had very little contact with his former wife since their divorce.

"I think I've only bumped into her twice at parties or charity affairs," Campbell said, "and even then it was just a case of hello and goodby.

"I'd heard occasional rumors (about her relationship with Kennedy and the underworld figures) but I never game them too much credence.

"I feel awfully sorry if she's finding herself under pressure, so to speak, It's hard for me to understand how these things come about. I think she has perhaps victimized herself by her associations."

Campbell said he does not know how his former wife met either Kennedy or Giancana and Rosselli.

"What mutual friends we had," he said, "you could count on the fingers of one hand. How she ever met the President, I don't know. I'm completely nonplussed about that."

Describing his former wife as "completely apolitical," Campbell said he did not think she could have had any role in the Castro assassination plot.

Even if Mrs. Exner was involved, Campbell said, "I don't think it would have been a thinking involvement. Without her knowledge, there might have been (contact between the White House and the underworld figures tied to the Castro plot.)

"I don't think she would have been privy to any information," Campbell concluded.

Campbell said he met his wife-to-be at a party in 1952, when, he said, she belonged to "the young Hollywood set."

"She wasn't an outgoing person," he said. "She was a bit introverted. She didn't have any deep convictions about anything at that time. There were no causes that she espoused."

Campbell appeared in more than a dozen movies in the 1950s and 60s. He portrayed mostly heavies, including the starring role in "Cell 2455 Death Row," a film about sex criminal Caryl Chessman, who was executed in the gas chamber at San Quentin.

Although she has kept records of her relationships with the slain President and the two Mafia kingpins, Mrs. Exner denied reports she had been unsuccessful in earlier efforts to sell a book, or that she currently is interested in writing one or looking for an agent.

Kennedy Friend Denies Plot Role

By JOHN M. CREWDSON
Special to The New York Times

SAN DIEGO, Dec. 17—Judith Campbell Exner maintained today that, although she had had a close personal relationship with President Kennedy while she was dating two leaders of a Chicago crime syndicate, she had never acted as an intermediary between the Mafia and the White House.

At a news conference here called to dispel what she termed "wild-eyed speculation," Mrs. Exner, who is about 41 years old, said she had never discussed with Mr. Kennedy her relationships with the late Sam Giancana, then head of the Chicago syndicate, or John Rosselli, an associate of Mr. Giancana.

Nor, she said, had she ever been aware during the time she was seeing President Kennedy and the two crime figures that Mr. Giancana and Mr. Rosselli, were helping the Central Intelligence Agency to recruit agents in an unsuccessful plot to assassinate Prime Minister Fidel Castro of Cuba.

Mr. Castro's name, the woman said, was never mentioned in the numerous telephone conversations she had with Mr. Kennedy, beginning in March 1961, or during what she said were a number of private White

United Press International
Judith Campbell Exner at news conference in San Diego

House lunches in the President's office.

Mrs. Exner, whose tan face was partly hidden behind saucer-shaped sunglasses, said that all of her discussions with the President, whom she said she had also seen on some occasions while he was traveling outside of Washington, were entirely "of a personal nature."

Mrs. Exner declined to com-

ment on a report that she had spent some time with Mr. Kennedy in Palm Beach, Fla., but she said that she had paid for whatever trips she had taken to meet Mr. Kennedy when he was traveling around the country.

She added that, although she had not worked during the two

Continued on Page 52, Column 1

The New York Times
Published: December 18, 1975
Copyright © The New York Times

Kennedy Friend Denies Role in Plot to Kill Castro

Continued From Page 1 Col. 6

years that she was close to Mr. Kennedy, she "was always financially able to take care of myself." She said she got her money from her family.

She repeatedly declined to elaborate on her relationship with any of the three men, and replied with a "no comment" when asked whether she had also known the late Robert F. Kennedy, the President's brother, who served as Attorney General in the Kennedy Administration.

A Government source said, however, that Mrs. Exner was known to have attended "a party or two" with Robert Kennedy when he was the Attorney General.

In a prepared statement read before reporters and cameramen crowded into a suite at the downtown Westgate Hotel, Mrs. Exner, who was accompanied by her attorney, Brian Monaghan, and her husband of eight months, Daniel Exner, said that she hoped to "set the record straight" about her relationships with the Mafia which have been the subject of leaks to newsmen from the Senate Select Committee on Intelligence, and about what she called "distortions" concerning her friendship with "Jack Kennedy" by former White House aides.

The first account of Mr. Kennedy's relationship with the woman, then known as Judith Katherine Campbell, was published in The Washington Post on Nov. 16. The Post article reported that Senate investigators had been intrigued by, but had later discounted, the possibility that Miss Campbell might have learned of anti-Castro plots from one of the Mafia leaders and passed on her knowledge of them to President Kennedy.

The Senate committee's report on the C.I.A. assassination plots, released four days later, concluded that there was no evidence to show that Mr. Kennedy or any of his aides had been made aware of the plots while they were under consideration between 1960 and 1962.

Associated Press

Judith Campbell Exner in 1960, the year she said she met Mr. Kennedy.

Mentioned Briefly

The report mentioned the Campbell relationship briefly, but did not give her name or sex or identify her as other than a "close friend" of Mr. Kennedy who had also known Mr. Giancana and Mr. Rosselli. The committee said, however, that it had no reason to believe the friend had had any knowledge of the involvement of her friends in a plan to kill Mr. Castro.

Mrs. Exner said today that subsequent reports by the Scripps-Howard news organization, The Chicago Daily News, The New York Times "and other papers" had implied "that I was a go-between for the Mafia," and that leaks of her secret testimony before the committee had been "distorted so as to implicate me in these bizarre assassination conspiracies."

All the news accounts of the matter have noted, however, that the Senate committee concluded that Miss Campbell did not know of the conspiracies. But she insisted today that her sole motive for summoning reporters was nonetheless to clear her name. She said she had no wish to sell the rest of her story to book publishers or to the news media.

Safire's Accusation

William Safire, a columnist for The Times, accused the Senate committee in an article published Monday of having sought to cover up the details of the Kennedy-Campbell relationship on partisan grounds, but the committee's chairman, Senator Frank Church, Democrat of Idaho, said the decision to include only the barest information about the matter in the assassination report was approved by all the members of the committee—Republicans as well as Democrats—after it was established that the matter was not relevant to the topic of assassinations.

Senator John G. Tower, Republican of Texas, the panel's vice chairman, said last night that Senator Church had "bent over backwards to avoid the appearance of a coverup," and that he did not believe the committee had been used by Mr. Church or anyone else for "political purposes."

Mrs. Exner said in answer to questions regarding her relationship with Mr. Kennedy and the circumstances surrounding her introduction to him and to Mr. Giancana that she would "clarify" such details at a later time and under unspecified conditions.

She said she met Mr. Kennedy through a "mutual friend" in Las Vegas, Nev., in February 1960, when Mr. Kennedy, then a Democratic Senator from Massachusetts, was beginning his successful campaign for the Presidency.

There has been some speculation that that relationship might have been initiated by Mr. Giancana in the Mafia's interest, but Mrs. Exner said today that she had not met Mr. Giancana until March 1960, while attending a party in Miami Beach.

Mr. Giancana, who she said subsequently introduced her to Mr. Rosselli, ran his end of the Castro assassination plot from a suite in the Fontainebleau Hotel in Miami Beach. According to the Senate report, however, that plot was not conceived within the C.I.A. until the following August.

Mrs. Exner declined today to name the friend who introduced her to Mr. Kennedy and then to Mr. Giancana, but Senate sources identified him as Frank Sinatra, the singer.

Lawyers for Mr. Sinatra, whom Mrs. Exner described as a "friend," had no immediate comment on his alleged involvement.

Asked whether she had been aware at the time that Mr. Giancana and Mr. Rosselli were important figures in the Mafia, Mrs. Exner said at first that she "didn't really know," but conceded later that she "probably knew they were members of the underworld."

Although she said that, to her knowledge, Mr. Kennedy had not know that she was also seeing the two Mafia figures, Mrs. Exner added that she thought Mr. Giancana was aware of her relationship with the President, although she said she never told him of it or discussed it with the Chicago crime leader. Mr. Giancana was slain last June 20 at his home in Oak Park, Ill.

Mrs. Exner emphatically denied reports that she had called Mr. Kennedy at the White House from a telephone in Mr. Giancana's home. One source familiar with the records obtained by the Senate committee said they showed at least one such call from Oak Park, although not necessarily from the Giancana residence.

Asked whether she had ever called Mr. Kennedy from her own home in Los Angeles or anywhere else, Mrs. Exner, who seemed nervous during most of her 45-minute appearance, quickly answered, "Oh, yes."

According to Justice Department sources, the Federal Bureau of Investigation became aware of Miss Campbell not through her relationship with Mr. Kennedy, but in the course of an investigation of Mr. Giancana's activities in the crime syndicate.

One such source said today that the F.B.I. subsequently discovered that Miss Campbell had placed two calls to the White House switchboard from her home in Los Angeles, and that the apparent relationship between her and the President was eventually brought to the attention of Robert Kennedy and Kenneth O'Donnell, a special assistant to the President,

in a memorandum from the late J. Edgar Hoover, then director of the F.B.I, dated Feb. 27, 1962.

The Senate committee reportedly obtained from the John F. Kennedy Presidential Library copies of the telephone logs kept by Evelyn Lincoln, the President's private secretary, which showed 70 telephone calls to the White House from Miss Campbell between March 29, 1961, and March 22, 1962.

Telephone Log

William Moss, the chief archivist at the Kennedy Library, said in a telephone interview today that Mrs. Lincoln's logs only showed calls made to the President's office in the White House, and not any calls he might have made to Miss Campbell or anyone else.

Some of the 70 calls, Mr. Moss said, were placed from Palm Springs, Calif., and Los Angeles, as well as other places around the country.

Mr. Moss added that there were no records at the library of any calls to or from Mr. Kennedy during periods in which he was away from the White House, and he said that, although none of the library's records of visitors to the Oval Office bore Miss Campbell's name, those records were not as inclusive as the ones kept by the Secret Service.

Jack Warner, a spokesman for the Secret Service in Washington, declined today to say whether his organization had any record that Mrs. Exner had ever been cleared for admission to the White House or to the President's office.

Mr. O'Donnell was traveling and could not be reached for comment. Mrs. Lincoln, according to the Senate report, told the committee that she had received a copy of Mr. Hoover's Feb. 27 memorandum describing Mrs. Exner's Mafia associations and "believed she would have shown it to the President."

Angie Novello, who was Robert Kennedy's secretary when he was Attorney General, said in a telephone interview today that, while she did not recall seeing the memorandum, it might have been delivered directly to the Attorney General by the F.B.I agent who then acted as the bureau's liaison with the Justice Department.

Worked in Primary

Mrs. Lincoln reportedly told the Senate panel that she recalled Mrs. Exner only as a worker in the President's California primary campaign in 1960, and did not believe the woman had ever seen Mr. Kennedy at the White House or anywhere else after his election in November 1960. Mr. O'Donnell reportedly endorsed this recollection.

Mrs. Exner expressed irritation today at what she characterized as efforts by Mrs. Lincoln and Mr. O'Donnell to sully or distort my personal relationship with Jack Kennedy."

"To me he was Jack Kennedy and not the President," Mrs. Exner said.

Mrs. Lincoln's friends said she was traveling in Europe and could not be reached for comment.

Mrs. Exner said that, whenever she called the White House, she would "always talk to Evelyn Lincoln first," and would then be put through to the President immediately, "if that was my purpose for calling."

Pressed by reporters to say what other reason she might have had for calling the White House, Mrs. Exner said she could think of none.

The Senate committee reported that the F.B.I. briefed Mr. Hoover on Miss Campbell's associations with the Mafia a second time, just before a March 22, 1962, luncheon meeting between Mr. Hoover and the President.

The committee said there was no record of whether that subject was discussed during the hour-long meeting, although another participant, who has asked not to be identified, said it never came up while he was present.

The committee report noted, however, that the last telephone call between Mr. Kennedy and Miss Campbell shown in Mrs. Lincoln's log took place a few hours after the Hoover luncheon.

Mrs. Exner said today she could not recall that conversation with Mr. Kennedy or ever having discussed Mr. Hoover or the Mafia with the President.

"I know nothing about that meeting other than what I've read," she said.

One source familiar with the evidence said there was "some indication" that Miss Campbell attempted to call the President after March 22, 1962, but that she was rebuffed.

Mrs. Exner said today, however, that "Jack Kennedy and I last talked in late 1962," about a year before the President was assassinated in Dallas on Nov. 22, 1963.

She said she last spoke to Mr. Giancana toward the end of 1964, and had not talked to Mr. Rosselli for "five or six years."

Mrs. Exner said that the Senate committee staff had read portions of the file compiled on her by the F.B.I. in the course of her testimony, and that what she heard seemed "prying, insidious and sounded more like a scandal sheet than a governmental investigation."

She and Mr. Monaghan, her attorney, said they intended to seek the contents of that file under the Freedom of Information Act.

An F.B.I. spokesman in Washington categorically denied that the bureau had used "illegal techniques" against Mrs. Exner in its investigation, or had "harassed" her, as she contended today.

Ex-Husband Comments

LOS ANGELES, Dec. 17 (AP) —Judith Campbell Exner was a "quiet, family kind of girl," her former husband, William Campbell, said here today.

Mr. Campbell an actor, and the former Judith Immoor were married on Oct. 25, 1952. when she was 18. They were divorced in 1958 and Mr. Campbell said he had lost contact with her.

He said he was never aware of her friendship with Mr. Kennedy, nor did he know that she had remarried.

"I only knew her as a very quiet, family kind of girl," he said. "She had two brothers and two sisters and her parents. She was a high school girl when I met her. It was a typical American home."

One sister was Susan Morrow, an actress who at one time was a contract player for Paramount Pictures and was briefly married to Gary Morton, a comedian. He is now married to Lucille Ball, the comedienne.

The New York Times
Published: December 18, 1975
Copyright © The New York Times

More Disclosures by Kennedy Friend Promised

SAN. DIEGO, Calif., Dec. 19 (UPI)—Judith Campbell Exner's attorney says that a book or television presentation will disclose more about her relationship with President Kennedy.

"We're looking at all alternatives," the attorney, Brian Monaghan, said yesterday. "We want the story told right. It may be a book, or series of articles or television interview, but it certainly is not going to be further news conferences."

Mrs. Exner, now the wife of the professional golfer, Dan Exner, emerged from 15 years of obscurity when information about her life was related in Senate committee testimony about C.I.A. assassination plots. She told a news conference Wednesday that she had a personal relationship with two Mafia figures at the same time she was seeing the late President.

But she never discussed her relationship with Mr. Kennedy when seeing the Chicago Mafia chief Sam Giancana and his associate John Rosselli, she told reporters.

Mr. Monaghan said that Mrs. Exner talked with representatives of CBS' "60 Minutes" program after the news conference.

A spokesman for George Hoover, executive producer of information services for CBS in New York, said that "60 Minutes" representatives were not bidding for the story.

"No money will ever be put up for this," he said.

Mrs. Exner denied having been unsuccessful in earlier attempts to sell a book or that she was interested in writing one or looking for an agent. But she said that she had sought Mr. Monaghan's advice.

Mr. Monaghan said that she had related her experiences in a series of tape recordings.

The New York Times

Published: December 20, 1975
Copyright © The New York Times

Put Your Dreams Away: The Sinatra Connection

In a recent essay about the way Senators Frank Church and John Tower were trying to conceal a connection between the Kennedy White House and the Mafia mobsters assigned to kill Fidel Castro, I concluded:

"Senator Church cannot slam the lid of Pandora's box back down now that he has glimpsed the evil that lurks therein. As that great matchmaker of Mafia hoodlums, good-looking women and a President of the United States used to croon: 'All—or nothing at all.'"

A Beverly Hills attorney, Milton A. Rudin, has kindly sent me a copy of a letter he wrote to The New York Times, which reads in part:

Put Your Dreams Away: The Sinatra Connection

ESSAY

By William Safire

In a recent essay about the way Senators Frank Church and John Tower were trying to conceal a connection between the Kennedy White House and the Mafia mobsters assigned to kill Fidel Castro, I concluded:

"Senator Church cannot slam the lid of Pandora's box back down now that he has glimpsed the evil that lurks therein. As that great matchmaker of Mafia hoodlums, good-looking women and a President of the United States used to croon: 'All—or nothing at all.'"

A Beverly Hills attorney, Milton A. Rudin, has kindly sent me a copy of a letter he wrote to The New York Times, which reads in part:

"There is no question in the minds of many readers that the last sentence refers to my client, Frank Sinatra."

After objecting to my "yellow journalism" in general, Mr. Sinatra's lawyer underscored the "e" in "women," and suggested that readers might infer from that word that his client had been acting as a procurer. He says he is not filing a libel action because of "the horrendous state of the law" on that subject, and because:

"Our client has not issued any statement concerning the stories which have appeared in the press concerning President Kennedy and Judith Campbell because he refuses to join in the chorus of ghoulish scandalmongers. A libel action would have the same effect. Even the printing of a retraction continues this shameful episode in the history of the American press."

At the risk of such shameful continuance, I concede one point: "Women," plural should have read "woman," singular. The Church committee's interim cover-up reported only one instance of a person introducing a friend of unspecified gender to Mr. Kennedy and also introducing that same friend to Mafioso Giancana.

Committee sources cited in many publications have identified that introducer as Mr. Sinatra, which charge he has not denied. Nor does his attorney deny it now, and it is logical to assume that he would have refuted the charge in his letter if Mr. Sinatra had not been the middleman, or matchmaker, in this particular White House-Mafia connection.

Accordingly, we in the ghoulish-scandalmonger set would like to know why the Church committee never called Mr. Sinatra to testify under oath, nor even had an investigator call him up. One man, presumably Mr. Sinatra, brought together a mobster and a woman, and a President and that same woman; the mobster was the one hired by the C.I.A. in that President's Administration to murder a head of state; as an investigation began in 1975, the mobster was silenced permanently with seven bullets. And Senator Church decided not to hear from the man who probably built the original bridge.

Here are a few of the questions

Senators Church and Tower were duty-bound to ask Mr. Sinatra. I regret the innuendo necessarily burdening these shots in the dark, but in view of the Senators' craven reluctance to ask them, and Mr. Sinatra's stated unwillingness to "issue a statement," I know of no other way to set the questions forth.

● When did you introduce Sam Giancana to Judith Campbell, if you did, and at whose request? When did you introduce Miss Campbell to either of the Kennedy brothers? Do you know if the Kennedys were ever aware of Miss Campbell's close association with the mobster Giancana and his lieutenant, John Roselli? Did the mobsters ask you to introduce her or anyone else to the Kennedys?

● Did you ever see Judith Campbell and John Kennedy together, or Messrs. Giancana and/or Roselli and Miss Campbell together? Did you make available premises controlled by you to any of them? Did Sam Giancana or John Roselli ever boast to you about Miss Campbell's calls and trips to the White House?

● To your knowledge, Mr. Sinatra, were any recordings made of any meetings between Judith Campbell and John Kennedy, or were any pictures taken of them that could have been used by organized crime for blackmail purposes? Were you aware of any communications between the President and the men hired to kill Fidel Castro through the woman you introduced to both? Did Sam Giancana tell you how he persuaded the C.I.A. to bug a Las Vegas hotel room on his behalf?

● What was the content of your last conversations with Sam Giancana, John Roselli, and Judith Campbell? Was Mr. Giancana fearful, and if so, did he tell you why?

● Did any member of the Kennedy family, including in-laws, tell you about the plot to kill Fidel Castro? Did Sam Giancana or John Roselli mention it to you?

● Was your association with Sam Giancana, which cost you the right to own part of a casino in Nevada, the cause of your break with the President? When President Kennedy changed his plans to stay with you in Palm Springs, and switched to the home of Bing Crosby, did Robert Kennedy give you the reason why? Did he mention a visit to the President by J. Edgar Hoover?

● Did you ever intervene with the Kennedys to get the Justice Department to stop an investigation?

● Before or after the Kennedy assassination in Dallas, did Sam Giancana or John Roselli ever mention the name of Jack Ruby to you?

Mr. Sinatra, who admirably refuses to abandon friends after their popularity fades, might emerge from such an interrogation with honor bright.

But we can put our dreams away for another day: Frank Church, dartgunning for the Presidency, needs Kennedy support and has accordingly aborted any future hearings of his cover-up committee. We are left to ponder what might have been learned if only "Old Blue-Eyes" could have been required to sing.

All in the Family: II

By William Safire

WASHINGTON, Jan. 28—In our last episode, readers were left breathless by revelations of an interlocking directorate of Old Kennedy Hands who set up the Church committee staff in a way that makes easy the cover-up of abuses of power in the sixties.

In today's episode, we go from cosy relationships to actual relatives.

1. *The brother-in-law.* Rule 6.4 of the Church committee calls for the committee to "endeavor to obtain voluntary counsel" for witnesses.

Sounds like an admirable service for indigents. In practice, this is how it worked: A Kennedy appointee named Daniel Rezneck, of Arnold and Porter, then head of the D.C. Bar Association, was asked to draw up a list of attorneys with top-secret clearances. His friend, John Denniston—a Government contract man at Covington and Burling—came up with a secret list of lawyers to receive the business (for a fee— "voluntary" has not meant free).

When Judith Campbell Exner was called, her lawyer also represented Robert Maheu (interesting lead) and begged off; a Church staffer then called the handful of approved lawyers to see who was available quickly. No volunteers.

Then, with the approval of F.A.O. Schwarz 3d, chief Church counsel, the woman who was President Kennedy's Mafia link was put in touch with a member of the law firm of the Kennedy brother-in-law, Sargent Shriver. Such referral is improper on its face; no investigating body can ethically recommend specific lawyers to witnesses. The Shriver firm did represent her at the committee and did discuss fees for future representation.

But the committee insists its staff did not know Mr. Shriver was in that law firm it told Mrs. Exner to call; Mr. Shriver insists the lawyer on his staff who took the job didn't clear it on high. If you believe all that, give my regards to the Tooth Fairy, but remember this incident when Mr. Shriver delivers his delegates to Mr. Church at the convention.

2. *The son-in-law.* One of the four "task forces" of the Church committee concerns itself with military intelligence abuses, and has been investigating the Defense Department and the National Security Agency.

Naturally, a key witness has been Robert McNamara, the Kennedy-Johnson Secretary of Defense whose computer-like mind has emptied its memory bank of all recollection of assassination plots.

Whom did Frank Church select to be the deputy chief of this military intelligence section? Answer: Barry Carter, a former Kissinger protégé, a brilliant mind, a likely future leader of the national security establishment, whose experience qualifies him in every way for the job. One small problem: for seven years, up to two years ago, he was Robert McNamara's son-in-law.

"Not one scintilla of evidence," to use John Tower's favorite phrase, suggests that Mr. McNamara's former son-in-law was not fervent and relentless in his pursuit of any transgressions by his former wife's father. Mr. Carter asserts he avoided the assassination area entirely, and points with justifiable pride to his work on the "Shamrock" intercepts of cable traffic. We shall see how the final report treats Kennedy-Johnson intelligence abuses in the military area.

But is this not what Senator Church would call in others "the appearance of conflict of interest"? The rough equivalent would have been for Leon Jaworski to hire Ed Cox or David Eisenhower to investigate Richard Nixon.

3. *The son.* From the very nave of the Church committee, sources report that when staffers went up to the Kennedy Library in Waltham, Mass., suspicious gaps were discovered in the telephone logs of the President's calls. Nor was there any record of a private telephone, installed in a tiny room just off the Oval Office, where Mr. Kennedy made private calls outside the White House switchboard.

One Church staffer, however, who has tried unsuccessfully to link President Eisenhower to the Lumumba assassination, was especially warmly received at the Kennedy Library.

He is Peter Fenn, and he is the son of Dan Fenn, the former assistant to President Kennedy who is now the director of that same Kennedy Library. Mr. Fenn the younger was given free access to the files of Robert Kennedy there by Mr. Fenn the elder, and cynics will question whether a vigorous search for Kennedy wrongdoing was conducted.

Now, if Frank Church—who needs Kennedy support in his Presidential candidacy—wants to do Ted Kennedy a favor by putting a 25-year-old kid at the public trough for $400 a week for six months, that's politics. But isn't it a bit unfair to young Mr. Fenn, who is Senator Church's son's best friend, to start him off in a situation with such an apparent conflict of interest? Let's assume he's a nice, honest, idealistic young man—why break him in on a cover-up?

Old-fashioned nepotism is not at issue here, nor are the young staffers culpable. Instead, we see what happens when a Certified Good Guy is convinced he has the press in his pocket: Arrogantly, brazenly, Frank Church has turned his investigation into a relative thing.

Published: January 29, 1976
Copyright © The New York Times

Court Refuses Mrs. Exner Quick Access to F.B.I. File

SAN FRANCISCO, April 24 (AP)—A Federal appeals court has delayed efforts by Judith Campbell Exner, who has told of having an affair with President Kennedy, to see the files on her kept by the Federal Bureau of Investigation.

The United States Court of Appeals for the Ninth Circuit granted the Government a temporary stay of two orders issued by a Federal judge in San Diego that the files be turned over immediately to Mrs. Exner. The bureau says Mrs. Exner must wait her turn among many seeking files.

The New York Times
Published: April 25, 1976

Copyright © The New York Times

●

To get a look at her F.B.I. file, **Judith Campbell Exner** will have to wait in line with 6,000 others, the Government said yesterday in papers filed in Federal court in San Diego. Release of the file had been deliberately blocked, according to the attorney for the self-identified "close personal" associate of President Kennedy and the late Sam Giancana, a Mafia leader. Government attorneys attributed the delay to the backlog, however, and said Mrs. Exner wanted special treatment "to meet a publisher's deadline" on her announced book.

The New York Times

Published: March 6, 1976
Copyright © The New York Times

No Sinatra Subpoena

Justice Department sources said earlier that Mr. Helms was under investigation on whether he ordered that the burglary be committed. The C.I.A. was allegedly trying to find out if the owner of the studio and his fiancée a former agency employee, might be involved in a security breach.

In another action, Mr. Church said, the committee said it saw no reason to subpoena Frank Sinatra, the singer, in connection with C.I.A. ties with the Mafia and the Kennedy Administration. Senator Church said the committee felt it had sufficient evidence on the matter in hand.

The committee approved by a vote of 7 to 0 a bill proposing Congressional oversight for the intelligence agencies.

Earlier today, William E. Colby, who will step down soon as Director of Central Intelligence, told the Government Operations Committee that he favored a joint Congressional oversight committee, but wanted it restricted to as few members as would be representative of the two houses of Congress to maintain security.

The New York Times

Published: January 24, 1976
Copyright © The New York Times

Slain Mafia Leader's Porcelains Are Auctioned

He was most proud of the monkey band — an orchestra of 17 pieces, all little monkeys. He really enjoyed that."

Miss Giancana said she hoped on Wednesday to bid on a pair of her father's silver cuff links.

Asked if the auction was linked to a tax lien, she replied: "On the legal end I have no comment. I can only

The New York Times/Gary Settle

er's art objects—a porcelain ; Inc. It sold for $825.

give you the humanistic part."

Mr. Giancana's name was in the news recently in connection with allegations that President Kennedy had a relationship with a woman who was also having a relationship with Mr. Giancana.

The woman, Judith Campbell Exner, has denied that she ever discussed her Giancana relationship with Mr. Kennedy.

Denies C.I.A. Knowledge

Nor, she said, had she been aware at the time she was seeing Mr. Kennedy that Mr. Giancana and another crime figure with whom she was involved, John Rosselli, were helping the Central Intelligence Agency recruit agents in an abortive plot to assassinate Prime Minister Fidel Castro of Cuba.

One man at the auction who said he had met Mr. Giancana on occasion was Chase Gilmore, an assistant auctioneer and the man who catalogued Mr. Giancana's possessions.

On a pre-auction tour of Mr. Giancana's figurines, which were crowded on a table, Mr. Gilmore said he had chatted with Mr. Giancana over the 10 years that Mr. Gilmore was manager of the Shangri-La, a once plush Chinese restaurant that is now a pornographic movie house.

"All that was before I got hepatitis and went to bed for nine months," Mr. Gilmore said, a period in which he studied antiques and changed careers.

Picking up a hand-painted plate of Killarney Castle in Ireland, he said, "Now this is class, whereas the other is, uh, merely decorative."

A photographer asked Mr.

Kennedy and Castro: 'No Smoking Gun but…'

By Richard J. Walton

In not directly linking President Kennedy to the assassination attempts on Fidel Castro, the Senate intelligence committee acted just the way the House Judiciary Committee wanted to act in the Watergate affair.

The House wanted in the worst way to avoid impeachment, though it, and the nation, were morally certain of Richard Nixon's guilt.

For a time it based its reluctance to act on the absence of absolutely irrefutable evidence, the "smoking gun." But then the White House tapes provided the "smoking gun" and the Judiciary Committee had no choice but to proceed with the steps that made President Nixon's resignation inevitable.

However, the intelligence committee, which is headed by Senator Frank Church, has not found a "smoking gun," so while it brought the accusation right to the late President John F. Kennedy's door, it did not open the door.

In not quite accusing President Kennedy, the committee was aided by another factor. With Mr. Nixon, the press was in full cry, helping the public become convinced that President Nixon was guilty. But that has not been so with Mr. Kennedy.

There was a flurry of stories when the Church committee released its report on political assassinations but then the press lost interest. It is difficult to escape the conclusion that the press is interested in seeking the truth about Mr. Kennedy than it was with Mr. Nixon.

The Senate committee relied on the narrowest, most legalistic interpretation of its mandate to avoid charging Mr. Kennedy with complicity in the attempts on Prime Minister Castro. But a jury might have found Mr. Kennedy guilty, so powerful is the weight of evidence and circumstance. And common sense will convince many that Mr. Kennedy had at least some knowledge of the schemes directed against Mr. Castro.

Mr. Kennedy's authorization of the Bay of Pigs operation demonstrates beyond question that he would have gone to great lengths to topple Mr. Castro. Before and, even more, after the Bay of Pigs, Mr. Kennedy was plainly obsessed with Mr. Castro, not only on the political level but on the personal as well.

Machismo was as much a part of

Marshall Arisman

'This was not idle talk'

Mr. Kennedy's character as it was of any Latin political leader. And Mr. Castro had humiliated him in front of the world. The evidence of the Church committee bristles with such tough talk as "get rid of," "knock off," "eliminate" Mr. Castro. This was not idle talk. The Kennedy Administration from the President on down prided itself on being made up of tough guys.

"Hard-nosed" was a compliment in those days. This was the Administration that radically escalated the military budget, sent the first combat troops to Vietnam, encouraged coups against Rafael Leonidas Trujillo of the Dominican Republic and Ngo Dinh Diem of South Vietnam in which both were killed, and, toughest of all, that confronted Nikita S. Khrushchev with the threat of nuclear war.

Not only were these genuine tough guys, but the evidence of the Church committee demonstrates that assassination was discussed by or in the presence of Secretary of Defense Robert McNamara; McGeorge Bundy, the national security adviser; and the President's brother, Robert.

The first two were intimate advisers, and his brother was, of course, the President's alter ego.

The evidence further demonstrates, beyond question, that the Central Intelligence Agency had absolutely no doubt that the President wanted Mr. Castro removed by any means necessary. Even the C.I.A. would not attempt to assassinate a world leader without absolute certainty that it was authorized. The C.I.A. was not dealing with the naive but with perhaps the most worldly men ever to occupy the White House.

It is beyond the bounds of credibility that the President's own brother, several of his top advisers, and responsible officials at several levels of several agencies could be involved in discussions of plans to kill Mr. Castro without President Kennedy's knowledge.

He, remember, prided himself on knowing what was going on at all levels of his Administration, to the extent of petrifying lower-echelon officials by telephoning them directly to find out what was going on in their areas.

Just as with Mr. Nixon's men in Watergate, the Kennedy men would have done such things only if they knew their boss approved.

Then there is this: About four months after Mr. Kennedy's assassination—what a terrible irony!—Senator George Smathers, in an oral history recording for the Kennedy Library, told of a conversation with the President.

Mr. Smathers said: "We had *further* [emphasis added] conversation of assassination of Fidel Castro . . . he was certain it could be accomplished —I remember that—it would be no problem." The President could have been so certain only if he had discussed assassination within his Administration.

Mr. Smathers has not denied his statement, which was called to the attention of the Church committee. He did tell the syndicated columnist John D. Lofton last summer that he was "irked as hell" that a written transcript of his interview had been put with the open material in the Kennedy Library, instead of being sealed until 1980, as he said he had specified.

The Smathers statement, plus the evidence published by the Church committee, seems to establish beyond reasonable doubt that Mr. Kennedy was aware of the plans against Castro. No smoking gun but a pretty solid case.

Richard J. Walton is author of "Cold War and Counterrevolution: The Foreign Policy of John F. Kennedy."

The New York Times
Published: December 10, 1975
Copyright © The New York Times

Crime Figure, Linked to Plot on Castro, Found Slain

MIAMI, Aug. 8 (AP)—The body of John Roselli, a key figure with San Giancana, the slain Chicago mobster. in a Central Intelligence Agency plan to assassinate Premier Fidel Castro of Cuba, has been found in a chain-wrapped 55-gallon drum floating in Biscayne Bay.

Mr. Roselli. 70 years old, was found yesterday by two fishermen. He had been missing since he left his sister's home on July 28 to play golf.

"These guys went to an incredible amount of trouble trying to make sure the body was never found," Dr. Ronald Wright, deputy chief medical examiner, said. "The lengths to which they went to insure the body would not be found clearly earmarks this as a true gangland-style killing."

The Dade County authorities said that Mr. Roselli had been asphyxiated. Earlier reports indicated that Mr. Roselli had been shot. Dr. Wright would only confirm that there was "a circular wound on the lower abdomen."

Mr. Roselli testified last year before the Senate Select Committee on Intelligence Activities that he and Mr. Giancana had been recruited in 1961 by the C.I.A. as a part of a plot to poison Mr. Castro. Mr. Roselli said that he had turned down the offer, for which he and Mr. Giancana were reportedly to

United Press International
John Roselli

have been paid $100,000. According to the Senate report on the plan, Mr. Roselli was the liaison between Mr. Giancana to carry out the assassination.

Giancana Murdered

Mr. Giancana was also supposed to testify before the Senate Committee, but on July 19, 1975, several days before his scheduled appearance, someone fired seven .22-caliber bullets into him in what the authorities said was a gang-land killing. That murder has never been solved.

The Intelligence Committee learned that Robert A. Maheu, a former top aide to the late Howard R. Hughes, was the liaison between the C.I.A. and the mobsters. Mr. Maheu, who has partly acknowledged his role in the assassination plan, split with Mr. Hughes long before the billionaire's death earlier this year.

The two fishermen found the oil drum floating in Dumbfoundling Bay, an arm of Biscayne Bay between North Miami and Miami Beach. The police said that because of the currents, it was not known where the drum had been thrown into the bay.

Dr. Wright said that the holes had been chopped in the barrel to make it sink and that the chains had been wrapped around it to weight it down. Gases formed by the decomposition and trapped inside body tissue and the barrel itself had brought it to the surface he said.

Car Was Found

Mr. Roselli had been reported missing on July 28 by his sister, with whom he had been living recently in Plantation, north of Miami. His car was found a few days later at Miami International Airport. His golf bags were still in the trunk.

Mr. Roselli was associated for many years with Mr. Giancana, who became the head of the Chicago rackets in the late 1930's and early 1940's.

Mr. Roselli was sent to Las Vegas, Nev., in the 1950's to operate the organized crime interests there but stayed under the control of the Chicago organization.

He went to Los Angeles in the early 1960's and was based there when Mr. Castro took over Cuba. Until then, organized crime had controlled gambling in Cuba.

Mr. Maheu has said that he recruited Mr. Roselli and Mr. Giancana to kill Mr. Castro at the request of the C.I.A. He said that the two men had been chosen because of contacts they had made in Cuba in the pre-Castro years.

Mr. Maheu said that the plot was timed to coincide with the Bay of Pigs invasion in April 1961 and was "always subject to a 'go' signal which, to my knowledge, never came."

Mr. Roselli told the Senate committee that he had made several trips to Cuba in high-powered boats furnished by the C.I.A. He said that the plan had included various methods for killing Mr. Castro, including sniper fire, explosives and poison capsules.

Mr. Roselli and Giancana were also linked with Judith Campbell Exner, who has said that she had "a relationship" with President John F. Kennedy. The names of Mr. Roselli and Mr. Giancana appear in F.B.I. reports released at Mrs. Exner's request for help in writing her memoirs.

The New York Times
Published: August 9, 1976
Copyright © The New York Times

Ex-Aides Say Justice Dept. Rejected a Sinatra Inquiry

By NICHOLAS GAGE

The Justice Department under Attorney General Robert F. Kennedy rejected or ignored repeated recommendations for a thorough investigation of Frank Sinatra and his relationships with Mafia leaders, according to former Federal officials.

They said that in May 1962, for example, the chief of the department's Organized Crime

---

Last of three articles.

Section, Edwyn Silberling, recommended to Attorney General Kennedy a thorough tax investigation of Mr. Sinatra, but it was rejected.

Several other recommendations were made within the department in 1962 and 1963 for investigations of Mr. Sinatra, his contacts with Mafia figures and his relationship with Judith Campbell (now Mrs. Judith Exner), whom Mr. Sinatra introduced to both the late Sam Giancana, the Mafia boss of Chicago, and President Kennedy.

But department records show that while Mr. Sinatra was interviewed by Federal agents and was asked to submit some affidavits, no thorough investigation was ever conducted by the department on Mr. Sinatra's Mafia ties.

Some former Justice officials feel that evidence available at that time did not warrant such an inquiry, but others believe that there was a reluctance to pursue an extensive investigation because of Mr. Sinatra's close ties to the Kennedy family.

Mr. Sinatra, through a spokesman, declined to be interviewed by The New York Times.

The rejected recommendations for investigation were disclosed in a two-month investigation by The New York Times of Mr. Giancana and John Roselli, another Mafia figure, and their relationships with Mr. Sinatra and Mrs.

Continued on Page 18, Column 4

Published: April 14, 1976
Copyright © The New York Times

Link of Kennedy Friend To Mafia Is Still a Puzzle

By NICHOLAS GAGE

The disclosure last December that President Kennedy and two major Mafia figures maintained close friendships with the same woman — Judith Campbell — has puzzled many private citizens, disturbed some law enforcement officials and aroused extensive speculation in and out of Government.

The speculation has been stimulated because the two

First of three articles.

Mafia figures, John Roselli and Sam Giancana, maintained the relationships with Mrs. Campbell at the very time she said she was having an affair with the President. And both men had been involved in the Central Intelligence Agency's abortive plots to assassinate Prime Minister Fidel Castro of Cuba.

But the Senate Select Committee on Intelligence, which investigated the C.I.A. plots, referred only briefly to Mrs. Campbell's relationships, devoting slightly more than a page to them in its 349-page report last December. The report did not identify Mrs. Campbell (now Mrs. Judith Exner) by name or sex, and left a number of questions unanswered.

Among them were whether Mrs. Campbell used her relationship with Mr. Kennedy to benefit the Mafia, and whether the President learned as a result of the Campbell friendship that the C.I.A. was working with the Mafia on a plot to kill Mr. Castro.

Interviews and Findings

During the last two months, The New York Times, in interviews with current and former Justice Department officials, participants in the C.I.A. plots and underworld figures, has examined these questions and found the following:

¶Several recommendations were made within the Justice Department in 1962 for a thorough investigation of Mrs.

Campbell's Mafia ties, but no inquiry was ever conducted. When high Justice officials learned about her friendship

Questions Remain De

Continued From Page 1, Col. 2

with President Kennedy in early 1962, they looked upon it as a "domestic matter," as one of them put it, and merely passed information on her to the White House.

¶Sam Giancana—who was slain last June — and John Roselli boasted to fellow gangsters about sharing the affections of a woman who was seeing the President, but they do not appear to have benefited further from their knowledge of Mrs. Campbell's friendship with Mr. Kennedy.

¶While the Senate committee found no evidence that President Kennedy knew about the C.I.A.-Mafia plots to kill Mr. Castro, the possibility appears high to some former Justice officials that Robert F. Kennedy, then the Attorney General, told his brother about the plots in view of what he learned about the relationships of Mr. Giancana, Mr. Roselli and Mrs. Campbell in 1962 and early

Associated Press
Judith Campbell Exner

her when she married Willia Campbell, an actor, a sho time later, according to th friend of the two Mafia leader

The couple was divorced 1958, and a year later sh began to date Mr. Sinatra, sh

Published: April 12, 1976
Copyright © The New York Times

Giancana, Mr. Roselli and Mrs. Campbell in 1962 and early 1963.

¶When the Senate committee investigated Mrs. Campbell's friendships, not only did the committee not call Frank Sinatra, who introduced Mrs. Campbell both to President Kennedy and to Mr. Giancana, but other key individuals were merely interviewed rather than questioned under oath, even though a deeper inquiry might have produced information affecting the committee's conclusion that President Kennedy did not know about the C.I.A.-Mafia plots against Mr. Castro.

Staying Out of Sight

A spokesman for the committee, Spencer Davis, said that the panel's mandate was to determine whether Mrs. Campbell was involved in an intelligence operation and not to conduct a broad investigation of her Mafia ties.

"We found that she was not engaged in intelligence and that was that," he said.

A close friend of the two Mafia figures said that Mrs. Campbell's initial contact with the Mafia was with Mr. Roselli, who was born in Italy, immigrated to Boston as a child, joined the Mafia in Chicago and later became involved in labor racketeering in Los Angeles.

Mr. Roselli, who has been staying out of sight since Mr. Giancana was slain last year, has told friends that he first met Mrs. Campbell in 1951— she was then Judith Immoor— when she was 17 years old and "hanging around the studios" in Hollywood. Mr. Roselli,

who had served three years in Federal prison for extorting money from the studios, was then associated with an independent production company. Miss Immoor had ambitions of becoming an actress.

Mr. Roselli stopped seeing her when she married William Campbell, an actor, a short time later, according to the friend of the two Mafia leaders.

The couple was divorced in 1958, and a year later she began to date Mr. Sinatra, she said in the outline for a book she plans to write. Mrs. Campbell said that she ended her affair with the singer because their tastes in sex differed, but continued to travel with the Sinatra crowd.

Sinatra's Reply

In reply to this assertion, Mr. Sinatra issued this statement: "Hell hath no fury like a hustler with a literary agent."

Mrs. Campbell said in the outline that Mr. Sinatra introduced her to John F. Kennedy on Feb. 7, 1960, in Las Vegas, Nev., and they made plans to meet in early March in New York, where they began to have an affair.

After her New York meeting with Mr. Kennedy, according to the outline, she accepted an invitation to meet Mr. Sinatra in Miami Beach, where he was performing at the Fontainebleau Hotel, and the entertainer introduced her there to Mr. Giancana.

Five months later Mr. Giancana and Mr. Roselli became involved with the C.I.A. in plots to kill Fidel Castro—recruiting Cuban agents who might be persuaded to poison Mr. Castro's food—but apparently they did not tell Mrs. Campbell about them. Mafia members traditionally do not confide in their women and Mr. Giancana and Mr. Roselli made no exception with Mrs. Campbell, according to the close friend of both men.

His contention is supported by participants in the plots, including Robert Maheu, who has acknowledged bringing together the Mafia and the C.I.A. Mrs. Campbell said in her book outline that she had "no knowledge of C.I.A. involvement with the Mafia."

The close friend of Mr. Giancana and Mr. Roselli said that, at that time, Mrs. Campbell was one of about 20 women, some of them well-known actresses, who were in the Sinatra crowd and were introduced to the entertainer's friends in public life and in the underworld.

"The difference with Judy was that she was pushy and reckless," the friend said. "She'd go to Johnny's place and call everyone she knew from his phone, or she'd call Sam at his home and at the Armory Lounge in Chicago, where he hung out. So the Feds picked up her tracks.

"The other girls were careful. They didn't call Sam or Johnny because they knew their phones were tapped. And they didn't call the White House, for God's sake!"

The Federal Bureau of Investigation first picked up Judith Campbell through electronic surveillance of Mr. Roselli in early 1961, according to Justice Department sources.

The F.B.I. checked out her long-distance calls over the next two years and found that she was in frequent contact with Mr. Roselli, Mr. Giancana and Mr. Sinatra.

For example, Government records show that during one four-week period, from June 8 to July 5, 1962, Mrs. Campbell called Mr. Giancana 23 times at his Chicago home and 37 times at the Armory Lounge from her Los Angeles residence at 8401 Fountain Avenue. During the same period, she called Mr. Sinatra 16 times at the Cal-Neva Lodge in Lake Tahoe, Nev., which he then owned.

70 Telephone Calls

Seven months before these calls, in November 1961, the F.B.I. found out that Mrs. Campbell had made two phone calls to the White House. They were followed by a third call early the following February. (The Senate committee found White House records showing that Mrs. Campbell had called a total of 70 times, but initially the F.B.I. knew of only three calls.)

On Feb. 27, 1962, J. Edgar Hoover, then director of the F.B.I., sent a memorandum to Attorney General Kennedy and to Kenneth O'Donnell, then special assistant to President Kennedy, saying that an investigation of Mr. Roselli disclosed that he had been in touch with a Judith Campbell. The memo also said that Mrs. Campbell was maintaining a relationship with Sam Giancana, "a prominent Chicago underworld figure," and that Mrs. Campbell had made calls to the White House from her home in Los Angeles.

It is not known how Robert Kennedy reacted to the memorandum, but a high official in the Justice Department at that time said that his staff did not take it very seriously.

"By that time a lot of stories were coming out of the Secret Service about the President's interest in women," one former official said. "We looked on it as a domestic matter and, as I recall, the whole thing was referred to Carmine Bellino, who handled personal stuff for the President."

Kennedy-Hoover Lunch

Another former Justice Department official also said that the matter was referred to Mr. Bellino, who was then a special consultant to the President. But Mr. Bellino said in an interview that he never heard of Mrs. Campbell until the recent articles in the press about her.

"The only personal matter I ever handled for the President was once when Jackie was spending too much money and he asked me to find out where it was all going," Mr. Bellino said.

The contradiction between the former Justice Department officials' recollections and Mr. Bellino's statement was never confronted by the Senate committee. The Justice officials who recall the matter being turned over to Mr. Bellino were not questioned under oath by the committee, but merely interviewed by staff members, whom they did not tell about Mr. Bellino.

Mr. Bellino, too, was never questioned under oath, but was merely interviewed at the committee's offices.

On March 22, less than a month after the Hoover memo was sent, President Kennedy and Mr. Hoover had lunch together, the Senate committee's report said. "According to White House logs," the report added, "the last telephone contact between the White House and the President's friend [Mrs. Campbell] occurred a few hours after the luncheon."

However, Mrs. Campbell said in her book outline that her relationship with the President continued for several months after that.

In the months following Mr. Hoover's memorandum of Feb. 27, the Justice Department received further information from the F.B.I. about Mrs. Campbell's close relationships with Mr. Giancana, Mr. Roselli and Mr. Sinatra.

The information was included in a series of reports prepared by Dougald McMillan, a Justice Department attorney studying the involvement of Mr. Sinatra with Mafia figures.

Mr. McMillan is still with the department and refused to discuss the matter, but former Justice officials who saw the reports said that they strongly recommended that Mrs. Campbell's relationships with the Mafia and with Mr. Sinatra be investigated.

Testimony Urged

They said that one of the reports urged that Mrs. Campbell be brought before a Federal grand jury, given immunity from prosecution and compelled to testify under oath about her Mafia contacts.

No action was taken on any of the recommendations by the Justice Department. Several officials who were asked about them said they did not remember reports specifically mentioning Mrs. Campbell.

But they said they did remember that several reports on Mr. Sinatra were prepared at the time, and it was in some of those reports that the recommendations about Mrs. Campbell were included.

The Sinatra reports apparently were seen by Attorney General Kennedy, because everything about Mr. Sinatra developed by the department was sent up to him at his request, according to William G. Hundley, former chief of the department's Organized Crime Section. Thus, Attorney General Kennedy presumably saw everything included in the reports about Mrs. Campbell.

Robert Kennedy learned on Feb. 27, 1962, in the memorandum from Mr. Hoover, that a woman was calling the White House who had a relationship with Mr. Giancana, one of the top Mafia bosses in the country and a main target of his department.

Involved in Plots

Just 10 weeks later, on May 7, 1962, according to the Senate committee's report, he was informed in a conference with C.I.A. officials that their agency had been involved with Mr. Giancana in plots to assassinate Prime Minister Castro.

In view of these two discoveries and what Robert Kennedy later learned about Mrs. Campbell in the Sinatra reports, some of Mr. Kennedy's former associates at the Justice Department believe that he told the President what he knew about Mr. Giancana, the C.I.A. plots and Mrs. Campbell.

"He had to; he told Jack everything," one of the former associates said.

But others feel that he did not inform President Kennedy.

"Any man would tell his brother, one would suppose," said Herbert J. Miller, who was head of the Justice Department's Criminal Division under Attorney General Kennedy. "But you must remember that the C.I.A. lied to Bobby and told him the plots against Castro had been terminated. So there was no compelling need to tell the President."

That the C.I.A. lied to Robert Kennedy about ending the assassination plots against Mr. Castro was confirmed in the committee's report through testimony from former C.I.A. officials.

Even if President Kennedy learned everything his brother knew about Mrs. Campbell and her Mafia friends, however, there is no evidence available to indicate that his relationship with her benefited them.

Wiretaps on Mr. Giancana and Mr. Roselli, as well as underworld informants who were close to them, confirm that they boasted about their relationship with Mrs. Campbell. But neither of these sources offer any indication that the two Mafia figures received any benefits from the Government as a result of what they knew about her, as they did for their involvement with the C.I.A., which once intervened to block their indictment on wiretap charges.

The Times investigation found no law-enforcement official who investigated Mr. Giancana and Mr. Roselli who could offer any evidence that they used the knowledge of Mrs. Campbell's friendship with President Kennedy to their advantage.

Tomorrow: Generous treatment for a Mafia boss.

MY STORY

By *Judith Exner. As told to Ovid Demaris.*
299 pp. New York: Grove Press. $8.95.

It would be understandable to equate Judith Campbell Exner with Elizabeth Ray: Both gained notoriety because of their alleged bedmates. While Miss Ray devoted herself to the legislative branch of the Federal Government, Mrs. Exner claimed liaisons with President Kennedy, Frank Sinatra and an important figure in a private consortium that does occasional contract business—one Sam Giancana.

This equation, however, is unfair. Mrs. Exner sought no publicity, at least until after a Senate committee investigating C.I.A.-Mafia connections summoned her to testify and press reports revealed her supposed connections to Kennedy and Giancana. It is also unfair because Mrs. Exner and ghostwriter Ovid Demaris have fashioned a curiously affecting book.

This is not the place to weigh Mrs. Exner's credibility, save to say that the welter of evidence she offers—addresses, telephone numbers, White House décor — makes the defensive protestations of the keepers of the Kennedy flame somewhat dubious. What can be said is that through spare, artless prose, Mrs. Exner has painted a sad, dispiriting view of men in power. Thackeray might have made it art: the furious competition of wealthy, powerful men for the body of an attractive, complaisant woman; the ways they identify and demand tokens of affection; the offering of gifts; Mrs. Exner's apparent willingness to lead a life in which (by the evidence of her book) she literally did *nothing* but dress, dance, dine, and so to bed.

To be sure, there is sufficient grist for the gossip mills in her account of her alleged lovers' sexual tastes. More interesting is the notion that three men of such unfathomable power found themselves so starved for affection that they became obsessed with the same object—for despite her defensive prose, a sex object is exactly what Mrs. Exner was.

The New York Times

Published: July 3, 1977

John Roselli and the CIA Family Jewels

New information and evidence is coming out all the time about the complex relationships between Exner, Kennedy, Roselli, Giancana and the CIA. One recent example of this is the CIA TOP SECRET *"Family Jewels"* documents that were released on June 25, 2007.

It seems strange that documents marked TOP SECRET would be released, until one reads them and realizes that they are largely old news that were leaked to journalists years ago and have long since become the grist of rumor mills.

Nevertheless, some of the revelations are new and shocking.

The item that made the biggest news when the Family Jewels came out was that the government particularly under the Nixon Administration was spying on political dissidents. Others may have found this shocking, but I was not shocked by this. I have always assumed that my telephone is tapped and that they have been spying on me since 1966. I am so deeply disappointed to find out that this seems not to be true.

However, I really am shocked to learn that during the Kennedy Administration the telephones of prominent newspaper journalists were tapped, such as for example ABC Reporter Britt Hume. Their telephones were tapped because certain news reporters consistently reported on top secret information that they were not supposed to know. The purpose of these telephone taps was to find out the sources of the leaks.

This was part of what was called "Project Mockingbird". It was, of course, highly illegal. It was approved by Attorney General Robert F. Kennedy and Secretary of Defense Robert McNamara.

The result of this project was that 12 Senators, 6 members of Congress, 12 Congressional Staff Members, a staff member of the White House, members of the Vice-President's Office and an

Assistant Attorney General were all identified as the sources of leaks. In fact, so much data and so many TOP SECRET documents were leaked to the newsmen that they could not use them all and distributed some of the material to other newsmen, which created the illusion that more newsmen were receiving the leaked material than was actually the case.

In short, the United States Government leaked like a sieve.

The Family Jewels documents were compiled by then CIA Director William Colby at the time that the Watergate Affair was unraveling. The previous CIA Director, James R. Schlesinger, had commissioned the report after two former CIA Employees, E. Howard Hunt and James McCord, had been implicated in the Watergate Break-in.

The purpose of assembling the *"Family Jewels"* was damage control, to identify areas of possible embarrassment to the CIA, should they ever become public, such as, for example, the unsuccessful attempts by the CIA to assassinate Congolese President Patrice Lumumba.

However the ultimate effect was the opposite. The "Family Jewels", which are dated May 16, 1973, put together in one neat pile all of the secrets of the CIA from 1959 forward. This infuriated Secretary of State Henry Kissinger. At a meeting with President Ford on January 4, 1975 in the Oval Office, Kissinger said:

> *"What is happening is worse than the days of McCarthy. You will end up with a CIA that does only reporting, no operations. He has turned over to the FBI the whole of his operation .... Helms said all these stories are just the tip of the iceberg. If they all come out, blood will flow. For example, Robert Kennedy personally managed the operation on the assassination of Castro. .... The Chilean thing, that is not in any report -- that is sort of blackmail on*

me."

Kissinger wanted for Colby to be suspended, but realizing how that could backfire suggested that he be transferred to a less sensitive position. Colby was eventually replaced with future president George H. W. Bush. Colby later died in a mysterious "canoeing accident" at night. There was immediate speculation that he had been murdered, as why would Colby, a real-life "spook" who had twice parachuted behind enemy lines during World War II, go canoeing in the Potomac River in the middle of the night without the life-jacket that he usually wore? This incident seems to be the inspiration for a similar scene in the 2004 version of the movie "*The Manchurian Candidate*".

The last quotation above, regarding "*The Chilean Thing*", probably refers to September 1970 when President Nixon informed the CIA that an Allende regime in Chile would not be acceptable, and the CIA attempted to kidnap a top supporter of Allende. This is similar to what happened in the United States Chess Federation in 2006, when USCF President Bill Goichberg tried to prevent Sam Sloan from taking office after Sloan had been democratically elected. It could not refer to the actual overthrow of Allende on September 11, 1973, because that occurred a few months after the date of the "*Family Jewels*" reports.

Although the Family Jewels documents, which are 702 pages long, deal with a wide variety of CIA operations, more attention is paid to John Roselli than to anybody else. This is because the CIA had contracted with Roselli to kill Fidel Castro.

Roselli was the ideal man for the job because, prior to the takeover of Cuba by Castro, he had been the supervisor of Mafia operations in casinos in Havana. After Castro had thrown out the mob and closed the casinos, Roselli still had been running forays into Cuba, using high speed power boats to cross the 90 miles from Florida to Cuba without being detected. One time his boat was shot out from under him by the Cuban Navy, but another boat rescued Roselli and carried him to safety.

Jack Anderson wrote in his column in the *Washington Post* for January 18, 1971:

> "The full story reads like a script of a James Bond Movie, complete with secret trysts at glittering Miami Beach Hotels and midnight powerboat dashes to secret landing spots on the Cuban coast.
>
> "For the first try, the CIA furnished Roselli with special poison capsules to slip into Castro's food. The poison was supposed to take three days to act. By the time Castro died, his system would have thrown off all traces of the poison and it would seem like a natural death. .... A couple of weeks later, just about the time for the plot to have been carried out, a report out of Havana said that Castro was sick, but he recovered."

Too bad our CIA can just never get a job done right! The Gang that couldn't shoot straight! Things are much better now however. They did such a fine job of detecting Saddam Hussein's *"weapons of mass destruction"*.

An aside to this issue is to compare the *"Family Jewels"* documents, with the so-called *"Killian"* documents that brought down CBS News Reporter Dan Rather during the 2004 Presidential Election Campaign. Dan Rather produced six pages of memorandums from 1972 which stated that future president George W. Bush had failed to report as required for National Guard duty in September 1972. Rather claimed that the memos had come from an "unimpeachable source" and had been authenticated by "experts". These memos were intended to demonstrate that Bush was unfit to serve as President of the United States.

By comparing the Killian documents from 1972 side-by-side with the *"Family Jewels"* documents from 1973 one can easily see that the Killian documents are fake. The Killian documents were obviously made with a modern computer word processor using Times New Roman typestyle proportional spacing fonts that did not even exist in 1972. For example, the "th" in 187th could not have been made by any typewriter that existed in 1972. The *"Family Jewels"* were created with an old fashioned manual typewriter. The comparison is ridiculous, not to mention the fact that the *"Family Jewels"* were created by the Director of the CIA whereas the Killian documents were supposedly created by a local National Guard grunt. The networks have every justification for kicking out Dan Rather. Even today, Dan Rather claims the Killian documents are genuine, even though the person who gave him the documents has admitted that they are fake.

The Family Jewels contain numerous shocking revelations regarding John Roselli. The CIA had ex-FBI agent Robert Maheu contact Roselli and claim that he represented businessmen who had been kicked out of Cuba by Castro and who were willing to pay $150,000 to have Castro bumped off. Later, on September 25, 1960, Roselli met Maheu in Miami and introduced him to *"Sam Gold"* and *"Joe"*. Sam Gold was, of course, our own lovable Sam Giancana. *"Joe"* was Santo Trafficante, Jr., the mob boss in Miami who had operated several legal casinos in Cuba until he had been kicked out by Castro.

The Family Jewels, on page 13, state that weeks later Maheu saw pictures of Sam Giancana and Santo Trafficante, Jr. in *Parade* magazine and identified them as being the same persons as *"Sam Gold"* and *"Joe"*. Both men were on the Attorney General's *"Ten Most Wanted"* list. Our super-sleuths had scored again! However, they did not have Giancana and Trafficante arrested. Rather they gave them the poison pills that were supposed to kill Castro, but failed.

To their credit, John Roselli and *"Sam Gold"* told Maheu that they did not want the $150,000. They were probably surprised by the ridiculously small amount that was being offered to kill Castro. One wonders how long it took them to realize that they were not dealing with disaffected businessmen but with the CIA itself.

Since they had spent years in Cuba prior to the revolution and probably knew everybody likely to want to engage in such an operation, it seems likely that Roselli and Trafficante realized almost from the beginning that they were dealing not with disaffected businessmen but with the US Government.

Both John Roselli and Sam Giancana had personal reasons for wanting to do business with the CIA. Roselli was an illegal alien. His real name was Filippo Sacco and he had been born in Esperia, Italy in Frosinone Province. As he was in the US illegally, he wanted to have some leverage to avoid deportation. Later, when he was being prosecuted, Roselli told the CIA that if the prosecution was not dropped he would reveal to newspaper reporters the plot to kill Castro. Richard Helms, Director of the CIA, made a decision not to help Roselli. Roselli, by then in federal prison, carried out his threat and the plot to kill Castro became public knowledge through Jack Anderson columns in the Washington Post dated January 18, 1970 entitled *"6 Attempts to Kill Castro Laid to CIA"* and in the subsequent column dated February 23, 1971 entitled *"Castro Stalker worked for the CIA"*. All this is detailed in the *"Family Jewels"* documents. Santo Trafficante, Jr., John Roselli and Sam Giancana are all on almost everybody's list of persons suspected of involvement in the Kennedy Assassination.

Reading these documents enables one to see your tax dollars at work, especially on page 14 where the CIA bugged Dan Rowan's Las Vegas hotel room at the request of Sam Giancana to find out if Rowan was sleeping with Phyllis McGuire and if McGuire was cheating on Giancana. One would have thought that these Mafia wise guys had lots of women.

Here are some of the more interesting *"TOP SECRET"* documents:

UNCLASSIFIED ☐ INTERNAL USE ONLY ☐ CONFIDENTIAL ☐ SECRET ☒

ROUTING AND RECORD SHEET

SUBJECT: (Optional)

FROM: Howard J. Osborn
Director of Security

EXTENSION | NO.
DATE 16 May 1973

TO: (Officer designation, room number, and building)	DATE RECEIVED	FORWARDED	OFFICER'S INITIALS	COMMENTS (Number each comment to show from whom to whom. Draw a line across column after each comment.)
1. Executive Secretary, CIA Management Committee				~~EYES ONLY~~
2.				
3.				
4.				(b)(1) (b)(3) (b)(5) (b)(6)
5.				
6.				
7.				APPROVED FOR RELEASE DATE: JUN 2007
8.				
9.				
10.				
11.				00001
12.				
13.				
14.				
15.				~~EYES ONLY~~

610 USE PREVIOUS EDITIONS ☒ SECRET ☐ CONFIDENTIAL ☐ INTERNAL USE ONLY ☐ UNCLASSIFIED

SECRET

EYES ONLY

16 May 1973

MEMORANDUM FOR: Executive Secretary,
CIA Management Committee

SUBJECT   : "Family Jewels"

1.   The purpose of this memorandum is to
forward for your personal review summaries of activities
conducted either by or under the sponsorship of the
Office of Security in the past which in my opinion conflict with the provisions of the National Security Act
of 1947.

2.   These activities cover the period from
March 1959 to date and represent as accurate a record
as is available in our files. Those activities which
took place prior to the date of my appointment as
Director of Security on 1 July 1964 have been developed
to a certain extent through the recollection of the
senior people in this Office who were involved or who
had knowledge of the activities at the time they
occurred.

3.   I have gone back to March 1959 because I
believe that the activities occurring since that time
still have a viable "flap potential" in that many of the
people involved, both Agency and non-Agency are still
alive and through their knowledge of the activity represent a possible potential threat or embarrassment to the
Agency. I would be glad to provide clarification or an
explanation of any of these activities if desired. You
have my assurance that unless otherwise stated each of
these activities was approved by higher authority--the

00002

SECRET

EYES ONLY

Director of Central Intelligence, the Deputy Director
of Central Intelligence, the Executive Director-
Comptroller, or the Deputy Director for Support.

Howard J. Bosch
Director of Security

Attachments

00003

"FAMILY JEWELS"

1.

2. Johnny Roselli -- The use of a member of the
    Mafia in an attempt to assassinate Fidel Castro.

3. Project MOCKINGBIRD -- During the period from 12
    March 1963 to 15 June 1963, this Office
    installed telephone taps on two Washington-
    based newsmen who were suspected of disclosing
    classified information obtained from a variety
    of governmental and congressional sources.

4. Yuriy Ivanovich Nosenko -- A KGB defector who from
    the period 13 August 1965 to 27 October 1967
    was confined in a specially constructed "jail"
    at [   ] He was literally confined in a
    cell behind bars with nothing but a cot in it
    for this period.

5. Various Surveillance and Support Activities --
    These are briefly summarized and range from
    the surveillance of newsmen to the provision
    of specialized support of local police officials
    in the Metropolitan area. I believe that each
    one is self-explanatory and, therefore, no further
    comment is needed here.

6. Equipment Support to Local Police -- Attached is a
    list provided me by the Director of Logistics
    (he will simply report these items in his
    report) which we have provided local police in
    the Metropolitan D. C. area over the past four
    or five years on indefinite loan. During the
    period when the Agency's installations in this
    area appeared to be a target of dissident elements

SUBJECT: Johnny Roselli

1.   In August 1960, Mr. Richard M. Bissell
approached Colonel Sheffield Edwards to determine if
the Office of Security had assets that may assist in a
sensitive mission requiring gangster-type action.   The
mission target was Fidel Castro.

2.   Because of its extreme sensitivity, only a
small group was made privy to the project.   The DCI was
briefed and gave his approval.   Colonel J. C. King,
Chief, WH Division, was briefed, but all details were
deliberately concealed from any of the JMWAVE officials.
Certain TSD and Communications personnel participated
in the initial planning stages, but were not witting of
the purpose of the mission.

3.   Robert A. Maheu, a cleared source of the
Office of Security, was contacted, briefed generally on
the project, and requested to ascertain if he could
develop an entree into the gangster elements as the first
step toward accomplishing the desired goal.

4.   Mr. Maheu advised that he had met one Johnny
Roselli on several occasions while visiting Las Vegas.
He only knew him casually through clients, but was given
to understand that he was a high-ranking member of the
"syndicate" and controlled all of the ice-making machines
on the Strip.   Maheu reasoned that, if Roselli was in
fact a member of the clan, he undoubtedly had connections
leading into the Cuban gambling interests.

5.   Maheu was asked to approach Roselli, who knew
Maheu as a personal relations executive handling domestic
and foreign accounts, and tell him that he had recently
been retained by a client who represented several international business firms which were suffering heavy financial
losses in Cuba as a result of Castro's action.   They were
convinced that Castro's removal was the answer to their

00012

problem and were willing to pay a price of $150,000
for its successful accomplishment. It was to be made
clear to Roselli that the United States Government was
not, and should not, become aware of this operation.

6. The pitch was made to Roselli on 14
September 1960 at the Hilton Plaza Hotel, New York City.
Mr. James O'Connell, Office of Security, was present
during this meeting and was identified to Roselli as an
employee of Maheu. O'Connell actively served as Roselli's
contact until May 1962 at which time he phased out due
to an overseas assignment. His initial reaction was to
avoid getting involved, but through Maheu's persuasion,
he agreed to introduce him to a friend, Sam Gold, who
knew the "Cuban crowd." Roselli made it clear he did
not want any money for his part and believed Sam would
feel the same way. Neither of these individuals were
ever paid out of Agency funds.

7. During the week of 25 September, Maheu was
introduced to Sam who was staying at the Fontainebleau
Hotel, Miami Beach. It was several weeks after his
meeting with Sam and Joe, who was identified to him as
a courier operating between Havana and Miami, that he
saw photographs of both of these individuals in the
Sunday supplemental "Parade." They were identified as
Momo Salvatore Giancana and Santos Trafficant, respectively.
Both were on the list of the Attorney General's ten most-
wanted men. The former was described as the Chicago
chieftain of the Cosa Nostra and successor to Al Capone,
and the latter, the Cosa Nostra boss of Cuban operations.
Maheu called this office immediately upon ascertaining
this information.

8. In discussing the possible methods of
accomplishing this mission, Sam suggested that they not
resort to firearms but, if he could be furnished some
type of potent pill, that could be placed in Castro's food
or drink, it would be a much more effective operation.
Sam indicated that he had a prospective nominee in the
person of Juan Orta, a Cuban official who had been receiving
kick-back payments from the gambling interests, who still had
access to Castro, and was in a financial bind.

00013

2

9. TSD was requested to produce six pills of high lethal content.

10. Joe delivered the pills to Orta. After several weeks of reported attempts, Orta apparently got cold feet and asked out of the assignment. He suggested another candidate who made several attempts without success.

11. Joe then indicated that Dr. Anthony Verona, one of the principal officers in the Cuban Exile Junta, had become disaffected with the apparent ineffectual progress of the Junta and was willing to handle the mission through his own resources.

12. He asked, as a prerequisite to the deal, that he be given $10,000 for organizational expenses and requested $1,000 worth of communications equipment.

13. Dr. Verona's potential was never fully exploited, as the project was canceled shortly after the Bay of Pigs episode. Verona was advised that the offer was withdrawn, and the pills were retrieved.

14. Of significant interest was an incident which involved a request levied by Sam upon Maheu.

> At the height of the project negotiations, Sam expressed concern about his girlfriend, Phyllis McGuire, who he learned was getting much attention from Dan Rowan while both were booked at a Las Vegas night club. Sam asked Maheu to put a bug in Rowan's room to determine the extent of his intimacy with Miss McGuire. The technician involved in the assignment was discovered in the process, arrested, and taken to the Sheriff's office for questioning. He called Maheu and informed him that he had been detained by the police. This call was made in the presence of the Sheriff's personnel.

> Subsequently, the Department of Justice announced its intention to prosecute Maheu along

with the technician. On 7 February 1962, the Director of Security briefed the Attorney General, Robert Kennedy, on the circumstances leading up to Maheu's involvement in the wiretap. At our request, prosecution was dropped.

15. In May 1962, Mr. William Harvey took over as Case Officer, and it is not known by this office whether Roselli was used operationally from that point on.

16. It was subsequently learned from the FBI that Roselli had been convicted on six counts involving illegal entry into the United States. Our records do not reflect the date of conviction, but it is believed to have been sometime during November 1967.

17. On 2 December 1968, Roselli, along with four other individuals, was convicted of conspiracy to cheat members of the Friars Club of $400,000 in a rigged gin rummy game.

18. Mr. Harvey reported to the Office of Security of his contacts with Roselli during November and December 1967 and January 1968. It was his belief that Johnny would not seek out the Agency for assistance in the deportation proceedings unless he actually faced deportation. Roselli expressed confidence that he would win an appeal.

19. On 17 November 1970, Maheu called James O'Connell, Roselli's first Case Officer, to advise that Maheu's attorney, Ed Morgan, had received a call from a Thomas Waddin, Roselli's lawyer, who stated that all avenues of appeal had been exhausted, and his client now faces deportation. Waddin indicated that, if someone did not intercede on Roselli's behalf, he would make a complete expose of his activities with the Agency.

20. On 18 November 1970, Mr. Helms was briefed on the latest development in this case, and it was decided that the Agency would not in any way assist Roselli. Maheu was so advised of the Agency's position, and he was in

complete agreement with our stand. He further advised
that he was not concerned about any publicity as it
affected him personally should Roselli decide to tell
all.

21. Subsequently, Roselli or someone on his
behalf furnished Jack Anderson details of the operation.
Attached are two Anderson columns dealing with this
matter.

22. The last known residence of Roselli was the
Federal Penitentiary in Seattle, Washington.

Attachments

00016

PROJECT MOCKINGBIRD

Project Mockingbird, a telephone intercept activity, was conducted between 12 March 1963 and 15 June 1963, and targeted two Washington-based newsmen who, at the time, had been publishing news articles based on, and frequently quoting, classified materials of this Agency and others, including Top Secret and Special Intelligence.

Telephone intercept connections were installed at the newmen's office and at each of their homes, for a total of 3. The connections were established with the assistance of a telephone company official who responded to a personal request by the Director of Security, Col. Sheffield Edwards. Col. Edwards' authority for the activity was Mr. John A. McCone, Director of Central Intelligence. The latter conducted the activity in coordination with the Attorney General (Mr. Robert Kennedy), the Secretary of Defense (Mr. Robert McNamara), and the Director of the Defense Intelligence Agency (Gen. Joseph Carroll). In addition to Office of Security personnel directly involved in the intercepts and research of materials acquired therefrom, only 3 other Agency officials are on record as witting of the activity: the Deputy Director of Central Intelligence (General Marshall S. Carter), the Inspector General (Lyman Kirkpatrick) and the General Counsel. (Mr. Lawrence Houston).

The intercept activity was particularly productive in identifying contacts of the newsmen, their method of operation and many of their sources of information. For example, it was determined that during the period they received data from 13 newsmen, 12 of whom were identified; 12 senators and 6 members of Congress, all identified; 21 Congressional staff members, of whom 11 were identified; 16 government employees, including a staff member of the White House, members of the Vice President's office, an Assistant Attorney General, and other well-placed individuals. A number of other sources were partially or tentatively identified, but the short span of the activity precluded positive identification. It was observed that through these contacts the newsmen actually received more classified and official data than they could use, and passed some of the stories to other newsmen for release, establishing that many "leaks" appearing under other by-lines were actually from the sources of the target newsmen.

Since the termination of Project Mockingbird, those materials related to it which were retained, have been maintained under strict security access of two Office of Security professionals.

00021

the periods 6-9 October, 27 October-10 December 1971
and on 3 January 1972. In addition to physical surveillance, an observation post was maintained in the
Statler Hilton Hotel where observation could be maintained of the building housing his office. The surveillance was designed to determine Getler's sources
of classified information of interest to the Agency
which had appeared in a number of his columns.

D. CELOTEX II

At the direction of the DCI, surveillance was conducted of Jack Anderson and at various times his "leg
men," Britt Hume, Leslie Whitten, and Joseph Spear,
from 15 February to 12 April 1972. In addition to the
physical surveillance, an observation post was maintained in the Statler Hilton Hotel directly opposite
Anderson's office. The purpose of this surveillance
was to attempt to determine Anderson's sources for
highly classified Agency information appearing in his
syndicated columns.

E. BUTANE

At the direction of the DCI, a surveillance was
conducted on Victor L. Marchetti from 23 March to
20 April 1972. The purpose of this surveillance was
to determine his activities and contacts both with
Agency employees and other individuals in regard to
his proposed book and published magazine articles exposing Agency operations.

II. POLICE SUPPORT

A. During 1969, 1970, and 1971, on several occasions,
the Intelligence Division of the Metropolitan Police
Department was provided a communications system to
monitor major anti-Vietnam war demonstrations in the
Washington area. This system consisted of a radio
receiver and an Agent at the Intelligence Division
Headquarters and several automobiles from the Washington
Field Office equipped with radio receivers and trans-
mitters and manned by two WFO Agents, as well as a
representative of the Intelligence Division, Metropolitan
Police Department. The benefit to the Agency was, that
the communications over this system were monitored at
the Headquarters Building to provide instant notice of
possible actions by the dissidents against Agency in-
stallations.

00027

SEC../
V/

15 FEB 1972

MEMORANDUM FOR: Executive Director-Comptroller

SUBJECT   : ROSELLI, John

1. This memorandum is for your information only.

2. Reference is made to our recent conversation regarding the Agency's participation in political assassinations. Attached hereto is a memorandum dated 19 November 1970 which was furnished to Mr. Helms setting forth the circumstances of the Subject's activities on behalf of the Agency. Initially Roselli was unwitting of Government interest, but as time went on, he suspected that the U. S. Government was involved and specifically the CIA.

3. Roselli is presently serving a prison sentence for conspiracy in a Federal penitentiary in Seattle, Washington and awaits deportation upon completion of his current sentence.

4. This Agency was aware that Roselli intended to expose his participation in the plot should we not intervene on his behalf. The DCI decided to ignore his threats and take a calculated risk as to the consequences that may occur with the disclosure of his story. This was subsequently done by Roselli or someone on his behalf furnishing Jack Anderson details of the incident. Attached hereto are two of Anderson's articles dealing with Roselli. Anderson is also Editor of the Washington Bureau of the Washington Post, Sunday supplemental "Parade."

5. Individuals who were aware of this project were: Messrs. Dulles, Bissell, Colonel J. C. King, Colonel Sheffield Edwards,

SECRET
EYES ONLY

00041

William Harvey, and James P. O'Connell. Also included were
Robert A. Maheu and his attorneys Edward P. Morgan and Edward
Bennett Williams.

    6. On 26 February 1971 arrangements were made with
Immigration and Naturalization Service Commissioner Raymond
Farrell to flag any action that may be taken by his organization
regarding deportation proceedings against Roselli. On 26 January
1972 James F. Green, Associate Commissioner for I&NS, advised
that they were deferring any deportation action for another year
and would again call it to our attention upon expiration of the
deferral.

                            Howard J. Osborn
                            Director of Security

Atts

MEMORANDUM FOR: Director of Central Intelligence

SUBJECT : ROSELLI, Johnny

1. This memorandum is for information only.

2. In August 1960, Mr. Richard M. Bissell approached Colonel Sheffield Edwards to determine if the Office of Security had assets that may assist in a sensitive mission requiring gangster-type action. The mission target was Fidel Castro.

3. Because of its extreme sensitivity, only a small group was made privy to the project. The DCI was briefed and gave his approval. Colonel J. C. King, Chief, WH Division, was briefed, but all details were deliberately concealed from any of the JMWAVE officials. Certain TSD and Commo personnel participated in the initial planning stages, but were not witting of the purpose of the mission.

4. Robert A. Maheu was contacted, briefed generally on the project, and requested to ascertain if he could develop an entree into the gangster elements as the first step toward accomplishing the desired goal.

5. Mr. Maheu advised that he had met one Johnny Roselli on several occasions while visiting Las Vegas. He only knew him casually through clients, but was given to understand that he was a high-ranking member of the "syndicate" and controlled all of the ice-making machines on the Strip. Maheu reasoned that, if Roselli was in fact a member of the clan, he undoubtedly had connections leading into the Cuban gambling interests.

00044

6. Maheu was asked to approach Roselli, who knew Maheu as a personal relations executive handling domestic and foreign accounts, and tell him that he had recently been retained by a client who represented several international business firms which were suffering heavy financial losses in Cuba as a result of Castro's action. They were convinced that Castro's removal was the answer to their problem and were willing to pay a price of $150,000 for its successful accomplishment. It was to be made clear to Roselli that the U. S. Government was not, and should not, become aware of this operation.

7. The pitch was made to Roselli on 14 September 1960 at the Hilton Plaza Hotel, New York City. His initial reaction was to avoid getting involved but, through Maheu's persuasion, he agreed to introduce him to a friend, Sam Gold, who knew the "Cuban crowd." Roselli made it clear he did not want any money for his part and believed Sam would feel the same way. Neither of these individuals was ever paid out of Agency funds.

8. During the week of 25 September, Maheu was introduced to Sam who was staying at the Fontainebleau Hotel, Miami Beach. It was several weeks after his meeting with Sam and Joe, who was identified to him as a courier operating between Havana and Miami, that he saw photographs of both of these individuals in the Sunday supplemental "Parade." They were identified as Momo Salvatore Giancana and Santos Trafficant, respectively. Both were on the list of the Attorney General's ten most-wanted men. The former was described as the Chicago chieftain of the Cosa Nostra and successor to Al Capone, and the latter, the Cosa Nostra boss of Cuban operations. Maheu called this office immediately upon ascertaining this information.

9. In discussing the possible methods of accomplishing this mission, Sam suggested that they not resort to firearms but, if he could be furnished some type of potent pill, that could be placed in Castro's food or drink, it would be a much more effective operation. Sam indicated that he had a prospective nominee in the person of Juan Orta, a Cuban official who had been receiving kickback payments from the gambling interests, who still had access to Castro, and was in a financial bind.

2

10. TSD was requested to produce six pills of high lethal content.

11. Joe delivered the pills to Orta. After several weeks of reported attempts, Orta apparently got cold feet and asked out of the assignment. He suggested another candidate who made several attempts without success.

12. Joe then indicated that Dr. Anthony Verona, one of the principal officers in the Cuban Exile Junta, had become disaffected with the apparent ineffectual progress of the Junta and was willing to handle the mission through his own resources.

13. He asked, as a prerequisite to the deal, that he be given $10,000 for organizational expenses and requested $1,000 worth of communications equipment.

14. Dr. Verona's potential was never fully exploited, as the project was canceled shortly after the Bay of Pigs episode. Verona was advised that the offer was withdrawn, and the pills were retrieved.

15. Of significant interest was an incident which involved a request levied by Sam upon Maheu.

At the height of the project negotiations, Sam expressed concern about his girlfriend, Phyllis McGuire, who he learned was getting much attention from Dan Rowan while both were booked at a Las Vegas night club. Sam asked Maheu to put a bug in Rowan's room to determine the extent of his intimacy with Miss McGuire. The technician involved in the assignment was discovered in the process, arrested, and taken to the Sheriff's office for questioning. He called Maheu and informed him that he had been detained by the police. This call was made in the presence of the Sheriff's personnel.

Subsequently, the Department of Justice announced its intention to prosecute Maheu along with the technician. On 7 February 1962, the Director of

3

Security briefed the Attorney General, Robert
Kennedy, on the circumstances leading up to
Maheu's involvement in the wiretap. At our re-
quest, prosecution was dropped.

16. In May 1962, Mr. William Harvey took over as Case
Officer, and it is not known by this Office whether Roselli was
used operationally from that point on.

17. It was subsequently learned from the FBI that Roselli
had been convicted on six counts involving illegal entry into the
United States. Our records do not reflect the date of conviction,
but it is believed to have been sometime during November 1967.

18. On 2 December 1968, Roselli, along with four other
individuals, was convicted of conspiracy to cheat members of the
Friars Club of $400,000 in a rigged gin gummy game.

19. Mr. Harvey reported to the Office of Security of his
contacts with Roselli during November and December 1967 and
January 1968. It was his belief that Johnny would not seek out
the Agency for assistance in the deportation proceedings unless
he actually faced deportation. Roselli expressed confidence that
he would win an appeal.

20. On 17 November 1970, Maheu called James O'Connell,
Roselli's first Case Officer, to advise that Maheu's attorney, Ed
Morgan, had received a call from a Thomas Waddin, Roselli's
lawyer, who stated that all avenues of appeal had been exhausted,
and his client now faces deportation. Waddin indicated that, if
someone did not intercede on Roselli's behalf, he would make
a complete expose of his activities with the Agency.

21. On 18 November 1970, you were briefed on the latest
development in this case, and it was decided that the Agency
would not in any way assist Roselli. Maheu was so advised of
the Agency's position, and he was in complete agreement with
our stand. He further advised that he was not concerned about

4

any publicity as it affected him personally should Roselli decide to tell all. He stated he would advise us promptly of any developments that he may become aware of in this matter.

Howard J. Osborn
Director of Security

<u>Retirement Information - E. Howard Hunt</u>

1. Date of retirement: 30 April 1970

2. System: CIA Retirement and Disability System

3. Grade and salary at time of retirement: GS-15, Step 8 - $28,226

4. Creditable civilian service used in computing annuity:

    17 May 1948 to 8 June 1948   - Economic Cooperation Administration

    9 June 1948 to 19 February 1949   - State (ECA)

    8 November 1949 to 30 April 1970 - CIA

5. Annuity:

    At retirement - $1,020 per month

    At present   - $1,181 per month (which includes cost-of-living
                                       increases since date of retirement)

6. At the time of retirement Mr. Hunt did not elect survivorship benefits.
This meant that upon his death, his wife would not draw a survivorship
annuity. By letter of 5 April 1971 he raised the question of changing
his election but was informed by the General Counsel on 6 May 1971 that
this could not be done. By letter dated 5 May 1972 Mr. Hunt asked Mr.
Houston to raise with the Director the possibility of being recalled to
duty for a short period of time, after which he could retire again and
elect survivorship benefits. By letter of 16 May 1972 Mr. Houston advised
Mr. Hunt that to call him back to duty solely for the purpose of permitting
him to change survivorship benefits would be in violation of the spirit of
the CIA Retirement Act.

00170

TOP SECRET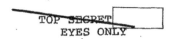
EYES ONLY

7 May 1973

MEMORANDUM FOR: Director of Central Intelligence

VIA   : Deputy Director for Intelligence

FROM   : Director of Current Intelligence

SUBJECT   : Activity Related to Domestic Events

1. In late 1967 OCI participated in the preparation of several short intelligence memoranda dealing with the foreign connections of US organizations and activists involved in the anti-war movement. The main purpose of these reports, prepared at the request of the White House, was to determine whether any links existed between international Communist elements or foreign governments and the American peace movement. The conclusion reached was that there was some evidence of ad hoc contacts between anti-war activists at home and abroad but no evidence of direction or formal coordination.

2. In October 1967 President Johnson expressed interest in this subject and ordered a high level interdepartmental survey. In response to his personal request to the DCI, Mr. Helms asked the CI Staff to collect whatever information was available through our own sources and through liaison with the FBI and to pass it to OCI, which was directed to prepare a memorandum from the DCI to the President.

3. A book message requirement was sent to all stations to report whatever information was on hand relevant to this subject. Although agent reports on Communist front operations overseas were of some value, the primary source of information on the activities of US activists—and that was quite limited—was sensitive intercepts produced by NSA, which had been similarly tasked by the White House.

TOP SECRET
EYES ONLY

MEMORANDUM

THE WHITE HOUSE

WASHINGTON

SECRET/NODIS/XGDS

MEMORANDUM OF CONVERSATION

PARTICIPANTS: President Gerald R. Ford
Dr. Henry A. Kissinger, Secretary of State
   and Assistant to the President
   for National Security Affairs
Lt. General Brent Scowcroft, Deputy Assistant
   to the President for National Security Affairs

DATE AND TIME: Saturday, January 4, 1975
9:40 a.m. - 12:20 p.m.

PLACE: The Oval Office
The White House

Kissinger: What is happening is worse than in the days of McCarthy.
You will end up with a CIA that does only reporting, and not operations.
He has turned over to the FBI the whole of his operation. He has offered
to resign and I refused. It is not my prerogative, but I said not until you
are proved guilty of criminal conduct.

The President: I agree.

Kissinger: Helms said all these stories are just the tip of the iceberg.
If they come out, blood will flow. For example, Robert Kennedy personally managed the operation on the assassination of Castro.

[He described some of the other stories.]

I told him Buchen would warn him and he won't say anything incriminating.

The President: I know Dick Helms and think very highly of him.

Kissinger: The Chilean thing -- that is not in any report. That is sort
of blackmail on me.

SECRET/NODIS/XGDS

CLASSIFIED BY Henry A. Kissinger
EXEMPT FROM GENERAL DECLASSIFICATION
SCHEDULE OF EXECUTIVE ORDER 11652
EXEMPTION CATEGORY 5(b) (1, 3)
AUTOMATICALLY DECLASSIFIED ON Imp. to det.

RELEASED PER P.L. 102-526 (JFK ACT)
NARA
DATE 2/29/99
(JFK NR) 108-886

JFK ARRB
KUS/SCOW 178100410294

The President: What can we do? We can get Griswold, Lemnitzer, Friend-ly, Reagan, Jack Connor, Shannon, Dillon.

Kissinger: You might think of Rusk. This will get very rough and you need people around who know the Presidency, and the national interest. What Colby has done is a disgrace.

The President: Should we suspend him?

Kissinger: No, but after the investigation is over you could move him and put   in someone of towering integrity.

When the FBI has a hunting license into the CIA, this could end up worse for the country than Watergate.

The President: Would Rusk have known any of this stuff?

Kissinger: Why don't you ask him?

[Discussed the Moorer spying incident and what he did to protect the institution of the JCS.]

[Rumsfeld enters to talk about Rusk.]

Kissinger: [Discusses some of the legislative restrictions.]

The President: [Talks to Rusk.]

[Tries to call Dave Packard.]

[Buchen and Marsh come in.]

[The Blue Ribbon announcement is reviewed.]

RELEASED PER P.L. 102-526 (JFK ACT)
DATE 01/29/99
NARA

111th Fighter Interceptor Squadron
P. O. Box 34567
Houston, Texas 77034

01 August 1972

MEMORANDUM FOR RECORD

SUBJECT: Bush, George W. lst Lt.3244754FG
Suspension of Flight status

1. On this date I ordered that lst Lt. Bush be suspended from flight status due to failure to perform to USAF/TexANG standards and failure to meet annual physical examination (flight) as ordered.

2. I conveyed my verbal orders to commander, 147 th Ftr Intrcp Gp with request for orders for suspension and convening of a flight review board IAW AFM 35-13.

3. I recommended transfer of this officer to the 9921 st Air Reserve Squadron in May and forwarded his AF Form 1288 to 147 th Ftr Intrcp Gp headquarters. The transfer was not allowed. Officer has made no attempt to meet his training certification or flight physical. Officer expresses desire to transfer out of state including assignment to non-flying billets.

4. On recommendation of Harris, I also suggested that we fill this critical billet with a more seasoned pilot from the list of qualified Vietnam pilots that have rotated. Recommendations were received but not confirmed.

JERRY B. KILLIAN
Lt. Colonel

This is one page from the notorious Killian documents and is not part of the "Family Jewels". It is presented here for purposes of comparison. The Killian documents were presented by Dan Rather on September 8, 2004 on the CBS News Show "60 Minutes". They purported to show that Lt. George W. Bush had failed to report for a physical examination and had been suspended from flying. The purpose of this presentation was to bring about the defeat of George W. Bush in his re-election campaign for US President.

However, the Killian documents were obvious forgeries, because they had been composed on a modern computer using Microsoft Word and Times New Roman proportional spacing fonts. Times New Roman fonts had not yet been invented in 1972. The result was a backfire. The fact that opponents of Bush tried to use forged documents to bring about his election defeat contributed to his election victory.

Judith Exner filed suit against the FBI for the release of their files concerning her. The following is an excerpt from the judge's oral ruling on her case:

IN THE UNITED STATES DISTRICT COURT
SOUTHERN DISTRICT OF CALIFORNIA

HONORABLE EDWARD J. SCHWARTZ, JUDGE PRESIDING

JUDITH KATHERINE EXNER, Plaintiff, -vs- FEDERAL BUREAU OF INVES- TIGATION, et al., Defendants.	No. 76-0089 S HEARING MOTION TO STAY PENDING APPEAL

Now, I think I should say that I have no particular concern with Mrs. Exner as a person or what her motives may be. Evidently, it is alleged that she is going to write a book or is in the course of writing a book. She may have other motives. She has alleged that there is some fear of danger to her life because of the statements that have been leaked in the press coverage of possible underworld connections.

She's also stated that she would like to know what's in the file: so that she can set the record straight, so to speak, if the file contains erroneous information. Again, I think that the Court should take into consideration the fact that, for whatever reason or whatever motives, Mrs. Exner kept the information that is now the hub of this controversy to herself for a period of perhaps 15 or 16 years, that she didn't write any books, she didn't publish any of this information, and then she was subpoenaed before a Senate Committee and required to testify.

I'm sure she was informed that the proceedings were secret, and then she found that the proceedings, at least insofar as they pertained to her, had been leaked obviously—and I can't imagine any other way than through some Government source.

Then, when the stories began to hit the press and Mrs. Exner was made the subject of a great deal of notoriety and publicity, she then brought this action to see if she could have a look at the information and materials that are filed.

PROLOGUE

The media attack on Judith Campbell Exner has been one of the most disgraceful performances on record. I can't recall a more vicious onslaught, a more hysterical outpouring of poisoned pen polemic—disguised as hard news wherever possible—all of it slanted to denigrate and assign the blame for untold crimes and misdemeanors in high and low places on the shoulders of one defenseless woman. In Watergate, at least, the shotgun attack was democratic in assessing guilt on a whole gang of felons.

The wrath of a righteous press is a sight to behold. Not one tempered word to be found anywhere. Legends are not easily surrendered. The press will fight to preserve its manufactured illusions, its Camelots and Good Ships Lollipop, and God help anyone who inadvertently threatens them.

Imagine my state of mind when I was invited to meet this pariah, this instant "mob moll" or "tramp" or "party girl" or "hooker"—pick your own epithet, and whatever it is, rest assured it has been reported somewhere as fact. I went to San Diego to have dinner with Dan and Katherine Exner, the name she is now using. She was christened Judith Eileen Katherine Immoor; the Campbell comes from her former marriage to movie actor William Campbell.

Actually, the first time I heard the name Judith Campbell Exner was during a television interview on a morning talk show in Nashville. I was doing the author's bicycle trick: a five-week, twenty-one-city publicity tour to promote my latest book, a biography of J. Edgar Hoover entitled THE DIRECTOR. I was at the tail end of the tour and thoroughly exhausted. I was not paying too close attention to current news. I had been jumping on airplanes and out of cabs, rushing to late evening radio and early morning television shows, and was beginning to think that the whole world was concentrating exclusively on my book.

The morning of this particular show in Nashville, I had not read the story concerning the Exners' press conference in San Diego. My host was one of those intrepid quizzers who loves to impress the home folk with his clever repartee. Always, of course, at the expense of his guests, be they local bumpkins or Nobel laureates.

"I'm going to put you on the spot," he said, "and I want a straight answer." He paused to wink at the camera, a signal to his fans that I was in for it. "Why did your publisher delete the Judith Campbell Exner material from your book?" He waggled an accusing finger at me. "Now, don't deny it. I know all about the publishing game." He was smiling but the glint in his eyes was that of a fox hotfooting it into a henhouse. "Boy, you guys are something else," he said to the camera, shaking his head in great bewilderment. "You don't mind dirtying Nixon, but when it comes to Kennedy, well, that's a whole other ball game."

As it turned out, his scenario of the Exner "expose" was a garbled version of a distorted news service report, and it went something like this: J. Edgar Hoover had blackmailed President Kennedy with information gained from wiretaps that linked Kennedy with a girlfriend of Sam Giancana and John Roselli, two Mafia bosses the CIA had hired to murder Fidel Castro. This liaison with Exner had put them all in bed together, along with Frank Sinatra, who had arranged the introduction, at Giancana's urging, when Kennedy had visited Las Vegas during his 1960 presidential campaign. In other words, the mob had a plant in the White House, a very neat little package that Hoover had exploited to maintain himself in office.

4

Fascinating. But where had the press gleaned this hot stuff? The answer is easy: from the Senate Committee on Intelligence Operations, chaired by Frank Church, who had done his damnedest to keep the lid on Camelot. The committee's eleven senators had voted unanimously not to reveal the name or even gender of Judith Campbell, as she was known during the years in question. However, the section in the report alluding to her was a little too intriguing to go unnoticed by the press.

A verbatim excerpt, complete with the Committee's footnotes, follows:

As elaborated in the previous sections of this report, all living CIA officials who were involved in the underworld assassination attempt or who were in a position to have known of the attempt have testified that they never discussed the assassination plot with the President. By May 1961, however, the Attorney General and Hoover were aware that the CIA had earlier used Giancana in an operation against Cuba and FBI files contained two memoranda which, if simultaneously reviewed, would have led one to conclude that the CIA operation had involved assassination.[1] There is no evidence that anyone within the FBI concluded that the CIA had used Giancana in an assassination attempt. The Committee has uncovered a chain of events, however, which would have given Hoover an opportunity to have assembled the entire picture and to have reported the information to the President.

Evidence before the Committee indicates that a close friend of President Kennedy had frequent contact with the President from the end of 1960 through mid-1962. FBI reports and testimony indicate that the President's friend

1. The two memoranda, which are discussed in considerable detail *supra*, were the October 18, 1960, memorandum linking Giancana to an assassination plot (but not mentioning CIA) and the May 22, 1961, memorandum linking Giancana to a CIA operation against Cuba involving "dirty business" (but not mentioning assassination).

5

was also a close friend of John Roselli and Sam Giancana and saw them often during this same period.[2]

On February 27, 1962, Hoover sent identical copies of a memorandum to the Attorney General and Kenneth O'Donnell, Special Assistant to the President. The memorandum stated that information developed in connection with a concentrated FBI investigation of John Roselli revealed that Roselli had been in contact with the President's friend. The memorandum also reported that the individual was maintaining an association with Sam Giancana, described as "a prominent Chicago underworld figure." Hoover's memorandum also stated that a review of the telephone toll calls from the President's friend's residence revealed calls to the White House. The President's secretary ultimately received a copy of the memorandum and said she believed she would have shown it to the President.

The association of the President's friend with the "hoodlums" and the person's connection with the President was again brought to Hoover's attention in a memorandum preparing him for a meeting with the President planned for March 22, 1962. Courtney Evans testified that Hoover generally required a detailed summary of information in the FBI files for drafting important memoranda or preparing for significant meetings. (Evans, 8/28/75, pp. 70, 72). The FBI files on Giancana then contained information disclosing Giancana's connection with the CIA as well as his involvement in assassination plotting (Memoranda of 10/18/60 and 5/22/61).

On March 22, Hoover had a private luncheon with President Kennedy. There is no record of what transpired at that luncheon. According to the White House logs, the

2. White House telephone logs show 70 instances of phone contact between the White House and the President's friend whose testimony confirms frequent phone contact with the President himself.
Both the President's friend and Roselli testified that the friend did not know about either the assassination operation or the wiretap case. Giancana was killed before he was available for questioning.

6

last telephone contact between the White House and the President's friend occurred a few hours after the luncheon.

The fact that the President and Hoover had a luncheon at which one topic was presumably that the President's friend was also a friend of Giancana and Roselli raises several possibilities. The first is, assuming that Hoover did in fact receive a summary of FBI information relating to Giancana prior to his luncheon with the President, whether that summary reminded the Director that Giancana had been involved in a CIA operation against Cuba that included "dirty business" and further indicated that Giancana had talked about an assassination attempt against Castro. A second is whether Hoover would then have taken the luncheon as an opportunity to fulfill his duty to bring this information to the President's attention.[1] What actually transpired at that luncheon may never be known, as both participants are dead and the FBI files contain no records relating to it.

On November 16, 1975, four days before the committee released its report, the Washington *Post*, after some heavy agonizing in editorial aeries, decided it had no choice but to identify Judy as the President's "close friend." The story, under the headline: "Probers Doubt Kennedy Knew of Poison Plot Against Castro," appeared on Page 6A. The thrust of the article was directed at what it termed "a bizarre White House episode"—to wit, the relationship between President Kennedy and a woman involved with two Mafia figures, who in turn were involved with the CIA in plots to assassinate Castro. As a result of its prosaic headline and innocuous position, the story slipped by relatively unnoticed.

1. The President, thus notified, might then have inquired further of the CIA. The Presidential calendar indicates that the President had meetings at which most CIA officials witting [sic] of the assassination plot were present during the period from February 27 through April 2, 1962. All of those persons, however, have testified that the President never asked them about the assassination plot.

Having performed its journalistic duty, the *Post,* the fearless vanguard in exposing Watergate, did not further pursue the story.

Others, of course, picked up the cudgel, but the story was a sleeper for nearly a month before it exploded into banner headlines around the world. Like Watergate, its genesis was in leaked documents.

Since that morning in Nashville, the story has gone from bad to godawful. Some of the stories were so outrageous that they would be comical if not so tragic. Being the co-author of this book has been an enlightening experience. It has given me a whole new perspective on the press, one which is not pretty to behold. However, the purpose of this book is not to take issue with the press, but rather to set the record straight, to tell it as it truly happened with Judith Campbell, and not as imagined by those who delight in speculating on the aberrations of the high and mighty. There is no question in my mind that this book would not have been written if the press had given her a fair shake. It is a safe enough assumption, considering that she lived with this knowledge for sixteen years.

It was a pleasant surprise to meet the Exners. They are just about complete opposites from the image presented in the press. She is not ''a rather ordinary woman,'' as Robert Sam Anson described her in *New Times,* but a very beautiful woman, with luxurious raven hair that is always immaculately groomed. She has classic features, with soft blue eyes and a warm, disarming smile. It is easy to see why she attracted the attention of men who had unlimited access to female pulchritude. In those days, she must have been a stunning beauty. Even more important, she is a lady with impeccable taste. She is thoughtful, gentle, well-mannered, intelligent, and properly reserved.

Contrary to reports that he is short and slight, Daniel R. Exner is six feet and weighs one hundred eighty. The press has made great sport of the fact that he is younger than his wife, but Dan is twenty-nine, going on forty-nine. He has crammed in more experiences during those few years than most people do in a lifetime.

8

Their preoccupation during dinner was that the book be written in good taste. Judith told me she wanted to tell the full story, the whole truth, but without pandering to prurient appetites. I couldn't have agreed more. Later in the evening, over coffee and brandy, I asked them directly why they had decided to write a book. The answer convinced me that their interest involved far more than money.

"When all of this started after her appearance before the Church committee, we had three choices," Dan said. "We could allow it to continue and just suffer with it. We could run and hide. Or we could stay and fight. She was not emotionally, or physically, in any kind of shape to allow it to continue. You can, in fact, run and hide. You can, in fact, disappear. But it has a tremendous price to it. So you come down to staying and fighting. There is no way this is going to continue without our doing a super effort to fight back. I don't care which side is after her, who it is, she can't take it."

Dan placed his hand gently over hers and she nodded in agreement. The expression in her eyes was of pain, not anger, when she spoke: "When the phone call came from my sister that an investigator for the Church committee was at her house, and she was hysterical on the phone because he had threatened to physically drag her to Washington unless she revealed our whereabouts, my remark to Dan was: 'My God, I knew it was going to happen. I knew it was going to come back.' That's just the feeling I had inside. It was like, merciful God, is it ever going to end? And Dan took over. I was at a point where I couldn't function. I don't know what I would have done if I had been alone. I only know that I had reached the end. There wasn't any way I could go through it again. And that was partially because of what had happened before, and partially because of the death of my mother and father, and what I had experienced through that. I knew I was at a point in my life where I could not take up where I had left off. To just have it happen again. And Dan just took over. From his attitude, slowly but surely, I got strength within me. If they shot him, if they took him away from me, I want to tell you, I couldn't continue."

"I talked to my father, who is a physician," Dan said, his hand still covering hers. "He was in the midst of this as it was happening. And emotionally and physically, he said, most candidly, she couldn't do that. She was just about to fall down."

"I'll tell you," Judith said, "sometimes I really think someone is watching over me because within the period of time all this was happening, the sequence of events, and Dan being the kind of person he is, a fighter—just don't push him in a corner because he's going to fight—I just thank God that he and I found each other. That we became what we are to each other. Without him I was absolutely lost. If you agree to write this book, you will get to a point in my story where I gave up. The fact that I was saved, the hospital records will show, is pure accident. It was all due to this—"

She paused and Dan put his arms around her. "Take a deep breath," she said, "I'm okay. While I was carrying my baby—God—" she stopped and turned to Dan, unable to continue.

"While she was carrying her child," Dan said, not taking his eyes from hers, "among all the other things that were happening, the Federal Bureau of Investigation just about put her away. They hounded her, they watched her, they trailed her, they tapped her phone, they bugged her home, they accosted her on the street, they broke into her home, they went to her friends, they went to her parents, without any regard for her, without any regard for her life, for her child's life. And because of that, she tried to kill herself. When she realized that killing herself wasn't the answer, and that her child was going to be born, and that he had nothing to look forward to other than what was being done to her, for his benefit, and his benefit only, she gave him up."

"After a year," she barely whispered, tears running freely down her cheeks.

"It was a long, long hard walk," Dan said. "And it isn't going to happen twice."

"It took a year for me to give him up."

"She could offer him nothing but what was being done to her."

10

"My brother wanted him, my sister wanted him, but I knew that he could not be near me and not know that I was his mother." She shook her head and closed her eyes. "Sometimes I wish I was stronger. I know I did the right thing for him. My brother Freddie in Tahoe had him for a period of time—you know, this was when he was a tiny, tiny baby. In fact, he was born at seven months. I almost didn't have him. He was in an incubator for many, many weeks. Freddie wanted to adopt him. He had him baptized. My baby had pneumonia while he was up there, and had the last sacraments while he was up there. They were never going to talk to me again because I would not sign the adoption papers. I knew there wasn't a way in the world I could have anyone in my family—my mother and father said, 'keep your child, we'll bring him up'—but the thing that was hounding at me was that this child deserved a mother and father, he deserved to be out of this mess. There was no way he could survive as my son. If he had a mother and father, at least he has a fair chance. If something happened to him then, at least I gave him a chance. The other way, there was so much stacked against him that there wasn't any way he could make it. He had to be so strong to start with, had to have so many built-in resentments that he would grow up with, there was no way he could survive unscarred. It wasn't fair. For his own safety, I could never tell him who his father was. And I would never tell him."

Later that evening, after she had composed herself, we again went into the reasons for writing a book.

"It isn't just the lies of Evelyn Lincoln and Dave Powers and Kenny O'Donnell, and others," she said, "or the leak from the committee. Or that night when I watched the news after my press conference and realized that no one was going to report it fairly. They sensationalized it, and it's been going downhill ever since."

"These things play a large part in our deciding to write a book," Dan said, "but the most important thing is that she just can't sit back and take any more of it. It's time to say halt. Stop, no more. It's time to stand up and fight back the best way we know how. With a book, surely, and with lawsuits wherever necessary. We've been sitting here like clay pigeons for too long. From this time forward, the enemy will be engaged at every turn. If it takes every penny we own, if it takes every ounce of our strength, if it takes our very lives, so be it.

"It's starting up all over again, just like it was before," Judith said. "We have again been followed, as I was followed constantly in the past. You never feel safe. You never know who is following you. That's it, no more. I'm putting my story down. It's going to be published, the whole story. I don't know whether someone's afraid of what I'm going to say. I just don't know why they are still after me.

"*They* could mean anybody. I didn't know anything about the CIA in those days. It's obvious to me now why they did what they did. It wasn't anything that I was doing wrong. Our own damn government was doing something wrong. They were the ones working with the hoodlums. They were the ones with the close association with them, the government. But I was paying the price for it. And I'm not going to pay it anymore without fighting back.

"As I said, the harassment from the FBI was horrendous. There probably was a tremendous conflict at the time. The CIA was protecting Sam and Johnny, the FBI was trying to get them, the White House was scared to death that the FBI might get them—after the White House found out, or even if they knew all along what was going on. I was caught right in the middle of it. The CIA was afraid because I was going to the White House, and because I did know Sam and Johnny. They wanted to know, I guess, what I was doing every time I went to the powder room. I think they all spend their lives looking over their own shoulders. I doubt if they could even trust their own mothers. So it was my association with those two people, and what the CIA connection was with them—I wasn't the one who was paranoid. I think they were. They had to know where I was, what I was doing, what I was saying, who I was seeing, and I can't live through that anymore. I almost didn't live through it then.

"It's hard to describe the feeling I get whenever the FBI stops me on the street. It is usually in a parking lot, and two

12

of them come at me from opposite directions. They call, 'Judy' and hold out their identification. They say, 'We'd like to talk to you,' and I just—I have finally reached a point where I don't even acknowledge them. I just turn around and get in my car and drive off. Just like they are not even there. They say, 'Wait, we'd like to ask you a couple of questions,' and I act like nothing is there. No one is talking.

"I act indifferent but my heart starts to go, and I really get weak-kneed. It's part anger, and part fear, too. And frustration. The feeling is how am I ever going to get it to end? When is it going to end? How will it end? What will eventually happen? I feel I have no control over the situation. That there is just nothing I can do about it. I am at their mercy.

"Of course, the surveillance has slowed down in recent years and for a while I even thought I was free of them. But now, in a sense, it's worse than it was. I'm being called every name in the book. Maybe if I was a different kind of person, if I'd had a different kind of mother and father, I'd be able to shrug my shoulders at some of the things that are being said about me. I can't. That kind of thing is too important to me. The relationships I've had, whether it be Sam, or Jack, are too important to me, there's too much respect wound up in them. It was not just a matter of two people meeting and going to bed together. It was not a fling. But that's the light it's being put in. That isn't me. I didn't live that way. I'm no angel. I didn't have a great many affairs, but, yes, I was single for many, many years, and I also went with a couple of people who were nobodies. And yes I had affairs. You know, I'm forty-two years old. I'm not an old maid. So I don't try to paint myself as an angel, but neither am I a whore. And neither am I a conspirator. They were strictly man-woman relationships. Two people who cared for each other. Because it was Sam Giancana—bull. It was Sam. The remark that I made to the newspapers that he was not the President to me. He was Jack Kennedy. The papers tried to make it sound flippant. I'm sure I thought about the fact that he was President. I'm sure that at times I was thrilled with it, but I'm sure that I was thrilled with it because I was proud of him. I wasn't saying, 'My God, look at me, I'm going with the President.' I was proud of him, proud that he had attained that position."

As I lay in bed that night, unable to sleep, thinking of all we had discussed, far more, of course, than reported here, I knew I wanted to write this book. I knew there was far more to this story than sensational headlines. This was a woman who had suffered, a woman who understood what had happened to her, in good and bad times, who could articulate her feelings, who was sensitive, and who was so damned vulnerable.

All right, she admits she is no angel, but who wants to write about angels. She has a story to tell that is unique, and I would gladly topple all the Camelots and King Arthurs, or Sir Lancelots, to give her that chance. As Dan would say, sure, there are some bad dudes around, but they don't wear different colored hats. There is no one in a white hat walking through these pages. As far as I'm concerned—and I have spent considerable time chronicling the adventures of hoodlums, as well as the misadventures of businessmen and politicians—Francis Ford Coppola, who directed *The Godfather*, says it best: "Men of power and the criminals in our society are distinguished only by their situation, not their morality." I think some women know this better than anybody. Judith Campbell is one of those women.

1

I remember people, moments and places. I can see Frank and Jack and Sam—so many faces, expressions, images that flash before my mind's eye. But people are really voices. I can feel their sound, their words course through my veins and warm my soul. Moments are love and music; songs that break my heart. Places are light and color, smells and sound, and I feel a great tenderness for the way they were then and will never be again.

Life is but a moment in time, a grain of sand, the blink of an eye. So why does it seem like a millennium? Death alters our perceptions of loved ones. It makes us remember what we should forget. They killed Sam, with bullets, as they killed Jack. But I knew them when the dream of Camelot was real, when life was the moment, when their worlds never collided—or so it seemed.

When I think of my father I hear thunder. He was a tall man with a barrel chest, and the sound would rumble and ricochet off the walls like thunderclaps on a summer night.

I guess I've always been afraid of my father. When I was at a very impressionable age, when I was so shy and timid, and World War II had started, we lived then in a huge twenty-four room house overlooking the ocean in Pacific Palisades, which is a suburb of Los Angeles. The navy was having bombing practice just off the coast and the noise terrified me. My mother and father were arguing a great deal

15

then and his voice became all mixed up with the noise of the guns. His voice always made it sound like the war was right in our house. I became even more timid, more frightened, and I used to dream about the sound of his voice. Even today, at my age, sometimes at night I can still hear the bombing and his voice is part of it.

My father was German and my mother was Irish. They both had explosive tempers. But it was my father that I feared. He was so formidable. I never could get close to him. He wouldn't allow it. He had so little patience. He couldn't help us with school problems because he expected us to understand whatever he was explaining the first time around. He would yell at us, in this booming voice that paralyzed me with fear.

I was a momma's girl. Whenever anything happened, I'd run to my mother. My most vivid impression of my mother is that she lived for her family. I remember when the money was scarce and there was no food in the cupboard, my mother would prepare a magnificent meal. She could bake from nothing. From absolutely nothing. She dressed us three girls alike until my oldest sister Joan was about twelve. Always white starched pinafores over our dresses. She was very finicky about our clothes and our hair. We always looked like we stepped right out of a washing machine. When we didn't have a maid, she did it herself.

Both my parents were born in New York. My father's name was Frederick Immoor and my mother's was Katherine Shea. I never knew my paternal grandfather. He died before I was born. Grandma Immoor lived to a ripe old age, but she was a hard, cold, frugal woman. Grandpa Shea died when I was in my late twenties. He had that Irish temper, but from stories my mother told me, he was a sailor as a young man and lived quite an adventurous life. Grandma Shea was the typical Irish grandmother, the kind the movies used to portray in the old days—the short, heavyset woman with the brogue and the bun in the back or on either side of her head. She was adorable.

My mother was at least five foot eight and she had the most magnificent red hair and soft blue eyes. As a young woman she was a great beauty. She modeled at Bonwit's in the days when that position was something very special. She was quite artistic. She could create marvelous designs with flowers. Whenever her friends gave a luncheon or shower, any special occasion, they would ask for her help in creating decorations. She could take a few pieces of net, some wire and some ribbon and make the most attractive centerpieces. And she loved doing it. She made all our Christmas stockings, and each one was an individual creation unlike any other.

My mother was an extremely loving, outgoing person. You felt her love. But she had that Irish temper. She was outspoken. She wasn't timid for a second. She was a strong woman. There were times when she was stronger than my father.

When things got impossible between them, my father was the one who deserted us. My mother was the one left behind with the five children. She kept everything together, kept everything going. I think she recognized what was happening within my father, the frustrations he felt when he botched it financially. He left us three times but always came back. Divorce was never even mentioned.

My father was an architect, a good one, too, but he had some problems at different times in his life. Part of it was his temper. He was very difficult to work with. He left some firms simply because of his own disposition. He was impossible to be around at times. Yet he was much in demand, for he had a great talent in his field. When he did leave a firm, whether it was because of his temper, or perhaps he didn't like the way things were done, or for any other reason, there were all kinds of firms who wanted his services. He was known as an impossible human being, and still he managed to direct some very important projects. In his later years, he became an expert in the design and construction of hospitals. He was the project director for the building of St. Vincent Hospital in Los Angeles. He built hospitals in San Francisco and throughout the Southwest.

In those days he was associated with Daniel, Mann, Johnson and Mendenhall. Not long before he retired, he was asked to survey veterans' hospitals and recommend which

17

were to be closed down and which were to be kept open. The government had contracted with the Daniel, Mann firm and they assigned the job to my father. At various times in his career, he also worked for major movie studios designing elaborate sets.

The other problem my father had was that he came from an immensely wealthy family. My father was probably the worst money manager that ever was. He never got the hang of living on less than he was accustomed to while growing up. Our life was always an economic seesaw. It was either everything in the world you could ever want, or nothing at all. He had money coming from his father, but he lost most of it in bad investments and high living.

He loved big homes. Our house in Pacific Palisades was a four-story Mediterranean villa built down a hillside with a dazzling view of the Pacific. Later it was bought by Joseph Cotton and featured in the *Los Angeles Times Home Magazine*[1] under the caption: ''Elegance, in the grand manner.'' But the house frightened me. I remember that part of the living room took up two floors. It had a handpainted vaulted ceiling and the room was so massive that if I ever got caught at the other end of it by myself, I wouldn't move until someone came in. I was a very timid child.

I was born in New York City on January 11, 1934. Although my parents were from the east, we moved to California before I was a year old. I was the fourth child in a family of two boys and three girls. Fred, who was named after my father, is the oldest. Then there's Joan, Jacqueline, myself, and Allen, the baby, who is eight years younger.

I don't really know the reason for our moving to California when I was a year old. I don't know whether my father was just transferred or whether it was a problem. It's something that was never discussed. I don't know too much about my family. My mother didn't sit down and tell me the heartaches of the past. She told me only the good things about the family.

[1]May 26, 1957.

18

When I think back to as far as I can go, I remember always my shyness. I was a shy, introverted child. A very private child. I was not outgoing. I hung onto my mother a good deal. Whatever happened, I'd always run to my mother. Later on I had my outs with my mother, terrible times with her. But when I was young, I didn't want her to be away from me. Not to the extent where it was a problem. But I didn't make friends very easily. I didn't have a great many friends. It took a while for me to cultivate friendships. But when I did find a friend, now that was my friend. You were my friend, if you wanted to be, for life. I never have taken to people easily.

My mother was my friend. My father was not. I don't want to get ahead of my story, but I should state that I did get to know my father before he died. After my mother passed away, he was a beaten man. My relationship with him was far better, far closer than it had ever been. I felt for him. He blamed himself for a lot of things that happened while I was taking care of my mother. The fact that he couldn't handle it bothered him deeply. I used to try to make him feel better about it. I could almost feel what he was going through.

When I was growing up my parents always did everything together, and with the family. They shopped together, we took rides together, we dined out together, we went to the movies together, to various events together. That didn't seem unusual to me then. I don't know how many families are like that. In meeting other people, I've seen the parents doing things without the children, and I have thought that perhaps in some given areas we were an unusual family. In other ways, of course, I guess you could call us Middle America. I don't really know.

My father wasn't the kind of man who had a night out. He was pretty much a homebody. My parents didn't do a great deal of socializing, but they did have some interesting friends. People today wonder why there are so many prominent names surrounding my life, but it was not unusual for me to be around notable people. My parents were friends of theatrical and movie people. Bert Lahr was a friend and so were Dolores and Bob Hope, who were also friends of my aunt Jean who was then married to a man named Horton. Dolores's mother was a close friend of my aunt Jean.

My parents enjoyed entertaining at home. They did very little drinking by themselves. And when they did drink, they were both happy drinkers. It wasn't a matter of having a martini before dinner every night. Usually at Sunday dinner there would be wine or champagne. Before the Sunday dinner, which was usually at three or four in the afternoon, my dad would make my mother a whiskey sour, which she always enjoyed so much. It wasn't that they disapproved of drinking, it just wasn't their pattern of living.

My mother's social functions were connected with her church. She did the flowers for the altar, she was very involved with the Catholic schools. She gave luncheons for her women church friends. She was not a social climber. Needless to say, my mother was a staunch Catholic. My father was a Lutheran. Perhaps the best evidence of my mother's strength is that my father was converted to Catholicism when I was about fifteen.

I was brought up a Catholic and taught by the nuns mostly at all-girls schools. We lived in the Los Feliz area when I started school and I went to Mother of Good Council. During my first two years in school we lived in four different places. From the Los Angeles address, we moved to Balboa for about a year, and then to Phoenix for about six months. This moving around didn't help my insecurity and timidity. Jackie could charge right in and make friends right away. I would just sit by myself and brood. I was a very moody child. I experienced many traumas and many of my fears, or phobias, lingered for years. Some, no doubt, will follow me to the grave.

I have a terrible fear of suffocation. I can trace it back to the time we lived in Balboa. A friend of my parents, who was the head of Technicolor (I think his name was Fritche), came to visit my parents one Sunday. He brought his son who promptly pushed me off the end of our pier. I went in very deep and as I struggled to surface, my fear was that I would come up under the pier. That was because of a story my mother had told me about a girl who dove off a floating platform on a lake and was trapped underneath the platform.

Her body stayed there for days before they found it. Yet I love the water and love to swim. I just can't stand being submerged. Even when I'm in a boat, I don't want to sleep in the forward cabin, below the water line. I'm sure the boat will sink and I won't be able to escape.

When we moved from Phoenix to Pacific Palisades, I went to Saint Monica's Catholic School. As I look back on it now, I preferred the Catholic schools. I liked the discipline. The one time I attended a public school for a few months, I was shocked at the rowdiness of the students. They ran and screamed in the halls, they talked back to teachers, and to me that was total confusion. I was used to a tight ship, at school and at home.

My father was a strict disciplinarian, but not to the point where it was totally unreasonable. He wanted us to behave properly. It wasn't something he drummed into our heads. It was just something that was expected of us. We were brought up in such a way that we could go out in the world and be in any given situation and handle ourselves properly. And I admire him for that.

There were times when my father yelled just to give us a bad time. He may not have been angry, but I was never quite sure whether he was kidding or serious. I never knew when he was going to jump on me with both feet. He seldom got physical with us children, but he did get physical with my mother a couple of times, and that's when he would leave us. There would be this big blowup and the next morning he was gone.

His temper would flare to the point where he didn't have any control. The reason he didn't spank us a great deal was quite possibly because he knew he couldn't control himself when he reached a certain point. His anger was just overpowering.

Yet there was love there, too, although never a great show of affection. He would kid with us, as I said, give us a bad time. He'd laugh with us, and, of course, he did everything with the family. But even when he was kidding, you could hear him a mile away.

Both my parents were generous. I remember the soldiers'

21

lookout down the street from our house in the Palisades. During the war my mother would bake a cake and make lemonade every single day for the soldiers stationed there. Every Saturday my mom and dad would pick up a couple of servicemen on the coast highway and bring them home for the weekend. Some of them would return on their own laden down with coffee, sugar, steaks, butter, all scarce items during the war. My dad always loved to tell the story about the time one of the soldiers spilled a can of coffee on the kitchen floor. He was sweeping it up and was about to dump it in the trash bin when my dad came into the room and stopped him. "My God," he boomed. "I don't care what's in it. Don't throw that gold away."

During the war, with the bombing practice on the ocean below us, they couldn't even light a cigarette on the patio at night. All the heavy drapes throughout the house had to be drawn at dusk.

When times were good we lived off the fat of the land. Big houses, servants, the best of everything money could buy. The fights between my parents, like the money, or perhaps because of the money, fluctuated from minor to major. One of the worst fights I can remember happened when we lived in the Palisades. I heard them fighting in the night and the next morning my father was gone. I think I was about nine then because my brother Allen was just a little baby.

After a period of time, we went east to meet my father, who had been in contact with my mother. We went back to be with him. But first we went to visit Aunt Jean in Chicago. Her husband then was Allen Hendricks, and, as I understand it, he started the sprinkler systems used in department stores. They were wealthy and had a lovely home in, I think, Glenview.

When my mother left to meet my father in Long Branch, New Jersey, my sister Jackie and I stayed with my aunt for about a month. I did very badly. I had never been separated from my mother. I hated being there. My mother was my security blanket. I cried every single night. It got so bad that finally they just put us on a train to Long Branch.

22

Something very traumatic happened in Long Branch, something that completely changed my attitude on school, and quite possibly my whole life. Because of the month of school I had missed while with my aunt, I was held back a grade at the Star of the Sea Academy. From that moment on I hated school. I never got over it. Every day in school was sheer torture. I was so embarrassed about it. I think I was an average student. I never got bad grades. The fact that Jackie was not held back made me wonder about myself, it made me feel inferior, self-conscious to the point where I resented everybody and everything connected with school. But Jackie was brilliant in school. She never had to study, and she never got anything but A's. I admired her greatly, and I suppose I envied her quickness, her ability to learn with such ease that she made others feel like clods.

We lived in Long Branch—actually in West End—about four years. I was fourteen when we returned to California. We lived in North Hollywood for a few months, and this was the only time in my life that I attended a public school. It was only for a few months while I finished the eighth grade.

That summer we moved to a large house on Martel, just off Sunset, and Jackie and I went to Balboa to spend a few weeks with Aunt Jean, Uncle Allen and their daughter Patsy. They had a beautiful summer home on one of the small islands. I was fourteen that summer, and though I was still a momma's girl, I behaved far better than I had in Glenview. And besides, Los Angeles was only fifty or sixty miles up the road.

Balboa was a marvelous place for a vacation. We went swimming and sailing, ate ice cream by the ton, rode our bikes, and generally had a swell time.

Uncle Allen was the world's sweetest and jolliest human being. I just loved him. He was one of those people who could make you feel comfortable with just a look. He had the kindest eyes. Aunt Jean and Uncle Allen were like my parents in that they included Patsy and us in everything they did.

I'll never forget the night he took us out for hamburgers and then to a movie. When we got home that night, Uncle Allen went into the kitchen for a glass of milk, and, as usual, sneaked a little scotch in his milk. Because he had suffered a heart attack, he was not supposed to drink any alcoholic beverages. I remember he was stretched out on the sofa and sipping his milk when I went to bed.

The next thing I remember are my aunt's footsteps coming up the hall to my room. I looked up when she came into the room and I knew without her having to say anything that there was something terribly wrong. I had felt it in the sound of her footsteps.

"I think something's wrong with Uncle Allen," she said, and her face was chalk white.

I jumped out of bed and ran into the living room. Uncle Allen was lying on the sofa with his head turned and his face against the back of the sofa. I called his name but I knew from just the way he was lying there that something horrible had happened. I reached over and gently pressed against his shoulder until I could see his face. God, it was just all blue and the eyes were blank and staring. I couldn't help it. I screamed and ran up the hallway to my room. I think I even locked the door. I never went into that living room again. Two days later I broke out with chicken pox and nearly died. Instead of the poison coming out through the vesicles, it went back into my system. My mother and aunt had gone to Chicago with Uncle Allen's body, and my father and sister Joan took care of me in the Balboa house. For years I dreamed about Uncle Allen, and the dream always started with my aunt's footsteps coming up the hall.

I started at Immaculate Heart that fall. My big dream at Immaculate was to make up the year I had lost back in the fifth grade. Somehow I was able to talk the Mother Superior into letting me take extra courses so that I could complete my education in three years.

During this period my social life was quite limited. For one thing I was still very shy, and for another my dad was very strict about my dating. Believe me, I wasn't a rip-roaring teenager. I was invited into the Tick-Tockers and the Junior Silver Spoons—they are social organizations that work for hospitals and charities.

To add insult to injury my first date was a disaster. I remember the incident so well, but I can't recall the boy's name or what he looked like. I was fourteen and this boy had invited me to a dance at St. Charles, which was our church. My father was driving us and I waited in the car while he went into the house to fetch the boy. He came out alone. The boy had gotten into trouble and his parents had refused to let him go to the dance. I was embarrassed to death. I wanted to crawl under the seat. It was so humiliating for me to walk back in our house. The whole family thought it was hysterical. It's just the kind of thing parents get a boot out of, but when you're fourteen, and timid to start with, you want the whole world to cave in right on top of you.

My next date was with Tom Branigan. He was fifteen and six foot four, just one long drink of water, but I had a terrible crush on him. We must have looked like Mutt and Jeff together, but that never occurred to me then. To my young girl's eyes, he was simply divine. We went ''steady'' for a little while, but we didn't date all that much. I never could go out during the week. I was restricted to either Friday or Saturday night. As it luckily happened, Jackie's boyfriend had a 1934 Ford, a model that was very popular with my generation. My parents allowed us to double date, which meant that I got to ride to a few dances with Tom. I remember going to a big outdoors party that summer at a large estate in Toluca Lake. I remember it because I had such a crush on Tom at that time. It was the kind of love that moves mountains, but I was scared to death every time he looked at me.

Sometimes we went to the movies, but for many years I had a phobia about movies. When I was just a child my mother took me to see *Snow White and the Seven Dwarfs*. The witch so terrified me that for years I couldn't even enter a theater. One Saturday, to get me over this, my mother made it a condition with my sisters that they couldn't go to the movies that afternoon unless they took me. They bribed me with a huge bag of candy. I was sitting there frightened to death with a lapful of candy when suddenly an oil well came in. The candy flew up in the air and I flew out of the theater.

I never heard the end of it. They were furious. I didn't really start going to the movies again until I was about thirteen. I remember watching a movie called *Ten Little Indians* while standing in the back of the theater, ready to run at a moment's notice.

I think that mostly it was a fear of the dark, coupled with my fear of loud noises. I think it all goes back to the bombing practice and my father's voice when he fought with my mother. Even now, if I'm awakened by a loud noise at night, I can't sleep for the rest of the night. My heart just palpitates like crazy, even when I can identify the cause of the noise. The fear is something beyond my control.

I had been at Immaculate less than a year when my mother was almost killed in an automobile accident. She was alone in a car when a man ran a stop sign and hit her broadside. The impact sent her flying out the door on the passenger side and they found her sixty feet away. She had multiple fractures and contusions. To make matters worse, the doctor who worked on her in emergency was drunk. It wasn't until a month later that they found several cracks in her pelvic bone. The fracture in her arm was set incorrectly which resulted in its being permanently deformed.

Because of my affection for her and my rather fragile nature, I became completely irrational at the thought that my mother might die. I was in a state of semishock for weeks. My first visit to the hospital was so traumatic that I can't even remember it. It was at this point that another major decision was made concerning my future.

My father decided that it was best to keep me home from school until I could function normally so he hired a tutor, which seemed to be the perfect solution. The tutor came in the morning and worked with me for two or three hours. He gave me textbooks, a reading list, and plenty of homework. It was the same curriculum used in high school. The only difference was that I received his undivided attention. If I didn't understand something, it was instantly explained to me. I wasn't in a class with thirty other kids where I would have to wait my turn. Besides I never could raise my hand in class and ask a question in front of all the other kids. I hated to be called upon to recite. I still don't like being the center of attention. I don't like all eyes focused on me, waiting to hear what I have to say. That just isn't me. I don't enjoy it. To me that's a performer. Yet I don't mean to convey the impression that I'm wishy-washy. I'm timid and then I'm not. I know I have tremendous strength. Just don't get me mad because I forget about being timid. There are times when I think I have my father's temper. My temper, or whatever strength I do have, has gotten me out of serious trouble on several occasions. It has earned me respect where I don't think I would have gotten any without it—but that's getting ahead of this story.

I'm sure my parents discussed my continuing with the tutor, but I wasn't in on it. As it turned out I just continued that way, and was very happy about it. I completed all my studies within a year and a half. I passed all the tests for my diploma required by the state when you have a tutor. I was only sixteen and I had finally made up the year I had lost in the fifth grade.

In the end, I don't think it was really good for me. I think that if I had gone back to Immaculate Heart, as difficult and as embarrassing as it was, I think I would—well, I probably wouldn't have married Billy Campbell. It's almost a certainty that I wouldn't have married him. The exchange with other students would have helped me develop emotionally. I would have dated more, gaining more experience with boys. Consequently, I would have matured more quickly. As it was, it took a lot longer for me to understand certain basics necessary for a successful relationship with men.

It wasn't that I was completely sheltered. I had a certain social life. I knew people through my sister Jackie. For example, before I met Billy and fell over the deep end I used to date Robert Wagner, who was just beginning in pictures. He was more a good buddy than a boyfriend. I knew his parents well. I had been to their home. They called him R. J. instead of Bob—the "J" is his middle initial.

II

It was Bob Wagner who took me to a party at Billy Campbell's house and started me on that bumpy road to romantic disaster. I was sixteen and Billy was in his late twenties, but he told me he was in his early twenties. I didn't discover his real age until I saw a copy of his navy discharge papers after we were married. At the time I met him Billy was living with Danny Arnold, a writer and actor who recently created the Barney Miller television series, and actor John Agar, who was married briefly to Shirley Temple.

That was a peculiar evening. Originally someone had wanted to introduce my sister Jackie to Billy. For some reason she couldn't go to the party and Billy didn't lose any time in asking me for a date. Jackie was furious with me when I started seeing Billy. Later I discovered that Billy was seeing Jackie on the sly—but that was Billy's pattern. He was never without a girlfriend the whole time I knew him. He grabbed anything within reach. As long as it was warm, he was interested.

We dated for two years before our marriage and during that period my mother and father both tried to break it up nine million times. They were in complete agreement on their opposition to him. There was no argument there. At one time they wouldn't even allow him in the house.

How I wish I had listened to my parents. If only I had not been quite so naive, so young, so damned innocent. I can only refer back to the tutor and the fact that I missed something important by not continuing in school. Perhaps I would have been more interested in going to college and then Billy would never have entered my life, or he wouldn't have entered my life the way he did.

I compare myself to Jackie, who had a very active social life in high school. She was into every fad. She did whatever was *in*. She belonged to a sorority and she just had a good time all four years. She was very outgoing and that was the difference between us. She dated Billy behind my back, and she was furious because he dated me first, but she wouldn't have married him for anything on earth. She was just a lot sharper than I was. Right away she saw things in him that took me years to discover. By this time Jackie, who is fourteen months older, had already started in pictures. Still she dated Billy for quite a while. Billy would drive her to an appointment or a screen test, or they just happened to be at the same place and he would bring her home, always late. They had numerous flat tires, and you have no idea how little gas that car carried.

My parents could not deter me. I just ranted and raved and fought them at every turn. I just thought they were the worst parents that ever existed. When you have strict parents, it's natural to rebel. Sometimes I think I married Billy to get away from home because the situation had become intolerable. Though they were doing only what any loving parents would do for their children, I couldn't see that at all then.

Many evenings after Billy brought me home and I had gone up to my room on the second floor, I could hear him arguing with my parents. One night they threw him out and told him never to come back. I got absolutely frantic. I don't know what the devil got into me, but I decided to leave home at that very instant and go find Billy. I had a corner bedroom and directly under my window was a cement driveway. I sat on the window ledge facing out and instead of turning myself around and hanging down by my hands before dropping to the ground, I just jumped from that sitting position. I landed on one knee and on my chest. I can still feel the pain when I think of it. I couldn't breathe and I couldn't walk. Finally I crawled to the front door and banged on it, still unable to breathe. And that really terrified me.

My parents were dumbfounded. They didn't know what had happened. One moment they thought I was in my bedroom and the next I'm at the door on all fours, gasping for breath. All they could think of was getting an ambulance. I was taken to Midway Hospital. To this day, if I kneel in a certain way, pain shoots all the way up that leg.

Eventually my parents came around. I guess they decided that it was hopeless—or more to the point, that I was hopeless. After all, what can you do with a silly little girl in love.

Disaster nearly struck the day before the wedding. There were caterers delivering chairs and tables, workmen putting up green and white awnings and installing a dance floor in the garden. It was just at that point when a big wedding is planned that all hell breaks loose: what are we going to do about this and about that, or the cake can't be here until such and such time, and so on. My father blew his stack. He refused to have anything to do with the wedding. He declared to the neighborhood in his booming voice: "I wouldn't walk her down the aisle to marry *him* for anything in the world. She's going to have to do it on her own. And that's final!" By the next morning he was fine. In fact, he cried at the altar.

The wedding was at three o'clock at St. Ambrose in West Hollywood and required special permission because you're supposed to be married before noon in the Catholic church.[1] There was a garden reception at our home with six hundred guests invited. There were white chairs and tables with white and green umbrellas, a small dance orchestra, and ten maids serving champagne and hors d'oeuvres.

My wedding gown was an elaborate three-tiered creation consisting of seventy-five yards of French tulle and chantilly

[1] The whole experience has been so distasteful that I can't remember the exact date of our wedding. It was either late October or late November, 1952.

lace. What a waste! When I went up to change before we left on our honeymoon, Billy's mother was crying her eyes out. My mother was so busy trying to make everyone happy that she had held back her tears. Billy's mother looked at her and said: "You have nothing to be unhappy about. You're gaining a son. I'm losing one and gaining nothing in return." She had been drinking and a moment later she vomited all over my mother's bedspread. After that it was all downhill.

Billy was her whole life. He worshipped her. Everything he did he did for his mother. He didn't like his father, who was a martinet, and the feeling was mutual. His mother was weak and his father was a bully, a very coarse man. His father completely overpowered his mother. He ran the whole show, even to doing the grocery shopping. He wouldn't even let his wife make out a grocery list.

Not long after we were married we went back to Belleville, New Jersey, to visit his parents. It was a disaster. His mother took an overdose of sleeping pills. She pulled through but she blamed me for all her troubles.

Billy's father had no respect for his son. He thought Billy was a weakling and in a sense Billy was an extremely weak man. When I knew him he had very little courage. He was a talker, not a doer. Sometimes he talked too much and to the wrong person, and on such occasions he could be backed into a corner so easily that it was embarrassing. Billy was too quick to criticize other actors. I think it's part of what ruined him in the business. He never had a nice word to say about anybody, but he would never criticize people to their faces. Of course, word got back to them and it hurt him. Gossip moves fast in Hollywood. It's a small incestuous town.

Before our marriage, of course, I saw Billy with different eyes. Because of the imperious strength of my father, I interpreted Billy's weakness as gentleness. I think I was impressed with the fact that he was impressed with himself. I thought it showed a certain confidence. His main topic of conversation was himself. The moment I strayed off that subject, he immediately lost interest. As I was to learn, that's a common trait in many actors. They live in a circumscribed world. The only wars they care about are those between New York bankers and studio chiefs. If it's not printed in the *Hollywood Reporter* or *Daily Variety*, it's not worth reading.

In a sense, Billy did the same thing to me that my parents were doing. They didn't want me to see him and Billy always kept me just on the edge where I wasn't quite sure he loved me. In his own way, Billy was keeping me at arm's length. I was fighting with my parents to see Billy and I was fighting with Billy to hang on in a number of crucial areas. Oh, I think he knew what he was doing. He was remote and displayed no jealousy, two attitudes that are very frustrating when you think you're madly in love. Love usually generates a little confusion, but with Billy it was total chaos.

Marrying Billy was like going from one keeper to another. Someone else was going to look after me. I think because of the problems that I had with Billy it took me a longer time to mature, simply because I was such a young eighteen. It was a process of growing up without my mother and father being there, and with Billy being gone most of the time, away either on location or out with the boys or his girlfriends. I was alone a great deal and could have completely withdrawn within myself—God only knows what would have happened to me. Luckily I was strong enough to avoid moving in that direction. It was a process of growing up one tiny step at a time.

I suppose Billy loved me in his own peculiar way, which was the only way he knew. Love to him was sex, and sex was just something you did at every opportunity to prove your manhood. It was strictly a biological function. He got an itch and he scratched it. Instantly! He couldn't have cared less how I felt. I thought I knew a lot about love then, but I knew nothing about sex. At first I was happy to give him that satisfaction. I never gave my own feelings a moment's notice. His happiness was all that mattered. It sounds strange now when I say, "God, if I knew then what I know now, I wouldn't have gone near him." He was such a dull, selfish human being. That was in the days before we knew about chauvinist pigs. I was nothing more than a possession. I was a pretty young girl from a good family who was totally devoted to her husband. He placed a great deal of importance on his position. He liked how we looked together. When we had parties at my parent's beautiful home, he could be very proud of the picture we presented.

Billy's drinking and eating habits had much in common with his sexual appetite. Whatever he drank he gulped right down, whether it was beer or brandy. Down the hatch. When I cooked dinner I had to fix his plate first. By the time I had fixed my plate he was already finished. I don't remember his ever cutting his food, I think he inhaled it. Then he wanted to get away from the table. In the beginning he would say, "Do you mind if I go watch TV?" What was I going to say? "No, you have to sit here with me." Before long, however, he stopped asking and just left me alone at the table.

Once he was full he left the table; once he was physically satisfied he rolled over and went to sleep. His lovemaking meant that he loaned me his body for one minute. There were long periods that he didn't come near me and it wasn't until much later that I learned that those were the times he was involved in hot and heavy romances and was just too exhausted to pay any attention to me. I was his little passive wife. And he assumed that I was happy and satisfied.

I remember what Van Heflin's wife, Frances, told me once. She was a colorful gal who always had a martini in her hand, she was great. She said: "I have the picture that Billy picks you up and sets you on the bed at night, undresses you like a child, slips this little wool flannel nightgown over your head, ties the bow at the neck and tucks you under the covers." I was nothing more than a doll, a toy that he played with when he was bored.

When he wasn't talking about Billy, or criticizing other actors, he talked about sports. When he watched football he would have two games on radio and one on television. It was never a question of "Honey, would you like to see something?" I was so intent on pleasing him that I kept telling myself that things were exactly the way they should be in a happy marriage.

This is a part of my life I hate to talk about. I know that I have to because they were formative years, and I did promise

33

to tell the full story. But I honestly resent giving Billy this much attention. I know what he will do with it. His career is at a low ebb and he needs something to jump on to get publicity. Even if it doesn't help his career, it's all right with him as long as he gets to say something, as long as he gets his picture in the paper. He's already given several interviews in which he said that my dad borrowed money from him, and that my mom was a stage mother, who did nothing but groom Jackie for stardom. He said my mother would have done it to me if he hadn't stepped in. Of course I didn't really have any talent anyway. Oh, I'd tried to be an actress, but it just hadn't worked out. Just plain flat-out lies. Not an ounce of truth in any of it. Like reciting in class, being an actress was the last thing on earth I aspired to.

There was a time, in fact, when I had an opportunity to be a singer. When we lived in Long Branch an Italian girl lived next door to us whose parents were even more strict than mine. She was taking singing lessons and Jackie and I would go over to her house and I just started singing with her. No one knew I could sing. I didn't know it myself. One day I came home and put a Jane Powell record on the phonograph and starting singing the *Italian Street Song* along with her. My mother and father almost fainted. My father was an opera buff. He had a large collection of classical records and every Saturday we would listen to the Metropolitan Opera on the radio. Once you are familiar with classical music, especially with Italian operas, it's easy to sing along with a record and imitate the sound of the words. I loved *Un Bel Di* from *Madame Butterfly*. I liked melodic arias, music from *La Boheme*, that kind of music.

I was a coloratura when I was thirteen. Our large house at 720 Ocean Avenue in West End was right along the ocean front, across from the Colony Surf Club. When I sang people in the homes on both sides of ours would come out, and people walking by would stop and sit for the whole time I was singing. I had a natural voice. I had no training at that time. I guess the expression would be a "God-given" voice.

That summer I sang at the West End Casino a couple of

times. It was an exclusive beach club with a large ballroom. The audience was marvelous. I sang at the Colony Surf Club also and at the Versailles, where I even forgot some of the words but just went on without any embarrassment. It was really strange. There I was standing in front of all those people, their eyes focused on me, their ears attuned to my every note, and it didn't bother me at all. But God knows I couldn't have spoken two words to them. It was as if I could hide behind my voice so that they didn't really see me. They were hearing music that came from inside of me, but that wasn't really me, not the private, innermost, secret me.

On our way to California we drove to Charleston, South Carolina, to pick up my brother Freddie who was being discharged from the army. There was a delay of a few days, and one evening I sang in an auditorium jam-packed with servicemen, thousands of them, and they gave me a tremendous ovation. The next week I got the mumps and we had to stay another two weeks in Charleston.

When I turned fourteen I became very self-conscious. Everybody was going, "My, my, you've got to do something with her. You can't let this talent go to waste. She must study." It was then that I began to be frightened by it and became more and more aware of myself, until finally I wouldn't sing in front of anybody. I'd sing at home, but I wouldn't sing for anyone except myself. My career collapsed before it even got off the ground. Contrary to what Billy said, my parents didn't push it one way or the other.

Not long before I married Billy, one of Jackie's agents, either Walter or Paul Kohner, was talking to my mother on the phone and he heard me singing in the background. He said, "My God, who's that singing?" My mother said, "That's Judy." He said, "That's Judy? Why haven't you told me about her? Can we do something with her?" My mother said, "I don't know, I doubt it.' He said, "I'd like to come over and hear her sing." My mother asked me and I said, "Well, all right." But deep down I knew it would never work. The minute he walked in through the door my throat constricted.

Sometime later, after I married Billy, the Kohners set up

an audition for Joe Pasternak at MGM studios, in a large room in the Thalberg building. I stood by a big grand piano and tried to loosen my voice, but it felt really tight. I did sing for Pasternak but it wasn't right. Pasternak told them, "She's got a tremendous talent, but she's got to relax. Tell her to continue to study and I want to see her again in four months." I did study with a woman but I didn't pursue a singing career, I never went back to Pasternak or anybody else. It was just something I did for my own pleasure.

The strange thing is that when I talk about my life, particularly my life with Billy, it's as if it happened to someone else. Possibly that's because I'm such a different person now. It took me a long time to wake up and discover that I was a person, too. I went through a period during which I became very afraid at night. The minute it began to get dark, I had a feeling inside me that can only be described as panic. When we'd go out to dinner, I couldn't sit in a restaurant for any length of time because I'd start to feel sick to my stomach. Nighttime became unbearable. I thought I was going out of my mind. I couldn't watch any show about mental illness. I think that was a turning point for me. Either I was going to go stark raving mad, or I was going to start to think for myself and grow up.

I was alone so much of the time and I didn't really see a lot of Billy. I wasn't allowed to go on location with him because he always had a new girlfriend to take along, usually one of the actresses in the picture. He went away on vacations by himself. I went on one location only because Jackie had a small part in the picture. Even when he went into Schwab's (a drugstore on Sunset that's a hangout for a certain class of actors and buffs), I always had to wait in the car. I suppose he just didn't want to create the impression that he was tied down to one person.

He was a fight fan and he would go to the fights all the time. "I'm going to the fights tonight," he would say, and before I could reply he was gone. A few times I found there weren't even any fights that night. Needless to say I wasn't invited to any sporting event.

My social life with him was only in people's homes for dinners and parties, and at our home when we entertained. Parties were where Billy would really shine. He always managed to get somebody in the kitchen or hallway for a little party of his own.

The whole group we socialized with was notorious for playing around. I don't say that all of them did, but there were plenty who kept up with Billy. Steve Forest was really a chaser. Once I was supposed to go horseback riding with him and his wife Chris, but he neglected to tell Chris about it. Then he told me she couldn't go, but had asked that we go ahead anyway. The whole day was sheer agony. Steve was one of those relentless pursuers. Luckily I had a horse under me and could get away. It was a constant chase.

When Billy was away and I would have dinner with them, I'd no sooner get back home than the phone would ring and it would be Steve asking me to meet him someplace. He thought he was so charming that I'd give in at some point. He was good looking but he ruined it with this overbearing attitude. He thought he was irresistible, and that makes a man very unattractive.

Others in the group included Mike and Mary Lou Connors (he was known as Touch Connors then), John and Millie Erickson, Hugh O'Brien, Charlton and Lydia Heston, and Lloyd and Dottie Bridges—I just have to laugh when I think about Lloyd Bridges. He was the most persistent of players. His wife Dottie was overweight, but Lloyd didn't care what she looked like. All he cared about was his waistline, the size of his muscles, that he stood up straight, kept his stomach sucked in, his tan the right shade—narcissism in its most basic state.

Gary Morton, who was once married to my sister Jackie and is now Lucille Ball's husband, used to do a hilarious routine about a guy preening and prancing beside a swimming pool with his stomach sucked in, muscles flexed, who would ask, "Any girls around?" When the answer was no, everything collapsed. "Okay," he'd say, "let's go swimming."

We called Lloyd Bridges "Bud." Well, Bud would corner me at every party, and for a while I was flattered by the attention. I didn't get it from Billy and I must say he was a lot smoother than Steve Forest. I visited Bud on the *Sea Hunt* set a few times. My father called him the cross-eyed underwater cowboy. Bud is dreadfully bowlegged, but I didn't care about that or about his physique. In a sense, seeing him gave me a feeling of freedom. He was fun to be with, very pleasant, good-natured, and loved the attention of attractive women. He was Mr. Charm.

One of the most amusing evenings I can remember spending when I was married to Billy was the time we went to dinner at the home of our houseboy. We knew he was gay and we knew he had money, but we had no idea how rich or how swishy he really was until we arrived at his home.

He dropped hints that he worked only because he loved doing it. And only for certain people. I know he took great pleasure in going through my wardrobe. he thought I had the most divine clothes. He came to clean three times a week and he did the catering when we had parties. He was an accomplished cook and he could bake the most magnificent pastries.

Among some of Billy's friends that he worked for was Bobby Van, the dancer, who was then married to Diane Garrett. The Vans were also invited to dinner that evening and we arrived together at this fabulous home, which was on two or three levels and elegantly furnished.

The next shock came when he opened the door. He was wearing a black sheath dress with at that time fashionable sheer material above the bustline and long puffed sleeves of the same material going to the wrist. The dress had a shaped bustline and he wore a strapless bra with falsies. His hair was blond and rather short, but he had the front brushed up so that it looked like the kind of hairdo a woman with short hair might wear. I had an aunt who wore her hair exactly like that. He had flowers pinned around the back so that they just cupped around the real short part of his hair. He had a great pair of legs and wore plastic Springalator shoes that had a sheer plastic strip across the arch and no sling in the back and were very high heeled. His hose were very sheer and their seams perfectly straight.

We were just dumbfounded when he opened that door. Luckily, we had big smiles on our faces and hellos on our lips. It took us a moment to realize that a man had answered the door. Knowing his preference was one thing, but seeing him in drag was another story.

He served a sumptuous dinner but we ate rather quickly. We played it straight because we didn't want to offend him. The fact that we knew he was gay was probably the reason he felt he could do this in front of us, be completely himself without fearing that we might turn around in disgust and walk out. He didn't feel he was offending us by doing it.

After dinner he put on an elaborate fashion show, modeling five different coats: a silver mink, a black diamond, a white, and two others I can't remember. He modeled cocktail dresses, long evening dresses, dressing gowns, and his patter was going a mile a minute as he swished around with material flowing and his arms moving like a Vogue model. He got away with it because he laughed at himself before we had a chance to. He was amused at our being amused at the whole situation, which made it even more amusing, but comfortable. It wasn't at all awkward.

By the end of the fashion show I think the men felt like "Well, okay, we've seen it all. This has gone far enough." But for me it was a perfectly delightful evening.

Far more delightful I might add than most of the evenings spent at the homes of Billy's actor friends. Perhaps I should qualify the word friend. Billy was just a young struggling actor when I met him. He was under contract at Warner Brothers and he went from there to MGM and later to Universal. They all had plans for him at one time or another, but there was a certain something in his personality that really hurt him. He wasn't a bad actor in the beginning, but the big plans never materialized. Yet Billy was working and this was Hollywood in the 1950's. If you were under contract, you were popular, you had friends. I mean if you gave a party, people would come to your party, and you'd be invited to their parties. As long as you were under contract, you were "in" and everyone stayed friendly with the actors who were working. It was survival.

As far as Billy was concerned I could go anywhere I wanted. He didn't care what I did as long as I left him alone. But until my mother taught me to drive I was stranded at home. Home was a modest house in the Hollywood Hills above Chateau Marmonte. After I learned to drive I took his Oldsmobile and he bought himself a Thunderbird. Then I started going places. I started going to the beach with Marlene Wessel, who became my best friend. Her parents owned clothing stores in Whittier and through her I did some modeling for the Anne Fogarty line. The representatives of the Anne Fogarty Company, a very nice couple, didn't like using professional models because of the style of the dresses—more sweet than sophisticated. It was fun, and it was something to do. It was about this time that I began to sketch the faces of children. Later I began to work in charcoal and oil.

I kept busy. I took extension courses at UCLA. Marlene and I went to Palm Springs. Once we went to Las Vegas. Slowly but surely I began asserting myself. I became a fantastic door slammer. I shattered quite a few full-length door mirrors. If there was a mirror on a door that I slammed, it had to go. Thank God I'm not superstitious.

Then one night I finally gathered up the courage to confront Billy at a party. He had been so revolting all evening long. Yet when I walked into the kitchen and found him pawing this girl, I didn't know where to turn. The only thing I could think of was what he was doing. So I said, "I'm going home and you're going with me." You know, Big Gutsy, me. He said, "No, I'm not going home." So then I said something about the girl being a tramp, some ridiculous thing, and he whacked me right across the face. When I think back on it now, I'm grateful to Billy for that blow. It did more to straighten me out than anything that happened in our marriage. I thought, "What are you doing to yourself? Do you like living in torture? Do you like being humiliated?"

As these thoughts flashed through my head, I was driving away from the party which was at a house on top of the Hollywood Hills. My eyes were blurred with tears and the road was steep and narrow and crooked. I don't know how I survived driving down that mountain. It was a scene right out of a Bette Davis movie.

From that time on my life began to change seriously. Actually in the last two years of our marriage I saw very little of Billy. Then one day while Billy was on location in Panama I met someone I had known before, and had disliked for a long while. He went with Jackie at one time and suddenly I really fell for him. His name is Travis Kleefeld, and he used the stage name Tony Travis. He was of medium build and very attractive. He loved to have a good time and he had a great sense of humor. He was crazy about women, a terrible flirt, but discreet about it. If he was cheating, it wasn't done openly to hurt me.

We were both violently jealous. He'd get mad if I even looked sideways, and I'd get mad when he looked straight ahead. That kind of attitude in the player atmosphere we lived in doomed our relationship from the beginning. Yet we lived together nearly two years before breaking up. In the meantime, we had terrible fights but they never lasted for any great length of time although each one added to the tension that was slowly building up.

At first his jealousy fed my ego. The fact that someone could get so mad at me just because I looked at another man was a new experience. Billy never gave a damn where I went or what I did—that is, until he found out I was leaving him. When he first heard that I had fallen for Travis, fallen for another man, he just couldn't believe it. As I was to learn later, his ego refused to accept it.

III

It's almost impossible to describe the exhilaration I felt being out of Billy's house, the great feeling that came over me the day I walked out. It was like the whole world was welcoming me with open arms.

I rented a small apartment in a Regency-style building just off Doheny, near Sunset. I kept some clothes and a few of my things in the apartment because it was my anchor, a place I could call my own. I never again wanted to be totally dependent on a man. My life with Billy made it really impossible for me to completely trust a man for many, many years.

Somewhere in the back of my mind I think I realized that going from Billy to Travis was like going from home to Billy. I was running away, I was seeking shelter, and really not being on my own. I wasn't learning to live with myself. Again I was leaning on someone else. It wasn't until I broke up with Travis that I started dating the way most girls date when they're in high school. But even with Travis, I started to learn more about other people in relation to me, not in relation to my husband. I'd never had any personal contact with people just for myself. I was Billy's shadow for so many years that it took time before I could step out confidently into the light. Gradually, I started to enjoy life and people in a different way, but I still didn't trust them. There wasn't a man alive I trusted.

Meanwhile back in the Hollywood Hills Billy had gone

berserk. Instead of sending him a "Dear John" letter when he was on location in Panama (I think they were shooting a war movie), I waited until he telephoned one night and then suddenly I blurted out that I was leaving him for good. Of course he didn't believe me. He gave it his usual response: "Oh, take it easy. You're just a little upset. You'll calm down."

By the time he got back to town I had flown the coop. I had taken the sterling dishes and trays my parents and relatives had given us for our wedding, my clothes, and my easels and paints. I didn't take another thing, not a dish, not a stick of furniture, not a book, not even a record, and there were many that I treasured.

When I first moved in with Travis he was living in an apartment belonging to Jackie Loughry, who later married Jack Webb. Travis had swapped his New York apartment for it. Then one Sunday morning Billy came looking for me with blood in his eyes.

There was a knock at the door and Travis asked who it was. Billy yelled, "Let me in. I know my wife's in there."

God, I had on only a robe and we were on the second floor and there was no back door. Billy stood in front of the only exit. As I ran toward the back bedroom, I could hear Travis saying, "No, she isn't here." The back bedroom was being used as a storage place and there was junk everywhere. I slipped out of my robe and grabbed my dress. I remember it was a black and white check with a full skirt—the style then was to wear two or three stiff petticoats underneath for a ballooning effect—and a long-sleeved tailored jacket that ended right under the bustline. I managed to slip into the dress but I had nothing else on when the front door opened and Billy came rushing in, ranting and raving at the top of his lungs. I looked under the bed and thought, "You can't hide there, that's the first place anybody looks." I opened the doors of the closet which was loaded with clothes and things piled up on the floor. I got one shoe on and struggled to squeeze myself between the clothes. While doing this, I managed to get a sleeve of the jacket over my right arm. I closed the doors just as Billy burst into the room, screaming bloody murder. But just as the doors shut I got a glimpse of my three petticoats standing stiffly in a corner of the room and I just knew Billy would recognize them.

The first thing Billy did was look under the bed. Then he headed for the closet and threw both doors open. My right arm, the one with the sleeve, was sticking out of the clothes a good three inches, but he was so mad that he didn't even notice it. If he had looked he would have known that it was a real arm in that sleeve. He pushed clothes around and growled viciously. How he didn't even feel me standing there I'll never know. I was close to having a heart attack. I knew that if he found me he'd kill me. He was that violently angry. I don't think there's a worse anger than that derived from a wounded ego. Especially when that ego belongs to an egotist.

Finally, now even more frustrated, he left the apartment, still screaming and yelling, "I'm going to find her." After the door was closed and locked behind him I got out of the closet and dressed. Then I called Marlene Wessel, who lived only two blocks away, to set up an alibi. But as I was talking to Marlene, I heard Billy's voice in the background and it was then that I realized she was carrying on with Billy. While I was still on the phone she told Billy where I was calling from.

The panic was on again. While I was telephoning, Travis's brother-in-law, Jim Wilson, had come into the apartment and Travis had told him what was happening. Jim said, "Come on," and he grabbed me and pulled me down the stairs to his Jaguar sedan parked in the driveway. He pushed me down on the floor of the back seat and put a blanket over me. Just as he was backing out of the driveway, Billy came barreling down the street and skidded to a screeching stop in front of the apartment house. He jumped out of the car and ran up the steps just as I was making my getaway.

Two months later Billy paid us a call in the middle of the night. We were then staying in Bobby Van's apartment. Billy was drunk and violent. When Travis refused to open the door, Billy tore the screen off the window next to the door and began pounding on the glass so hard that Travis had to go out and talk to him. Billy tried to hit him and Travis came back in and called the police. When they arrived Billy started to cry. He said, "My wife is in there and we're not divorced and I love her. I want her back." The cops felt sorry for him. They kept glancing suspiciously at Travis, but Billy was so drunk they had to cart him away.

For two years Billy was a madman. He drank twenty-four hours a day. He called me at all hours of the day and night, and he'd cry on the phone. He promised to take me anyplace in the world I wanted to go if only I would come back to him. He called my sisters and my parents. He even tried to break into my parents' home. He turned into the most pathetic creature. He even married a girl who looked like me. The love and then the hate I had felt for him now turned to pity.

I filed for divorce in April 1958, and it was final on April 24, 1959—that date I do remember. The divorce attorneys wanted to do all kinds of dreadful things to Billy, but I refused to go along with them. They wanted him followed, they wanted him to pay all the income tax, they wanted two thousand dollars a month alimony. I asked for five hundred dollars a month and it was scheduled to run five years, but at the end of two years I just couldn't stand it any longer. I didn't want his money. I didn't want anything from him. I signed it all back for a lump-sum settlement of six thousand dollars. Besides I didn't need his money. Through my father I was getting money from Grandma Immoor. At least that's what my father told me, but I've often thought that it came from him and my mother. For many years my father claimed me as a dependent and provided quite handsomely for my well-being.

Travis was a singer. He had a good voice, but he too had his problems, and had been in analysis for five years before we started living together. Travis's problems started when his father committed suicide. His father had been a very successful builder and was quite wealthy. After the war, he had built thousands of tract homes in the valleys surrounding Los Angeles.

With Travis I began to move in different circles. Many of his friends were wealthy businessmen. Some had winter homes in Palm Springs and we began going there regularly, staying either at the Racquet Club or at the homes of friends like Bob Whittaker who headed a large financial empire. Other good friends included Dick Elwood, who was in electronics, and Marshall Edson, who owned the Little Club in Beverly Hills.

Travis's friends became my friends. I wasn't as withdrawn. For the first time in my adult life, I started communicating with people. Instead of saying, "How do you do?" I'd talk with them. I had a completely different attitude. I learned to enjoy conversations with people. They were not people who sat around talking about themselves, or about their next picture. There were some actors in the group, but they were on a different level.

I had this new found freedom, but I was still shy in given areas and I still couldn't put myself in a position where I knew attention was focused on me. For example, Travis and his mother, Sylvia, were both members of the Beverly Hills Tennis Club. We spent considerable time there and at first I just sat and watched. I avoided taking lessons because I wasn't totally comfortable doing it. The learning process, when you look awkward, is what bothered me. If there was no one around, I enjoyed playing games. That was the ideal situation.

When I was a little girl people would come up to my mother and say, "What a beautiful child. She's going to be a great beauty when she grows up." I never quite believed it. I never was that thrilled with my appearance. Once I grew out of the little girl stage, it took many years before I would wear a bathing suit and then only in fairly private places. There were too many girls who looked so sensational in bikinis. They made me feel like something inside of me was missing. I felt I just couldn't stack up. Slowly, I got over some of these feelings, but not entirely. After a while I even took tennis lessons, and that was a giant step forward.

Falling in love with Travis at that time was the best thing that could have happened to me. For the first time in my life, I was important to a man. He taught me what it was to be made love to and to make love. He was very open in his lovemaking. I learned that when you love someone there is no good and bad, there are no boundaries for those two people. I felt joy in making love. With Billy it had been a biological function, with Travis it was total freedom without guilt.

Also with Travis I was back more or less in my natural element. He enjoyed good food, fine wines, caviar—his whole family loved caviar—and I was back to living the way I had and enjoying the things I had grown up with.

For a long time there wasn't any doubt in my mind that we would be married when my divorce became final. But the insecurity we both felt in ourselves really intensified our jealousy. I think jealousy and a little possessiveness is good when you're in love. It's natural. But when it goes beyond that point then that's a problem you have within yourself. The greater the insecurity, the greater the jealousy.

When I think back on it, I feel that I was the one who caused the breakup. We were having difficulty together and in some ways I think I was growing beyond that way of life. I had kept my apartment because I couldn't live with the idea that Travis was keeping me. I knew so many girls in that situation. My apartment was my shelter. In the event of an argument, I had a place of my own to mend my wounds. After two years with Travis, I felt I needed to be completely on my own. Yet I was afraid to let go.

Finally, in August 1959, I went to New York for two weeks on a trial separation with Alice Wallace, who was a former model for Oleg Cassini, and we stayed at the Plaza. Time goes very fast when you're in New York on a vacation. You sleep late in the morning, you meet friends for lunch, you go shopping, you meet friends for cocktails at four, and by the time you finish with cocktails, it's time to go back and change for dinner engagements. Alice was contacting a number of people she hadn't seen in a while.

Alice Wallace was a lovely woman. She later married Kem Dibbs, who worked for Bob Whittaker as a personal aide. He arranged all the entertaining for Bob. Many of Bob's subsidiaries worked on government contracts, and I remember dinners and parties for generals and government officials.

Kem could always come up with a bevy of pretty girls to decorate the room.

When I came back from New York, Travis and I had dinner and we talked it out. The next day I moved into my sister Jackie's Beverly Hills apartment. It was one of those things: I couldn't live with him and I couldn't live without him. But I knew I had to try. We saw a great deal of each other in the next few months. It wasn't as if I had completely cut that cord. But it was different now. I was completely and totally on my own. Travis eventually became a great friend of mine in succeeding years. I could call and cry on his shoulder. He was that kind of person. At that point in my life, I can't think of anyone who could have been better for me. He was there when I needed him. Contrary to what has been written about me, I am a one-man woman. When I am with someone, I don't see the other men in the room. I'm grateful that Travis was that man at that moment.

IV

The first indication I had that Frank Sinatra was interested in meeting me was when Nick Sevano approached me one night while I was having dinner with friends at Puccini's.

Nick said, "I really would like you to meet Frank."

I had known Nick for a number of years. I think he was connected with Paramount when Jackie was under contract. I said, "Thanks, but I've met Frank at parties."

Nick laughed. "You know what I mean. Would you like to go out with him?"

"Yes," I said, without hestitation. "I'd like to go out with him."

Frank called a couple of days later and invited me to dinner but I already had plans for that evening. A few nights later, again at Puccini's, Frank himself approached our booth. He had been sitting at a large table with a group of friends and I could feel that he was watching me. He sat down and we talked briefly. He was extremely charming. Before going back to his table, he said he'd call me again, and I didn't discourage him. I've never been a game player in any relationship. I have never worked out any kind of strategy that keeps a man guessing. Some women spend all their time playing games.

Frank called me the very next day and he didn't waste any time. He said he was going to Hawaii, and would I like to go

49

with him. We had quite a discussion. I liked the prospect of going to Hawaii and of seeing Frank, getting to know him, but I wasn't giddy about it.

I refused to go on the same plane with him but I promised to meet him there. He didn't sound too happy about it, but I tried to explain that I just didn't like the way that looked. I was sensitive about it. I could see what my getting on a plane with Frank Sinatra would look like to other people, and how it would sound in the gossip columns. I wanted to see him, I wanted to go to Hawaii, but I didn't want to go that way. He came around, but I think he thought I was going to stand him up.

I took the midnight flight on November 9, 1959, and I arrived at 6:45 the next morning—they were still flying propeller planes at that time. I went directly to the Surfrider Hotel. They didn't have a reservation in my name, but they gave me room 1509. I just stretched out on the bed until Frank called later in the morning and asked me to come up to his penthouse suite. There were two suites on the penthouse floor, one at each end, with two rooms in between. Frank had one suite, Pat and Peter Lawford had the other, and Dr. Leone Krohn (they called him Red) and his wife, Ester, occupied one of the rooms. I was given the other.

My nerves were strung pretty tight when I walked into Frank's suite. I hadn't been with him except for that brief moment at Puccini's. We had talked on the phone, but phone conversations are a lot easier if the person I'm talking with takes the initiative. If they wait for me to direct the conversation, then the phone is not easy for me. Frank was an artist on the phone. He had everything under control, and that was just fine with me. The rapport we seemed to have established on the phone left me anticipating the time we would be together. There is no question that I was attracted to him, and I was looking forward to a good time, but I certainly wasn't thinking of falling in love. I was still trying to get over Travis.

Frank, Peter, Pat, Red, Ester, and Al Hart were in the suite when I arrived.

50

AUTHOR'S NOTE: *A former liquor distributor who had con-nections with Joseph Fusco, a Chicago gangster who started out in the rackets as a beer-runner for Al Capone, Al Hart later headed the City National Bank of Beverly Hills.*

There were others, as there always were others around Frank, but he never bothered introducing them. They were hangers-on, bodyguards, gofers, flunkies, men who were always there but who never spoke unless spoken to. They moved in and out of the suite, but you hardly noticed them at all. It was almost the same with Al Hart. He was in and out, and I seem to remember him being there that first day, but it could have been the next day. He sticks in my mind because of the comical image he presented when he walked out in swim trunks. They were of a jersey material, jockey style, very tight, and his paunch and saddlebags hung over his waistline like an innertube. None of the parts—legs, arms, torso, head—seemed to go together. He reminded me of a koala bear.

It was a leisurely afternoon. We sat out on the patio, which ran the whole length of the penthouse floor, a tremendous area, and though the drinking was pretty heavy, the conversation was light and airy. There was a lot of hip talk. Frank and Pete—somehow Pete never seemed right for Peter Lawford—communicated in a language of their own. It was a mixture of slang, a vernacular that originated with hip musicians, comics, hoodlums and teenagers. Their favorite words were gas and gasser, clyde, bunter, cool, crazy, harvey, fink, mother, hacked, smashed, pissed, charley, and, of course, ring-a-ding, or ring-a-ding-ding, depending on the enthusiasm of the moment. The meaning of many of these expressions seemed to change daily. This was at a time when Frank was known as The Leader (he was also The General, The Dago, The Pope) of the Rat Pack, which he inherited from the late Humphrey Bogart. The name of the group was later refined to the Clan. Besides Lawford, the membership included Dean Martin, Sammy Davis, Jr., Joey Bishop, Sammy Cahn, Sy Devore, Mike Romanoff, Jimmy Van Heusen, and for a time, Eddie Fisher and Elizabeth Taylor.

Much of their conversation, as I was soon to learn, was inconsequential. They communicated by using only the punch lines, or buffo lines, as they called them, to *in* jokes. If you didn't know the joke, you had no idea what the words meant. They might just as well have been talking Chinese. Much of the time I sat there smiling while they slapped their thighs and guffawed. There was little said worth remembering. When people use words or talk about subjects or people that I'm not familiar with, I have a tendency to daydream.

Pete made the only remark that afternoon that I can recall. It got me off to a bad start with Pat Lawford almost immediately.

Pete turned to his wife and said, "Look how beautiful Judy's hair is. Isn't it marvelous? Pat, why can't your hair look like Judy's?" That's not what you say to your wife, especially a Kennedy wife. Of course, at that time I knew nothing about the Kennedys. I was not a politically oriented person. I knew the names of California senators, but I knew little about senators from other states. Just the same, it didn't take me long to get a bearing on Pat Lawford. There was no question that she was the strong one in that family. She's such a strong woman. Looking back on it now, Pete is all flowery speeches and no guts. The expression I've heard used is that Pete is a steer, not a bull. I think that fits him and perhaps it also fits the other men married to Kennedy women. They marry weaker men. Anytime I see Sargent Shriver and his wife on television, when she talks, I see Pat and hear Pat. There's a certain strength there, and when Shriver talks I get the same feeling that I would get from Lawford. There's something unmistakable about the Kennedy women. They are their father. They've got the same strength as the men in the family. Except perhaps for Teddy. Somehow I feel less strength from Teddy than Pat. That could be because he was the baby of the family. Very often there's a change in personality with the baby.

Prior to Pete's observation about my hair, Pat had just remarked that the humidity in Hawaii was doing terrible things to her hair. It was obvious from looking at her that her problem involved more than humidity. The humidity was terrible, but Pat doesn't have the greatest hair in the world to work with. Besides she doesn't seem to care that much about her appearance. I've known many people like her. Because they are so terribly wealthy, they kind of flaunt it. The attitude is, "I've got so much, why care?" It's a sort of Howard Hughes syndrome.

Pat could be an attractive woman. All it takes is a little pride in yourself. If you can't have pride in yourself, there's something missing somewhere. It's so much nicer to look upon something that's pleasant than something that is deliberately ugly. When a woman is deliberately disheveled or doesn't give a damn about herself, that's very distasteful, and it's just as distasteful with a man. Pat never seemed to care what she wore. Her favorite outfit was blue jeans and a blouse. On the other hand, Pete was a fashion plate.

Speaking about things that are distasteful, Frank's favorite colors are orange and black. It's a color scheme that makes me feel like I'm at a Halloween party. All his swim trunks were a vivid orange or black. His idea of a sharp outfit would consist of black slacks, an orange shirt, and a black alpaca golf sweater. The only flower I ever saw in any of his homes or hotel suites was the bird of paradise. There were at least twenty-five of them in that penthouse suite. You couldn't turn your head an inch without having another one staring at you. The motif of his Palm Springs home was orange and black. And when I say orange, I mean orange orange.

That afternoon I called a record shop, and ordered a copy of every album Frank had made, with instructions that they get them elsewhere if they didn't stock them all. I still have a copy of the bill from the House of Music, $47.87 for nine albums. They were delivered to his suite, and although Frank never said very much about it, they were played constantly.

That first evening there was a barbeque on the patio for about twenty people. The view of the city, the soft night air, the moon, the stars—it was all magnificent. I couldn't get over how beautiful it was. The setting was absolutely entrancing.

It was a perfect evening. I sat next to Frank and he was very attentive and very charming. As always, there was a lot of kidding and laughter. Everybody was smiling, and, as I was soon to learn, whenever Frank was happy, everybody was happy. And grateful. Because when Frank scowled, there were no happy faces around.

After dinner, when everybody had wandered off, Frank and I sat on a couch on the patio. I felt relaxed and contented. We listened to his records and now and then he would hum a few bars. It was very romantic.

Then his mood seemed to change when the song *Here's My Rainy Day* was playing. It's a very touching song and for some reason I had the feeling that he associated it with Ava Gardner. He became quiet, very sad looking, as he listened to it. Later he said the song had a special meaning for him, but I didn't pursue it.

We kissed. He was gentle, and really very sweet. After a while he stood up, took my hand, and said softly, "Let's go inside." He put his arm around my waist and steered me into his bedroom. He was very gentle, romantic, expressive, sensual, and very active when we made love, and very loving afterward. He seemed genuinely concerned that I was happy and just kept his arms around me all night long. We made love again during the night and when we awakened in the morning. It was the most idyllic night I ever spent with Frank.

It was a lazy week. People kept coming in and out of Frank's suite. We sat in the sun—Frank worked hard on his tan—and drank Jack Daniels. One day flowed into the other without any noticeable transition. Much of it was not memorable, but there were moments that remain with me.

Frank and I went shopping one day, just the two of us, and we had great fun. We went to a market and he was like a kid in a candy store. We bought milk, bread, cheese, and piled all kinds of delicacies into a shopping cart. He got such a kick out of it that it was obviously a long time since he had been in a market. For a moment he was able to act like an ordinary shopper. People paid very little attention to him, which was surprising since he was then at the peak of his career. The only damper on the day was when we went into a department store. I bought a purse, hose, a scarf, and a full petticoat, and he wasn't too thrilled when I wouldn't let him pay for them. But it was no major catastrophe. We even walked back to the hotel holding hands.

On the third night we went to a Japanese restaurant. We had a private room and sat on pillows while two Japanese girls cooked the dinner at our table. Pat was getting annoyed at the attention Frank and Pete were paying the girls, and vice versa—Japanese girls know how to stroke a man's ego. Pat whispered a few snide remarks about the girls. She thought the boys were going overboard in their attention, but they were just having a good time; much of it, I think, was designed to pull our leg. Finally, completely exasperated, Pat scribbled on a cocktail napkin and passed it over to me. The first thing I noticed was the strength and boldness of her handwriting. It looked more like a man's writing, with the letters going straight up and down. She wrote: "I still think they're full of shit!" She had shit underlined about seven times. Pat's language is basic. There's nothing flowery about her speech. When she wants to emphasize a point, she has no hesitation about using four-letter words.

One afternoon while everybody was sitting around in the living room, two Japanese girls—pretty, delicate little things—were escorted into Frank's bedroom. Frank and Pete stood up and Frank said something about it being time for their massage. It was so blatantly obvious. You just knew what the score was. Neither one was just getting a massage, there just wasn't a chance. The funny thing is that I don't remember really caring. Pat was furious. To Red Krohn and Ester, who were close to Frank, there was nothing unusual about it.

That evening Frank excused himself and said he was going to lie down a while. He didn't feel too sharp. Pat and the others disappeared and the first thing I knew there was just Pete and me sitting there finishing our drinks. Pete came over and sat next to me on the sofa, and after a little light banter, he just casually suggested that we take a walk on the beach. The way he said it, it was plain he had other things on his mind besides walking. I told him I didn't think so. The British accent got a little more pronounced as he leaned forward to look deep into my eyes. "But darling," he said, touching my hand, "don't worry, Frank will never know." He was a little high and coming on a little too strong. I took my hand away and stood up. "Thank you," I replied, "but I really don't think so." He stood up and gave me his most boyish grin. "Look, I'll call Pat and tell her I'm going to take a walk on the beach. Come on, why not?" I figured the easiest way out of it was to play along. "All right," I said. "Let me go to my room first. I want to freshen up and get a wrap. It may be a little chilly out there. When you get downstairs, call me and I'll meet you on the beach." I felt like adding, "If I'm late, start without me." I went to my room, locked my door, and went to bed. The phone rang a long time but I didn't pick it up.

The next morning, which was Saturday, Frank seemed a little perturbed. "What happened?" he asked. "Why didn't you just come in when you wanted to go to bed?"

"I went to my room," I said. "I thought you weren't feeling well."

He let it go at that but I could tell he was disappointed. Although we had been sleeping together since the first night, I kept my clothes and cosmetics in my own room down the hall. When I wanted to set my hair or do my face, or shower and freshen up, I had a room I could go to. I never would have moved into his room, even if it meant getting a room on a different floor. I still needed that little shelter away from everybody, a place I could call my own, preferably a place I could pay for with my own money. That made me feel independent.

Pete had an even longer face when he came into the suite, but he had the good grace not to mention it. That afternoon the four of us—Frank, Pete, Pat and I—went to play golf. I should say we went to the golf course. I rode in an electric cart with Frank but I certainly didn't play golf.

Something strange began to happen out there. Frank was

getting sullen and I could see that it had nothing to do with his game. He and Pete did a lot of talking as they fooled around the greens, and I had the feeling that they were talking about me. Later, when I looked back on it, I felt that Pete might have said something about me to Frank. I was the new girl in the crowd. Pete was a trusted friend. It occurred to me that Pete might have wanted to protect himself in case I said something to Frank about the night before. I could visualize him saying something like, "Boy, is she something. I don't know how you feel about her, Frank, but be careful." Then he could twist it around and say that I had suggested a walk on the beach, and he being the good trusted friend that he was, had naturally rejected my advances.

That evening we went out to dinner and it was a nightmare. There were about twelve of us seated at a rectangular table, and Frank and I were facing a dark-haired woman and her husband, who was loaded. In fact, everybody was pretty well loaded. The dark-haired woman, in her middle thirties, was completely enthralled with Frank, who was gradually getting vicious with everyone except her. He would stare at her, openly flirting, and had no interest in anyone else. He totally ignored me. A couple of times I asked him what was wrong, and he just looked at me and there was a surly expression on his face as he snapped, "Nothing."

If I had known what he was really like I would have told him to go stuff it. I'd have gone back to the hotel for my bags and would have been on a plane back to the mainland that night. But I was confused. I thought, how can this charming, loving person all of a sudden turn so ugly?"

"What did I do?" I asked again. "If I did something, please tell me."

He looked like he was going to spit on me. "Nothing," he said, and if he could have just turned his back to me, I think he would have. I finally just didn't talk to him.

I've had time to think about Frank Sinatra and his Jekyll and Hyde personality. This will come up again in the book, but for the moment I'd like to say that I was not totally unaware of his reputation as a tough guy. I had read about his bodyguards and his fights in public places. Without trying to analyze him, it's possible that much of it has to do with the fact that he's a tiny man with a big man complex. Frank gets considerably shorter when he takes his shoes off. He's heavyset today but his bone structure is small. His wrists are delicate. In his mind he feels he's a big man, that he has power, and the way he proves it is to push people around.

Everybody around Frank walks on eggs all the time. Everybody is smiling and happy when Frank is smiling and happy, but the minute Frank starts to frown, everybody is quiet and fearful. No one dares talk back to him. He berates everybody mercilessly and they take it and take it. It's a very distasteful atmosphere to be in. I resent seeing people who are recognized for their own accomplishments take his tongue lashing and kow-tow to him in the bargain. Frank knows what he's doing. He was always careful about what he said to Pat, since she was a Kennedy, but he just pulverized Pete at will.

Once he gets someone under his thumb, it's never-ending. He will just mistreat that person whenever it suits him, whenever he gets in one of his black moods and needs to abuse something or someone. He will do it to those who will take it. And he'll try it with some who won't, but not too often. I think when Frank gets into fights or when people are hurt by his bodyguards, it's because he picked the wrong person to give a bad time to. There are people who say, "I don't give a damn whether you're Frank Sinatra or Jesus Christ. Nobody talks to me like that."

When we got to the hotel that night, I went directly to my room. I asked Red Krohn to come in and I said, "What's the matter? What's happening?" He said, "Don't pay any attention to it. He'll be okay." So I left it at that. When I went in the next day and saw that Frank was the same way, I told him I was leaving. I said I had things to take care of at home and he didn't even look at me. I went back to my room, called the airlines and booked a midnight flight.

Red Krohn came to my room and I said, "I'm really very upset about all this. I don't know what's going on and I'm very hurt by it and very insulted by this treatment."

I made an excuse at that point because my ego was hurting.

I told Red, "Well, it worked out for the best, really. It's made me realize that I'm very much in love with someone else." I was referring to Travis, and boy, I was so happy that I could fall back on that. It seemed the perfect lie. All I wanted was for Red to go back and tell that to Frank. It was such a childish thing to do.

That evening they gave me a going away party, like everything was just fine, everything was peaches and cream, but Judy had to leave, you know, and don't we all love Judy. If I had been strong enough, I think I would have taken Frank and thrown him over the balcony. On the other hand, I didn't want to let him know that it bothered me that much.

The party that evening in Frank's suite was just a replay of the night before. The dark-haired woman was there and he was still flirting, still just giving her such a snow job. The vile mood he was in, I think he was daring her husband to do something about it. I didn't even want to sit next to him. It was a long evening. I just couldn't wait to get out of there, but finally it was time for my exit and I didn't even say goodbye to Frank. Everyone at the party gave me their leis and Pete took me to the airport in a limousine. The leis were put in a large box and Pete said he would see that they were checked through with my luggage. I never saw them again. I was furious. I could picture Pete getting them back after I walked away.

I don't have an ounce of respect for Pete Lawford. I think he's an ass. He makes the best flunky in the world because it's important to Pete to be with important people. He'll sacrifice himself, take a tremendous amount of punishment, just to be there with Frank. When Frank gets into one of his black moods and turns on him, Pete just sits there and takes it. And when Pat talked, he listened. If there was a disagreement in their conversation, it was Pat who had the last word. He kept his mouth shut. Later, I would learn from Sam Giancana that he too had no respect for Pete. More on that later.

Anyone would think that after that week in Hawaii I would have had my fill of Frank Sinatra. Not so. I arrived home the morning of November 16, and that evening when I returned from a dinner date with Travis and his mother, there was a message from Frank which my sister Jackie had left for me on about twenty feet of toilet paper.

The message started out with, "Hawaii called twice, Aloha, I told him you were out on your surfboard," and it went on in that vein across the room, the paper draped over chairs, lamps, sofa—wall-to-wall Western Union. The last line was something like, "Can I borrow ten bucks till Thursday?"

I was very excited, very thrilled, that he had called, because at that point I was more confused, more hurt than angry. I was sorry it had gone wrong and I was disappointed because I would have loved to have it continue the way it had been the first few days. It had been a frustrating experience. There was something about Frank that I really liked, and I was questioning myself, wondering whether I had been too quiet, not interesting enough, and I didn't like that thought. Perhaps he was just too worldly and I was too naive. I had agonized over it until I was kicking quite a hole in my ego, which was not that resilient to begin with.

Frank called at two the next afternoon. He was very concerned about whether I was all right. The thought that struck me was, "What did you think I was going to do? Go jump off a bridge because I was treated badly by Frank Sinatra?" Yet I sensed that he was uncomfortable, that perhaps he suffered a little when he mistreated someone that really didn't deserve it. He sort of apologized but he didn't offer any explanation and I didn't ask for one. He promised to call again and I said that would be fine. I had a peculiar reaction after he hung up. Instead of feeling giddy and girlish, I thought, "Well, you big shot, you feel guilty don't you?" It restored my ego somewhat.

Now that I was free of Travis, and had moved in with Jackie, the phone never stopped ringing. I don't mean to sound immodest, but I had met a lot of people when I was with Billy and Travis who were just waiting for the day I became unattached. It was the first time Judy Campbell was available. I could have had dates morning, noon and night. As I said earlier, for the first time in my life I began dating the way most girls date when they're in high school.

Life became so good. I slept until nine, sometimes ten if I was up very late, and tried to paint at least two hours every morning. I lunched with friends or went to the studio and had lunch with Jackie. I painted some more in the afternoon, or went shopping. I didn't have dinner at home one night a month. And I never went out to dinner in a restaurant alone or with just other women. To this day I don't like the picture it presents. When I travel alone on a train, I never leave my compartment. The same applies to hotels. When I'm alone, I live on room service.

I traded in my Olds 98 for a new Pontiac convertible. It was marvelous riding to Palm Springs with the top down. I visited the Whittakers, the Elwoods, Sam and Marilyn Sontag, all the people I had met through Travis. I became a regular weekend guest at the Racquet Club.

It took a few calls before I agreed to meet Frank in Palm Springs. I wanted to see him but I didn't want to just go rushing in. Our date was for the evening of December 7, and I drove up in the morning and checked in at the Racquet Club. I had an early dinner with the Sontags and at nine-thirty that evening I arrived at Frank's Palm Desert home, which is a few miles beyond Palm Springs.

I was surprised at the size of Frank's house. It was nice and comfortable, but compared to the opulent homes I had lived in and the homes of others I knew, it was a modest, quite ordinary house. It certainly was not the home of a famous movie star.

Even the living room was small. There was a wall bar and a piano at one end. Two beige couches faced each other in front of the fireplace, with a large coffee table between them. There were sliding glass doors leading out to a patio and pool, and the motif was orange and black Oriental.

The only impressive thing about Frank's bedroom, as I was to discover later that evening, were twin beds and a glass shower in the room itself. Luckily, there was another bathroom connecting with the bedroom which had a shower and tub. There was no way I would have used the bedroom shower.

Frank's houseboy, George, opened the door and Frank was right behind him. He seemed very relaxed and in fine spirits. He bussed me on the cheek and gave me a big wink. "I'm glad you could make it," he said, taking my elbow and guiding me into the living room. Besides Pat and Pete Lawford, there were three others in the room. Jack Entratter, who was president of the Sands hotel in Las Vegas, Jimmy Van Heusen, a song writer, and Johnny Formosa, who, as best as I could make out, had some connection with the Chicago underworld. Frank walked very carefully around him.

Before I arrived, Frank and Jimmy Van Heusen had been working on a song for a picture called *Oceans 11* that Frank was going to start shooting in Las Vegas. After the introductions they went back to work. Jimmy was at the piano and Frank was singing but moving around the room, and quite often he would come to the sofa and put his hand on my shoulder as he sang, all the while giving me that twinkle of his, flirting with me, but in a gentle way. It was the same kind of attentiveness he had first given me in Hawaii.

We had a spaghetti dinner, which I hate when I'm eating out because it's always such a messy thing to eat. But Frank, like most Italians, just loves it. After dinner we went back into the living room and Frank sat next to me, keeping his arm around my shoulders the whole time we sat there. From time to time he would give me a little squeeze, lean over to kiss my cheek, and say softly, "Are you all right? You want anything?" There was a lot of joking and laughter, but again I was very quiet and had very little to say.

Frank was particularly pleased that Formosa was there. He liked being with him, having him around. Frank always seemed partial to underworld types. You could tell when he was around someone like that. He enjoyed them more than anyone else. Sometimes I think he was just a frustrated hoodlum. It was an element that he thrived in.

But Frank made sharp distinctions between a genuine

hoodlum like Formosa and a man like Jack Entratter. Frank could be brutal with Entratter, who, like Pete Lawford, took it without a word of protest.

As the evening came to an end and people began leaving or disappearing into bedrooms, Frank leaned over and said, "You'll stay, won't you." I knew what he meant and I said, "Yes."

We made love and it was the same as it had been before. He was very gentle, very attentive, very loving, and very active. He did not expect to be made love to. We slept in each other's arms.

For breakfast the next morning, Frank had a scrambled egg and bacon sandwich on toasted sourdough bread. I never had that before and it was quite good. I've had it many times since then. It's a much tastier way of having scrambled eggs, if you're just having plain scrambled eggs. I'm a garbage scrambled egg eater—I empty the refrigerator and dump it all in.

Everyone just stretched out on chaise lounges around the pool and took the sun. Frank had a tap beer dispenser out on the patio and there was a lot of beer drinking. Jack Entratter and I hit tennis balls on Frank's court. Jack was about six foot four and three hundred pounds, but there was something wrong with his feet or his legs. He had difficulty moving around. I had to hit the ball right to him because he just stood there without moving. Nobody paid any attention to us and so it was fun.

That evening Frank and I and the Lawfords went to Romanoff's for dinner—his restaurant in Palm Springs wasn't open too many seasons. This was the first time I remember the name of Jack Kennedy coming up in the conversation. The whole evening was a political discussion, and Pat had the floor. I remember how amazed I was at the thought that her brother was making a bid for the presidency. Slowly it dawned on me who Jack Kennedy really was and then I could see the striking resemblance to his sister.

Frank was all ears as Pat analyzed Jack's chances in the coming primaries. He seemed so subdued and respectful.

Even Pete commanded his attention when he talked about Jack. The more Pete talked the more British he became until it was downright ridiculous.

After we made love that night Frank still had Jack Kennedy on his mind. "You know," he said, "I'll bet even money Jack gets the nomination."

"It sounds like something you really want," I said, struggling to keep my eyes open.

"Why not," he said. "Jack's a great guy. And don't forget, he's my friend. I know how to help my friends." He gave me a hug and I was soon sound asleep.

The next morning Frank was very quiet, not sullen yet, but slowly on his way there. I decided it was time for me to leave. I just couldn't figure him out. He seemed so complex. I think he wants to be so many different people that he doesn't know who he is. The one thing I knew was that I wasn't going to take any of his abuse. But I kept coming back to Frank because there is something compellingly attractive about him that draws you like a magnet. I think that's why so many stick to him even when he grinds his heel into their very soul.

Though Travis and I were no longer lovers we still saw a lot of each other and became, as I said, very close friends. That was before he married Carolyn Taper, Mark Taper's daughter, and I became that other woman. We went to Palm Springs on December 12, which was Frank's birthday, but I didn't see Frank. The week before I had ordered leather album covers as a gift for Frank. A day or two before his birthday I took them to his office in Beverly Hills and gave them to Gloria, his personal secretary. I later saw them on a shelf at his Beverly Hills home, but he never mentioned them to me.

That whole month of December, Travis and I spent more time in Palm Springs than in Beverly Hills. I was extremely fond of the Springs, but as I look back on it now, I can see that it wasn't exactly the paradise that I thought it was. We went to a different party every night. I say different, but actually all these parties were exactly alike. There were

64

cocktails and hors d'oeuvres, and no matter what time the party started, whether it was six-thirty or nine-thirty, dinner was always served, and it was almost always buffet, between eleven and midnight. There was a tremendous variety of food, but it was always the same variety, really not very imaginative. They were fun because a great many of the people we knew came to these parties in a very pleasant frame of mind.

Bob Whittaker had the most interesting parties. He often entertained important people from Washington. I remember dancing with Senator Ribicoff at one of Bob's parties. Bob doesn't believe in doing anything unless he can do it the very best way possible. If he served caviar, it was *Baluga*. If he served vodka, it was Russian. When Bob had a formal dinner, he would serve authentic dishes from the country he was favoring that evening. Bob's homes were designed for entertaining. Besides his Palm Springs home, he had a beautiful place at Lake Arrowhead and a grand old mansion on June Street in Los Angeles. Bob was the quietest, the gentlest, the most unassuming man I had ever met.

Scotty Rubin also threw some of the parties I attended. Scotty was typical of the rich, older man with the big house, the big car, and the big blond on his arm. There are certain men who always have a flashy girl on their arm. If straight skirts are in fashion, the flashy girl's skirt is cut so that it completely shows the contours of her body, with the slit just a little higher in the back. Her décolletage is a little lower, her hair is more lacquered, her false eyelashes a little longer, her mascara a little heavier—everything is a little flashier. The walk is a little different too. The stride is longer, the hips move a little more, and dignity hasn't a great deal to do with it.

Escorting this type of woman seems to work miracles for the ego of some men. The other men sit around saying, "Wow, see what Scotty's got tonight!" It lends itself to a certain type of men's humor. You see them whispering together, "Whoa, whoa, whoa!" and giving it that limp-wrist shake of the hand. Like the food at the party, flashy girls come in a variety of shades and sizes, but it's always the same variety. They are presented as "actresses," that's the standard line whether they are starlets or hookers. In New York, the term is model.

I used to get so irritated when my name would appear in the newspaper and they would call me an actress. It upset me because I wasn't an actress and I wasn't passing myself off as one. I didn't like the association. If you are an actress, that's fine, but if you're not, it creates a different picture. I never liked publicity, but you couldn't move in those circles without getting into the gossip columns. For example, when I came back from Hawaii, Harrison Carroll, who wrote a truly gossipy column for the old *Herald Express,* carried an item about it. He wrote, "Judy Campbell says she wasn't dating Frank Sinatra as such but that they did get around together in Hawaii since they were in a group and saw a lot of each other. Frankie was enjoying a couple of weeks over there with Peter Lawford and his wife and kids." Harrison called me often but most of the time I was able to dissuade him from using my name.

Life in Palm Springs moves at a slower pace than in Los Angeles or New York. The weather in winter is ideal, warm and dry, and you can get your tan, all of which is conducive to feeling good. People go there to have a good time, to play tennis and golf, to swim, to sit out in the sun, to party, but it's not a racing kind of party life. There is a cocktail hour in New York that never seems to end. Lunch is a cocktail hour, four o'clock is a cocktail hour and so is seven o'clock. Much has been written about the loose life in California, and some of it is true, but New York doesn't take a back seat to any other place. Successful businessmen in New York stick their wives in the suburbs and stay in the city all week. New York wives probably do the same thing at their suburban country clubs that California wives do in Palm Springs or Beverly Hills. Or, for that matter, wives at some cheaper country club in the midwest. Men are men and women are women, whether they have a dime or a million. Both the poor and the rich get bored. They either play around or they don't. Geography has nothing to do with it. Perhaps it's a little more available in some areas, but if sex is what you really want, you can find it.

I liked the atmosphere at the Springs. The whole town was clean and compact and expensive enough to be exclusive. I thought it was sophisticated. I loved the Racquet Club and its ambience then, although I couldn't stand it today. Now I can see a certain phoniness. Even then I couldn't mix with the wives who spent all day in their little tennis skirts, flirting with the glamour boys (the young bit players who try to make it in the movies by pleasing the wives of successful Hollywood men), playing gin, discussing their affairs and gossiping about the affairs of others. They are players, hard as nails, and if you don't like the games they play, you're out.

Perhaps because my marriage to Billy had been so disastrous, it seemed to me that the married men were worse than the single ones. They were always looking, always hunting. You'd see them at parties with different girls and every once in a while you'd see them at a party with their wives. As far as I was concerned, I had made up my mind that if I got married again, I'd have to accept the fact that my husband would cheat.

No matter how long I live, I'll never forget January 5, 1960. That's the day I had dinner with Richard Ney, the actor who played the son of Greer Garson in *Mrs. Miniver* and who is now a stockbroker.

He picked me up in his Rolls, and when I say he drives slowly, I mean he crawls along the street. You get the feeling that he's living in another world; that he is not with us. He drives that car the way the car looks. I don't know quite how to express it, but I was really awestruck. His manner was so proper and precise. There was never a lull in his conversation. He always thought of something else to say. As the car slowly inched its way through the streets, I felt like he and the car had an agreement. He wasn't going to hurt the car and the car wasn't going to hurt him; he was going to take care of it and it was going to take care of him.

When we arrived at his house in the hills above Sunset, he

took my elbow gently and guided me into the house. There wasn't a chair that wasn't placed just properly for two people to spend an evening together. The dining room table, which I could see partly when I came into the living room, was already set. The lights were just right—they weren't too bright or too low. The hors d'oeuvres were already out. If he had someone in that house preparing things, you never felt it, you never knew it.

I felt I was being swept out of this world and almost as if, "My God, I wonder if I'm ever going to get back." And not only out of this world, but out of this time—I was going back in time to when Hollywood was something else.

He put on some romantic music, fixed the drinks, and sat for a few minutes, talking all the time. Then he took a gentle sip from his perfectly chilled martini, turned to me and said, "Would you like to dance?" I couldn't believe it. I didn't know what to say. I know that the movies have done this scene so that it looks very romantic. There is a fireplace and candlelight and the couple dances beautifully together. You may even feel envious as you watch the movie. But it just doesn't fit in real life. Nevertheless there we were dancing all alone in this room and I felt that pretty soon someone was going to say, "Cut! That's a print." I wasn't entirely sure that it was really happening. The dance was torture because I didn't know whether I was going to burst out laughing or run out of the place and yell "Help!"

When we sat down, and again I didn't even have to think of anything to say because he would not allow a lull in the conversation, I had a terrible urge to cross my legs. But I didn't dare because I was afraid that my hose would make a noise or my foot might accidently touch the coffee table. That noise would not have belonged in that scene. I was happy that I hadn't worn taffeta.

He put his arm up around my shoulder but it was as if he had looked at the clock and said, "Well, now it's time to put the arm around the shoulder." It was just exactly the right time before dinner was served.

When we entered the dining room, the candles were lit and the dinner was in serving dishes. He served and by now I was really getting nervous. What would I do if my knife clanked on my plate? Throughout dinner he sat very erect and he always had the proper thing to say.

After dinner he escorted me back to the living room. I had the feeling that instead of walking I was on rollers and he was just steering me around, with never a halt, to the right place. I floated down on the sofa. The liqueurs were on the coffee table and by now I was convinced that there was someone else in the house, perhaps an Oriental houseboy tiptoeing in his stocking feet. But I never heard a sound or saw a soul.

It was survival now. He offered me a liqueur and I took it. I was afraid not to have something in front of me. I had to be busy because strange as the evening had been, I didn't know what was coming up next. I wouldn't have been surprised to see him turn into a werewolf. There had to be some kind of drastic change. This couldn't continue.

So we sat for a couple of minutes, and I began to get the feeling that he was talking slower. Something was coming. This was the time to be more romantic—the clock said so, or the book said that after dinner you do such and such. Again this studied way of putting his arm around my shoulder and when he leaned over to kiss me I had the feeling that someone said, "Camera! Action!" because everything was perfect. His arms went around me and one hand reached the back of my head gently; his head lowered toward me and stopped when his face was in front of mine.

I was trying to be very quiet and nice, and I let him kiss me, but very gently. I'm surprised that I didn't stare at him wide-eyed. He kissed me again very gently and whatever his words were I just don't know because my head was going a mile a minute. My biggest fear was that I would start laughing. Finally, when he began to get a little more amorous, I made some outrageous excuse that I had to leave— something like I think I'm coming down with the plague— anything to get me out of there. He was surprised, but in a way that a person might be when he doesn't want you to know he's surprised. His eyes seemed to say, "But my performance was so great, why is this review so bad."

You could almost feel what was going on inside of him. I

sensed a little extra effort then in maintaining the conversation without a lull. But he did and he was very nice when he escorted me out to the Rolls. It took forever for him to back up. He let the motor run for ages, checked and rechecked the instruments, and checked and rechecked the rear-view mirror. Again it was, "Don't worry, I'm going to take care of you." We crawled down the hill and now I had the feeling that the wheels were not touching the road, that we were floating down the hill.

Even on Sunset Boulevard, with cars whizzing by and people crossing the street and lights flashing on and off, this car was just going slowly down the street and nobody touched it. To tell the truth, I don't think anybody else could see it.

When we arrived at my place, he just came around, opened the door, and escorted me to the front door. He held my shoulders gently as he leaned forward to kiss me and I turned my face and he gave me a light kiss on the cheek. I said, "Good night," thanked him for the lovely dinner and lovely evening, and apologized for having had to end it so early, all the time thinking, "God, if I don't get in that door soon I'm going to explode." He said he would definitely call me the next day and that he wanted to have dinner with me again soon, and perhaps I had a favorite restaurant we could go to. He waited until I was safely in the building before turning and walking very slowly back to his Rolls. I barely made it to my apartment before getting completely hysterical. I laughed and laughed until it hurt. He did call me the next day, and he called several times before he finally gave up. I think of him at times and wonder if he's real. There's an old expression that says a man, whether he's a king or a peasant, puts his pants on one leg at a time. That's not possible with Richard Ney: I have the feeling that he wishes his clothes on and off, he's that different from the rest of us.

Although I was dating a great deal during this period, I was more interested in having men as friends than as lovers. I've always preferred the company of men to that of women.

Marty Tamambaum and Sy Devore were two such friends. Sy was the most fashionable tailor in Beverly Hills and a member of Frank's Rat Pack. I think Marty was involved in horseracing and had all kinds of irons in the fire, none of which he ever talked about. Sy and Marty were the best of friends. Marty was also a close friend of Jerry Lewis, who comes up later in this story.

To this day I haven't been able to figure out Mort Viner. I don't know whether he was a talent agent, a business manager, or a hanger-on. All I know is that he seemed involved with the entertainment industry. Mort was Mr. Average—average height, average build, average age, average intelligence, average looks.

I had met Dean Martin about ten years earlier, but through Mort I became reacquainted with Dean. Early in January 1960, Mort and I had dinner at LaScala with Dean and his wife Jeanne. Jeanne was a good friend of Gloria Cahn (Sammy's wife). They were typical Hollywood wives. They were not very nice to a single attractive woman and tended to band together against outside threats. Yet they didn't feel threatened by starlets who would sleep with anybody's husband to get a part. There's such an overabundance of them that it's become just another facet of the business.

I was an unknown factor. They couldn't quite place me. Although I was more comfortable talking to men, I never paid much attention to their husbands simply because I didn't want them to reciprocate with their wives sitting there. I wasn't completely comfortable with the wives because I could feel them withdrawing, being cautious, and then I would have to try to prove myself. Very often I felt like saying, "Look, I don't care about your husband. I'm not the least interested. Now, do you want to be friends?" Of course I'd never say it, but it was a feeling I had whenever I was around Hollywood wives.

I was about seventeen and dating Billy the first time I met Dean Martin. Jackie was part of The Golden Circle at Paramount, which was a group of young people they were grooming for stardom. Barbara Rush was in the group. Paramount changed Jackie's name to Susan Morrow. Two of her early costarring roles were in *The Savage* with Charlton Heston and *Burning Forest* with John Payne.

One day while I was visiting her at Paramount, we went over to the set of a picture that I think was called *Sailor Beware,* and it starred Dean Martin and Jerry Lewis. To say that the boys were exuberant is to put it mildly. The next thing we knew the studio wanted Jackie to go to San Diego with Dean and Jerry to do a layout for a movie magazine. I was to accompany her. We were told the studio was sending a limousine to drive us to San Diego, but Jackie got suspicious and checked with the studio. The boys were pulling a fast one. It was their limousine and the picture layout was just part of their little scheme. Jackie was furious, but not as furious as Billy, who swore up and down that he was going to kill Dean. Danny Arnold had told him that Dean was trying to date me.

If Dean remembered the incident that evening at La Scala he gave no indication of it. His secret preoccupation that evening, as it was many of the evenings I was to spend with him, was with Mort Viner. Dean thought that Mort and Jeanne were seeing each other. I saw a lot of Dean in the next few months. He would call me at all hours of the day or night, and much of the time he just wanted to talk about Jeanne and Mort.

Even so, Dean and I had a pleasant relationship. I know that Dean is a player, but he never made a serious play for me. He would kid about it from time to time, but I don't think that Dean is a very virile man. He's a slow-moving, relaxed kind of human being; there's nothing pretentious about him. He likes to sit up and drink all night. I think he enjoyed our relationship because I wasn't after anything, and he didn't have to give a great deal of himself. He could be great fun to be with when he was in a good mood. He has a tremendous sense of humor. People around Dean always laughed a lot.

My next date with Frank was a total disaster. It made Hawaii really look like paradise. The evening started with dinner at Romanoff's in Beverly Hills. It was a long dinner, followed by some heavy drinking in the bar. By the time we got to Frank's house, my stomach was feeling a little queasy.

72

Sometimes when I dined out I wouldn't eat enough of my dinner and the liquor would hit me harder.

Frank was sympathetic. He said, "Go in the bedroom and go to bed. I've got to make a phone call and I'll be with you in a few minutes."

I remember I undressed in the bathroom and went to bed. I dozed off and the next thing I knew Frank was getting into bed beside me. He put his arms around me and as I turned to look at him I saw the bedroom door open and this tall black girl came in without a stitch of clothing on.

I blinked my eyes, trying to clear my vision, not really wanting to believe what I was seeing. She was smiling as she crawled in beside Frank.

I just absolutely froze. I went rigid: no one could have moved my arms or legs. You would have had to pry them loose with a steel bar, that's how stiff I was.

She immediately pulled down the covers and began to make love to him, orally, while I remained absolutely rigid. Frank realized what was happening when I started to shake. I was trying to keep from crying—I could feel it welling up inside of me, choking me, until I thought I was going to lose control. I wanted to run out but I knew I couldn't move a muscle.

Frank waited until she had completed the sex act before he eased her out of the bed and followed her into the bathroom. I could hear him whispering to her, and then they came out and he opened the bedroom door and she left. He got back into bed, put his arms around me and began apologizing. By then I was sobbing out of control. He said he was sorry, but he hadn't realized I would be so affected by it. He said he should have known better, or at least he should have first discussed it with me. When that didn't work, he tried to calm me down with reassurances that she was gone and wouldn't be coming back. I just crumpled. The last thing I remember before falling asleep was Frank cooing to me like one does to a baby that won't stop crying.

Frank was still sleeping when I got up the next morning and went into the next room to dress. A few minutes later he came into the room and put his arms around me. He was wearing a robe and there was a sheepish look on his face. "Are you all right?" he said. I nodded and he said, "I'm sorry about last night."

"It's okay," I said, "but I don't really want to talk about it."

"I don't blame you," he said. "It was a mistake. But how was I to know you'd take it so hard."

"Have I ever given you any indication that I would take it lightly?"

Frank laughed and pulled away from me. "Judy," he said, shaking his head. "You're so square I can't believe it."

I could feel anger rising inside of me. "Frank," I said, and my voice was shaking, "you may think I'm a prude, but it's just not my cup of tea." I could hear how stupid that sounded but I forged ahead anyway. "It's not something I'm interested in. But I'm not criticizing you. I don't care what your tastes are. That's your business. When someone closes the bedroom door, whatever goes on in there is their business, but it's got to be something the two people consent to. If they want to add a third, fourth, fifth or sixth, that's fine as long as it's what they all want. I have no objection to any of it as long as you don't try to include me in it against my will."

My voice was really off key by the time I got that mouthful out. I was looking down at the floor because I could feel myself—my insides—just shaking. I knew if I looked at him I would break down and cry. I wanted to make my point and yet I didn't want to talk about it. Several times I said, "I don't want to talk about it," and then I'd go off on a tangent. I could see that he was very uncomfortable, but instead of caring, I was pleased. I wanted him to be miserable.

When I finished dressing, he took my arm and guided me into the breakfast room. "Come on," he said, "I want you to have something to eat with me. I don't want you to leave feeling the way you do right now."

I sat at the table and had coffee, but I wanted to get out of there. I wasn't going to really calm down, if even then, but I knew the first thing I had to do was get out of there. I was on the edge of hysteria, and the last thing I wanted was to get

74

hysterical in front of Frank. Nor did I want to leave in anger. I knew he was genuinely sorry for what had happened. That's probably why we remained friends.

My problem was that I knew how Frank could be. His physical contacts with me had been most pleasant. After making love, he was loving. He was understanding when I was upset. He could be a very thoughtful, very attentive, very gentle person. He just was not consistent. You couldn't spend too much time with him and expect him to be that way all the time. I had seen his black moods and I would see them again. I knew how he treated the people around him. His attitude reminded me of someone kicking a poor defenseless mutt in the ribs. He was venting whatever ugliness was inside of him, taking it out on whoever was handiest, whoever was closest. People around Frank were always trying to explain him. They all had a different explanation or reason for the way he behaved. He was something different to everyone because they each had to find an excuse for taking his abuse. Whatever was lacking in them showed up in Frank.

Now I had seen still another side of Frank and I was terribly disappointed. There was something about him at given times that I just adored. It was so frustrating to think, "My God, why does this man have to change so at times?" Although I was blaming him, I still had the feeling that there was something wrong with me. I was too quiet, not outgoing enough, and I just couldn't adjust to Frank and the people around him.

Perhaps if I had been in love with Frank, I would have tried harder to please him. I was infatuated with him. I just adored him when he was being nice. He knows how to make you feel like a complete woman.

Frank sent me home in a limousine and later in the day called me. He was still being apologetic. "I just wanted to check and see how you are doing," he said.

I said I was fine and he said, "Good to hear." Then he started telling me that he was going to start filming *Oceans 11* in Las Vegas with the Clan. They were going to shoot in the daytime and put on a show at the Sands at night.

"Why don't you come up and see the show? We're going

to be there for quite a while, and I thought maybe you'd enjoy a little change. Come on, say yes, it'll be a gas."

I remember saying something like, "No more antics, no more rabbits out of the hat?" I said it lightheartedly and he laughed, and I could sense that he was relieved. It was as if I had pardoned him.

Another good friend who liked to talk about his wife was Ray Anthony. Ray was an orchestra leader and married to Mamie Van Doren. He carried a torch for her all his life. But he was fun to be with. Back in January 1960, Ray was enjoying another of his many comebacks.

On January 12, we went to a party at the home of Joe Perrin, whom I had known for many years. There was a story Joe loved to tell about the Saturday morning he took Aly Kahn to my home to meet Jackie. That was after Aly and Rita Hayworth had separated, and Jackie was a beautiful girl with flaming red hair that looked very much like Rita's.

It was the old story. If you can't have the original, get a good copy. The only problem was that Jackie was a very independent headstrong girl who was not impressed by celebrities. Just minutes before Joe and Aly were to arrive at our home, Jackie said to my mother, "Tell Joe I had to go somewhere," and off she went. My father was working in the garden, all grubby, and my mother was making out her shopping list because Saturday was the day they did their weekly shopping—by then the cupboards were bare.

When Joe arrived with Aly Kahn—Jackie had neglected to mention him—my mother invited them in and asked if they would like something to eat, not thinking for a minute that they would accept. All she had left was a Coke and a couple of hot dogs. They said they'd be delighted. So Aly, one of the world's richest men, sat in our kitchen and shared a Coke with my mom and dad and had half a hot dog. Joe has told the story a thousand times, exaggerating it a little more each time, about how embarrassed and yet how dignified my mother was through it all. Of course, what Joe never realized was that my mother would have been just as embarrassed and just as dignified if it had happened with one of our neighbors.

76

Frank called again and insisted that I come to Las Vegas to see the show, which according to the reviews was a blockbuster—it starred Frank, Dean, Peter Lawford, Sammy Davis, and Joey Bishop. Frank wouldn't take no for an answer. We made a date for dinner after the late show on January 23, which was a Saturday, and that morning I flew to Las Vegas with Dick and Marilyn Elwood.

After checking into our rooms we met in the lounge for a drink, and within minutes Dean Martin was at our table, smiling at us in that soft way of his, and saying, "Hi, there, how are you today. Are you going to be here long?"

I introduced him to the Elwoods and he sat down. "Hey, it's good to see you again," he said. "Going to see the show tonight?"

I said yes and before I could say another word, he said, "Okay, I want you folks to sit at my table, you hear? No arguments, now."

I hated to tell him. "Frank has already invited us," I said. Dean didn't bat an eye. "That's fine," he said. "Maybe I'll see you after the show. You staying here at the hotel?"

This was before he had confided his suspicions about Jeanne and Mort Viner. When he stood up to leave, he very casually said, "Have you seen Mort lately?"

It was one of the funniest, one of the best shows I've ever seen. There was a barrel of talent up on that stage. They were all great ad-libbers. The only weak link was Lawford, the one with the least talent, and the least amount of respect from anybody. Pete was the butt of all the jokes. He was there because he was in *Oceans 11*, and I think he was in that picture because he was married to Pat Kennedy. Sammy Davis was one of the most versatile performers in the business, an unbelievable talent. Dean was on the same level as Frank, and Frank always treated Dean as an equal. Dean was a star in his own right and Frank showed his respect. Frank knew better than to berate Dean. He knew that Dean wouldn't have put up with it for a second.

Sammy Davis was another story. He idolized Frank. Whenever Sammy was around Frank, I often had the feeling that Sammy would have crawled on his knees for Frank.

77

Joey Bishop's star was at its peak then; he was very quick witted and worked well with the group. But as far as Joey was concerned Frank was the boss. I always had great admiration for Joey's talent as a comic. Years before I had been in New York with Jackie when she was married to Gary Morton, and the three of us had run into Joey at the Stage Delicatessen. He walked us back to our hotel and on the way did a very funny, very clever routine. He mimicked a boy trying to walk me home after school. He imitated all the antics of a young boy showing off. He jumped over fire hydrants, walked the curb, walked backwards, ran up stairs into an apartment house, jumped off the stairs, faked a somersault, pretended he was carrying my books. It was hysterical. Gary was laughing so hard he could barely walk.

I never asked Joey if he remembered that evening. When I was first married to Billy I used to be amazed sometimes when an actor that we had spent a whole evening with did not remember me. Then I realized that a lot of performers are not aware of anyone but themselves. They just don't know that anybody else is around. This is particularly true when that someone doesn't sit there and talk about them all night long, which I never was prone to do. I never enter a conversation or feed a conversation in which someone is talking about himself all the time. I will listen politely but I won't encourage it. I won't keep asking questions to keep it going because I think it's a bore to watch people flex their egos.

After the show Dean was the first one to join us in the lounge. He had a drink with us while we waited for Frank, who came in about a half hour later with a huge group of people. We sat around drinking for a couple of hours before going to an Italian restaurant for dinner, and then back to the lounge for more drinks. Frank and his friends knew how to drink. The details of that evening, like the details of so many other evenings with Frank and Dean, are locked in limbo. They are all the same. You drink, you make jokes, you eat spaghetti, you drink some more and make more jokes, and pretty soon the sun starts coming up and it's time to go to bed.

When people started drifting off, I excused myself and

went to my room. The phone woke me up around noon. Frank wanted to know what had happened to me.

"Nothing," I said. "I just got tired and went to bed."

"Well, that's great," he said, and I could tell he was a little peeved. "I thought you came here to see me."

"Yes, I did, Frank," I said. "I came to see you and the show."

"Okay, so why didn't you wait?"

I knew I had to tell him in plain language. "Look, Frank, I came here at your invitation to see the show." I paused, not sure if I should go on, then said to myself, "the hell with him." Then I said: "But not to sleep with you. I'm not ready for that yet, Frank."

"Oh, Christ," he said, "haven't you gotten over that yet?"

"No," I said, and I just let the word hang there.

There was a long pause and I could hear his breathing. "All right, **goddamnit**, but promise me you're going to stay a couple more days. I want a chance to talk to you. You and I have got to talk this thing out."

"I told you, Frank. I don't want to talk about it."

"Will you stay a couple more days, **goddamnit**? That's all I'm asking. Now, promise me."

"All right, Frank. I'll stay."

"Go back to bed," he said, and the warmth was back in his voice. "Sleep warm, baby."

Dick Elwood left that afternoon and Marilyn moved into my room with me. That evening we had dinner with Ray Anthony, who was appearing in one of the lounges. After dinner we had a drink with Frank and then we went to see his late show. Then we had more drinks in the lounge with the whole group. When Frank went to gamble, Dean asked me to go see the Mary Kay Trio. It was then that Dean started asking me questions about Mort and Jeanne. Although I told him I didn't know anything about it, and I didn't (even if I *had* known something I certainly wouldn't have told him), it made no difference at all. Once he had caught my ear, there was just no letting go. I had drinks with Dean in the afternoon, in the evening before and after each show, we had breakfast together, and the times we weren't together he would telephone from whatever movie location they were shooting in that day. When I went back to Beverly Hills on Wednesday, without having been alone with Frank for a single minute, Dean called me at least twice a day. He created endless convolutions to this "affair" which could have been a figment of his imagination. What is ironic about it, and this is probably par for the course, is that throughout this period the movie magazines were writing about poor Jeanne sitting at home with the kids while her wayward husband was playing the field.

Gossip moves like prairie fire in Hollywood. This reminds me of the night I went with Sy Devore to an opening at the Coconut Grove. Sy went to the men's room and came back shaking his head.

"You're not going to believe what I just heard," Sy said. "I just ran into newspapermen and they wanted to know what I was doing with Dean's girl. I told them, 'You guys are out of your mind. She's not Dean's girl.' I don't think they believed me."

From then on, whenever I saw Sy, he would say, "Oh, I know whose girl you are," and would just laugh his head off.

As I said, I preferred the company of men to that of women. Sy is a good example of what I mean. Sy was no romantic hero, and he wasn't all that interesting, but he was a good person and very pleasant company. It's nice when you're single to have people to spend time with that you don't have to fight off. That's why I had a tendency to hang onto friends who were not all that exciting but who were enjoyable and safe. I could go out and have dinner, see a play, a concert, a nightclub show, or just have a few drinks and laughs. I certainly didn't want to have an affair with every man I went out with.

If to enjoy sex a woman has to go to bed with a great many men, or with every man she goes out with, then I think she has a serious problem. I know that the newspapers have painted me as a scarlet woman, and I suppose I am to some people, for it is, after all, a question of individual morals. As strange as it may sound to some people, I really am a prude. I attribute that to my strict upbringing and Catholic teachings. They are appendages that I can't shake loose. The mistakes that I have made have troubled me far beyond their importance. Once society paints that scarlet letter on you, all distinction is lost. But there is a vast difference between a hooker, a nymphomaniac and someone who has had some affairs in her lifetime.

There is a certain quirk in some men that makes it perfectly fine for them to run around, but they just can't live with the thought that their wife might be cheating. Dean was becoming obsessive, or so it seemed in our conversations. For example, he called one night from Las Vegas and asked me to check if Mort was at home. Then he said, "Is there any way you can find out if Jeanne's with him?"

"My God, Dean," I said, shocked at the prospect of what his request entailed, "you can't be serious."

He chuckled. "I'm going to make you my private eye."

"Oh, no, you're not."

"Come on, be a pal."

"Dean, I don't like any of this. I will call Mort to see if he's at home, but I can't—"

"It's okay," he interrupted, giving me another friendly chuckle. "I understand. But you know I'm really very worried about this."

"I know you are."

"Thanks, Judy, I'll call back in a few minutes."

I called Mort and he wasn't home. When Dean called back I took the opportunity to ask him for a favor. Marilyn had left a gold bracelet at the hotel and I asked him to inquire about it.

He called from Los Angeles the very next day and told me he was on his way to my place to deliver the bracelet. Jackie's apartment was on the second floor and when he arrived I met him at the door. Jackie was washing her hair, I think, or there were some other reasons, but I couldn't invite him in. He laughed and said, "That's okay, let's sit outside and talk awhile. I have a little time before my flight back to Vegas."

So we sat on the brick steps and talked for an hour about the perils of married life in Hollywood. I told him what I thought about Hollywood wives and he told me what he thought about Hollywood husbands. Then we switched sides. It was one of our most interesting conversations.

I had a special feeling about Dean as an individual. He was not like the rest of the Clan. He was the kind of person who wandered around by himself. He didn't need a retinue walking with him when he walked from one room to another. Dean walked alone, which is a rarity for a man in his position. But Dean was a loner in many ways. I don't think he could stand haivng a lot of people around him all the time the way Frank did. I was only in Dean's suite once and there wasn't another soul around. He didn't have that need for constant attention, for having people at his beck and call. All he had was Mack Gray to run his errands. He was around Dean sometimes, but he wasn't everpresent.

As I said, Dean enjoyed my company because he could sit and talk and not have to worry about being the romantic, glamorous movie star. I wasn't after a screen test, or money, or sex. I was just a friend. And a good listener. Some men like the idea of having a woman friend. I think that's why he sought my company. That along with the need to have a woman's viewpoint on his problem. So contrary to all rumors, there never was any romance involved.

Not long after Dean left Frank called again and within hours I was back in Las Vegas for another long weekend. To avoid the possibility that Frank would "comp" my bill, I checked into the Flamingo. My mind was made up that our relationship would be platonic.

I was supposed to spend the evening with Frank in his room, but I got tied up in the Garden Room with Dean, who really was moaning and groaning. To be truthful, I just didn't feel like going over and holding Frank's hand. Finally around three in the morning he paged me, and when I got on the phone greeted me with, "What the hell happened?"

"I'm having something to eat," I said, "and I got caught up in conversation."

"Well, for Christ's sake, I thought you were coming over."

There was more surprise than anger in his voice. It was as if he couldn't believe that anybody would stand him up. He was so used to people jumping when he snapped his fingers. "It's getting pretty late and I'm a little tired," I said. "It's been a long day. How about a rain check."

Two things were going to happen. Either the phone was going to melt in my hand or my eardrum would be shattered beyond repair. Frank surprised me. "Yeah, okay, I'm tired too. In fact, I'm taking the day off tomorrow. I'm just going to lay around here and take it easy. Come on over and spend the day with me."

"The whole day?"

"Yeah," and he mocked a growl. "I expect you here at eight sharp."

"In the morning?"

"You're damn right. We're shaping up around here."

"Good night, Frank. I'll see you tomorrow; in the afternoon."

The next day was remarkably tranquil. There is no way anyone can ever spend a day alone with Frank Sinatra. His quarters are a crossroads, with traffic moving in all directions, day and night. I think he would dry up and blow away if he were left totally alone.

Everything considered, it was a peaceful, pleasant day. I brought a book and sat out in the sun on his patio and read while Frank talked on the phone, glanced through a pile of scripts, dictated a few letters, acknowledged the comings and goings of an endless string of visitors, growled at flunkies, drank martinis, ate lunch, drank Jack Daniels, ate hors d'oeuvres, drank Jack Daniels, ate dinner, and drank more Jack Daniels. Frank was not feeling well that day. That was his way of recuperating from a grueling schedule of shooting a movie in the daytime and sometimes at night, and doing a couple of shows a night, plus a lot of drinking, gambling, talking, not to mention doing a few unmentionables. As for me, for the first time since I had met Frank I felt comfortable around him. The sex part was behind us. Although he kidded about it during the day, asking me to bring a little happiness to a tired man, I had been able to kid right back and hold my ground. I wasn't too sure he liked it, if only because he likes women to want him, but now I thought I knew how to handle him.

I left for Beverly Hills on Monday, February 1, and Frank called on Tuesday in the afternoon, to chide me for not having registered at the Sands.

"I had a good room for you," he said. "What's the matter with you anyway? What makes you so **goddamn** independent? I don't understand it. Afraid to get compromised, for a lousy room, why don't you grow up."

"Frank, I'm not going to listen to you if you keep going on."

"Okay, have it your way."

"Thanks."

"On one condition. Come over this weekend. I still want to talk to you."

I had already agreed to go with Mort Viner and a group that included Jeanne Martin, Gloria Cahn and Pat Newcombe, who was Marilyn Monroe's secretary and confidant.

I told Frank I would be there and he had no sooner hung up than Dean was on the phone wanting to know if I would be up over the weekend.

We took the eight o'clock flight on Friday evening. I sat with Mort, but Jeanne, Gloria and Pat acted like I wasn't even there. I realized they must have been listening to the gossip about Dean and me, but there was nothing I could do except weather the storm. Protestations were pointless. As I said, Hollywood wives are really bitchy. They completely ignored me the whole weekend. Sometimes when I found myself almost alone at a table with them, they acted as if I wasn't sitting there. If I hadn't been the kind of person that I am, there would have been a very bad scene. Instead I would act interested in anything they were saying and then would go back to my room and kick the furniture. I tried to avoid them whenever it could possibly be arranged.

Again I registered at the Flamingo. A half hour later, Mort and I went to a cocktail party in Dean's suite. An hour later the whole group had dinner in the Garden Room, then sat at Frank's table for the midnight show. I was happy to see that a new member had been added to Frank's retinue: Juliet Prowse was now Frank's number one girl. That made me feel even more liberated.

V

    Although it began as a typical Las Vegas weekend it ended, for me at least, quite differently, for this was the weekend I met Jack Kennedy. The first time I saw him was at ten o'clock Sunday evening (February 7, 1960). He and Teddy were at Frank's table in the Sands lounge. He looked so handsome in his pin-striped suit. Those strong white teeth and smiling Irish eyes. The introduction, as all introductions in that group, was so perfunctory that it took me a moment to realize this was actually Pat Lawford's brother. But of course the moment he opened his mouth there was no mistaking the Kennedy voice.

    I had a drink and someone said, "Who wants to have dinner?" Five of us (Peter Lawford, Gloria Cahn, Jack, Teddy, and I) had dinner in the Garden Room. There was nothing memorable about the dinner. Pete and Gloria competed in monopolizing the conversation. Every time Jack or Teddy tried to talk to me, Gloria butted right in with some inane political comment. Anything to keep the attention away from me and on herself. Pete expounded at interminable lengths on the filming and merits of *Oceans 11*.

    From dinner we joined the others in the Copa Room for the late show. I sat next to Teddy and Jack sat across from me. The show was so fast moving and riotous that it allowed little time for conversation. It was one long uninterrupted laugh from beginning to end. But I had seen it often and this made it possible for me to concentrate a little more attention on Jack. I could observe him without creating attention, and I must say I was tremendously impressed by his poise and wit and charm. He talked to all the women at the table, and when he listened, it was as if every nerve and muscle in his whole body was poised at attention. As I was to learn, Jack Kennedy was the world's greatest listener. I have never known anyone like him. When you talked to Jack there was total concentration and absorption. He really wanted to hear what you had to say. He had a habit when he listened of tilting his head slightly toward you, as if to facilitate the process, guarding against the possibility that a word might mischievously try to slip by him.

After the show we returned to the lounge for the ritual drinking session. Teddy was sitting next to me and after the first drink and a few pleasantries, he leaned over to ask if I would show him the town. Having spent three weekends in Las Vegas, I felt eminently qualified to give him the full tourist treatment. After all, the Las Vegas Strip in 1960 was one mile of wall-to-wall casinos and hotels. The rest was tumbleweeds and sand.

Casino hopping was and still is great sport in Las Vegas. We saw various lounge shows, played a little blackjack, had some drinks and lots of conversation. It was my first experience with the Kennedy interrogation, their need to know everything about your life, not only who you are but what you are. It was flattering and most enjoyable. What woman doesn't like to talk about herself when she has a truly devoted listener?

Our last stop was at the Flamingo Lounge. By now, with the drinks and conversation, we were both very relaxed with each other. As I look back on it, Teddy was such a rosy-cheeked little boy, very good looking, full of the Old Nick, a great teaser with a ready laugh, and eyes that never stopped flirting. But he had nowhere near the charm and sophistication or just plain likability of Jack. He was the baby brother walking in his older brother's shadow.

When it came time to say goodnight—it was closer to good morning—he insisted on escorting me to my room. He asked for my key, unlocked the door, and waved me into the room, bowing as I went in. He was right behind me, but I stopped abruptly at the end of a little alcove that led into the room and we nearly collided. He laughed and put his hands on my shoulders.

"Wait a minute," he said, quickly moving around me and into the room. There was a copy of *Time* on my bed that I had bought earlier in the day but had not yet looked at. He flipped it over, turned and pointed a finger at me. "All right," he said, grinning. "Let's test your memory. Describe the cover?" That was another Kennedy trait. They like to test you, just to see how observant you are, how quick or perceptive you are, how large a vocabulary you have, anything that will give them information about you. Generally, that smacks a little too pedagogic for my comfort, but this evening I was more amused than anything else. It seemed more like a clever ploy to get into my room.

I remained in the alcove, with the door open, and beckoned him with the crook of a finger. I felt like I could handle the situation in a pleasant way. Compared to the people I had been associating with, he was a baby. I had no idea then that he was already married.

"I thought you lived here," he said.

"Oh, I do."

"Well, then, come right in. Make yourself at home. If you feel like going to bed, don't mind me, just crawl right in and go to sleep. I'll sit here and read *Time*. I want to know what they have to say about Jack this week."

"Oh, very funny," I said, "but I'm getting a little tired standing out here and I know you wouldn't want me to lose my patience."

"Oh God, no," he said, laughing, "that's the last thing I want you to lose."

"Then be a good boy and say goodnight."

"All right," he said, stepping over to the alcove, "but you can't blame a guy for trying."

He put his hands on my shoulders again and looked at me very seriously. "I have to leave for Denver in an hour," he said. "Why don't you fly up with me. It will be great fun."

He looked so eager and sweet that I hated to disappoint

him. I tried to let him down gently. I told him I had come with friends and besides I couldn't just go flying off with someone I had met only a few hours earlier. He persisted and I tried to keep it light and airy.

"All right," he said, "I'm going to the airport and I'm going to call you. I'm going to wait until you agree to come with me."

"I'm afraid you're going to have a long wait. You better bring your sleeping bag."

"We'll see," he said, and leaned forward to give me a kiss just as I turned my head. He quickly pulled back to avoid an awkward situation.

He left and it seemed like I had just gotten into bed when the phone rang and it was Teddy calling from the airport. "Everything is all taken care of," he said. "The pilot has promised to wait for you. So please hurry over. Remember, the success or failure of the campaign rests on your beautiful shoulders."

I started laughing and he said, "It's not funny. This is a serious matter."

Although I was amused and flattered by his persistence, I tried hard to convince him that he was wasting precious time. Finally he hung up, but an hour later he was back on the phone to say that he had not taken his plane and he was waiting for me. I couldn't believe it. It seemed so incredible that he would do that when the campaign was obviously so important to so many people.

Jack called later to ask if I would have lunch with him and I said I would love to. He was having a press conference in the covered section between the casino and the pool area and he suggested that I meet him there around twelve-thirty.

I wore a burgundy Kimberley knit suit, with a soft black leather belt, black leather shoes and matching bag. My hair style was pretty much the way I wear it today, perhaps a couple of inches shorter. When I arrived he was addressing a group of newspapermen. I tried to be as quiet as a little mouse as I moved over to a bench across the way. Jack immediately saw me and called out: "Judy, I'll be right with you, we're just finishing up." I could have fallen off the bench in a dead faint. "Fine, take your time," I managed to vocalize to my complete surprise, my face turning every shade of red. All the newspapermen had turned around to look at me. Jack didn't seem to mind at all. He didn't even flinch.

When the press conference broke up, Jack came right over, and again I was struck by his good looks. He seemed so young and virile, so dashing, not at all the image I had of a politician.

"Do you mind having lunch on the patio of Frank's suite instead of going inside?" he said, his eyes looking directly into mine. "I want a chance to talk with you without the interruptions we would get in the restaurant."

That was absolutely fine with me. I was not anxious to be the center of attention. God knows, that was the last thing I ever wanted in life. "Yes," I said, "it's too beautiful a day to be inside."

It was lovely on Frank's patio. There was not another soul around. I don't have the faintest recollection of what we had for lunch. My memory works in peculiar ways. Sometimes I can remember every detail of a room that I saw only once twenty or thirty years ago and can't remember a word that was said by anybody. Other times it's just the opposite. On this day, I do remember a great deal of what we discussed because of his attentiveness and what seemed an almost insatiable interest in *what* and *who* I was. He asked about my parents, my brothers and sisters, and we discussed the merits of coming from a large family. He was one of nine children. He thought it was much more fun to come from a large family, and he compared it to what it would be like being an only child. I didn't realize it then, but he was feeling me out, trying to see how I felt about things. At one point, he asked me if I was a Democrat or a Republican, and I honestly confessed that I didn't know. He said, "Well, we'll change that." At that moment, I am sure he had every intention of converting me from nothing to something. His job was to convert people. He wanted to convert the world.

The main topic of conversation, once I had given him my

family history, was religion. He was surprised, I think, that I had stopped going to church after my divorce from Billy. Until then, as a devout Catholic, I had gone to mass every Sunday. I explained that I knew I would one day remarry, and for me to continue going to church knowing that I would then be excommunicated was just pure sham. I lost faith in the church because I knew I could buy my way back into it. All I had to do was tell a few lies, find someone to swear to them, and pay the required fee to have my marriage annulled. How hypocritical that seemed to me.

When I was growing up, the teachings of the Catholic Church were based on fear. Going to confession used to terrify me, even when confessing the simple things a child does. As I kneeled in the darkness of the confessional, waiting for the priest to slide open the little panel behind the mesh screen, I would start to tremble as I tried to remember the sins I would have to confess to God so that the priest could punish me and cleanse my soul before I could receive Him at communion the next morning. If I had to confess a lie, then I was panic-stricken at the thought that he might want me to explain that lie. What if I forgot to confess everything and then received communion while still in a state of sin? There were times when I thought a bolt of lightning would strike me dead just as the priest opened the panel—he either was going to have horns and fangs or a halo and a toothless grin. It's terrible what the Catholic Church does to children—the fear it instills remains hidden inside you all your life.

When Jack asked if I had any objection to a Catholic president, I said that if he had the same feeling inside him that I had as a child, or that my mother had all her life, then I was concerned about it. "So much of it is so unrealistic," I said. "So much of it is controlled by the Pope. It has to affect you as President."

He smiled. "That's interesting and it's precisely what I have to find out," he said. "That's why I have to expose myself to as many people as possible as soon as possible. I want them to see me and hear my views. I want them to believe in me, as a free thinking individual, and not to worry about the influence of the Pope. The issues I'm interested in have nothing to do with religion. As I see it, it's basically a question of educating non-Catholics.''

"I don't agree," I said, now completely engrossed in the subject. "Some non-Catholics may resent you at first, but I think you can win them over for the very reason that they don't really know all that much about the Church's method. The resistance, I think, will be with people who had a strict Catholic upbringing and later walked away from it. I'm sure there must be millions who have left or are on the borderline of leaving. You will get more opposition from them than from non-Catholics.''

He was smiling, no doubt amused by the intensity of my feelings when I talked about the Church. Jack's attitude was more sophisticated. Like so many educated Catholics, he was more interested in the philosophy of religion than in the methods by which it was implemented. Paradoxes did not trouble him. Most of them, he felt, were problems created at the teaching level by nuns and priests, not by scholars and philosophers. I have heard this argument before, and it never fails to confuse me. It was the last thing I wanted to pursue with Jack Kennedy on that beautiful day.

As I was to learn time and again during the entire presidential campaign, the Catholic issue was constantly on his mind. We talked about it often. Another important concern was his age. He was only forty-two on the day we sat out on Frank's patio—he was born May 29, 1917. If elected, he would be forty-three, just a few months older than Teddy Roosevelt, the youngest president.

Although he was concerned about his age, he felt that he could overcome it during the campaign. He thought people would forget about his age, but no matter how much he tried, for some people the religious issue would be irreconcilable. He thought it was terribly unfair to mix religion with politics. It was his feeling that if he had been good enough for the navy during the war, he was good enough to be president.

Jack was very proud of being Irish and Catholic, in that order. He was exceptionally proud of his family, particularly of his father. As the world was to learn, the Kennedys were close. You took on one Kennedy, you had to take on the whole family. They never made derogatory remarks about one another. The most I ever heard Jack say about a member of his family was his response when I told him about my evening with Teddy. He had asked whether I had a good time the night before, and I said, "Your brother Teddy is really something." Then I recounted Teddy's antics about my going to Denver with him. After my experience with Pete and Frank in Hawaii, I thought it best to speak out first.

Jack thought it was hilarious. "That little rascal," he said, shaking his head as if it were too funny to be true. "You'll have to excuse his youthful exuberance. He's still quite a kid in many ways, but his heart is in the right place. He's a little immature, but time will cure that. Right now he thinks politics is a game, and that's all right too. I'm glad he's having fun. The point is that he's carrying his share of the load. Teddy is working out just fine."

We sat over lunch nearly three hours. The time went by so quickly that I couldn't believe how late it was until I realized that I had about an hour to get ready for a five o'clock reception being held in Jack's honor in one of the banquet rooms at the Sands. I can take an hour just soaking in the tub. Ideally I like three hours to get ready for an evening out. Putting on my face takes no time at all. The only makeup I use is mascara and powder. What takes time is my bath, my hair, my nails, and selecting the proper attire for each occasion. Everything from top to bottom must be coordinated.

Our whole crowd was at the reception and I was never more talkative and friendly with them than I was that day. I would have done anything to keep a respectable distance from Jack. I felt terribly conspicuous every time he came near me. I had such mixed feelings about him; would always have mixed feelings where he was concerned. The fact that he was married, that he was a public figure, with all the dangers that implied; the fear that I might fall in love and be hurt again, or that perhaps it was just a passing fancy; the fear that we would have an affair and it would become serious, or that it would not be serious; the fear that I was heading for a hard fall, and could not stop any of it from happening. I knew something was going on inside me that I could not fully comprehend. I was becoming restless, anxious in ways I could not satisfy. I saw myself as a rudderless ship in a storm, being tossed in all directions, without the slightest bearing on where I was headed. Self-examination has always left me with an empty feeling, a sadness I can't explain even to myself.

There was no avoiding Jack at the reception—I don't mean to suggest that I was trying to avoid him, but I was so afraid that others would get ideas. Frankly, I don't really know what I wanted. I think I felt like a schoolgirl infatuated with the new boy from out of state that no one knows anything about. The mysterious stranger. Every time he made his way over to me in the crowd and I saw that big smile on his handsome face, my heart skipped a beat. It made me light-headed. I had this wonderful happy feeling and yet I was uneasy and uncomfortable. I thought that every time he came over and touched my hand, all eyes were focused on us.

Once when he came over, he said, "We have a date at eight o'clock. Don't forget."

"Oh," I said, and I know I must have had a big smile on my face.

"Jack Entratter offered us his table and I'd like for just the two of us to see the show. I have to go to Oregon later tonight, so this may be our last chance to be together for a while."

I must have looked disappointed because he said, "Don't worry, I plan to see a lot of you, campaign or no campaign, we can arrange it somehow if you're willing."

"I'm willing," I said. "Don't worry about that."

"Good. Now don't go away. We'll go directly from here to the Copa Room."

Entratter's booth was in the back, but elevated, with an unobstructed view of the stage. It was as private as one could be in a room with hundreds of people. It was dark enough to create a feeling of privacy. I don't think either one of us had the slightest notion of what was happening on the stage. By this time it was plain to both of us that we were deeply interested in each other. I was terribly impressed with him, and, as the saying goes, my heart was on my sleeve. But I could tell that the feeling was mutual. He wanted to be alone with me. He didn't want other people intruding on our conversation. It was the feeling that you get when someone just wants to talk to you. That was the way we both felt. Every time he reached for his drink, he gave my hand a little love pat or squeeze. Nothing more. He wasn't all over me. It made that furtive touch in the dark all the more thrilling.

After the show, as we were walking out of the Copa Room, we were overtaken by Gloria Cahn and Pat Newcombe who very skillfully formed a wedge between us and swept him off. I could hear Gloria frantically saying, "Come on, Senator, we're going to such and such for dinner. Everybody is going to be there." By then they had succeeded in separating us. They had him surrounded and were literally pulling him away with them. I watched him being propelled across the casino, with the crowd around him getting larger, and I remember Gloria turning to give me a last smug look just before they disappeared in the lobby.

I took a cab to the Flamingo and went directly to my room to kick away at the furniture before I exploded into a million little pieces. Yet I was more unhappy than angry. I felt terribly disappointed, particularly since he was leaving to campaign later that night and I might not see him ever again.

I don't remember what I did for the next two hours, but when the phone rang a little before twelve I just knew it was Jack.

"What happened to you?" he said. "What are you doing in your room?"

"Well, you were swept away," I said. "I thought you had plans that didn't include me."

"I almost died when we got to the restaurant and I realized you weren't with us. I asked a couple of people but they didn't know. Then Gloria said you had other plans for the evening."

"That doesn't surprise me in the least," I said, wondering why she was working so hard to do me in.

95

"Did I offend you in some way?" he asked, and he sounded so puzzled by it all. "Was it me?"

"Oh, no," I said. "Nothing like that. It's just that I had the feeling I wasn't wanted. Also I didn't know when you had to leave for Oregon."

"All right, then. Come on back over. We're going to see the late show and I would very much like for you to be with me."

I didn't know what to say. Again that dilemma. I wanted to see him, but I was hurt, and I would rather have had the others believe I had missed dinner because I had something else planned, than for them to think that I was sitting in my room waiting for his call.

While I was debating with myself, he said, "Please come over. There's no sense in my sitting through the show again unless you're with me. I'm going to wait for you at the entrance to the Copa Room and I won't go in until you get here."

He was waiting for me, but so were Gloria and Pat. The only consolation was that they didn't know he was waiting for me until I arrived. Gloria looked daggers at me and it gave me all the satisfaction in the world. Not only that, but Jack didn't say a word to them during the entire show. We sat in Entratter's booth again, and I was on Jack's left and they were on his right, and we acted like we were completely alone. You could feel it from head to toe how happy he was that I was with him. We exchanged telephone numbers and there was no question that this was the beginning of what would be a long and intimate relationship. He was so different from anyone I had known up to then that I just didn't know how to evaluate my emotions. Getting to know Jack Kennedy was going to be not just an experience, but an adventure.

After the show, we sat in the lounge a few minutes until he had to leave for the airport. He didn't say anything in front of the others, but from the way he looked at me I knew that everything was fine.

I went to my room and a few minutes later Dean called.

"How come you left?" he asked. Jeanne had already left for Beverly Hills.

"I was getting tired," I said.

"Come on back down, will you? Come have something to eat with me."

It was always hard saying no to Dean. I went down and we talked for a while, and then I went to bed and thought about Jack. I was anxious to be alone with my thoughts. I wanted to try and sort them out. The fact that he was married was bothering me, and yet it wasn't bothering me. The thought that he liked me was the most important of all.

Something wonderful was happening to me. I was lying in bed and smiling at the ceiling. I was almost giddy. It was a feeling that I had when I was young and had a crush on someone—that first meeting when you realize that he's someone special. It's all anticipation, hoping and wondering and feeling good. Then doubt creeps in: "I wonder if I'll ever see him again?" There was not much doubt that night. I slept well and woke up feeling like Scarlet O'Hara the morning after Rhett Butler carried her up the stairs.

I returned to Beverly Hills the next day and the first thing I did was to buy Jack's two books: *Why England Slept* and *Profiles in Courage*. I couldn't get him off my mind and I wanted to know everything about him I could possibly learn. I bought every book I could find concerning the Kennedys.

Jack called me from Fresno on February 12. Earlier in the day I had received a dozen red roses from him. He sounded pumped up and raring to go. There would be calls when he was completely exhausted and my heart would go out to him. I never have understood how a man can survive a presidential campaign. It boggles my mind to think about it. Going to all those places, meeting all those people, shaking all those hands, making all those speeches, eating all those cold dinners, attending all those meetings, not to mention the smoke-filled-room ones. If there is such a talent in homo sapiens classifiable as a natural born politician, Jack Kennedy had a genius amount of it. Politics wasn't something he learned in school or from his father. There was something about him that made people feel happy and safe in his presence. I think people felt his interest in them. Whoever he talked to, that person knew Jack Kennedy was talking to him, and to no one else, that he was interested in him, and wanted to hear his views exclusive of any other. When he shook your hand, you felt that he was really shaking your hand, that it was not just another hand along the way. He had a quality that touched people. They believed him when he told them what was good for them. He had a good face, an honest face, and the people liked and trusted what they saw.

We talked a long time that evening. He told me how much he missed me, how pleased he was we had met, and most important of all, he wanted to arrange another meeting. From that moment on, the phone calls never stopped. He called almost every day—no matter where he was, or how tired, he found the time and the energy to call me. Sometimes I called him, routing the calls through his secretary, Evelyn Lincoln, at her office in the Old Senate Office Building. She always knew where Jack could be reached. Most of the times I called her with a request to speak to Jack, it would be only a question of minutes before he returned my call.

I became an avid Kennedy follower. I read newspaper accounts, watched television, read magazines. My need to know more about him was insatiable. I read that while in Madison, Wisconsin, Jack began his day in darkness at the gate of a sausage works and ended it in Kenosha with a coffee hour for two hundred women. Jack trekked through snow in sheepskin-lined shoes but hatless as usual. With that marvelous head of hair, he didn't need a hat. He visited places like Beaver Dam, Waupun, Oshkosh, Appleton, West Bend, Mayville—sixteen cities in three days. Children were excused from school to see him, for the first time since William Jennings Bryan's campaign. I thought, "My God, a sausage works in freezing darkness in Wisconsin. Just to shake the frozen hands of a few workers." I truly felt for him. What a tortuous road candidates travel and so much of it in vain.

On the afternoon of February 24, I went to Warner

Brothers to have lunch with my sister Jackie. Afterwards we went to see Frank on the set of *Oceans 11*. He was extremely solicitous and gallant, making sure that chairs were provided for us so that we could watch the shooting of a scene. Later, over drinks in his dressing room, I asked what he was going to do next. He said he had an engagement at the Fontainebleau in Miami and that the Clan was planning on joining him for some of the shows. Their show had been a huge success at the Sands and Frank thought it would be "a gas" to repeat it in Miami. "Hey, why don't you come down for the opening. Always great to have a pretty girl up front."

I didn't accept, nor did I refuse. I said I would think about it. I wasn't about to make any plans that might later conflict with my seeing Jack. As luck would have it, we decided on the place and time for our next meeting that very evening when Jack called from Wisconsin. Throughout this period, we both had been anxious to see each other, but it was a question of finding a suitable time and place. I didn't feel comfortable just flying to a rendezvous point in some obscure part of the country. Because of the way I felt about his situation, being married and a candidate for the presidency, I didn't want to compromise him or myself. We discussed this at great lengths on the phone, at times for an hour or more. I didn't know how or where he found the time that he spent with me on the phone, and I didn't care really, as long as I could hear his voice—I read newspapers and magazines not because I cared all that much about politics, but just to see his name in print.

When he mentioned that he would be in New York on the evening of March 7, I told him I would be at the Plaza. He offered to get my airline ticket and to make my reservation at the Plaza, but I said I would take care of it myself.

"Are you sure that you're really coming?" he asked.

"Of course," I said. "My God, why do you ask?"

"Then why won't you let me make the necessary arrangements?"

"Because I feel more comfortable doing it myself."

"Well, for a moment I thought you might have changed your mind."

"I have every intention of being there. I want to see you, Jack, as much as you want to see me."

"I don't think that's possible, Judy, not the way I've missed you these past two weeks. I wish I had taken Teddy's idea and brought you along with me. I wish you were here tonight."

"I wish I were with you, Jack, I really do."

We talked in this vein for a while, and then before saying goodnight, he said, "I would be terribly disappointed if you weren't at the Plaza on March 7."

It wasn't until the next day that I realized that March 7 was the eve of the New Hampshire primary. What a man, I thought, to find time for me on a day when he would be campaigning all over the state in a last effort to gain votes.

When I arrived in New York, I remember seeing a headline in one of the newspapers to the effect that the stop-Kennedy drive had failed. Jack was the favorite Democratic candidate. It was exciting news. I called room service and ordered a drink to celebrate.

It was a long evening. It's one thing to get comfortable with someone on the phone, but a whole month had gone by since we had met and spent that brief moment together in Las Vegas. Talking and kidding with him on the phone was one thing, but in a little while he was going to be right here in this room with me. The longer I waited, the more nervous I became. I must have gotten up to look in the mirror a hundred times. Then I thought that perhaps I should have worn something else.

It's terrible waiting for a knock on the door. I could hear footsteps coming down the hall and my heart would stop until they went by. Finally there was a light tap on the door. He was all smiles and out of breath. I remember thinking that perhaps he had run up the stairs. My room was 1651—that would be some hike.

We looked at each other and at first he was a little hesitant.

I said, "Hi, Jack. How are you?" I didn't know what else to say.

100

He looked at me, still smiling, and said, "I'm sorry I'm late."

"That's all right," I said. "I understand. I know how busy you've been lately."

He closed the door and put his arms around me. "God," he said, "it's good to see you."

It takes me a long time to be at ease with people, and I think he felt it because he pulled back and held me at arm's length. "Let me take a good look at you. You look sensational." He kept his arm on my shoulder as we walked into the room. The bed just seemed to zoom in size. It looked to me like I had the smallest room and the biggest bed in the Plaza. There were two chairs and a small table at the other end of the room. There was a bottle of Jack Daniels, ice and two glasses on the table. As we walked toward the chairs, I offered him a drink, and he asked if I would prefer to go out for something to eat. I could tell that he wasn't too keen about it. I said, "Sit down and let's just talk. I would rather not be seen with you right now."

He was visibly relieved. I made drinks and we sat facing each other, drinks in hand, and began to make conversation. I asked if he would like to remove his jacket and he promptly stood up, removed it, draped it over the back of his chair and loosened his tie. Now it looked like I was planning to spend the evening in bed. My head was going in different directions. I wanted to be with him and I didn't want to be with him. It was easy to talk on the phone, but once something else started, I just knew how difficult it would be for both of us. I was afraid of getting hurt. I was just getting over Travis, and I wasn't sure I wanted to become deeply involved with anyone. Still it was happening to me and I was letting it happen.

That damn bed was getting bigger by the minute. Finally, after interminable small talk, Jack took the initiative. He stood me up and kissed me. It was all well and good, but I knew what was coming and something inside me was beginning to resist. He was amorous and just very loving. I realize today that I was overly sensitive about it. All of a sudden, I was discounting every phone call, every flower, everything. I just didn't want what was happening to happen.

By this time, he had maneuvered me over to the bed, and had gently pushed me on my back. His kisses were more passionate now and my head was beginning to reel. Suddenly, I pushed at him and said, "No, Jack."

He couldn't believe it. "What do you mean, no?"

"I just can't do this right now," I said. "I haven't seen you for a month."

"But we've talked on the phone every day. What's the matter?"

"Yes, we've talked on the phone, but I just can't say, 'Hello, there, how are you, have a drink, let's go to bed.' I feel so uncomfortable."

"But, Judy, don't you want to be close to me?"

"I do, Jack. I really do, but not this way. I need time to think it out."

I could see he was getting impatient. "I've waited so long to see you," he said. "I tried to see you before now, in other places, and it was your choice to see me in New York."

"I know that, Jack."

"And time-wise, you knew what you were getting into."

"I know, I know . . ."

He was getting more annoyed as the discussion went on. Finally, he stood up and walked over to the chair for his jacket. I sat there just feeling dreadful. I thought frantically: "What do I do now?" I knew that if he walked out that door, I was going to be just miserable. I had gotten myself into a situation I couldn't resolve. I wanted to be with him, but it was so abrupt, so cold and calculated. Somewhere, also, hidden in this jumble of thoughts was the question of what he would think of me, how it would look to him.

I knew he had been anticipating our meeting the way a man anticipates when two people start getting close. A woman anticipates in another way. Most women—I know I am—are incurable romantics. Love should be the way it used to be presented in the movies. You're romanced and the hero is gentle and charming and ever so considerate. Of course, it's not realistic. A woman can't be brought a rose, a single rose,

102

and have dinner by candlelight every night. If only violins had played outside the door to create a romantic mood. Anything to soften it.

I was absolutely desolate as he walked to the door. I sat there, a hurt soul, hoping he'd turn around and say he was sorry, that everything was all right. But he was leaving, there was no doubt about it.

He turned around and looked at me: "I'm really sorry," he said, his hand on the doorknob.

I said, "Jack, come here."

He came back to the bed and sat down, putting his arms around me. "Don't misunderstand this," he said. "I don't mean to be impatient. I know it probably looks that way, but I have been anticipating this moment for a long time. This has been the longest month."

I nodded. "It has for me, too, Jack."

"I could have walked in this room and picked you up and put you down on the bed." He stopped to kiss me. "I have so looked forward to being close to you, to making love to you, and then to just lie in bed and talk the way two people can talk after making love."

We kissed and after a while I went to the bathroom to disrobe. When I came back, Jack was already in bed. He was smiling as he reached out for me. I snuggled close to him under the covers. "I didn't mean to act badly," he said. "I was so disappointed. I hope you understand how much I've anticipated this moment." I placed a finger against his lips and he kissed it. Then we made love.

Once I had made up my mind, there was no hesitation. I am very emotional and very demonstrative with my love and in lovemaking. That is my nature. I am very active, but the man has to take the initiative. When people make love, they should make love to each other. I mention this because, as I was to learn in my relationship with Jack, his attitude was that he was there to be serviced. Partly this was due to his back problem, and partly I think he had been spoiled by women. There is a world of difference between a man who expects to be made love to and two people making love to each other.

103

This attitude, or inclination, was not apparent that first night. He couldn't have been more loving, more concerned about my feelings, more considerate, more gentle. There was no question that he cared deeply about me. I was happy that I had called him back. Yet I was concerned about where the affair was leading me. He was married and perhaps someday he would be the President of the United States. How does the President of the United States carry on an affair without arousing suspicion? At the same time, I was busy rationalizing, trying to convince myself that everything was fine because he truly cared about me. I couldn't picture anyone working that hard just to go to bed for one night. Anyone who put in that much time and effort and energy for a so-called conquest had to have a serious problem. Jack was the last man in the world to have that kind of problem.

After we had made love, we lay in each other's arms for a long time. Mostly we talked about ourselves, but he did relate anecdotes from the hustings. I loved the way he pronounced hustings. The tempo of the campaign seemed so hectic—frantic, really. I remember his reciting the wording of a sign made up by one of his aides: "As soon as the rush is over, I'm going to have a nervous breakdown. I worked for it. I owe it to myself, and nobody is going to deprive me of it."

Jack was a great teaser and had a marvelous sense of humor. And he could take it when you teased back, but there were areas where he was sensitive. One was the money his family was spending on his campaign. Other candidates had criticized him for this. Hubert Humphrey had charged that Jack was on a "spending spree." One of the sore points was the twin-engined Convair airplane Jack's father had purchased for him. I personally loved that airplane. It had made our evening possible. Jack hated that "little rich boy" image his opponents were trying to create.

What fascinated me about Jack was that he was the same in person as he was on the television screen. His mannerisms were natural. I don't think he ever sat down and tried to create an image. He wasn't two different people. Some

104

politicians deliberately use their hands in certain ways. They have been told that this is the way to be effective before an audience. Jack used his hands the same whether he was talking to millions on television or sitting up in bed after making love.

"I told Hubert that I will be happy to sit down and agree on a maximum spending figure," Jack said, his right hand sawing the air the way I had seen him do so often on television.

We were propped up on pillows drinking Jack Daniels. "Poor Hubert," I said. "There are so few Humphreys and so many Kennedys. Anybody could become President if they had a family as big and as hard working as yours. How can one country stomach so many Kennedys."

He laughed. "Don't forget the grandkids. Wait till they come along. We'll take over the whole country—maybe the world."

I loved the wonderful airy, light side of him. It was amazing to me that he could be so relaxed on the eve of the first important primary. Not once did he mention New Hampshire. He had an air of confidence that was unshakeable. Come hell or high water he was going to win. He was a winner. He came from a family of winners. They would do anything to win. They never thought of losing. His attitude with me was always on the up-side. If he was worried about anything, he never let me know it.

After he left in the wee hours of the morning, my emotions were still mixed. I was happy and I was sad, and that pretty much explains my relationship with Jack Kennedy. As time went on, I would vacillate between these two emotions, with the emphasis first on one and then the other, which kept me in a state of continuous anxiety.

What a delight it was to be awakened by a bellman with a dozen red roses. The card said, "Thinking of you—J." And then to hear that he had won in New Hampshire made it complete. He was on his way and I was so proud of him.

When he called later that day, he didn't even mention the primary. All he seemed interested in was us. He wanted to know if I had slept well, and did I get enough rest? He was sorry he couldn't have stayed longer; he was anxious to see me again, and he would call and try to set something definite in the next few days, perhaps in Washington, if that met with my approval. I, in turn, was saying the same things to him. Don't worry about it, I'm happy I was able to see you, and, yes, I would love to see you again, and Washington was a fine place.

It was then that I congratulated him on his victory in New Hampshire. "I guess we showed them we're going *All The Way*," Jack said. "That and *High Hopes* are our theme songs. Frank recorded two parodies. One of the lines goes, 'Oops, there goes the opposition—Kerplop!' " He laughed and it was such a hearty laugh. We laughed a lot on the telephone. We teased each other all the time. Jack went on to explain that he had a station wagon equipped with loudspeakers following him whenever he went out on the street to shake hands. "Frank's voice gets them out of the barbershop and general store. All I have to do is grab them and convince them that they've just shaken the hand of the next President of the United States."

Every time we talked on the phone, and I am referring to before and after our meeting at the Plaza, he invariably would ask, "Have you seen Frank lately?" I would answer, "No," or "Yes, I saw him on the set," or "He called last night and I wasn't home," or whatever was the circumstance at the moment. Jack would say, "Ohhh, you still want to see Frank?" I would say, "We're just friends, Jack." Then he'd say, "Okay, okay," in almost a little boy's "See if I care" voice. Then the very next day, "See Frank? Where did you go last night? I called and you weren't home." I would tell him I had been out to dinner with Travis, or Dick Elwood, or Jeff Chandler, or Dewey Martin, or Sy Devore, or whoever, and he would respond, "Is he a good friend, is he someone you're interested in." He wanted to be the star of the show. He was married and yet he was jealous. I was always reassuring him that they were only friends and that there was no personal involvement with any of them.''

On this day, however, I told Jack that I was leaving for Miami in two days to see Frank's opening at the Fontainebleau. He wanted to know how long I would stay and I said only a few days. ''Have a good time,'' he said, ''and I'll try to call you every day. Don't forget we have a date in Washington very soon.''

Toni Carroll flew to Miami with me. She had long since been divorced from David Wolper and had resumed her career as a nightclub singer. She was living in a small apartment off Central Park South. She was between engagements at the time and just leaped at the chance to get away from the snow. I had planned on staying only two days, but as it turned out I ended up staying much longer.

We got in late and both went straight to bed. The next day I left word for Frank that I was there with a friend and Tony, his valet, called to say that Frank was tied up that night but he wanted to know if we wanted to see the show. I said we would like to see the late show. ''Fine,'' he said, ''Frank wants to take care of the table and everything for the show. Do you want to have dinner late in there?'' It was Frank's way of smoothing things out when he wasn't available.

When Frank called to invite me to dinner the next day I had already made plans to see my uncle, Armand Cerami, that evening. I said I would stay on a few more days, and he said, ''Okay, I'll call you tomorrow.'' Toni left that afternoon.

I call Armand Cerami my uncle but he is my uncle's brother. Uncle Armand owns part of two Miami restaurants called Tony's Fishmarket and Tony Sweets.

The next night Frank called and invited me up to his suite. ''We'll have cocktails while I finish getting ready for the show,'' he said.

It was absolutely amazing. There were only two others in the room with Frank when I arrived. Tony, his valet, who let me in, and a man Frank introduced as Joe Fish.

AUTHOR'S NOTE: *Joe Fish was an alias for Joseph Fischetti, a cousin of Al Capone, and a brother of Charles and Rocco Fischetti, now deceased, but once high ranking mafiosi in the Chicago Syndicate.*

Frank was in a good mood. As I came into the room, he held out his arms and crooned, "A pretty girl is like a melody." Then he went, "boom, boom, boom," rotating his hips like a stripper. "Come on, baby, let's have a little kiss and hug, a little rock and roll," he sang, "it's been a long dry spell in Campbell land."

I walked across the room and sat down. "That's a likely story," I said.

"You have a cruel heart, Campbell. That's your German blood. *Achtung!*" He clicked his heels and slapped Joe Fish on the back. "Hey, Joe, what about this little Campbell chick?"

"Beautiful, Frank. Very beautiful."

"What would you say, Joe, if I told you that this little broad, with the cold German blood, has broken my heart. Not just once, Joe, but many times. You might even say often."

"That wouldn't surprise me, Frank. It breaks my heart just looking at her."

"Come on, you guys, cut it out, will you," I said, trying to suppress a giggle.

While Frank talked, Tony was all over him, first with a whisk broom, then a shoe brush, and finally straightening his tie and pocket handkerchief.

When Frank was ready, all four of us went down to the lower level and went through a door that brought us backstage. I watched the show from the wings. In those days Frank was magnificent. There is no other way to describe what he did on that stage. He would snap his fingers, sing a couple of bars, and the whole audience would fall under his spell. It was like watching mass hypnotism. Women would stare glassy-eyed while their burly husbands furtively brushed away tears as Frank took them on a sentimental journey.

Frank could evoke any mood he wished almost at will. He was a magician and a hypnotist. He stole hearts and made the old feel young again.

While Frank was onstage, people backstage were falling all over themselves trying to be nice to me. For days afterward, whenever I encountered any of them in the hotel, they would whisper, "That's the girl that was with Frank!" People can be so silly. I could just imagine what would have happened if they had seen me with Jack.

After the show, we went to Ricco's for dinner. It was the first time I tasted Italian baked clams and they were delicious. For some reason, my liking them delighted Joe Fish. Then we went to a burlesque place to see Hank Henry, an X-rated comic who was a friend of Frank. As we parted that evening, after I had gently deflected Frank's advances, he invited me to come to his penthouse suite for brunch the moment I was up.

Something happened the next day that I have often wondered about. We were out on Frank's patio, and Frank, I remember, was wearing his favorite orange trunks, and I had on slacks and a blouse, instead of the bikini he always wished I wore. I was standing looking over the balcony when Frank said, "You know, Campbell, you're really stupid."

I turned to look at him and he wasn't smiling. "Well, thanks a bunch," I said.

"I mean it. You're so beautiful, and you're bright, but you're so square. I've told you that before and I mean it. You don't know how to take advantage of the opportunities open to you. You don't walk through any of those open doors. Goddamnit, the things you could have if you weren't so fucking stupid."

"You have a strange way of complimenting someone."

"It's not a compliment," he said, his mouth twisting in disgust. "Do me a favor, will you? Don't be a sucker all your life. Wake up and realize what you've got in the palm of your hand. Sometimes you remind me of some silly schoolgirl. Get with it. Swing a little. You only live once, baby."

That was the first and only time Frank Sinatra offered me personal advice. I considered his evaluation a compliment. I was glad I was not the kind of person he wanted me to be. I wasn't as stupid as he imagined. I knew what he meant. I knew all about people going through open doors, or busting through them, and grabbing everything in sight. That had no interest for me. All I ever wanted in my life was love and peace of mind, to be *comfortable* with myself. I know this word comes up often in my story. It has a special meaning for me. I cannot function unless I am comfortable. I mean comfortable inside, with my thoughts, with my code of conduct, which may seem cockeyed to some people but it's what I'm stuck with, and what I must live with if I want to survive as a rational human being.

After deciding to stay on in Florida, I had changed the departure day for my flight back to New York to March 16. The day before I was to leave, Frank asked if I would mind dropping off one of his watches at Cartier's for repairs. I had scheduled an early flight, but it was cancelled because of a bomb scare. This was when the bombing of airplanes first started. I think Eastern Airlines had had one of its planes blown up a few days before. I made a reservation for later that night but I got cold feet and cancelled it.

The next day I called Frank to have Tony pick up the watch. I didn't want to be responsible for it. Frank asked if I wanted to see the show. I said that I was going to spend the day in the sun, relaxing, and was planning on going to bed early.

I found a fairly secluded spot above the cabanas near the pool, and was lying there, enjoying the sun in a Jax swimsuit, which was a modified bikini, when all of a sudden I heard, "Hey, Campbell, what are you doing down there!"

It was Frank from the balcony of his patio. He knew it would embarrass me and he was laughing like a loon. "Hey, where did you get the bikini, Campbell? Hey, I can see you!"

When I refused to acknowledge him, he shouted. "I mean you, there, Campbell, in the orange bikini. Come on up here!"

I must admit I was wearing an orange swimsuit, but it was

a very pale orange. By now, of course, everybody was either staring at me or laughing with Frank.

I clenched my teeth, turned over on my stomach, and buried my face in my arms. I wanted to get some color. I knew I would be going back to see Jack. He called almost daily, from places like West Virginia, Pennsylvania, Indiana, Wisconsin, Washington. Evelyn Lincoln and I became old telephone friends, or at least co-conspirators. She never failed to give Jack my messages and Jack never failed to return my calls. Every time I would mention that I had seen him on television, Jack would invariably ask, "How did I look? Did I come across?" Sometimes he even asked me if I liked his suit. He was always concerned about his appearance. I was complimentary when he asked, but I never paid gratuitous compliments. I just felt that people in the limelight received too many compliments as it was.

There may be a whole lot of things historians will take away from Jack, but no one can say that he wasn't attractive, or that he couldn't charm a crowd. He had a little boy charm for some and for others he was so sophisticated. God, some women would have done anything to get near him. He had sex appeal. And he knew it.

One night when he called I told him that Uncle Armand had contributed to his campaign—I may be wrong, but I think it was $20,000. I said, "See we have Democrats in the family." I was only kidding, but many months later when I was visiting him in the White House, he acknowledged that Uncle Armand was a good Democrat and even named the amount he had contributed. When it came to politics, there was very little that slipped by Jack Kennedy.

One night after Jack had asked me who I was seeing in Miami, he said something I have never forgotten. "You don't seem to care who I see," he said, and he actually sounded a little petulant.

"What do you mean?" I asked, really taken aback by the remark.

"You never ask who I'm seeing. Don't you care?"

"My God, Jack," I said, now even more incredulous. "I can read about you every day in the newspapers. You're on television every night. If I want to know where you are or who you're seeing, all I have to do is pick up a paper or switch on the dial.''

Years later, when I began to hear rumors about Jack's various extramarital relationships, I often wondered about that conversation.

As the song goes, the ''days dwindle down'' fairly rapidly in Miami. Some of my escorts there were Bill Orr and Hugh Benson, who were producers at Warner Brothers and were in Florida scouting locations for a television series. Another was Bob Neal, a young Texas oilman, who has been described by Pete Lawford as a ''real ladies man.'' According to a recent (1976) interview Pete gave to a tabloid, Jack once greeted Neal with, ''Ah, Bob, the man who lives the life we all want to lead.'' If Bob Neal is a ''real ladies man,'' then Don Knotts is Casanova. That comment by Pete makes about as much sense as the one he made in the same story concerning me: ''This lady [me], to my knowledge, I have never met. I never saw her in the company of the President, never saw her in the company of Frank Sinatra and never saw her in the company of Sam Giancana.''

Bob Neal was as docile an escort as I ever had. Not as interesting as some, perhaps, but certainly as safe. Bob's family was in oil and he lived accordingly. On March 23, I took Bob to one of Frank's parties. We had dined on Bob's yacht and had gone to see the late show, sitting at Frank's table. After the show, Tony had invited us to a party in Frank's suite.

The next evening I went with Bill Orr and Hugh Benson to see a Cuban show in one of the hotels. We sat at a long table with at least fifteen people, including Desi Arnaz, who couldn't take his eyes off me. Bill told me that everybody was going to Desi's suite after the show for a party—Desi had even invited the Cuban performers. Afterward in the parking lot, everybody was going every which way and I found myself in the car with two friends of Bill and Hugh, who had sat next to me at the table and who were connected with the Miss Universe Pageant.

Since it was getting chilly, on the way to Desi's hotel I asked them to stop at the Fontainebleau so I could get a wrap. I ran into the lobby and Tony, Frank's valet, was standing there watching me. There was a message from Dean under my door, which meant he had arrived, but I didn't have time to answer it. When I came back, Tony was standing beside the car talking to the two men. Upon arriving at Desi's hotel, which I think was the Diplomat, the man driving the car said, "You two go up and I'll be right with you." I didn't think anything of it.

The light went on quickly enough when I walked into Desi's suite. There were only three of us in there—my escort, Desi, and me. The next time I looked around there were only two—my escort had vanished. By now Desi was talking a mile a minute, but I wasn't listening. I was frantically thinking of a way out. Finally I just said, "Excuse me a moment," turned around and walked out the door without looking back once. I went down the elevator and took a cab to my hotel.

I spent most of my time with Dean the next couple of days. The whole Clan was now in for the show. Others included Sammy and Gloria Cahn, Jack Entratter, and Juliet Prowse. Each girl in Frank's life has a certain amount of time allotted to her. Jeanne Martin had not come and if Pat Lawford was there, I just don't remember. She became the kind of person that I didn't see even when she was sitting at the same table.

On March 26, Dean and Jack Entratter took me to a party in the Poodle Bar at the Fontainebleau. We came in about two in the morning and Frank was sitting at the head of the table with Juliet on his right. I said, "Hi, Frank—" but the rest of the words stuck in my throat as he turned to look at me, his eyes narrowed and cold as ice. I thought, "Oh God, not again," and hurried away from him. The moment I sat down, Frank stood up, and I knew I was in for it. He was quite drunk, leaning forward, with a finger pointing right at me. He proceeded to dress me down for what he thought had occurred the night before at the so-called Arnaz party.

It was like instant fire. My head was exploding and my legs were shaking so badly that I was afraid to stand up. I looked at Jack Entratter, who was sitting on my right, and I said, "Jack, I have to get out of here. Will you help me?"

"Boy," Jack said, also struggling to stand up, "I'll tell you, the mood he's in, that's a good idea."

So Jack, who had trouble walking, helped me walk out of that room in front of all those people. I think if I had had a weapon in my hand, I would have killed Frank. I was that blood-curdling furious with him.

The next night was the big farewell party—the last night of the show. I had already made plans to go with Bob Neal and I was angry enough to keep the date regardless of Frank's ugliness. I slept late that morning and when I got up I decided to spend the day in my room, relaxing, reading magazines and *The New York Times* which I had delivered to my room every day. Through the pages of the *Times*, I could keep track of Jack and of the campaign on a day-to-day basis.

I read in that Sunday's *Times* that the Missouri state committee was urging that the state's slate be pledged to Stuart Symington. I laughed because former President Truman was for Symington, and I remembered Jack telling me that "the old bastard will come around." Jack, as always, was convinced that his rivals would be unable to form a coalition against him. He was the front runner, the man to beat, and opponents were coming out of the woodwork every day. Now Sam Rayburn was promoting Lyndon Johnson. Even Rose Kennedy was out in Wisconsin campaigning for her son. In Eau Claire, she had met with three Protestant clergymen who were opposing Jack on religious grounds. The Catholic issue remained unresolved.

Around four o'clock that afternoon there was a knock on my door and when I asked who it was, Jack Entratter said, "I'd like to see you for a minute, Judy."

I was wearing a caftan-style robe, which was perfectly proper for the occasion. I opened the door and said, "Hi, Jack, what's going on?" Instead of answering, he pushed me aside and barged right into the room, closing the door behind him. All he had on was a robe and slippers.

"What the devil are you doing here dressed like that?" I

asked, backing away as he tried to grab me. "Get the hell out of here," I shouted, "and don't ever come back." He got hold of me and began pulling me toward the bed, all the while saying, "Come on, Judy, what's the matter with you?" He was a big hulk of a man but his legs were weak. I shoved as hard as I could and he stumbled, letting go of me as he reached for something to steady himself. I ran to the door, opened it, and shouted, "Out!"

He was crouching on one knee in the middle of the room, his face contorted with anger, and I knew that if he had had good legs he would have leaped at me. Instead he struggled to his feet and as he went out the door, he said, "Who the hell do you think you are?"

I closed the door and leaned against it, my own legs barely able to support me. I felt sick to my stomach. I thought to myself: "What is wrong with me? What could have made him think that he could barge into my room like that?" This coming on top of the incidents with Desi Arnaz and Frank was more than I could cope with. I just sat on my bed and cried.

By the time Bob Neal picked me up that evening I had forced myself to stop thinking about what had happened. I was determined to go to Frank's party and not let anyone know how upset and unhappy they had made me. I wore an ice blue *peau de soie* cocktail dress with matching shoes and bag, which I had worn only once before, for the party at Dean's house. I had a necklace made for the dress, strands of matching ice blue beads. There is nothing like clothing to lift a woman's spirits.

VI

The party was in the French Room. There was a reception area and beyond it a large dining room and dance floor. We arrived at the cocktail hour and it was jammed with people. As we walked around greeting friends, Bob spotted Joe Fish and Skinny D'Amato and started toward them. At first I didn't see Frank, and by the time we got there it was too late. He was behind Skinny and caught up in conversation with a man I had never seen before. Joe Fish said, "Hey, Frank, look who's here."

Frank turned and actually smiled. I couldn't believe my eyes. "Come here, Judy," he said. "I want you to meet a good friend of mine, Sam Flood."

I offered my hand, but instead of shaking it, Sam Flood held it in his two hands. "It's a pleasure, Judy," he said, giving my hand a little squeeze but still holding on. He was middle-aged, of medium build and ruddy complexion, but with penetrating dark eyes. "Do you mind if I say something, Judy?"

"Not at all—I think."

He laughed, and it was a hearty laugh, the kind you hear from people who laugh a lot. "You're far too beautiful to be wearing junk—excuse me—I mean costume jewelry. A beautiful girl like you should be wearing real pearls and diamonds and rubies."

"A girl like me does sometimes."

"No offense, please," he said. "Real pleasure meeting you. Hope to see you again soon."

He released my hand and Bob and I continued to circulate.

AUTHOR'S NOTE. *Sam Flood was one of at least sixteen aliases used by Sam Giancana, whose real name was Momo Salvatore Giangono. As the author of* Captive City, *a book about crime and corruption in Chicago, I learned a great deal about Giancana, the criminal, as viewed by various records, but next to nothing about his personal life. Consequently, getting to know Giancana through Judy's reminiscences was a new experience for me.*

Born on May 24, 1908, his rap sheet dated back to 1925 and listed more than seventy arrests for crimes including contributing to delinquency, vagrancy, burglary, assault and battery, larceny, fugitive, assault to kill, damage by violence, conspiracy to operate a "book," possession of burglar tools and concealed weapons, bombing suspect, gambling, fictitious driver's license, murder—prime suspect in countless murder investigations, three before the age of twenty. In one murder indictment at the age of eighteen, in which he was released on bail, the sole prosecution witness was murdered before the trial. With all that, he was convicted only twice: thirty days for auto theft and four years for operating a still.

His first important job was as chauffeur and bodyguard for "Machine Gun" Jack McGurn (nee Jack De-more), a syndicate killer and a prime suspect along with Tony Accardo in the St. Valentine's Day Massacre. By 1932 Giancana was known as one of the fastest "wheelmen" on the West Side. And by 1948 he was described in police records as "in charge of the rough stuff department for Tony Accardo." In 1950 he was one of the principal Chicago area hoodlums and was considered a "general overseer" of illegal gambling in Chicago. In 1951 he was spending "considerable time

117

in Florida but never at the same time as Tony Accardo as one or the other is always around the local area to make sure that business is conducted as usual." In 1952 he had "gambling interests in Cuba" and was a "big man in the shrimp industry." Also in 1952, he was attending a "meeting between Sheriff Kelly of Miami and Murray (the Camel) Humphreys, Jake (Greasy Thumb) Guzik, Gus (Shotgun) Alex, and Tony (Big Tuna) Accardo in Miami." In 1953 Giancana and Accardo and Guzik were "holding conferences in Reno and Las Vegas with other kingpins of the national syndicate." In 1954 "Judges John A. Sbarbaro and Joseph A. Pine attended the wake of Giancana's wife, Angeline, along with politicians and hoodlums." In 1956 he was "proclaimed 'Enforcer' during a dinner party at the Tam O'Shanter Country Club." The coronation ceremony was deceptively simple. Accardo merely placed a hand on Giancana's shoulder and said, "I want you to meet my good friend, Sam Giancana." He was forty-eight when he became the boss of all bosses of the Chicago Syndicate. Although he was not as precocious in gaining the leadership as his predecessors—Al Capone, Frank Nitti and Tony Accardo—he ruled longer than any of them.

Once described by a police official as "a snarling, sarcastic, ill-mannered, ill-tempered, sadistic psychopath," Giancana was a sixth-grade dropout at the age of fourteen. His lack of education was reflected in a psychological evaluation performed in 1940 at Terre Haute prison. The tests indicated he was still the equivalent of a sixth grader in knowledge, with a general IQ of 71 verbal and 93 nonverbal, with poor accuracy and good speed. Drafted by the U.S. Army in 1943, he was rejected as "a constitutional psychopath" with an "inadequate personality and strong anti-social trends." Actually, when they asked what he did for a living he said he was a thief. It is possible that he knew what he was doing.

As the chief executive officer, the president, so to

speak, of this vast criminal enterprise, this "constitutional psychopath" was responsible for its day-to-day success. Under him were vice presidents, department heads, district supervisors and straw bosses. This executive staff of approximately a thousand men commanded a force conservatively estimated at over fifty-thousand—about one percent of the population of Cook County—consisting of burglars, hijackers, fences, counterfeiters, extortioners, narcotics peddlers, loansharks, collectors, torturers, assassins, crooked cops, venal judges and politicians, union and business fronts, plus an array of gamblers including bookies, steerers, and policy runners. The annual "revenue" in Cook County was estimated at more than $2 billion, a figure arrived at by local authorities and newspapers—federal sources placed the gambling take alone at more than $1 billion.

In terms of leadership, this made Giancana the most powerful archcriminal in the world. Where New York rackets were divided among four or five separate organizations, Giancana was the ostensible ruler of a single syndicate with interests extending as far west as Hawaii. His immediate perimeter stretched from Cleveland to Kansas City, from Hot Springs to New Orleans. Trusted lieutenants operated lucrative rackets in Florida, the West Indies, Arizona, Nevada and California. The Chicago branch of the international crime conglomerate has always been the most politically insulated and police-pampered "family" this side of Sicily.

This, then, was Sam Giancana on paper. What follows are the impressions of someone who knew him in a far different way.

Dean joined us and as we wandered around I noticed that Sam Flood's eyes never left me. I was used to people watching me or doing double takes, calling attention to someone else: "Look at her!" I seldom paid any attention to it. But this evening I was very much aware of his eyes on me. There was a little smile on his face whenever I looked at him. Although he wasn't what I would call handsome, he was a pleasant enough looking man, who seemed very sure of himself. I noticed another man, a big bruiser, standing a short distance away. He never took his eyes off Sam Flood. Later I would learn that he was John Matassa, who was one of his bodyguards, chauffeurs, and trusted emissaries. His devotion to Sam was remarkable. I have no doubt that he would have sacrificed his life for him without a second thought.

Once we went into the dining room I forgot about Sam Flood. He got lost in the shuffle. There were two main tables. Frank and Juliet with their group had one; Dean, Bob Neal, and I with our group had the other. It was a long evening. I danced with Dean and with Bob, drank a little too much, and got a terrible headache. Everyone was having a good time. It was noisy, lots of laughter as always, and I think also the pressure of Frank being at the next table got to me. It was like sitting near a time bomb. Finally, I told Bob and Dean I was tired and asked them to excuse me. As I walked by Frank's table I said, "Good night, Frank. Thanks!" There was more sarcasm than gratitude in my voice. I walked away before he could think of anything to say.

I talked to Jack the next day and agreed to see him in Washington on April 6, the day after the Wisconsin primary. I was supposed to have flown to Washington on March 24 but I missed my flight—I missed many planes and trains in those days—and when I called Jack, he said he was returning to Wisconsin the next day and would not be back in Washington until April 6.

It was time to leave Florida. I had been there two weeks and my bill, because of a lot of shopping, was close to two thousand dollars. To avoid any problem with the desk when checking out, I tried to reach Joe Fish to see if he would OK my check. Although no one had said anything to me about him, I was under the impression that he either owned the hotel or was one of its top executives.

In between calls while trying to track down Joe Fish, I received one from Betty Winikus, whom I had known for several years. She went with Brad Dexter, a bit actor who a few years later saved Frank's life when he got caught in a riptide in Hawaii. From then on, Brad and Betty were around Frank every chance they had. Brad even got a couple of small parts in Frank's movies. Betty knew everybody in Hollywood. When she walked into a restaurant there wasn't anybody important in there she didn't know. She was invited to all the parties; she obviously had good connections, but I never really knew her story.

Betty was calling to see if I would have dinner with her and a friend. I explained about my interest in finding Joe Fish, and she said, "Don't worry about it. I'll talk to somebody."

I said, "Thanks, Betty."

"Don't mention it. Look, I'll meet you in your room about seven-thirty and we'll go up to his suite."

"You mean have dinner in his suite?"

"No, Judy, we'll have dinner at the Eden Roc."

"Okay, Betty, but I have to catch a plane at ten."

"Don't worry, we'll have you there in plenty of time."

The gentleman was Sam Flood—it would be months before I knew his real name. When we arrived in his suite, he invited us in for a drink. There was not another soul there. Betty did most of the talking. It seemed as if she felt compelled to keep things moving right along all by herself. Sam—he had corrected me when I called him Mr. Flood—sat there with that little smile on his face. His eyes were friendly, but again he never took them off me.

Dinner at Eden Roc was hasty, but the conversation was pleasant and surprisingly easy. I talked about my family and he told me that he was a widower. He asked me what I did and I said I was an artist, that I worked in charcoal and oils. At the time I was mainly doing children's faces. He expressed a desire to see some of my work, and whenever anyone said that, I used to kid about it, doing a switch on the old line: "Ah, you want to come see my etchings?"

"You bet," he said. "I'd like that very much."

"If I ever have a show, which I hope to have very soon, I'll send you a special invitation."

He asked where I would be staying in New York, and wanted to know if he could call me, and I said, "Yes, that's fine." The answer even surprised me. There were very few people I would say that to on a first meeting. The fact was that I enjoyed his company. He was a calm, low key person—so much more mature than the younger people I knew. It was partly what impressed me about Jack. They had a different way of handling themselves.

From the way people behaved around him, Sam was obviously a man of "position." I was used to seeing the help jump whenever Frank walked into a restaurant, but with Sam they fell all over each other trying to please him. And he, on the other hand, acted like royalty, completely ignoring their existence, which seemed to spur them to even greater effort. The more I watched the various performances, including Betty's, the more intrigued I became with Sam. But I wasn't about to ask him what he did for a living. For all I knew, he could have been president of General Motors. Because of my shyness, I have always avoided asking questions that could make me look foolish. Besides what difference did it make at the moment? Later, when I began to suspect, I found that I didn't want to know anything.

I paid a terrible price for my association with Sam, but I have never been one to judge people because of what others have said about them. I believe in finding out for myself. This is not a conscious effort—it's just the way I am constituted. If I like a person, I like that person until I find out that person is not a friend. Then, and only then, do I say, "Go away."

After dinner we went back to the Fontainebleau to pick up my luggage. As we walked into the lobby, I asked Betty if she had talked to anyone about clearing my check, and Sam said, "Just a minute." He walked over to the cashier and was back in two minutes flat. He handed me my bill and it was marked "Paid."

I looked at him. "What are you doing?"

"Don't worry about it," he said. "It's all taken care of."

"No, I can't have you do that. I'll give you a check."

"No, Judy, please, I want to do it." He had a big grin on

his face, proud as a peacock for what he had done, no doubt expecting me to be all giddy about it and say, "Oh, goodness, thank you so much."

I said, "It's ridiculous. There's no way I can accept this. I'm either going to give the cashier my check, or I'll give it to you, but only if you promise to cash it."

"Okay, okay," he said, "give me the check."

I wrote out a check and gave it to him. Betty was getting a big kick out of it. She later told the story over and over again, embellishing it as she went along, until finally Sam had not only paid my hotel bill but had also paid for my trip to Miami. She never mentioned that I had given Sam a check, which he did cash.

I stayed at Toni Carroll's place in New York, and was awakened around noon by the delivery of five dozen yellow roses from Sam. Whenever I received flowers from Sam, it was always five dozen yellow roses. I know that yellow roses mean jealousy, but I never understood the significance of five dozen. Sam called shortly after the flowers arrived and again later that day.

That evening I went to dinner with Morris Levy. I had met him through a friend of Travis, Frank Satinstein, whose family, I think, owned American Bookbinding in New York. He also either produced or directed the original Jackie Gleason shows. I had a rather peculiar experience with Frank Satinstein. He had a girlfriend, Jennifer, who was really gorgeous, and he wanted me to do a portrait of her. Then it came out that he wanted a nude portrait, and it further came about that he wanted to be there when I painted the nude portrait of Jennifer. Then I started getting calls from Jennifer in the morning and she wanted to come over to see me. Then I severed my relationship with Frank Satinstein and his Jennifer.

Morris Levy would probably be considered unattractive by most people. He looked very much like Telly Savalas, and had a certain charm that you find with some very unattractive men. He talked with "dese, dem and dose" but in a light, kind of charming way. He was a character, but he was also a friend I could call and say, "Morris, I'm bored, want to go out to dinner?" I have never understood Morris's connections. As far as I knew, he owned Roulette Records, Birdland, and the Round Table restaurant. Later I discovered that one of Sam's sons-in-law worked for Roulette Records.

Sometimes when I called Morris would say, "Not tonight, Judy. I'm having certain people over." He was another one who enjoyed the company of hoods and hookers. He once gave a party for a hoodlum by the name of Johnny Dio when Dio was either coming out of jail or going in. He would not have me around when those people were there.

I could call him at midnight and he would whiz over to take me out to the Stage Delicatessen for a cup of coffee. There never was any romance between us. I doubt that I was the kind of woman he would have been sexually interested in. His leanings, I suspected, were more exotic. I don't know how to explain my relationship with some of these men. Without meaning to sound immodest, perhaps I flattered their egos. I was a beautiful girl, always impeccably groomed and with an elegant wardrobe, and they liked being seen with me. Once we got beyond that stage, I think they enjoyed having a woman as a friend or drinking buddy, someone to whom they could tell their troubles and find a sympathetic ear. In some ways, Morris wanted less from me and gave me more of himself, and more fun, too, than anyone I knew in those days.

Although he was tough and had rough friends, he was always a gentleman with me. And extremely protective. He had a magnificent apartment on Central Park South, and one night when he was entertaining friends, someone brought out a small vial and poured a white powder-like substance into a tiny spoon and sniffed it. Then he passed it around and others sniffed it.

"What is that?" I asked.

"It's nothing for you," Morris said.

"Well, thanks a lot."

"You better thank me," he said, "because that's nothing for you, *ever*."

They all laughed and later, after his friends had left,

Morris told me it was cocaine.

One of Morris's friends was Sarah Vaughan. I stood in awe of her, and that hasn't happened too often in my life. She has such an incredible talent. I went with Morris to her home in New Jersey. She had some music in her hand and she transposed it to another key, all up in her head, never went near the piano. I was enthralled. I just couldn't believe what I was hearing. For a moment I had a glimpse into her world, the world of great musicians, people with gut-level genius, who live and breathe a music that's in their very soul. Frank was talented, but there was no comparison. They lived in different worlds.

By now, between Jack and Sam, I was spending a great deal of time on the telephone. Sam was calling from Chicago two and three times a day, trying to suggest a time when we could see each other. My response at that point was, "Have you deposited that check?" And he would say, "Now what makes you think I wouldn't deposit that check?" I would say, "If you don't deposit it, I'm not going to see you." "Well," he would say, "it looks like I'm going to have to deposit that check, because I sure do want to see you."

Not only was he bombarding me with telephone calls, but every single day I would get five dozen yellow roses. I had to throw them out even before they started to wilt. And always in a green glass vase. I collected them when I was back in California. Everyone in my family has a collection of those green glass vases.

As the days went by, I discovered that Sam had a good sense of humor and just loved to tease. He loved to get my goat. He just thought that was the funniest thing on earth. I couldn't stay mad at him because his laugh was so hearty. His sense of humor wasn't like Jack's, who was so bright and really so quick and so witty. It was more elemental, a little more mundane, but very pleasant just the same. Everything with Sam was lollipops and roses. If I'd accepted it, I think he would have sent me the Hope Diamond. Instead he was sending me what he thought I couldn't refuse—every woman loves to receive flowers. I adored getting flowers and he could tell that I was getting a big kick out of it. He was winning me over right where I lived.

He wanted to visit me in New York but I told him I was going to Washington. Then he wanted us to meet in Florida, or in Chicago where he could show me his town. He would say, "What time did you say you were arriving?" I would laugh. "I didn't tell you I was arriving at all, Sam." "Oh, I must have misunderstood." He would laugh, thinking he was being quite clever. "If you ever get me there at all, you're not going to get me there by tricking me." He would say, "Okay, straight forward, will you come?" I would say, "No." "Well, then I've got to try another way."

He would ask who I was seeing in New York, and when I told him he would say, "You can find time to go out with that jerk, why can't you let me come and see you or come see me?" His tone was always light, always very friendly, never heavy.

On April 4, the day before I left for Washington, Sam called four times. During his last call, he said, "How long will you be in Washington?"

"Probably about a day."

"Why don't you fly to Chicago from there. Give me a chance to show you a good time in my home town. I promise you that everything is going to be on the up and up. You'll be as safe here as in your mother's arms."

"Maybe I'll take you up on it," I said. "Let me think about it."

His persistence was making me a little nervous. It's not easy to put someone off two and three times a day, especially when you're sitting in a room full of his flowers. By the end of the week, he had pretty well broken through my defenses.

When he called the next afternoon—I was to leave for Washington at nine-thirty that evening—I told him that it looked promising, but I would call him from Washington with the final decision. It was then that he gave me the telephone number of the Armory Lounge in Forest Park. I was to ask for Butch or Joe Pignatello, and they would put me in touch with Sam Flood. The Armory was operated by Carmine and Doris Fanelli.

126

Meanwhile, of course, Jack was also calling every day, wanting to make sure that I would be in Washington at the appointed time. Since I had missed that plane in Miami, he wasn't too sure whether he could depend on me. He would say, "You better be here Wednesday or I'm coming up there to get you."

"Don't worry, I'll be there," I would assure him.

"That's what you said the last time." Jack was kidding and yet it had something to do with an attitude men in certain positions have toward women. They are used to snapping their fingers and having women run to them. It has to do with wealth and power and fame. With Jack it was all of that plus great charm, erudition and sex appeal—an irresistible combination.

I missed my flight that evening. I met Uncle Armand and some of his friends for cocktails at the Pierre and dinner in the Plaza's Persian Room. Then it was the Village Vanguard and on to Birdland for Count Basie and Joe Williams.

I flew to Washington the next morning. Before boarding the plane I bought several newspapers. I had thought about the Wisconsin primary the night before, wondering how Jack had fared, but it had been too late when I returned to the hotel to get any news report on television. I pored over the newspapers, happy at what the headlines proclaimed, but very unhappy when I realized that Jack's margin of fifty-six percent of the popular vote came entirely from heavily Catholic districts. He was badly defeated in the four Protestant districts. He barely squeaked by in the one unclassified district. The meaning was crystal clear. It was a Catholic-Protestant contest. Jack was still the *Catholic* candidate for President. The columnists were bursting with dire predictions about the upcoming West Virginia primary, where the population was ninety-five percent Protestant.

If Jack had been a Protestant, his vote margin would have been considered a landslide. Yet it was Hubert Humphrey who was acting like the winner. "I'm encouraged and exhilarated and sorry it's all over," he told newsmen. He was going directly to Washington and on to West Virginia the next day. "I was going to try and get a ride with Jack on his plane, but he thought I ought to catch the next bus. Why don't you fellows come along? We're selling popcorn concessions down there." Humphrey was described as laughing and joking, very jubilant about what he called his "moral victory." "I always told you fellows politics could be fun, didn't I?"

I stopped reading. Poor Jack, I thought, his religion would destroy him. By the time I arrived at the Sheraton Park in Washington, I had a terrible empty feeling gnawing at me. But when I came into the room and found a dozen red roses from Jack, I felt better. I ordered a drink and took a long hot bath. That always works miracles for whatever ails me.

Then I stretched out on the bed and called Evelyn Lincoln, who had made my reservation, to see what instructions Jack had for me. She was extremely cordial as always, and told me how happy Jack would be that I was in Washington. I was to go to Jack's Georgetown house at seven-thirty that evening. The address was 3307 N Street, Northwest.

Since Evelyn Lincoln has now chosen to deny any knowledge of our relationship, I have decided to list some of the addresses and telephone numbers given to me by her and Jack during the time we saw each other.

When I first knew Jack, Evelyn lived at 3132 Sixteenth Street, Northwest, apartment 507, telephone AD 4-5745. Other numbers were MA 4-1011, MA 4-9335, HO 2-5632. Her number at the Old Senate Office building, room 362, was CA 4-3121, extension 3341. The private number was RE 7-0064. After the election, Evelyn moved to 1440 Rock Creek Ford Road, Northwest, apartment 402, and the number was TA 9-5552.

Jack's Georgetown home number was FE 8-2325; in New York it was PL 5-7600 and EL 5-4878, and his apartment was at 277 Park Avenue. The White House was NA 8-1414. At Hyannis, I could reach Evelyn at the Yachtman Hotel, Spring 5-4600. In Palm Beach, numbers for Jack were TE 2-7117 and TE 3-4622; Evelyn's, at the Palm Beach Towers, was TE 3-5761.

Later in the day, Jack called to welcome me to

Washington. "I wish I could show you the city," he said, "but—" I said, "Jack, please, you don't have to apologize. You know how I feel about being seen in public with you. All I want is to be with you."

I listened closely to his tone, trying to detect his mood, but it was impossible. He seemed very cheerful, as he always did to me in those days. He wanted to know if I liked my room. Did I need anything at all? When he offered to send a car to pick me up, I told him I preferred taking a cab.

His call helped lift my spirits, but now I had butterflies. I didn't relish the idea of going to his home. That was Jackie's home. As much as I was beginning to care for him, I had serious misgivings about the evening.

I wore a black knit suit and a brand new black diamond mink coat with horizontal fur that I had bought in New York that week. Jack answered the door and his eyebrows went up when he saw me.

"You look fantastic," he said, as he helped me out of the coat. He leaned over and gave me a kiss on the cheek. He was grinning from ear to ear and from head to toe. It was that kind of genuine welcome. That's saying a lot for Jack, because he was naturally reserved. He was affectionate, but he never gushed. We were similar in that respect, and that was probably the attraction between us. We weren't all over each other, and I think he liked that—I know I did.

As we came into the living room, a large man stood up and Jack introduced us, but I have never remembered his name. He was very tall, large in stature, and from what was said, I gathered he was a railroad lobbyist. I was almost relieved to see him. It is hard to describe the feeling, but, as I said, I was sensitive about seeing Jack in his wife's home. I couldn't even think of it as being his home. I had come to Jackie's house to see her husband. I was thinking how I had suffered through Billy's affairs, and now I was doing the same thing to another woman. Unfortunately, my interest in Jack, my need to be with him, was stronger than my conscience.

We had a drink, and while we made small talk, I looked around the room and tried to figure out the style or period of the furnishings. The living room was small—all the rooms were small—and the house was long, skinny and tall. It was typical Eastern architecture, designed to provide all the living space a narrow lot allows.

The couch and chairs were soft, very billowy. The colors were light, with soft floral prints, to create a feeling of comfort, and there were a lot of delicate-looking pieces from various French periods. Since I had read that Jackie had magnificent taste, the room was a disappointment. There was too much around, too much clutter for a small room.

Dinner started with a cold soup, which is something I avoid like the plague—too many hidden calories. Jackie loved French cuisine, but Jack, as I was to learn, had an Irish palate. Finger bowls were brought out after the soup, and then it was down to basics: meat and potatoes.

Meanwhile, Jack and the lobbyist were analyzing the Wisconsin primary. From what I gathered, Humphrey's optimism was ill-founded. Jack thought that regardless of the religious vote, Hubert's defeat in Wisconsin, a neighboring state of his native Minnesota, meant that he couldn't deliver anywhere else in the Midwest. If a politician couldn't deliver his base, he was finished, Jack said. Both Jack and the lobbyist felt that Humphrey's decision to campaign in West Virginia would prove fatal to him. A victory would only deadlock the convention, opening the way for some of the peripheral candidates, but his defeat in West Virginia would make Jack's nomination a certainty. There was no question in Jack's mind that he would win in West Virginia, regardless of the religious issue. The Kennedy spirit was indomitable. I was so proud of him.

Once he had disposed of Hubert, Jack began discussing the kind of staff he wanted as President. He seemed particularly troubled about Evelyn Lincoln. He wondered whether she was capable of handling the broader responsibilities of the White House. When he asked for my opinion, I said she seemed extremely efficient and loyal, putting as much em-

130

phasis on the word loyal as I could without making it an issue.

We had an after dinner drink in the living room and then the lobbyist left. Jack escorted him to the door and when he came back into the room, he sat next to me on the sofa.

"This has been a long evening," he said. "It was very hard sitting away from you when all I wanted to do was to come over and put my arms around you like this."

We kissed and he said, "Let me show you the rest of the house." We wandered through various rooms until we came to the master bedroom, which was upstairs at the front of the house. There were twin beds with pale green spreads, very filmy and delicate.

He put his arms around me and we sat on one of the beds. We kissed and he was almost immediately amorous. I went to the bathroom to undress, and when I came back into the room, the lights were very low and Jack was already in bed.

"I've missed you so much," I said, as I went into his arms.

We kissed passionately, and he said, with his lips still on mine, "Do you think you could love me?"

"I'm afraid I could," I whispered, and it was so true. I was so afraid that it was happening to me. I was really mixed up. The thought of loving him made me happy one moment and unhappy the next. I wanted to be with him, but I hated being in his bedroom, having that close a contact with his wife. And I worried about the servants, of what they thought of my being there, and I couldn't quite understand how he could do that with the servants in the house. Yet every time I really started to think about it, whether it was in his home in Georgetown or later in the White House, I would whitewash it with excuses—the servants probably knew they weren't happily married. To be perfectly honest about it, I think I was caught up a little with the intrigue of it. The sneaking around, a mild form of cloak-and-dagger, the anticipation, and "Boy, we didn't get caught!"

I adored Jack's possessiveness after we made love. He

didn't want to let go. He would lie with his arms around me and I would rest my head on his chest and listen to the beat of his heart as we talked for hours. Much of it was pillow talk, light and teasing, nothing ever too serious, but this evening he said something that really took me aback.

"If I don't get the nomination—"

I said, "What?" without waiting for him to finish. It was the first negative thought I had heard him express. "I didn't really hear you say 'if'!"

"Let me finish," he laughed.

"I can't believe my ears. Jack Kennedy, the erstwhile candidate for the Presidency of the United States, has just said, 'If I don't get the nomination.' "

He squeezed me. "Will you shut up. This is important."

"Important? I have a good mind to call your mother. I can only hope she doesn't tell your father. He'll take your little plane away from you."

"All right, you had your fun, now it's my turn. If—now don't say anything, I know it's a big if—but if I don't get the nomination, we're going off and sit on a deserted beach somewhere for a whole month, maybe longer, just the two of us. We're going to hide from the world."

I knew how much he loved the water and the beach. "Oh, tell me another one."

"What's wrong with this one? Think of some romantic, faraway place you'd like to go to."

All right, I thought, two can play this game. "You mean where it's warm and we can make love in the sunlight and moonlight."

"Yes, and never wear clothes."

"That's going too far," I said.

"Do you mean you wouldn't give up your wardrobe for me?"

"I'd give up anything for you, Jack, anything but that."

It was all in fun, or so I thought.

It was very late when I reluctantly decided that it was time for me to leave. As I sat up, Jack said, "Is it possible for you to be in Miami on the twelfth?"

"Yes, if we can see each other."

132

He explained that he was going to Indiana, Arizona, and West Virginia, covering some twenty or thirty towns and cities in a campaign swing, and it would be extremely difficult for him to call me. He would be in Miami for just that one day and I promised that I would be waiting for him at the Fontainebleau, at whatever time was convenient for him.

While I dressed Jack called for a cab, and then put on his robe and went downstairs to get my coat. We watched for the cab out the bedroom window.

As he helped me into the coat, he said, "What a beautiful coat."

"I'm very proud of it," I said. "I just bought it this past week."

"You shouldn't be spending that kind of money on a coat."

"Well, I wanted it. I'm not married. If I want something, I have to buy it for myself."

"I don't see why," he said. "Plenty of people would love to buy this coat for you."

"I don't want plenty of people to buy my coat for me. I'm very happy buying my own coat for me. Then no one can come and take it off my back."

We laughed and he said, "How about my buying it for you. I'd never take it off your back."

"Oh, no," I said. "This coat is bought and paid for and I don't really want to discuss it."

"Judy, be reasonable. There's so little I can do for you. Please, let me buy the coat."

"I've told you, Jack. It's already bought and paid for."

"Let me do something, please."

He wasn't kidding anymore. It was obvious that he wanted to do something for me, and though I knew he could well afford it, I had a rule about men giving me expensive gifts. I had seen too many gals running around with mink coats and diamonds and living in apartments paid for by married men. That was not my style. It was important to me that I paid my own way.

In a way, I told Jack, the coat was a gift from Billy. The

month before I had signed away my alimony payments for a cash settlement. But that did not satisfy him. He wanted me to understand that if things were different, he wouldn't want to buy me a mink coat. "That just isn't my way," he said. "But the situation being what it is, you won't let me pay for your room or your plane tickets, and you're the one coming to see me. Let me do something for you. This is something you love, so let me be a part of it."

The discussion went on until the cab arrived. Then he said, "We'll talk about it later. I haven't given up."

What Jack couldn't understand was that I was hanging onto myself for the first time in my life. I was taking care of me and paying my own way. I was doing for myself, and I was living my own life on my own terms, coming and going as I pleased. I was my own keeper, and I loved that freedom.

We walked downstairs and he said, "Call me at my office in the morning. Do you know what time you're leaving?"

I said, "No." I had told him I was going to Chicago to visit friends, for I had already made up my mind to go see Sam.

"Well, make sure you call me before you go."

He waited at the front door until I reached the cab. I looked up and smiled at him, and he nodded and closed the door.

The phone rang almost the moment I walked into my room. It was Jack wanting to know if everything was all right. I said I was fine and he gave me his home number. "Now, you call me if you need anything during the night." That surprised me. It made me think that I was more concerned about his wife than he was.

I was tired but I lay in bed a long time and thought about Jack. I was happy that he wanted to buy the mink coat for me, that he thought that much of me, that he truly wanted to do something for me. I was on the edge of falling in love, but I was fighting it because he was married and deep down I knew the relationship was doomed to failure. In some ways, I was an emotional cripple. I was so afraid of getting hurt. I was instinctively holding back.

134

The fact that he might be President one day was not what attracted me. And I was not bowled over by the fact that he was interested in me, or that Sam was interested, or Frank, or Dean, or anybody. I expected it. I have often wondered about myself. As insecure as I was in given areas, I was never surprised by the attention showered on me. I think a psychiatrist would say I had a problem.

When I called his office the next day, Evelyn said he had already left for Indiana. I took the train for Chicago at five-thirty that evening. I love trains, especially the old Eastern trains. I used to take a bedroom, drawing room, living room suite and it was tremendous—it could accommodate a family of three. I ordered drinks and dinner, and sat back in the splendor of my privacy, and thought about Jack and Sam. Although it may sound strange to the reader, this was a time in my life when I was exploring. I was infatuated with Jack, not really in love yet, but I couldn't just sit home and wait for his calls which came at all hours of the day or night. He was on the go constantly. He had something else to occupy his time. It was exciting for me to be going to Chicago instead of just going back to New York and moping about Jack. It was a new adventure. I didn't feel any pressure from Sam and I was looking forward to seeing new places and meeting new people. In my mind, I was not going to Chicago to see another man, to become emotionally involved with anyone. I was in a happy frame of mind. I liked the idea of being with someone that really wanted to be with me.

It never occurred to me that I wouldn't be able to control the situation. I may have been a little naive but I was a big girl. No one ever talked me into the bedroom. I felt myself getting stronger all the time. But I had my insecurities. I wasn't alone, however; I don't care who you are, or how strong you are, we are all vulnerable in some ways.

Jack Kennedy was insecure in certain areas. He was insecure as to how he looked when he dressed. He always needed to be reassured that he looked just right. He used to ask me all the time, especially after he was in the White

House, "Do you like this suit? How does it look?" He would ask it over and over again. He needed the confidence that comes from reassurance.

If you look at the women in that family, I think they dressed because the law says you have to wear clothes. But once the public eye zeroed in on them, they took a little more care. Their mother was probably a very elegant woman, but I think all the children took after the father.

I don't think Jack realized just how great he looked. But that's not unusual. Very often you'll find the most attractive people will look in the mirror the most because they are told so often—I think it's part of my insecurity—that they are so beautiful. And you think, "Am I really?" Then you get used to people looking at you and you become very conscious of always looking right. That's a very fine line. You can become overly conscious of how you look and constantly worry about it, like some actors and actresses, who often go off the deep end worrying about their looks. They never think they look quite right, or perfect enough.

Jack was used to dressing a certain way because it was required of a young man going places. Now, suddenly, he knew he had to make sure that he looked elegant. His natural inclination was to be sloppy—that is, Palm Beach and Hyannisport sloppy chic: old trousers, sweatshirt, and scuffed loafers without socks. That was fine for weekends but not for the limelight, not for the President of the United States, not for the most powerful leader in the free world. Everything had to be perfect. If he walked the wrong way, someone was going to put it in the newspaper. If he got a cinder in his eye, someone was going to have him going blind. The same applied to the way he dressed. He was a conservative dresser, and sometimes a conservative dresser is just a safe dresser. A very conservative dresser is someone who wants to feel safe in what they wear, and I think that was Jack's basic insecurity.

VII

We pulled into Chicago at eight-thirty the next morning. I looked out the window and there was Sam smiling at me. I was thrilled. Finally I knew someone who cared enough to meet me. I slipped into my mink and hurried to meet him. Sam was there to take my hand as I stepped off the train.

"Ah, I finally got you here," he said.

"Don't get too cocky," I said. "I may get back on the train and go home."

"Boy, you're really hard on a guy."

The porter started bringing out my matched luggage and I said, "How strong are you?"

Sam started to laugh after three large suitcases were brought out—by the time it got to number seven he was hysterical. Joseph Pignatello, a short, stocky man with black hair, who was another of Sam's many chauffeurs, was scratching his head and looking frantically for a redcap.

As I stood there in the grime of that railroad depot, I was truly happy. Because I didn't have a romantic attachment, I felt free and comfortable. Sometimes the more you care about someone, the uneasier you are, because you anticipate every move you make, you want to be right in everything you say or do. Sam was just somebody who was amusing and was just showering me with attention. There was no emotional tie and therefore no anxiety. I could just relax and have a good time.

I don't know how Joe ever got all that luggage in that little black Ford. It was in the trunk, the front seat, the floor in back.

"My God, Sam," I said, as I sat with my feet on a suitcase, "why are we riding in this terrible little car?"

"Well, what did you expect?" he said, laughing. "Isn't this good enough for you?"

Sam thought that my distaste for little cars was the funniest thing in the world. That was the one thing about him that used to drive me crazy. He always traveled in a little black Ford or a taxicab.

"Besides, what were you doing on the train?"

"I love trains."

"Ah, go on, you're afraid to fly?"

"Are you kidding? I fly all the time."

"Then you must have been stalling."

"What do you mean?"

"The train takes longer. You just hated coming to Chicago."

"I tell you, I really love trains."

"Tell me another story."

That's the way it went with Sam. We kidded a lot, but his attitude was one of being flattered that I had come to see him. I think he was getting a big kick out of the fact that I didn't know who he was. That he could fool me, that I would come to visit him because I liked him, and not because of what he could do for me. As I was to learn in time, Sam could do a lot for people, particularly people in the entertainment business, or he could do a lot to them.

My reservation was at the Ambassador East. I think it was the John Barrymore Suite, which was the one I stayed in most of the times I came to Chicago. Lo and behold, there were five dozen yellow roses in a green glass vase. I thanked him and after he was sure I liked the suite, he said he would be back around noon.

I suppose the reader is wondering at this point what I could see in Sam. Besides what I have already said about his sense of humor and his attentiveness, he was always well dressed, very neat, and always conducted himself, at least in my presence, like a gentleman. He created a nice impression. He wasn't handsome, but everything was where it should be. His whole attitude, his personality, the way he treated me was very appealing, not physically or emotionally attractive, but as a friend, someone who was enjoyable.

Now, as I read about Sam, I find another whole side of him of which I was never a part. Perhaps he always looked like a hoodlum to the police or to the public at large. All I can say is that he was different when he was with me. At that time, it was all that mattered to me.

When he picked me up that afternoon, he said, "Come on, I'm going to drive you out to a place. I have to see some people. Then I'll show you around."

The place turned out to be the Armory, and it wasn't much of a place—perhaps I should say it wouldn't be much of a place in California, but in the Midwest or East, it was perfectly respectable. Typical Eastern saloon-type place. There was a jukebox and the bar was the length of one side of the room. There was a pay phone on the wall near the kitchen entrance that Sam kept pretty busy. There was a dining room and behind it was a back room, kind of a storeroom, with a table and chairs. We sat there one night to watch television returns of a local election. Sam would often have a "meet"—I learned to use that expression after hearing so often "we've got a meet"—in the back room with important people. However, he conducted a lot of business at our booth in the bar right in front of me. As he did on that first day. But it was in Sicilian.

Sometimes in the middle of one of those rapid fire discussions, he would turn to me and say, "Bet you can't understand that?" The smile on his face was as if, "I'm really putting one over on you."

I would reply, "You don't know. One of these days I'm going to understand every word you're saying."

"Honey," he would say, "there is no way on earth that will ever happen. We're Sicilians and we talk our own dialect. We know how to do it."

"I'll go to Berlitz."

He just about fell over laughing. "You can go anywhere you want, but nobody will ever teach you our dialect. When I don't want you to understand, believe me, you won't understand."

Months later he would say, "You don't want to hear what I've got to say to these people."

When I finally realized who he was, I appreciated the fact that whatever he was doing, he was making sure that I was not a part of it. I was particularly appreciative when I saw some of the characters who came to see him. They may have been comical in their appearance and speech, but I am sure there was nothing very humorous about their business. It occurred to me that the ones who looked the most comical were perhaps the most dangerous. The strange ones—but I didn't think about it that way then. I had no fear of Sam. No fear that anything would ever happen to me because of Sam or with Sam or by Sam. That, I know, was terribly naive. There are times when I wonder who or what I was in those days.

Sam used to disappear for a month or more at a time, and I wouldn't hear a word from him. I would say to him upon his return, "My God, why couldn't you call? Why couldn't you let me know you were all right? I was afraid something had happened to you."

"It was a time when I shouldn't be in touch with you," he would reply, or "It's better for you that I wasn't in touch." That is all he would say about it. It always gave me the feeling that he was protecting me.

I was seeing a different environment and it was exciting. I was watching Sam and really wondering about him. But I wasn't about to ask him what was going on. On that first day or any other day. I felt that if he wanted me to know anything he would tell me. Or maybe he assumed I knew and that would be terribly embarrassing if all of a sudden I would say, "What do you do for a living?" And he would look at me and say, "Where have you been anyway, hiding in a closet all your life?"

Doris and Carmine Fanelli ran the Armory. She did all the

cooking and baking, and Carmine tended bar and managed the business. Sam loved to tease Carmine. When I was introduced to Carmine, Sam said, "Turn around Carmine—now, doesn't he look like a taxicab with the back doors swung open." Poor Carmine. His ears did stick out like opened doors.

For dinner that evening we went to Whitehall, which in those days was a private club. Sam liked their steak Diane—they cooked it at your table and the aroma was sheer ambrosia. And again as I had observed in Florida, the owner, the *maître d'*, the wine steward, the waiter, everybody was just showering him with slavish attention. Their performance was so obsequious that it was distasteful. Every other word was punctuated with "sir" and bows—I had the feeling that mentally they were walking on their knees.

What bothered me even more was Sam's aloofness. I don't believe in getting chummy with your waiter or *maître d'* but I do believe in common decency. When you're asked a question—"How is your steak?" or "Is everything all right?"—I think some kind of comment is deserved. When someone is trying very hard to make things right for you, the least you can do is acknowledge it with a yea or nay.

There were times when Sam ignored everybody except me. He did a little of it that night, and the more he got to know me, the more imperious he became with others. I got the impression that unless he made a conscious effort, those people didn't exist for him. I didn't know it then, but he was the *Padrone*, the Godfather, if you will, and how well they knew it. One word from Sam and that restaurant would be closed. The unions would strike, the city would revoke its various licenses, its trash wouldn't be collected, a bomb might go off, fire might break out—in other words, instant and complete disaster.

To be fair about it, I don't have any evidence that any of the above ever happened, but I do know that because of their respect—and anxiety—for him, and their need to endlessly express it with words and deeds, it was impossible for Sam to respond to everybody hovering around him. He held a position of highest "honor" in his world and his cool demeanor was no less than expected. This did not only apply to the help, but to anybody who made contact with him. For example, nobody ever approached Sam's table unless he wished them to approach. There was no buddy-buddy back-slapping good-time-Charlie stuff around Sam. On occasion, Sam would embrace other Italian men of respect, but there was a distinct protocol that was rigorously followed at all times.

Sam was a martini drinker and he drank his fair share. Later in our relationship, I began to notice that when Sam got a little in his cups, he became more abrupt with people—not with me— and this caused great consternation for whoever was at the receiving end. I could well imagine the poor fellow spending hours agonizing over it, no doubt wondering where he had gone wrong in the past and what dire fate awaited him in the future.

As for our own relationship, it was one of gradual attraction for me. It was almost a year and a half before we became intimate. Being a normal male, Sam tried to change that situation, but after I told him about my feelings for Jack, he didn't push it beyond the teasing stage for at least a year. His patience so impressed me at the time that I actually felt guilty.

I told him, "I'm sorry, I just can't carry on two affairs. I love being with you, but if you want more than friendship, then I'm going to have to stop seeing you." I knew that if I had an affair with Sam, if I went to bed with him, it wasn't going to be something that happened because I drank too much one night and made a mistake.

His response was, "It's okay, don't worry about it. Everything is fine the way it is."

As I look back, it's possible that Sam got exactly what he wanted from our relationship. Now that I know of his involvement with the Central Intelligence Agency, it is possible that I was used almost from the beginning. I don't exactly know how it was done, but perhaps it will become more evident as my story unfolds. Except for occasional observations, I think, it would be a mistake at this point for me to indulge in theories. I will continue to tell my story, as honestly and clearly as I remember it happening, or the way it seemed to be happening at that time.

It never occurred to me that Sam's interest in me was simply because of my association with Jack Kennedy. Of course there were people who wanted to be my friend because of my relationship with Jack, backslappers who wanted "little favors," but Sam never asked me for anything, and so I never connected Sam with any of that. Whatever may have been Sam's motivation in the beginning, I do know that he later fell deeply in love with me, and what he did then violates a lot of the theories that certain people find so much pleasure in expounding.

When I told Sam I was going to see Jack in Florida on the twelfth he said, "Well, why don't you fly down with me on the ninth. I have some business down there."

"That's fine, Sam, as long as I pay my way."

He shook his head. "Now, wait a minute, honey. Fair is fair, but you're overdoing it. I've cashed your check—I didn't want to, but I did. And you've paid the freight coming up here to see me. Now it's my turn to do a little something for you."

"You have done plenty. You've shown me a wonderful time."

"I want to do this, honey. And I want to take care of your reservation down there too. Wait! I swear, it's not costing me a dime. It's on the house. Let them pick up the tab. Hell, they comp people right and left all the time."

"You're not pulling my leg?"

"Now, would I pull your leg?" And he laughed. "But don't give me ideas like that. You know how I feel."

Later, when Joe Pignatello handed me my ticket, I saw that it was made out to a Miss Moore—my first alias. We took Delta on the morning of the ninth and we played gin all the way to Florida. Playing gin with Sam was not the world's greatest pastime. I don't know whether he cheated, but there was just no way I could play cards with him. He would knock so fast I barely had time to arrange my cards. He thought that was hilarious.

143

Joe Fish met us at the airport with a limousine and Sam just looked at me and shrugged his shoulders. At the Fontainebleau I had a large corner suite, and I think Sam had his suite on the same floor.

That evening we went with Joe Fish to the Eden Roc to see Sammy Davis, Jr. Our table was directly center front and Sammy just about played the whole show to our table. This nightclub custom has a lot in common with bullfighting, when the matador dedicates his kill to a pretty lady. In this case, the attraction was Sam. At first I thought that Sam was in one of his aloof moods, for he completely ignored Sammy, but as I soon learned Sam hated blacks, a trait that annoyed and embarrassed me no end.

As far as Sam was concerned, all blacks were stupid, lazy, and not to be trusted. He would refer to them as niggers, a term I have always loathed, and I would nudge him and say, "Don't use that word." I would be indignant, and he would just laugh. The more I objected, the more he did it. Finally I decided that it was best for all concerned if I just ignored it. His hatred was so ingrained that it was hopeless for me to try to change him. He was particularly offensive with cab drivers. He would tease them in a derogatory way, call them "boy," and mimic them with expressions like "Sho'nuff, now."

We went to Palm Beach the next day and this time instead of riding in an old Ford, we rode in an old white and blue Buick, a hideously cumbersome piece of junk.

"What is this car we're riding in?" I saw that little smile on his face and instantly realized that I had taken the bait.

"Why, don't you like it? Look at this man," he said, pointing to the heavyset Italian driving it, "you've got a chauffeur and everything. What are you complaining about? You're going out in style."

"You're impossible," I said. "This car is embarrassing."

"I disagree. I think it's very nice. Don't you pick on my car."

As I look back on the conversation, it sounds kind of inane, but to me it was just lighthearted banter on a beautiful day. This was my first visit to Palm Beach and I was looking

144

forward to seeing the city and Sam's home. Although he never mentioned it, I have since read somewhere that his wife died of a stroke in that house.

The strange thing about Sam's house was that I confuse it in my mind with the house that Jack used the times we met in Palm Beach. Both houses were near the water and typical of what might be typed as Florida subdivision architecture, long and low, with large lawns, large swimming pools, and glassed-in breakfast rooms—both had glass-topped wrought iron tables and wrought iron chairs. The only difference I can remember between the two houses was that Sam's pool was on the left side of the house and Jack's was on the right. Sam's color scheme was muted rose and green, Jack's was more of a grass green.

Sam's proudest possession was a collection of original china figurines, German or Dutch, which he proudly displayed in a lighted glass case in the living room. While he gave me the grand tour of the house and the grounds, his caretaker cooked spaghetti, that eternal Italian sustenance for all occasions. I hate to eat the messy stuff when I'm out, but this was really sensational.

For the rest of the day we basked in the sun and talked about traveling in Europe and South America, two continents Sam had traveled in extensively. Since I had never been abroad, he was more than willing to show me the world if only I said the word. Jewelry was another subject on which Sam could talk for hours. He knew more about jewelry and owned more of it than anyone I have ever known.

The very next day we just had to go look at pearl necklaces at a jeweler Sam knew on Worth Avenue, who also had a store in the Fontainebleau. Shopping on this street is a unique experience. You see all the famous names of stores you find on Fifth Avenue and in Beverly Hills, but here everything has been drastically scaled down in size. Worth Avenue is a miniature street with miniature stores, something out of a child's toyland. The only things of normal size are the prices.

When it came to shopping, Sam was just like me—we both were natural born shoppers. He enjoyed it more than any man I had ever known. That, in my book, was a huge plus in his

145

favor. In those days, shopping was my opiate. I had the world's strongest shopping legs and the most tireless eye. I would hate to calculate the hours I have spent looking at lovely things in lovely stores. If I didn't shop every day, even for a few minutes, I felt like there was something missing when I went to bed that night. That may be a slight exaggeration, but I hope it conveys my passion for this great female sport. I still love it, but the passion has cooled somewhat.

That day in Palm Beach, I bought a pearl necklace with a one-and-a-half carat marquis diamond in the clasp, ringed with small diamonds. Naturally Sam wanted to pay for it, but I declined so firmly that he threw his arms up in disgust. It cost me three thousand dollars, but I now suspect it was worth far more. To me it was a necklace of perfectly matched cultured pearls, but months later Sam wanted to know if I had had it x-rayed. When I replied I had not, he said, "Do me a favor and have it x-rayed." I never did and I have since wondered if perhaps the pearls were not real. The fate of this necklace, along with the rest of my jewelry, will be explained later on.

On our way back to Miami in the old Buick, Sam handed me a small package and said, "Don't give me any trouble." It was a turquoise and diamond earring and ring set. I thanked him and he said, "You were standing right there and you didn't even see me buy this." It always delighted him to put something over on me.

Sam left the next day, which was the twelfth, and I waited for Jack in my room. It was a long wait, and when he finally did arrive, he looked so tired I felt sorry for him. I should clarify this by saying that Jack always looked good to me. He could look vivacious when he was dead tired. Even so the strain would show. This was especially evident when he took cortisone. His face would puff up until his features were distorted.

He closed the door and we embraced. Then we walked over to the sofa and sat down. I had an assortment of finger sandwiches and Jack asked for a soft drink.

146

"God," he said, stretching his feet out on the coffee table, "it's great to see you, and it's great to sit down."

"You look tired."

"I believe it. This is the world's fastest and longest marathon."

"Why do you do it? You're killing yourself. I don't understand it."

"Welcome to the club. Sometimes I wonder if I understand it myself."

I knew he didn't mean it. It was his way of curtailing that line of conversation. "I missed not receiving your calls," I said. We had talked on the phone only three times since I had seen him in Washington.

He leaned over and kissed me. "I can't tell you how much I missed you," he said. "Even in the heat of this campaign I think of you so often. We couldn't have met at a worse time. I'm the busiest I've ever been in my life."

"I wish we could do something about it."

"Judy, I do too. Fortunately, the campaign won't last forever."

"It seems like forever to me."

He smiled. "Don't forget your promise. We may go sit on that island sooner than you think."

"Don't be silly. You're going to get the nomination."

"You never know. We may be lucky."

"Be serious for a minute. Even if you did lose it, God forbid, you have personal commitments. You couldn't just take off like that in a million years."

"I am being serious. I can't go into it right now, but there will be some changes in my life if I don't get the nomination."

That's all he would say at that time and I didn't press it. Later, through various conversations, I got the impression that it was Jackie who was planning to leave him if he didn't become President. In recent years, of course, there has been considerable speculation to the effect that Joe Kennedy had promised Jackie a certain sum of money to preserve the marriage in the event of Jack's election. I have no idea how much credence to give this gossip. All I know is that I was sticking my head in the sand. I was playing the game according to his rules. I didn't want to discuss his wife and from all indications the feeling was mutual. I find it amusing now when I read accounts by women claiming affairs with Jack who say he criticized Jackie or discussed the other women in his life. I can't imagine him doing that. It's completely out of character. The whole time I knew Jack Kennedy, he never once mentioned another woman in my presence. Nor did he criticize Jackie. The most he ever said was that their marriage was not a happy one. It hadn't worked out as they had hoped. Good or bad, I didn't want to hear anything about her. Nor would I have respected him if he had talked about her in my presence. Besides he had too much respect for her to bring it down to that level. Because their marriage wasn't working didn't mean he had any less respect for her.

Oh, but he loved gossip. He adored it. That was something he was always asking me about on the telephone and in person. He would say, "Who's Frank seeing now?" or "I heard Frank is seeing so-and-so and isn't she married?" I would say, "I don't know any gossip." He would say, "Come on, let me in on a little of it. You're around those people, you see things going on." "If you want gossip, pick up a movie magazine." He would act shocked. "I don't want that phony stuff. I want the real inside dope." I think he wanted to know a little dirt about everybody. He wanted to be one step ahead. He never wanted to be the last one to know anything.

I was always fascinated by the way Jack's mind worked. Although he would ask me if I had seen Frank, and tease me a little about it, he would never ask me specific questions about the people I was seeing. If I told him I went to visit friends in Chicago, he would never ask for their names. He would say, "Did you have a good time?" If I said, "Yes," he would reply, "Oh, that's great."

For example, I told him I had gone with friends to shop in Palm Beach, and he said, "Did you find something nice?" If he had asked me outright for the names of the friends, I

148

would have told him the truth. It wasn't that I was hiding anything from him. He either was not a prying individual, or he believed in the old adage of what you don't know won't hurt you.

He stayed not more than an hour that day. He relaxed, he had something to eat, we talked, and he left. There was no lovemaking. He apologized profusely for not staying longer, but he felt that even a little time together was better than no time at all, a sentiment with which I fully concurred.

As he was leaving he handed me an envelope. "Don't open it until after I leave," he said.

"What is this? What did you do?"

"It's a personal note for you," he said. "Just this once, will you listen to me and not question it."

"Okay," I said, "don't give me a bad time."

He laughed and hugged me. "I promise you, Judy, our next meeting will be longer."

"I'll second that motion," I said.

He must have been clear out of the hotel before I opened the envelope. I found two one-thousand-dollar bills and a note on a plain sheet of paper to the effect that he still wanted to pay for my mink coat. If I wouldn't let him do that, then he wanted me to use the money for something special. What could I do now? When is it time to stop arguing and accept a gift gracefully?

I don't quite understand it, but there was something about accepting gifts that chipped away at my freedom. On the other hand, I was always giving expensive gifts to those I loved. Sometimes I think compulsive givers make poor receivers. That was true with Sam and Jack, which I will talk about later, and Frank, of course, as far as I know, never even acknowledges gifts. As I grew older, I became more understanding, more receptive, but for a while my stubborn pride irritated people who were only trying to show me their love.

I sat with the note and the two bills in my hand a long time, thinking about Jack. I was happy I had come to Florida to see him. I was particularly thrilled at the fact that we had sat and talked instead of making love. This told me far more about his love for me than if he had rushed in with just sex on his mind. It made me feel that his plans for me concerned the future. In other words, I could tell myself that it was not just a fling. I badly needed that kind of reassurance. I think Jack knew it. He was so sensitive to people, and by now, with all that chatter on the telephone, he knew me inside out. He probably knew me better than I knew myself.

Later in the day I called Morris Levy in New York. I was undecided on what to do next, but Morris solved that problem for me. Unfortunately it was bad news. Our good friend, Marty Tannenbaum, had suffered a serious heart attack and was hospitalized in Great Neck, Long Island. I flew to New York the next day and again stayed in Toni's apartment. I called Marty's sister—Marty was divorced and his sister took care of his two children—and she arranged with the hospital for me to visit Marty at a time when he was not allowed any visitors.

I stayed two days, flew to California for a quick visit, and came right back to New York. Sam was at the Hampshire House, Jack was all over the place charming voters, God was in his heaven, and all was well with American Tel & Tel—just keep those calls coming.

On the afternoon of April 22, Sam called to ask if I would mind coming over to his suite for a few minutes around six o'clock. He had something he wanted to show me. Ordinarily I would have rejected the invitation out of hand. However, by now I thought I knew Sam well enough to believe him when he said it was important.

I knew that was a mistake the moment Sam opened the door. He had that little mischievous grin on his face as he gave me a quick peck on the cheek and turned to introduce me to his guests. Sitting on the sofa big as life, with drinks in hand, were Bob Wagner and Natalie Wood. We just stared at one another with eyes like saucers. It seemed hours before Bob stood up and said, "Hey, it's good to see you, Judy. How are you?" Natalie murmured her greeting and at that point I could have kicked Sam. I may not have known his real name, but by now I was reasonably convinced that his line of business had nothing to do with General Motors. If it did, it wasn't something that GM was reporting to its stockholders in its annual report. Yet what difference did it make that his name was Giancana instead of Flood? Both names meant absolutely nothing to me. Unless you're a celebrity, what's in a name? Outside of Chicago, in 1960 how many people had ever heard his name?

As we sat down and continued staring in confused embarrassment, I realized that Sam had planned it exactly that way. It was his idea of fun. A good joke. He had pulled a fast one on somebody—but who? For reasons I couldn't fully grasp, I felt compromised, as I'm sure did Bob and Natalie.

Sam was talking about nothing, happy as a lark, but I wasn't listening. I was frantically trying to unravel the puzzle. Then it hit me. While in Chicago, I had mentioned to Sam that it was Bob who introduced me to Billy when I was only sixteen. And that I knew Natalie in the days when she dated Nick Adams, who was part of the group of young actors I knew in the years I was married to Billy. Nick afterwards fell victim to that lethal combination of sleeping pills and booze that has taken such a tragic toll in Hollywood.

While I sat there wondering what they must be thinking of my visiting a man's hotel room, they probably were equally busy wondering about what I thought of their having a social drink with the Godfather of the Chicago mafia—I assume he wasn't Sam Flood to them.

There were long embarrassing lulls in the conversation. Sam was the only one not visibly confused. In an effort to fill one of the lulls—the three of us were desperately searching for something to say—I mentioned that Toni's birthday was coming up and I had to think of a gift before she left for a singing engagement at the Statler in San Antonio.

Sam jumped up and hurried to the bedroom. A moment later I heard him calling, "Hey, Judy, come in here a minute. I want to show you something." I couldn't even smile when I stood up. Bob and Natalie tried to smile, but they weren't doing too well either.

When I walked into the bedroom, Sam closed the door and said, "Take your pick." His top dresser drawer was open

151

and it was full of jewelry—rings, bracelets, necklaces, but mostly watches—all the finest makes like Movados and Corums, all diamond-studded, and all terribly expensive.

There were three watches lined up on the dresser. "Take these for yourself," he said, "they're the best, and pick one out of the drawer for Toni."

I felt like stamping my foot. "Don't you ever give up?"

"Okay, okay, but pick one for Toni, but don't tell her it's from me."

Not being in any mood for an argument, I picked the plainest one I could find. "I'll give this one to Toni, but I don't want a watch. Now can we go back in the other room? I don't like being in here like this."

This nearly doubled him over with laughter. He had a sharp laugh, and at this point I was sure they could hear him throughout the whole damn hotel.

I dropped Toni's watch into my purse and walked out of the room. I sat for only a few minutes before I excused myself. Sam said he would call me later and I just couldn't get out of there fast enough. By the time I got back to Toni's apartment, I was so upset I didn't want to be there when Sam called. Toni was out on a date and that seemed like a perfect idea at the time. I knew just the man who could cheer me up—I had dinner with Morris Levy.

Sam said he was disappointed when he called the next day. He was under the impression that we had a date the night before. I wasn't upset anymore, but I wasn't about to let him dictate to me. It was time for an understanding. "I've never considered 'I'll call you later' a definite date," I said. "Lots of friends say they will call me later, and if I stayed home waiting for their calls, I would never be free to have a date."

"You're absolutely right," he said. "So how about lunch? *Today.*"

"I'm having lunch with Toni."

"Okay, bring her along."

Toni was delighted—but delighted is hardly the word to express her enthusiasm. First I had made the mistake of telling her the truth about the watch when I gave it to her that morning. Now Sam had invited her to lunch. You could see

152

The program Ted Kennedy autographed for Judith's mother at
the 1960 Democratic National Convention in Los Angeles.

WESTERN UNION
TELEGRAM

LA112 A109 SSA096 L

P WWY229 PD=FAX WASHINGON DC 15 NFT=

MISS JUDY CAMPBELL=

1200 NORTH FLORES LOSA=

BECAUSE OF DISTANCE AND TIME INVOLVED YOUR INVITATIONS
AND TICKETS THAT ARE SET ASIDE FOR YOU MAY BE PICKED UP
AT THE INAUGURAL TICKET OFFICE 921 SEVENTEENTH STREET
NW WASHINGTON DC FROM 9 AM TO 9 PM STARTING MONDAY
JANUARY 16 PLEASE BRING THIS TELEGRAM WITH YOU TO
PROPERLY IDENTIFY YOURSELF WHEN PICKING UP YOUR
CREDENTIALS IF YOU ARE NOT PLANNING TO ATTEND PLEASE
END 1

WESTERN UNION
TELEGRAM

P WWY229   LONG 2

ADVISE ME WARM REGARDS=

ROBERT J BURKHARDT EXECUTIVE DIRECTOR
INAUGURAL COMMITTEE 1961 LIBERTY LOAN BLDG
14TH AND D STREETS SW WASHINGTON DC=

921 NW 9 AM 9 PM 16 1961 14 D SW=

The telegram from the Inaugural Committee.

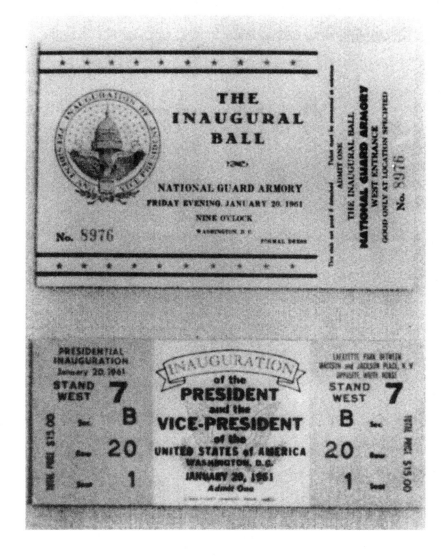

Tickets for the Inaugural Ball and Inauguration.

INAUGURAL ACTIVITIES

Calendar and Information

RECEPTION FOR DISTINGUISHED LADIES

Wednesday, January 18   National Gallery of Art, 3 to 6 p.m.

By Invitation

RECEPTION HONORING THE
VICE PRESIDENT-ELECT AND MRS. LYNDON B. JOHNSON

Wednesday, January 18   Statler Hilton Hotel, 6 to 8 p.m.

$5.00

Public Sale

YOUNG DEMOCRATS' RECEPTION AND DANCE

Wednesday, January 18   Mayflower Hotel, 7 p.m. to 1 a.m.

$8.00

Tickets Available Through The Young Democrats' Inaugural Festivity Committee

GOVERNORS' RECEPTION

Thursday, January 19   Sheraton Park Hotel, 3 to 6 p.m.

By Invitation

INAUGURAL CONCERT

Thursday, January 19   Constitution Hall, 8:15 p.m.

$5.00, $7.50, $10.00, $12.50, $15.00, Boxes (seating 5) $125.00, if available

Public Sale

DEMOCRATIC GALA

Thursday, January 19   National Guard Armory, 8:45 p.m.

$100.00 Contribution to the Democratic National Committee

Tickets Available Through The Democratic National Committee

OFFICIAL INAUGURAL CEREMONY

Friday, January 20   The Capitol, 12 noon

By Invitation

PARADE

Friday, January 20   2 p.m.

$3.00, $5.00, $6.00, $8.00, $10.00 $12.00 $15.00,

Boxes (opposite Pres. Reviewing Stand) $25.00 per seat

Public Sale

INAUGURAL BALL

Friday, January 20   9 p.m. to 2 a.m.

$25.00 per person, Boxes (seating 8) $320.00, Box seats $40.00 per person

By Invitation

3.

EDWARD H. FOLEY, Chairman, Inaugural Committee 1961

(over)

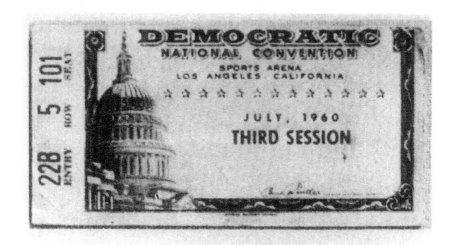

get well soon —

Friends &

Evelyn Lincoln

1. Ticket for the Democratic National Convention.

2. The card that came with a dozen red roses from Jack Kennedy when Judith was ill—Evelyn Lincoln was Jack's secretary.

3. Inaugural activities Judith was invited to attend.

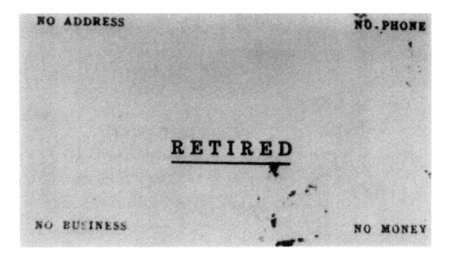

NO ADDRESS   NO.PHONE

RETIRED

NO BUSINESS   NO MONEY

Under the Fifth Amendment to the Constitution of The United States, I respectfully decline to answer, on the grounds that my answer may tend to incriminate me.

The two sides of Sam Giancana's business card.

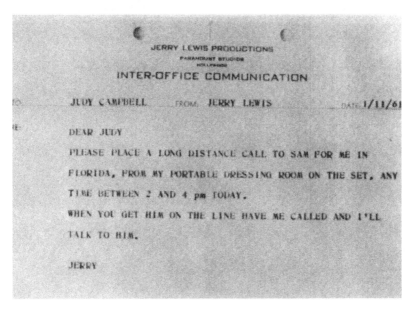

The Congressional Directory Jack autographed in a White House bedroom during one of Judith's visits.

The memo from Jerry Lewis asking Judith to contact Sam Giancana.

Judith, age six, was in her Little Bo Peep outfit, holding her cat, when this picture was taken on Pearl Harbor Day. The picture later appeared in *The Saturday Evening Post.*

Dan and Judith Exner.

1.

2.

3.

4.

1. As a young woman, Judith's mother modeled at Bonwit Telier in the days when that position was something special. She was five foot eight and had "the most magnificent red hair and soft blue eyes."

2. Judith's father, who was an architect, was a tall man with a barrel chest, whose "voice would rumble and richochet off the walls like thunder claps on a summer night."

3. During World War II, Judith lived in this twenty-four-room Mediterranean villa in Pacific Palisades.

4. Judith, age twelve, wearing her first fur jacket, with sister Jackie and brother Allen.

5. Judith at far right, with sister Joan at far left, sister Jackie, and friend in Balboa the summer Uncle Allen died.

5.

A photograph of Judith taken in 1962 by
Mervyn LeRoy's photographer.

Dick Elwood and Judith at the Malibu luau
in the summer of 1961.

1.

2.

1. Sam Giancana's Oak Park home.

2. John Roselli and his nephew in a villa at La Costa.

Photo: National Enquirer

3.

Photo: National Enquirer

4.

3. The Sands, Las Vegas.

4. The Mayflower Hotel, Washington, D.C.

Next page: Judith, age twenty-four, dressed for an evening out.

the light bulbs flashing in her eyes and you could almost hear the bells going off in her head. "Boy, oh, boy," she's thinking, "Sam wants to get to me." She ran into the bathroom and a moment later emerged dressed to kill. She had on her tightest, lowest-cut dress, her longest eyelashes, her reddest lipstick, her shiniest hairspray, and her biggest mink coat. I was grateful that the invitation was for lunch. Otherwise she could have worn her red taffeta, which was skin tight, with special emphasis on her well-rounded derriere and forty-four-inch bosom. Seeing this voluptuous five foot nine creature undulating on spike heels was enough to give some men a coronary.

She wasn't quite sure about Sam, didn't have all the particulars, but I had told her enough to start her wheels spinning. She was a nightclub singer with two records to promote, and she had been around the business long enough to know that talent could carry you just so far. More often than not, and this was especially true with beginners, it was *who* and not *what* you knew that made that dream come true.

We were complete opposites, but I liked Toni. It was fine with me if she wanted to impress Sam. More power to her. Sam was just another friend. I had no claim on him, nor did I want one. As it turned out, lunch was pretty much a disaster. Toni talked about her records, talked about her career, talked nonstop from the time we sat down until we left. Sam didn't say more than five sentences. He listened, he was a good listener, and I could see him sizing her up. He would look over at me and wink. It should have been obvious even to Toni that he was not impressed.

That evening at the Latin Quarter Sam asked me, "What are you doing with her? How did you two ever get to be friends?"

"I think she's a lovely gal," I said.

"Oh, sure, she's a beaut. Did you see what she was trying to pull off right in front of you?"

I knew what he was getting at but I wasn't about to give him the satisfaction. "Whatever it was, I noticed you didn't miss any of it."

"I'm not talking about that. She thought I could do her some good."

I gave him my most innocent look. "How could you do her any good?"

That little smile was back on his face. He was happy to be still putting one over on me. "Well, people get funny ideas at times. Couldn't be anything you said to her, could it?"

"I told her the truth. What else could I do?"

"Yeah, go on. I'm all ears."

"I told her you either were a jeweler or a cat burglar."

There were two other men at the table with us, a Jimmy and a Tom—introductions by Sam seldom got beyond first names—and all three roared with laughter.

On April 27, Jack called from Hinton, West Virginia, with good news. He was coming to Washington the next day to vote on a mine safety bill. It was another opportunity for us to get together and because of his hectic schedule I promised to wait for him at the Mayflower Hotel, as I had done at the Fontainebleau, without setting a definite time for the rendezvous. Jack sounded cheerful, and well that he should, for he had just scored a major victory in Pennsylvania, receiving seventy-five percent of the Democratic ballots in a write-in campaign.

But late that evening, after I had returned from a dinner date with Charles Evans (Charles and Bob Evans owned Evan-Picone—that was many years before Bob became head of Paramount Pictures), Jack called to say that there had been a change of plans. He had to make a quick trip to Indiana before returning to West Virginia.

He sounded so sad. "It's not the end of the world," I said, trying to cheer him out of his doldrums. "It's politics that makes the world go round, not love. What do song writers really know?"

"They know how I feel about you," he said. "They just don't know about my other commitments. Fortunately, it's not a permanent condition. It may even be shorter than you think."

"In that event, I've got the island picked out."

154

"That's my girl. Wherever it is, it will be paradise with you there."

A week later I·was in Chicago, again at the Ambassador East, but I was experiencing severe abdominal pain, a condition that had been recurring for several months. There were cysts on my ovaries and I was being treated by Dr. Krohn, but the medication was not doing the job. I knew the answer was surgery, but I was determined to postpone the inevitable as long as possible, even if it meant living with pain.

As always, Sam wanted to show me a good time. He devoted nearly all of his waking moments to me. It was a flattering and convincing statement of his interest. We talked and joked and laughed and ate and drank and had a marvelous time. Somehow he conducted his business, meeting with people at the Armory and at the Villa Venice, a restaurant and nightclub in Northbrook, some thirty miles northwest of Chicago. My impression was that Sam owned the place, and the fact that the biggest names in show business played there, including Sinatra, was impressive considering that the Villa Venice was nothing more than a mammoth neighborhood joint.

Only three things annoyed me about Sam in those days. First, of course, was his need to shower me with gifts and the battles that would ensue when I refused to accept them; I hated the terrible little cars we ran around in, and I couldn't understand his racial prejudice, which seemed irrational and pointlessly cruel.

One example was the night we went to the Chez Paree to see Sammy Davis, Jr. Again Sammy directed his performance to our table, and again Sam ignored him. This time, however, Sammy came to our table after the show. He greeted us, a big smile on his face, and Sam turned away from him. Sammy caught the movement and quickly turned his attention to me, asking me when I got in, where I was staying, how did I like Chicago? It was polite conversation, but with a nervous edge as he kept glancing at Sam, who was impatiently drumming his fingers on the table.

"Hey," Sammy said, turning his full attention to Sam,

155

"would you good people join me and a few friends for a little *soirée*?"

Sam abruptly stood up. "No, no, we can't," he said. "We don't have the time."

"Well, I thought—"

"Just forget it, okay? I told you, we don't have the time!"

Sammy gave me an anxious look and backed away. "Sure, okay, see you good people later."

On the way back to the hotel I was furious. "What's the matter with you?"

"Why are you mad? What did I do?"

"You know what you did."

"I thought I was charming as can be."

"Don't be ridiculous. You were downright rude to Sammy."

"Aw, don't worry about that nigger. He can take it."

"That's disgusting."

"Aw, come on, don't get excited. You're too sensitive. I'll bet you anything Sammy didn't even notice it."

"Don't worry, he noticed it."

Sam started to laugh. "Did I ever tell you about the time I threw cherry bombs under Sammy's chair? Now, that he noticed."

"You're crazy."

"I got both Sammy and that fruitcake Lawford in Frank's suite at the Fontainebleau. I rolled a couple of cherry bombs under their chairs and scared the shit—excuse me—the be-jesus out of them. They jumped so high their heads nearly hit the ceiling."

"But why?"

"Why not? One's a nigger and the other's a fruitcake. Gave them a little thrill. Nothing to get excited about."

The phone was ringing when I walked into my room and it was Sammy wanting to know why Sam was mad at him. "Did I do something wrong?" he asked.

"No, Sammy, there's nothing to worry about. Sam was just giving you a bad time, just horsing around."

"God, I was really worried. I thought I did something to offend him and didn't realize it."

156

"Forget it, Sammy, he was just showing his muscle."

The pain finally got the best of my determination. I returned to Los Angeles on May 7, moved in with my parents
in their new home off Laurel Canyon, and began a series of
tests, along with new medication, but the pain only got worse.

The only bright moments in my life were the calls from
Sam and Jack, whose campaign was going great guns. He
was sweeping every primary. He won in Indiana and Ne-
braska hands down. But West Virginia had him really worried. When he called on May 10, the day West Virginians
went to the polls, he sounded so gloomy I couldn't believe it.
I thought he was acting. He said he was in Washington,
hiding from the press, because he was convinced he was
going to lose the primary, and with it, his chances for the
nomination.

"In that event," I said, "I better start packing."

"That's what I wanted to hear," he said. "To the loser
goes the spoils."

"I beg your pardon," I said, summoning my most indignant tone.

He laughed and all was well again. And so it was in West
Virginia that day. Jack won a smashing victory, knocking
Humphrey completely out of the race. In the next few days,
Jack won primaries in Maryland and Oregon, giving him
seven straight victories.

Medically, I was not doing as well with my own battle.
My gynecologist, Dr. Krohn, whom I had met when I was
with Frank in Hawaii, finally decided that the inevitable day
had arrived. The cysts were increasing and surgery was the
only solution. I was admitted to Cedars of Lebanon on May
23 and was operated on the next morning. Almost all of one
ovary was removed and some nerves in my tubes were
severed because of scar tissue—I don't remember all the
details anymore, it's all wrapped up in medical jargon. As a
gratuitous gesture, they removed my appendix.

When I came to later in the day, my mother, father, sister
Jackie, brother Allen, and Travis were all lined up on one
side of the bed looking down at me. My first impression was

that they looked frightened and I said, "My God, is something wrong?"

They smiled and I felt better, but only for a moment. I became so violently sick to my stomach, a reaction from the anesthetic, that the nurses couldn't hold me down, even when they warned me that raising my head could cause a spinal headache. And did it ever. I had to lie flat on my back for two weeks. Every time I raised my head I felt like the back of it was going to explode.

I was in the hospital seven days and on every single one of those days I received phone calls from Jack and Sam, along with Jack's one dozen red roses and Sam's five dozen yellow roses. Jack's card read: "Get well soon—Friends of Evelyn Lincoln." Sam's were in a more jocular vein. "I wish I could take a vacation," or "Some people know how to live," words to that effect. Then I received flowers from my parents, from Travis, from the Elwoods, from so many friends that the place looked and smelled like a funeral parlor.

Because of my spinal headache I left the hospital in an ambulance. I had rented one of those fine old houses on Roxbury Drive, between Santa Monica and Sunset Boulevards in Beverly Hills, and hired a practical nurse. I was settling down to the task of getting well before Jack and his Democrats came to town in July for their convention.

On May 31, the day after I checked out of the hospital, Jack came to Los Angeles to speak at a testimonial dinner for Governor Pat Brown. He called from the Hilton and said, "Can I stop by? I only have a few minutes, but I'd like to see you, make sure everything is fine, that you're doing all right."

I was so thrilled I sat right up and just about lost my head in the excitement. The explosion in the back of my skull knocked me right down again. Pain or not, there was no holding me back now. With the help of my nurse, I slipped into my most beautiful negligee and really primped for hours before I was satisfied with my appearance.

I heard the car stop in the driveway, heard the door open and close, the doorbell, voices in the hallway, then the bedroom door opened and Jack walked in with a dozen red roses. There was a big smile on his face as he leaned over to kiss me. As his lips touched mine, I could hear the motor still running in the driveway.

"God, you look great," he said. "You look like you haven't been sick a single minute."

"I've always been able to fool you," I said.

"I think you've been lying to me. You just want a little sympathy."

"Some day I'll show you where that butcher sliced me open like a chicken."

He took my hand and squeezed it. "I can't wait," he said. "You hurry and get well."

We had talked only a few minutes when he stood up and apologized for having to leave. "It just kills me to have to run like this, but I wanted to see you, to make sure you're okay. Take good care of yourself and I'll call you later on."

One moment he was there and the next he was gone. That's how fast it went. I heard his footsteps going down the hall, the front door opening and closing, the car door slamming shut, and the motor noise gradually fading down the street. I was in seventh heaven. How thoughtful that had been. With his busy schedule, he still had found time on a hot day to drive across town in that miserable Los Angeles traffic just to bring me flowers and a smile. I think I loved him more at that moment than at any other time I can remember.

Sam was also doing his best but in a different way. He sent John Matassa to see me. Earlier, while I was in the hospital, he had sent Joe Pignatello with instructions to pay for my hospital bill, but I quickly rescinded that order. Now it was Matassa with a white envelope in his hand. "Sam told me to give you this and he doesn't want any guff," he said, trying to hand me the envelope.

I was in bed, propped up on a couple of pillows, making progress in my struggle to once again become perpendicular like the rest of the human race. "What are you doing?"

"Don't get upset, you'll be happy when you look inside."

I opened it and saw a stack of hundred dollar bills. "I

don't want it," I said, trying to thrust it back into his hand. "You better take it back to Sam."

John looked like I had slapped him across the face. This was an important assignment for him, having to come out to see Sam's girl, making sure that Sam's wishes were fulfilled. "He's sure going to be sore if you don't take this money."

"It's not your fault. You've done your job."

"No, you're gonna get me in trouble because Sam told me, 'Don't you come back here unless she's taken this money.' Sam said, 'I'm worried about her. I don't see how she keeps herself going.' "

"That sounds like a rehearsed speech. Go back and tell Sam that I said he gave you a rehearsed speech and that you did very well but I'm not buying it."

He looked like he was going to cry. It was a strange scene. There I was in bed, propped up on silk pillows, the imperious queen, and there he was beside the bed, the big gorilla on the verge of tears. He could have throttled a man with one hand, and probably had for all I knew, but he would have kissed Sam's feet for one quick glance of recognition. Now he was failing in his mission. "All right," I said, taking a couple of bills from the envelope, "this will get you back in his good graces. Go back and tell Sam I took what I needed."

He must have called Sam the moment he left the house because Sam was on the phone within an hour. "You are unbelievable," he yelled. "A guy tries to do something nice for a gal and look what she does. She throws it back in his face."

His need to give me money and presents was becoming very frustrating to both of us. It was now an obsession with him. But it was far worse for him than for me. I wish I could remember some of his expressions in those heated moments. They used to knock me over. He would get so exasperated that his character would actually change. I could see, or visualize on the phone, his poise dissolving as he reverted to type, back to the mannerisms and colloquialisms made so popular in gangster films. What was there to fear from Hollywood? Sometimes it was all I could do to keep a straight face. It would crack me up. Even his appearance would change. He became a different person. The little cigar that he constantly chewed on would slip to a corner of his mouth and flop up and down as the flurry of words, many incoherent, fought for expression.

I used to get the biggest kick out of him. He became a very special part of my life. I loved his phone calls. Even when he was exasperated, he was a joy. He demanded nothing from me, or of me, and he wanted to give me the world. That was supremely flattering. No woman, I don't care who she is, can help but be impressed by this quality of attention from a man.

VIII

Monday, July 11, the opening day of the Democratic National Convention in Los Angeles, was a good day for Jack. Like most Americans, I was glued to my television set, and no doubt as hopelessly lost in the nuance of politics as everybody else. What was Governor Brown up to? What about Lawrence of Pennsylvania? Would Humphrey deliver Minnesota to Stevenson? It was a day of nail-biting suspense. Yet the consensus among commentators was that Jack's chances for a first ballot nomination looked good.

Jack was running the show from suite 8315 in the Biltmore Hotel in downtown Los Angeles, miles away from the convention which was being held in the Sports Arena. And miles away from my home on Roxbury Drive. Jack had promised we would get together but I had not heard from him in two days. When the call came early that evening I nearly broke one of my own commandments. He invited me to have dinner with him at Puccini's, one of Frank's favorite restaurants and one I think he owned an interest in. I don't remember if Jack said Frank was giving a dinner for him, or that we would be dining alone, all I know is that the invitation threw me into a tailspin. I wanted to go so badly. That might be my only chance to see him that week, which had to be the busiest week of his life. On the other hand, it was such a reckless thing to do that it stunned me. I couldn't believe that a man in his position would take such a foolish chance at the most crucial time in his life. My thought then was that he wanted to demonstrate his love at any cost. This was his way of saying that I was more important to him than his career. I know better now, but at that moment I was overwhelmed.

Finally I said, "I'd love to go, Jack, but I can't really. It's not worth the risk."

"Don't worry about that," he said. "It's perfectly safe. There won't be any problem."

"I'd rather not. I'm sorry—"

"It's all right, Judy. Dinner is going to be early. Could you come over to the Beverly Hilton after? I'll send someone over to pick you up."

"I'd love to, Jack, but I'll come over myself. Just call me when you get back from dinner."

It was before ten when Jack called again. "Are you sure you don't want someone to drive you?"

"No, just give me directions."

"It's room seven twenty-four and it's listed under Peter's name. If anyone should ask you where you're going, just give them Peter's name and say that you want to see Kenny O'Donnell."

I said I would be right over and I was there within twenty minutes. I knocked at the door and there was no answer. I waited a moment and knocked again. Still no answer. Now I was getting angry. All of a sudden I didn't like being in that hallway. I wasn't comfortable. I knocked one more time, still got no answer, and I left. When I arrived home the phone rang. Jack said, "Where are you?" I was furious. "Jack, I was there and I knocked and there was no answer." He seemed shocked. "But, Judy, I'm here. I'm right here!" "Well, I don't know what the problem is." I checked the number and I had gone to the right door. He said, "Please, come back. I'm sorry that happened. I've been right here all along."

After some coaxing and more conversation, I finally agreed to return. This time the door opened on my first knock. The room was full of people and Jack came right over to greet me. When he escorted me to the couch he looked really pumped up. "I'm sorry about all these people, but have a drink and I'll be with you in a few minutes."

There were six or seven men and one woman in the room. She was a tall, thin, secretarial type in her late twenties, with brownish hair and rather sharp features. She kept circling the room like a bird of prey, never lighting anywhere.

Then Peter and Pat walked in and seemed absolutely stunned to see me sitting there. I said hello and it took them a moment to regain their composure. I caught Jack's eye and he smiled and went on talking to a heavyset man, not even acknowledging their arrival. They looked at me and looked at Jack and somehow figured out they weren't welcome because they didn't even sit down. The next time I looked in their direction, they were gone.

Jack came over and said, "I'm sorry about the mixup, but everybody's going now. Just hold on because I want to spend some time alone with you."

He went back and people started drifting out. As much as he wanted them to leave, he still had something personal to say to each and every one before they left. Then he came back to the couch and sat down, sighing with relief. The only person left in the room was Kenny O'Donnell, who was wandering around, nervous as a cat.

Jack took my hand and said, "Let's go into the other room, I want to talk to you."

We went into the bedroom and sat on the end of the bed. As I looked up, I saw that the tall, thin woman was standing at the other end of the room. She gave me a little smile and went into the bathroom, closing the door. While I was trying to figure out what she was doing there, I heard Jack say something about the three of us going to bed together. I will never remember his exact words because I just couldn't believe my ears.

I think I said something like, "Oh God, Jack, how could you?" He said, "But it's all right, don't be afraid, I know you'll enjoy it." I thought, "Oh Lord, what's wrong with me?" He tried to kiss me and I pulled away. There was an anxious look on his face and I could see that he was puzzled

164

by my rejection. I was crushed. I just couldn't believe it. He never stopped talking. He assured me the girl was safe, that she would never talk about it to a single soul, that there was nothing wrong with a *ménage à trois*, that it was practiced widely, and, over and over again, that I would enjoy it—"I know you, I know you'll enjoy it."

It was a repeat of the night with Frank and finally I found myself giving Jack the same lecture—if you like it, fine, do it, but leave me out of it. I also lectured him on having the girl there without first asking me about it. I said things like "having your nerve," and the next thing I knew I was crying from sheer frustration and anger.

Realizing the gravity of his mistake, Jack quickly shifted gears. He got up and went into the bathroom, and when he came back, he put his arms around me. "I hope you're not angry with me," he said.

"I can't tell you how disappointed I am in you," I replied, trying to pull out of his embrace. "You didn't have to present this the way you did. You could have first asked me about it," I repeated.

"I'm really sorry," he said. "It was a stupid mistake."

I couldn't let go. "If you cared as much about me as you say you do, how could you have put me in this position?" I wanted him to know that I was angry and embarrassed, but I didn't want to let him know how terribly he had hurt me. This was far more devastating than the experience with Frank, who has a reputation as a swinger, and though I liked him, my affection for Jack went so much deeper.

"I do care for you," he said. "Please don't let this make you doubt the way I feel about you."

I kept on with my tirade. "How can I help but doubt how you feel when you—"

"I can't tell you how sorry I am. I think you're reacting too strongly to it. It's not that important. It's something you have the right to decide for yourself."

I pulled away. "What's the use. You're just completely losing the point. I'm tired and I want to go home."

"I just hate to see you leave like this."

For a moment it was as though Frank was sitting there saying those exact words. "Stay a while. I've sent her away. We're alone."

"Jack, not in a million years." I stood up and straightened my clothes.

He looked up, and the tension and pressure of the past few months were etched on his face. For the first time that evening I felt sorry for him, and truly wanted to put my arms around him, to comfort him, to tell him that it was all right, but I couldn't do it. "Will you call me here when you get home?"

"No, I want to go home and think this over."

He shook his head and stood up. "I really did it, didn't I?" he said.

"You puzzle me," I said. "I would think you had enough on your mind without cooking up something like this."

He forced a smile. "It wasn't easy," he said.

I started toward the door and stopped. "Don't you say one word about this when we walk out of this room."

"I won't. But I still want you to call me when you get home."

"I'll see how I feel when I get home."

Kenny was still in the other room, and obviously waiting for us. As we walked toward the door, Jack stopped and said, "Would it be an inconvenience for you to drop Kenny off at Jack Haley's place on Rossmore?"

I said no, but of course it was an inconvenience, although one Jack no doubt thought would help cool me off. He was smiling, his old confident self, when he kissed me on the cheek and said goodbye. "Don't forget," he said, "I'm going to wait right here for your call."

Kenny O'Donnell is another refugee from Camelot who has suffered a lapse of memory as far as I am concerned.

AUTHOR'S NOTE *In an interview published in the Boston Herald-American on December 23, 1975, O'Donnell labeled all reports about the former President's ex-*

tramarital sex life as lies. "They are all lies," he said, "but there is no way to stop it. They will keep it going. I think there is a campaign on to give it to the Kennedys." Later in an Associated Press interview, he said, "I think the guy they are after is Ted." Asked about the "seventy or more" phone conversations between Judy and Jack reported by the Church committee, Kenny said it was ". . . ridiculous. Some gal in California would call Evelyn Lincoln and ask to speak to the President. Evelyn Lincoln, a nice lady, would take a call from anybody. But that doesn't mean the caller actually spoke to the President. No one outside of Bobby Kennedy and Vice President Lyndon Johnson had access to the President's office without first getting clearance from me. Every morning I would get a list of phone calls he had received the night before. I never heard of this woman who now insinuates she had been his mistress."

Being Jack Kennedy's mistress is the last thing that Judy would ever want to insinuate because it would be as false as any of O'Donnell's insinuations. "She now admits she is going to write a book," he continued. "That's what this is all about. It's just a sex story now, and not a very good one at that." As far as Jack was concerned, Kenny said he was "very discreet and very proud of being President of the United States. There is not much he did in his life, after 1957, that I didn't know about or Dave Powers didn't know about." The Secret Service, he said, recorded every visitor and there are no records of women who visited Kennedy secretly. "There were no secret passages or anything like that."

But that evening he was full of questions disguised as chit-chat, a low-key pumping that never fools anyone but the pumper. He wanted to know where I was born, where I lived, what I did for a living, how long I had known Jack, a very curious man. I gave him nothing specific, and though he was persistent, he was careful not to push. He would change his

167

line of questioning, rephrase the questions, all innocuous on the surface, but probing nonetheless.

Gently, I turned the tables on him. As much as I hate to pry, I felt I had to do something. I said it was a fine evening and then wondered what he did for a living, what were Jack's chances at the convention, and what role did he play in the scheme of things. As a result, I learned that he was a professional politician, that Jack would win on the first ballot, and that he, Kenneth P. O'Donnell, was the architect of the Kennedy phenomenon. "I traveled with him every day of his life," he said. "The chain of command is from Jack to me to Bobby." This was all very interesting, and in the meantime, the miles were spinning by without further interrogation. When I pulled up in front of the Haley apartment house, I was still fuming. Then I felt his arm on my shoulder and his face was right in front of mine. All I could see were those lips coming at me. I jerked my head back and his chin hit my cheekbone. He pulled away and there was the strangest expression on his face. The corners of his mouth had curled into a leer, but his eyes seemed to be pleading for understanding.

"What in God's name do you think you're doing?"

"Well, uh—wait, don't get excited, take it easy, all I—"

I don't know what he was about to say. He never got it out. His mouth was stuffed with my words. "Get out of this car this minute!" He moved, but not fast enough. "Go on, get the hell out!" By now he was tripping over his own feet getting out. I yelled, "Close the door!" Then I reached over and locked it.

How I got home is a mystery. My eyes were blinded with tears. All I know is that I am lucky I didn't kill myself. When I got home I couldn't remember anything about the drive. I couldn't remember any of the stop signs, lights, streets, turns—everything was a complete blank. All I could think of was that I had tried to do this *nice* gentleman who worked for *nice* Jack a favor and look at what had happened. I had driven twice to the Beverly Hilton and look at what had happened.

I filled a tumbler full of ice and Jack Daniels and sat in a hot tub. It all seemed so unfair. It was so exasperating to be

168

so vulnerable. This was something that had troubled me for a long time. A woman seems to have no place to go in some areas. How do you make your position clear? All right, so I went to see a married man. I realize that is not right. I am not condoning it but why should it make me common property? Why all of a sudden should those around him think that I am fair game for anybody? Why can't two attractive women go into a restaurant at night without creating the impression that they are available? Women's liberation has changed some of the practices, but it hasn't changed the thoughts in men's minds. The evening, the booze, the hot bath, it was a good time for self-pity. I felt I had earned the right. When the phone rang, I scowled at it and took another swallow. This was not the time for lengthy explanations. I was beginning to revel in my misery.

I slept most of the next day. The phone rang several times and the one time I did pick it up it was Jack, sounding full of vim and vigor and pushed for time. "I called last night and there was no answer," he said.

My head was throbbing. "I didn't feel like answering the phone."

"You're really upset with me, aren't you?"

"I'm more confused than upset."

"God, I wish I hadn't done that. Will you please try to forget it?"

"We'll see if I can. I really don't want to talk about it anymore." I felt weird saying those words. It seemed like *deja vu* but it sounded more like a broken record.

"I'd like to talk to you some more, but it's impossible now. Are you coming to the convention? Evelyn is holding four tickets for you."

"I don't think I will but my mother wants to go."

"I wish you'd come with her. Whatever you decide, the tickets are waiting here for you. Call Evelyn and she'll make all the arrangements."

At the end I softened. "Good luck tomorrow, Jack. I truly mean it."

"Thanks, Judy. I'll call you the first chance I get. Just take it easy and think kind thoughts."

169

We said goodbye and I felt better. I called my mother and she was delighted. My father was tied up at the office and so my mother asked a friend, Marie Marz, to go with her. My mother later told me what happened when she and Marie went to the Biltmore for the tickets.

The place was a madhouse. But when she introduced herself to Evelyn Lincoln, Evelyn stood up and said, "Oh, Mrs. Immoor, you've got to meet Senator Kennedy." My mother was thrilled beyond belief because she adored him. To her he was not only a good Irish Catholic politician, which is high enough in her eyes, but she suspected I was in love with him and she saw how happy it made me. Evelyn opened a door and said, "Senator! Senator! Judy's mother is here!" Like that. Jack came bounding out and said, "Oh, I am so happy to meet you!" And just made a big fuss over her and Marie. Then he said, "Isn't Judy with you?" She could see that he was disappointed, and she said, "No, she isn't feeling well." My mother gave the best excuses in the world—she used to do it for me all the time. "She went through quite a bit when she was operated on and had quite a difficult time. She's not feeling strong enough yet." Jack commiserated with her. "Oh, I'm so sorry to hear that. I'll have to call and see how she's doing. She is such a wonderful girl." Mom said, "Yes, she is, and I'm sure she'll be happy to hear from you."

My mother thought the whole Kennedy family was magnificent. She was absolutely ecstatic at the convention when she found herself seated right next to them. Ted even autographed her ticket. My mother was proud as a peacock. She had no doubts ever that Jack would be nominated and become President. Once she got something in her head, there was no way in the world to change it. In the next two years she would talk with Jack on the phone many times, and love every minute of it. And she loved talking with Sam on the phone. She liked them both because they thought her daughter was "special." She was that kind of mother.

I received a dozen red roses on the thirteenth and all it said on the card was, "I'm sorry." What happened at the convention on that day is history now. Jack won on the first ballot. I sent him a telegram, addressed to Evelyn, congratulating him on his victory. When he called on Thursday, I said, "Thanks for the flowers. You must feel guilty."

"I didn't send them just because I feel guilty," he said, and I detected a little defensiveness in his voice.

"Well, if you don't you should." I laughed and it broke the tension. I knew he didn't have a great deal of time to talk but we had a nice conversation.

"I'm going to try to see you before I leave," he said in closing.

"Well, don't worry about it."

"Oh, I don't like the way that sounds."

"All I mean is that you're too busy right now to worry about things like that. When this is over, we'll see what we can do about seeing each other." We said goodbye on that note and I felt that the episode at the Beverly Hilton was behind us.

As much as my mother liked Jack and Sam, she despised Frank Sinatra and anyone with that kind of swinging reputation. Actually, she disliked and distrusted most actors. Both Jackie and I had married actors and with predicted results. In her opinion actors were shiftless egomaniacs, devoid of any ethical standards, and that's all there was to it. With me it was a little more complex. Two weeks later I was in Atlantic City with Frank, getting set up for another disastrous experience.

I flew to New York on the twentieth and went to visit Marty Tamambaum in Great Neck. Marty had an apartment in the Navarro, 17E, which was at 112 Central Park South, a marvelous location, and since he was going to hibernate on Long Island while recuperating from his heart attack, I made plans to sublease his apartment. New York was the ideal place for me, close to Washington and Chicago, and a place where I had many friends. I enjoyed the Eastern lifestyle, the restaurants, nightclubs, theater, the late hours, for I had become a night person. I loved going to Reubens or Lindy's or the Stage Delicatessen at four in the morning for pastrami and coffee. Those were the days when I never had to worry about dieting. It was as though my figure had been cast in a mold and there was nothing I could do to change it.

On the twenty-fifth Frank sent a limousine to the Navarro to bring me to the Claridge Hotel in Atlantic City. Joe Fish and Skinny D'Amato, along with others of the entourage, the faceless ones, were in Frank's suite when I arrived. Frank was in his Dr. Jekyll mood, although he couldn't have been too happy about appearing in Skinny's 500 Club, a booking that was as dubious as any he had in Chicago. I don't have any specifics, but from conversations between Sam and others, I have the impression that many top performers were forced to appear in certain clubs by underworld edict. In fact, Sam and Johnny Roselli used to laugh about the things they made performers do. Their control over jukeboxes and nightclubs, from the lowest to the plushest, is more pervasive than most people realize. This gives them power over certain recording companies, radio, television, and movie productions. I once heard Sam say that Tony Bennett was kept from working for a number of years because he wouldn't follow orders. When he straightened out and got on the circuit laid out for him, then big things began happening in his career. I have no way of verifying any of this beyond the fact that it was a favorite topic of conversation among Sam and his friends, and it involved a long list of famous entertainers. I saw enough of them pay homage to Sam and Johnny to believe there was some truth in it.

I was in Atlantic City three days, in a room connecting with Frank's suite, and each day Frank's kidding was becoming more amorous. On the twenty-seventh, as I was helping him get ready for his show, he said something that really stopped me. I remember I was straightening his tie, and he took both my hands in his and looked right at me. "You know, baby, if I marry again, you're the kind of girl I should marry."

"Thanks for the compliment," I said, a little flustered, but determined not to pursue that line, "but our tastes are not compatible."

"Well, maybe you'd be worth giving up a little swinging." He smiled and kissed me, still holding my hands, and I kissed him back until I realized he had something else in mind. I pulled away and he said, "Come on, will you sleep in here tonight?"

"Oh Frank," I said, "that's such a corny line."

He looked at me, the expression on his face hardening, changing from a smile to a knowing look. "You'd be surprised how often it works," he said, turning away from me and calling for Tony, who hurried in with his whisk broom.

That evening, after the show, Frank wanted to go bar-hopping. Joe Fish, Skinny, three or four faceless ones, and I started out with Dr. Jekyll and ended up with Mr. Hyde in his most extreme transformation. Nobody dared say a word as he cursed and flailed at the faceless ones in one of the most obscene performances I have ever witnessed. In one terrible place with a large horseshoe bar, Frank picked up a couple of aging hookers and proceeded to demonstrate his command of their vernacular until finally dismissing them with, "Oh, shit, get the fuck away from me, you pigs."

That was my final outing with Frank Sinatra.

On August 2 I went to the Four Seasons and El Morocco with Eddie Torres and Charlie Kahn, who were as inseparable as Siamese twins. You never saw one without the other. Eddie was tall, Latin-looking, dignified, quiet, reserved; Charlie was short, robust, red-faced, a Jewish Phil Regan type, happy-go-lucky, talkative, and knew everybody. They were the classic opposites, but I have never known two better friends.

When I first knew Eddie, he was connected with the Fremont Hotel in downtown Las Vegas. Later on he moved over to the Riviera Hotel on the Strip. I will never forget the time I called Eddie to place a bet on the election. That is how naive I was in those days. I called from Los Angeles to Las Vegas and wanted to know what the odds were on the election. Eddie said, "Well, I don't really know, Judy, but how are you?" "What do you mean you don't know?" "When are you coming over to Vegas?" "Eddie, I want to bet on the election." "Oh, that's very nice, Judy. Call again sometime, always nice hearing from you." "But Eddie, where do I place my bet? I want to bet on Jack Kennedy. Why can't you take it?" "Look, Judy, I'm sorry but I've got a call coming in from Paris. Talk to you later, okay." The next time I saw him he said, "My God, woman, what is wrong with you? Don't you know there's a law against interstate betting?"

I had known Eddie and Charlie for years, had met them through Marty Tannenbaum, and every time Eddie came to visit his family in New Jersey and I happened to be in New York, they would always give me a call to see if I was free for dinner. They liked to eat at The Colony and to drink at Elmers, the quaint name for El Morocco, which was a cha-cha-cha kind of in-place for jet setters and nouveau riche types. It was where everybody went to see and be 'seen by everybody else. I went for the same reason. That's why it was always too crowded.

On August 3, Jack called from Hyannis to ask if he could drop by the Navarro the next day. We had made our peace. I am not one to hold something inside and brood over it. He had apologized, had done all he could to make things right again, and I had only two ways to go—forget or forgive him. Once I decided on the latter course, I got it out of my head. I knew I cared deeply about him and wanted to go on seeing him.

Except that it would be later in the day, he could not give me a specific time for his visit. I said it was fine, that I was painting again, and I would be home all day. The day I moved into the Navarro I had bought two complete sets of oils, sable brushes, canvases, and an aluminum easel that folded up into a tube for traveling. I started work on a very skinny nude girl who was standing in front of a mirror with a towel wrapped around her. I had gotten the idea from a Walter Keane poster, but I did it entirely in shades of blue. My father used to ride me about the way I painted women. I never made them voluptuous, and my father called them banana tits and that's exactly the way they looked. They were terribly unsexy.

174

My deepest fascination was with children's faces. Again I owe it to Keane, who painted children with sad faces and wide-eyed innocence. I wanted to capture that sadness and innocence. Children don't know what is happening to them, are not aware of the sadness in their life. Little children in tattered clothes, emaciated, victims in a world they don't understand and yet there is a deep sadness in their eyes. The lost children of the world. Having been a timid and frightened child, I could empathize with that concept. I am very sensitive to the unhappiness of a child. Adults can take care of themselves, hopefully, but a child has no place to turn.

As I look back on my paintings of children in those days, there was nothing but sheer tragedy in most of them. I had a feeling that I needed to shake people up. I was involved with people who lived a kind of superficial life, and perhaps my judgment of them was superficial, but I had this feeling that there was a great deal of sadness in the world. Perhaps I felt that my own life was superficial. There had to be something more to care about and I think I recognized it in the sadness of children. Childhood is supposed to be a happy time, in the ideal fantasy, but there are far more sad children than happy ones in this world, far more of them go hungry than not.

So there I was, the poor, sad, little rich girl at the easel. With Rachmaninoff on the hi-fi, filling the room with his melodic beauty, I would sip *Clos de Vough* and paint my sad children. The more the image took on life, the more emotional I became, until finally I would become blinded by my own tears. I think it was an important release for me, because deep down, regardless of what I was doing, I was still a sad unhappy child.

I often painted through the night, sometimes I would paint for days without leaving the house. I became obsessed with what I was doing and wouldn't even answer the phone. Jack understood that kind of drive. I think he liked the fact that I could get so lost in my work, and recognized that there were times when I didn't want to do anything else. The difference between our drives, his for politics and power and mine for art and beauty, was that I didn't have mine all the time.

175

The moment he walked in that day I said, "My, that island of yours must certainly have been nice today." He had this great tan and looked like a million. "All that nice sand and ocean, so idyllic for a romantic interlude."

He grabbed me and laughed. "God, you really know where to get a guy, don't you? That's really dirty pool."

"It beats stuffy, greasy, smoggy, steamy old New York in August. I once knew a handsome man who wanted to take me away to a deserted island and make love around the clock—I think that is the way he phrased it—but that was a long time ago. Memory gets hazy—"

He was hugging me and laughing. "Don't worry, we may be leaving sooner than you think. This election is not won by a long shot."

"But that can't be any problem now," I said. "I just read in the paper only yesterday that Truman has given you his Presidential seal of approval."

"That old bastard," he said, but it sounded more like *bahstard*, "has no other option. I'm the only game in town. I think he'd support the devil before he would Nixon."

Later, after we had made love, and he was holding me in his arms, he said, "Wouldn't it be nice if we could have that time together."

I raised my head to look at him and there was such a wistful look in his eyes. Jack was very loving and attentive after making love. He said all the things a woman wants to hear, but that look was something that stayed with me a long time.

I was so confused about love. There are moments during and after the act of love when words are not to be taken to heart. Many times Jack said, "Oh, I love you." At those moments his feelings for me were strong, but there is love and then there is *love*. I don't know how much he loved me, or if he loved me at all. If I thought I knew then, I don't know now. After my divorce from Billy and my experience with Travis, I was skeptical of intimacies expressed in bed. Several people have told me they loved me, but I don't think I ever quite believed them. I don't think I believed that anybody ever really meant it. And if they did, I knew it wasn't going to last. No matter how much you loved someone and they said they loved you it still wasn't going to work out. So I took the words "I love you" and let them sit inside me just where they wouldn't hurt. Or so I thought.

Real love for me is all consuming. For Jack, as I was to discover after he was in the White House, love was just another element in his life. It was completely excluded from all the other items on his daily schedule. There was a niche for each one: his career, his Presidency, his political party, his family, his children, his wife, or perhaps the image of the First Lady, me, his cronies, and so on down the line.

Before leaving that day, Jack said, "Will you be home tomorrow?"

"Will I see you if I'm home?"

"I think so. At least, I'm really going to try."

"Then I'll be here."

"Good. I want to see as much of you as I can, but I know as the campaign heats up, it's going to get progressively more difficult to find the time. The idea is to make plans whenever there's the remotest possibility of a meeting. You're good for me, Judy, you really are."

And he was good for me. I painted through most of that night and slept late the next morning. When Jack came that afternoon, he looked sensational and his mood was absolutely irrepressible.

"Vell, how var you today, Mrs. Feinberg [or was it Steinberg]," he said, shaking my hand like an anxious politician. "How's de hosiery bizness?"

He flopped on the couch and roared with laughter.

"How about letting me in on the joke?"

"I can't," he said, pulling me down next to him, "you don't know the secret code. You're just a girl. You don't even have a code ring."

"Let me smell your breath."

A moment later he started getting amorous and I never did find out what it was all about. While in bed I told him of my trip to Atlantic City and about Frank's black mood. That

177

tickled him. He thought Frank's temperament was a riot. He was amused at the havoc Frank could cause and at the way people around him would cower in fear.

On August 8 and 9, I again went to the Colony and El Morocco with Eddie Torres and Charlie Kahn. I saw Jack at the Navarro on the eleventh and not long after he left he called to ask if I would contact Evelyn at her home and tell her not to meet him because he would be delayed. When I called Evelyn, she thanked me for relaying the message and then she asked, "How is he?" That kind of stopped me for a moment. "Why, he's fine. Racing around. He dropped over for just a moment." Afterwards I wondered why I had added that little disclaimer.

Jack was back again on the sixteenth and on that day we made plans for another visit at his Georgetown house. I missed my plane on the eighteenth and Evelyn changed my reservation at the Mayflower to the nineteenth. That evening I again took a cab to his home.

What is remarkable about this visit is that it was almost a total recreation of the previous one. There was a guest for dinner, a man whose face and name I've long since forgotten, and again during dinner Jack brought up the question of Evelyn's competence to serve him in the White House. It seemed to be troubling him terribly and for some reason he thought I could shed light on the problem.

My response was the same as before. "She's loyal as you could ever want anyone," I said. "If she has been good enough for you all these years, she ought to be good enough for you in the White House."

Later, in bed, I kidded him about his going to Independence the next day. There had been a story in the morning paper about it. Jack called him that old *bahstard* again, but he seemed tickled pink at the prospect that Truman might take to the stump on his behalf.

It was early morning before the taxi came to pick me up. This time Jack waited at the front door until I rode away. He didn't wave, that wasn't his style, but I did. Before leaving for New York the next day I went to the Old Senate Office Building to pick up my train ticket from Evelyn because Jack had insisted on buying it. I didn't see Jack, for he had long since left for Independence.

By nightfall I was back on the Manhattan merry-go-round. A few days later Marty Tannenbaum introduced me to Jerry Lewis, who immediately wanted to know all about my *shtick*. He obviously did not remember our meeting years before. When I said I was a Sunday artist, he asked if I would be interested in working for him. He explained that he had a picture coming up, *Ladies Man,* and he thought he might be able to find a way of utilizing my artistic "proclivities." Jerry, when he was being the debonair ladies man, had his own proclivity for big words. He would never use a small word when three big ones would do the job. When Jerry is coming on, he quickly goes overboard. You expect him to start speaking French. Although he is very serious about his flirting, from a woman's viewpoint it is funnier than his pratfalls.

He called six or seven times the next day with invitations for lunch, cocktails, dinner, theater, nightclub, and struck out each time.

Then on the twenty-third he came up with a novel idea. He called and said, "Would you come over for lunch?"

"I'm afraid not."

"Well, what about later? I have to go see someone very interesting. I could pick you up in my limousine and on the way over there we could talk about that job I offered you. I'm going over to Sophie Tucker's. Have you ever met her?"

"No, I haven't."

"Well, would you like to meet her? She really is a legendary figure. One of the greatest living stars of our time."

Now he had me. How could I refuse to meet this fascinating woman? So Jerry picked me up in his limousine and immediately got on the phone, playing the important executive to the hilt. As the limousine pulled up in front of her apartment house, Jerry said, "Damnit, I didn't get a chance to call England. That's all right, it'll keep. Did you know that tomorrow we're previewing *Cinderfella* here in New

179

York? I've got a million things on the agenda but this old gal is so marvelous that I can't come to this city without paying my tribute. For me it's like returning to—to—you know, oh, what the hell, you know the place I mean."

I thought, the womb?—but I didn't say anything. He ushered me into Sophie's presence and said, "This is Judy, my secretary."

My mouth must have dropped open. Sophie looked at me and at him as if to say, "I know what your act is, sonny."

Walking into her apartment was like stepping into an old Gloria Swanson movie. The motif was Roaring Twenties, and it even smelled like it. There seemed to be a lot of doillies, knick-knacks, end tables, floor lamps with fringe on the shades, throw rugs, pictures and doodads all over the walls, and heavy plush furniture. The only thing missing was wax fruit in a hobnailed milk glass bowl.

Sophie was everything I expected. This big broad with a face sculptured in concrete. When she laughed that whole room was filled with her sound, and when she talked the lamps quaked. They heard what she had to say. She didn't care what anyone thought of her. If she wanted to use a four-letter word, and you didn't like it, then you had better put cotton in your ears or leave. Because she was going to say whatever she pleased. She really made my day.

I went to Jerry's preview with Morris Levy and Marty Tannenbaum. From there we went to Danny's Hideaway and on to the Imperial where we met with Jerry and his entourage, which was bigger than Frank's, probably bigger than anybody's.

Jerry went back to Hollywood the next day and called me several times in relation to the job. He was beginning to sound sincere. His offer came at a time when I needed help. I was experiencing frequent depressions. My drinking had increased, I wasn't eating properly, and I would go for days without sound sleep. When I did finally sleep, my dreams were terribly disturbing. I would wake up completely exhausted. I began calling Dr. Sherman in Beverly Hills, who was the psychiatrist I had consulted after my breakup with Travis. I should have been happy, but my life was crumbling. I didn't know what was happening to me.

Basically, I am meant to be married. I am meant to be with one man and to give my whole life to that one man. My marriage had failed, and the pain it had caused me in those early years when I still thought I loved Billy had gone so deep that I couldn't bear to think about it. My relationship with Travis had also failed. I was falling in love with Jack, but I still thought I could stop it. I was almost glad that I couldn't see him more often. That's probably why I missed so many trains and planes going to see him. It wasn't a conscious effort, but perhaps I was trying to keep myself at arm's length.

I was a bundle of confusion. As I said, I hated his being married and I liked his being married. I wanted to see him and yet I didn't want to be in that situation. But I continued because I knew this was really my only protection. I didn't have to commit myself to him. If I didn't give all of me, I couldn't be hurt all that much.

In the event that he lost the election, I was afraid to contemplate what would happen between us. Would he get a divorce? What did he expect of me? Could I commit myself completely to him? It was all too new, too close to Travis, and in a way, even Frank, too close to the pain of failure.

I was living in an artificial world, one created in self-defense. "Look, see, I'm on my own. I'm my own boss. No one can hurt me. I can come and go as I please. If you don't like it, so what!" The problem was that I couldn't function very well that way. Being alone, without a man of my own to share my love, left a void that no amount of running could fill.

My painting was not filling the void. I was doing it to please myself, and Dr. Sherman suggested that I find another form of expression. I needed to do something more constructive with my life. So I decided to accept Jerry's offer. Up to this point, nothing in my life had worked out as anticipated, why I then found this prospect such a pleasing one shows the degree of my desperation.

Jerry came to New York on September 2 and I flew to

California with him on September 4. He sat with me for a while, trying to "visualize" for me the "concept" of my "project" with his production of *Ladies Man;* he dictated a flurry of memos to his secretary; he discussed musical arrangements with someone else; he never stopped talking or moving the entire flight. His attention span where others were concerned was severely limited. He concentrates best when he is listening to himself. He may have been listening to himself talking to someone, listening to a record of himself, reading something he had written, or listening to someone reading it to him, listening to someone compliment him or discuss him or his movies. He would listen to you on other subjects, but better make it quick if you don't want to get caught talking to yourself. Jerry had a million things to do and many miles to travel before he lay to rest—each day.

His Jekyll-and-Hyde syndrome made Frank's seem like a model of stability. Jerry could swing from the heights of euphoria to the depths of hell in the blink of an eye. This could happen many times in the course of a single day. He was one of those people who was happiest when he was unhappiest. He could make a problem out of just absolutely nothing, and carry on like he was demented, cry like a baby, then snap right out of it, laugh and joke, and the next moment he was right back in the doldrums.

Jerry was another one who flagellated those closest to him, but he made up for it by giving expensive presents to the victims. He kept one Beverly Hills jeweler busy engraving gold lighters, tie tacs, cuff links, pencils, bracelets, earrings, key chains, charms, etc. to reward those he had punished. Anyone around Jerry for any length of time had to collect tons of this stuff. The difference between Jerry's and Frank's flunkies was that Jerry was a workaholic. Jerry worked until midnight, and later, and when Jerry worked, everybody worked.

I don't mean to analyze Jerry, but having known Gary Morton and other comics, it seems to me that comics generally have one thing in common—insecurity. They clown to gain attention but it is also a clever camouflage. When they make people laugh it covers up for other inadequacies. Their clowning as they walk into a room throws people off balance. No one is looking at them for anything else. They are not looking at them for interesting conversation, for good manners or proper conduct. They are looking at them to laugh, to be entertained, and comics learn that trick in childhood. Nobody cares if they are unattractive. How many comics look like Johnny Carson? Most of them look like Milton Berle, Buddy Hackett, Gary Morton, Henny Youngman, Danny Thomas, Jerry Lewis, Bob Hope, Jimmy Durante, Alan King, Paul Lynd, Jonathan Winters—the list is as long as you care to make it.

Before leaving New York, Sam had asked me to deliver a message when I arrived in Los Angeles. He wanted me to contact Red Skelton's manager and instruct him to call Sam at the Armory, which I did the moment I checked into the Beverly Hills Hotel. That evening I went to my parents' home to help celebrate Allen's birthday. He was seventeen, a sweet little boy who towered over me.

I had several meetings with Jerry at Paramount to discuss the concept of my "special project." He hadn't yet "formulated" it in his mind, but he wanted some kind of booklet that would "commemorate" the work that went into designing the sets for *Ladies Man*, but the "germ" of this idea was still in a "formative state."

"Don't worry," he said, "I will get it settled in my mind before long. What I want to know now is whether you'd be interested in tackling it."

"Yes, I'm interested," I said, "as long as I don't have to punch a clock."

"Oh, don't worry about that. This is a special assignment. You can come and go as you wish. All I ask is that you get the job done on schedule."

"Of course," I said, not having the faintest notion of the job or schedule involved.

"I'm going to give you your own office," he said, "with your name over the door in bold type. Unfortunately, I can't pay you much at this juncture—that's the only problem. I've already got so many people on my staff, so much dead wood, that I've got to start chopping it down pretty soon."

How much do you charge someone to give you therapy? "I'm not interested in a big salary."

"What's the minimum you would need?"

"Is a hundred a week all right?"

"Oh, that's fine," he said, jumping out of his chair. "I'm going to have that office readied and the sign made for you right away."

"When do I start?"

"Well, as you know, we're not clear yet on the concept. We need to clarify that somewhat before we put you on the payroll. But it won't be long. We're going to record some music tonight. Why don't you come over around ten-thirty?"

I had another session with Dr. Sherman that evening. He thought the job was tailor-made for me. "I don't want to steer you," he said, "but I think you need to do something constructive at this time in your life. You're not happy and this will give you an opportunity to concentrate on something else besides Jack Kennedy."

Instead of going to the studio that evening, I called Sam and we had a long talk, the kind that was always so relaxing for me. Sam was good for me, as I said, because I was not emotionally involved with him. He was a friend, one that I was beginning to rely on more all the time. His advice was simple: "Come to Chicago and relax for a few days."

IX

The next morning, September 14, my mother had breakfast with me at the hotel and then took me to the airport. Sam and Joe were waiting at O'Hare when I arrived and we went directly to the Armory. Doris fixed a superb antipasto—everything imaginable—and we began on martinis. Thus started five exquisite days.

As always I had my suite at the Ambassador East, but we were together from early afternoon to early morning every single one of those days. There are moments from that trip I will never forget. There was the night we had dinner at the Singapore and the bowing and scraping reached new heights. At least four people greeted him when we entered: "Would you prefer your usual table, sir?"

Sam barely nodded his head and the *maître d'* called out, "Clear that table over there." Waiters and busboys were falling all over themselves. Sam didn't say a word. The more they kowtowed the more aloof he became.

They seemed terrified of him. I felt like I was watching the Three Stooges in a haunted house. I knew something disastrous was going to happen, somebody was going to stumble and spill something, and Sam was going to be furious. Then all hell would break loose. It had never happened in my presence but there had to be a reason for this performance. It reminded me of the times my father wanted silence at the table and said, "No laughing." You knew the first thing you were going to do was laugh. When my cousin Patsy lived with us for a while, she spilled a glass of milk every single night at the dinner table because she was so afraid she was going to spill that glass of milk. This was the same thing. You knew something had to happen.

Although nothing happened that night, I was sure something did the moment we walked out. Sam's favorite table probably collapsed. The kinetic energy released by the management probably ignited and the whole building blew up as we rounded the corner.

Later in the car, I said, "You must be some kind of bully. That was a comic opera in there. They were falling all over themselves."

"What a thing to say," he said. "I was so good, so humble, so quiet. I never said a word to anybody. You had my undivided attention."

It was true. I started to laugh and then he was laughing. We had the greatest time reenacting that comic opera—the Singapore fugue, as we called it.

What was so refreshing about Sam was that he didn't have those highs and lows of so many people I knew—Travis, Frank, and now Jerry. Whatever was going on inside of Sam, if it was something other than what I saw, was carefully concealed from me. I liked what I saw in him. I was always sure of how things would go when I was with him. I felt—and this may sound strange knowing what I know now—safe and secure. My head would be free of doubt and of the pressure that brought on the depressions. I was happy when I was with Sam.

We were at the Armory one afternoon and Sam said, "Come on, I've got a stop to make." So we jumped into his little black car—I was now calling it his "limousine"—and drove to 1147 South Wenonah Avenue in Oak Park. We pulled into the driveway of a red brick house, walked down steps, and entered a basement that had been converted into a kitchen and family room area. Sam introduced me to his sister Rose and her husband Richard Flood, which gave me food for thought. My first impression was that I had misunderstood him—that Rose was his sister-in-law and Richard his brother.

186

I asked him about it and he said, "No, Rose is my sister."

"That's strange," I said, "her marrying someone with the same surname. Is Richard a cousin?"

"No, no," he said, and there was that twinkle in his eye.

I thought, "Oh, no, I'm not biting this time." "That's very interesting," I said, as he led me up the stairs to what was the main floor.

"If you want to see something interesting, look at this," he said, pointing to a glass case and his magnificent collection of china figurines, the same kind I had seen in his Florida home. They were his wife's and he seemed especially fond of them. He was so careful in handling them.

Although he never said anything about it, I soon realized that this was his home. It surprised me because it was such an ordinary place, with typical heavy Italian furniture. Years later I used to get hysterical whenever I read about Sam's "Oak Park mansion." This was in the same category as his "pink Cadillacs" and "flashy convertibles." Sam was either playing games with me or somebody out there, probably the same somebody that wrote so many lies about me, has a fertile imagination. From the books and articles I've read, it only takes one fertile imagination and hundreds of copycats to turn fiction into fact.

What was not ordinary, however, was Sam's collection of jewelry. He showed me through the whole house, including his bedroom suite on the second floor, which didn't run the full length of the house but was more like a large attic. He had a bedroom, sitting room, bathroom and large walk-in closet to accommodate his extensive wardrobe.

I waited in the sitting room while he changed and when he came out there was a mischievous twinkle in his eye. There was an even brighter twinkle in his hand. It was a ring with a twenty-seven-carat canary diamond with blue white diamonds circling it. It was magnificent.

"Put it on," he said, handing it to me. I did and he said, "It looks beautiful on you."

"God, it would look beautiful on Tugboat Annie." I started to take it off and he said, "Don't, I want you to keep it." That ring looked so beautiful on my hand I didn't know what to say. Finally, I said, "Sam, you're crazy."

"I'm serious about this," he said. "This belonged to my wife and I would like for you to have it."

"I adore you for offering it to me. I understand the sentimental attachment you must have for it, and I can't tell you how flattered I am by your offer, but, please, don't ask me to accept it."

"Why not, honey. It's only a ring, a piece of jewelry. It's no big deal. You're just too sensitive about these things. Nobody is trying to buy you. I wish you'd get that out of your head. This doesn't entitle me to anything special. I'm not trying to trap you into anything. Okay?"

"Sam, I wouldn't be comfortable accepting a valuable ring like this on that basis. And I don't want you to be offended. We're good friends and I just love being with you. I love our relationship."

"I do too and it's great. Who's complaining."

"It would be different if our relationship was more intimate—"

"Well, you know we can change that anytime you're ready."

"I understand and I appreciate your feelings, but this has to be the way it is for now." Possibly I was leading him on. I used the words "for now" quite often during similar discussions. Somewhere in the back of my head, I was using Sam as my ace in the hole, the relief pitcher warming up in the bullpen. This was not a conscious effort at the time, but something arrived at now in retrospect.

My feeling about Sam was that he had had a good marriage. I think this not only because of the way he talked about his wife, but from observing his youngest daughter, Francine, who just adored him. Ordinarily, when parents don't have a good marriage it is reflected in the children.

We had a busy five days. We shopped on Michigan Avenue. We lunched and dined in places like Mike Fish, the Imperial House, the Trade Wind—not exactly Pavillon or The Colony, but interesting all the same. We spent the late

188

hours in smoky piano bars. Sam's favorite song was *You're Nobody 'Till Somebody Loves You,* and wherever we went he would always request that song. One big blond with a gutsy voice in a Little Italy bar sang it from the time we walked in until we left.

Sam was feeling pretty happy by now, and the first thing I knew he was singing right along with her. Usually something like this would embarrass me, but he was having such a good time, and he thought he was being so subtle that I could only laugh. Of course, no one would dare even say a single word to him.

Then he began to play with the words, wanting to make sure that I got the message: "I'm nobody 'till somebody like you loves me—all the way," and "You're nobody 'till somebody like me loves you—all the way." He twisted it every which way. As if that wasn't enough, he would lean over and whisper: "When are you going to make me somebody?" I would shrug and smile at him over the rim of my champagne glass—the strangest little places would come up with Dom Perignon when Sam ordered it.

It was that evening that he showed me his money clip with the initials SMG and said, "I'll bet you don't know what that means?" When I shook my head, he laughed and put it back in his pocket. He wasn't about to tell me his real name. That privilege would be left to the FBI at a future time.

Sam was a pretty fair drinker, but I never saw him sloppy drunk or mean drunk. There were times when he was happy-high that he liked to ride me about the Kennedy family. It was obvious that he didn't like them. He used to say that Joe Kennedy was one of the biggest crooks that ever lived.

My response was, "I don't want to hear that, Sam."

He'd say, "What's the matter? Can't you stand the truth."

"That's not what you're doing, you're trying to get my goat."

"No, I'm not. I'm giving it to you straight. He was a big thief."

"Be that as it may, I'm not seeing Joe Kennedy."

"The problem is that you can't separate one Kennedy from another. Maybe Jack would be okay if you could get rid of that damn family."

Whatever Sam had to say about Jack and his family, it was done in a teasing way. He never seriously discussed Jack with me. He never directly attacked him. It was always through his family. He often intimated that he knew a great deal of derogatory information about Joe Kennedy's background. I didn't want to hear it and I doubt that he would have told me even if I had asked him. There were areas that were automatically *verboten* without his having to articulate the guidelines.

Before returning to Los Angeles I went to New York because Jack thought there might be an opportunity for us to see each other. I drank and painted and talked to Jack, Sam and my psychiatrist on the phone. After ten days I realized that Jack, like God, was everywhere except at the Navarro. In that brief period, he was in Charlestown, West Virginia; Washington D.C.; Johnson City, Bristol, Kingsport, Knoxville, and Memphis, Tennessee; Sioux City and Ford Dodge, Iowa; Sioux Falls, South Dakota; Billings, Montana; Cheyenne and Casper, Wyoming; Denver, Colorado; Salt Lake City, Utah; Chicago, Illinois; Cleveland, Ohio; Chicago and Cleveland again; Painsville, Lorain, Elyria, Mansfield, Akron, and Canton, Ohio; Albany, Buffalo, Rochester, Lockport, Troy, Schenectady, Amsterdam, Ilion, Utica, Rome, Oneida, and Syracuse, New York.

Jack's second visit to Chicago, as noted above, was for his first television debate with Nixon on September 26. Jack stayed at the Ambassador East—we met there once after he was President. Perhaps I am prejudiced, but the contrast between Jack and Nixon on television was startling to me.

Jack's performance was flawless. He came across as a man who was calm, deliberate and mature far beyond his years. Besides appearing unshaven, Nixon was haggard, perspiring, and nervous as a cat. While Jack ignored Nixon's comments and addressed himself to the audience, Nixon's attention was riveted on Jack, as he took issue with every position expressed. This defensive attitude made him sound like a high school debater, one more interested in scoring points on little details than in proposing political solutions for the future. Jack was concerned about peace and freedom and getting "America started moving again." Nixon lauded the "progress" of the Eisenhower administration. It was no contest. Jack went into the first of the four debates as the underdog and when it was all over the positions were reversed.

I gave up my vigil on the twenty-ninth and returned home, except that I had no home of my own. I moved in with my parents and started apartment hunting. In the meantime, Jerry's concept was slowly evolving. In it's final evolution, after at least a score of "in-depth brainstorming" sessions, the concept became a booklet that would contain photos, sketches, articles and descriptive copy to "dramatize" everything that happened on the set from beginning to end. It was to be used for publicity, but I had a feeling that years later Jerry would sit back and relive those great moments when he produced, directed, wrote and starred in *Ladies Man.*

While I waited to become a paid member of Jerry's staff, I continued seeing Dr. Sherman. I painted, shopped, went to Palm Springs, dated almost every night, and even went to cocktail parties given by Kennedy supporters like Barry Sullivan. I saw Ted Kennedy at one of Barry's parties. He did a double take and just as he said, "Hey, hi there, how are you?" somebody whisked him away before I could answer. With all of these diversions, I was still confused and depressed. Fall was a long, painful season.

I finally found an apartment at 1200 North Flores Avenue, below the Sunset Strip and east of Doheny, and moved in on November 3. My apartment was on the second floor, number 201, and I took great delight in decorating and furnishing it. It was a fairly new apartment, not as large as I would have liked, but I was able to take it with the understanding that I would move when I found a larger place. This meant that I was shopping more for the future than the present. It was a one-bedroom apartment, with an L shaped living-dining room and a nice size kitchen.

191

It was here that I received my first visit from the FBI. There was a knock at the door and when I asked who it was, a man said, "Judy Campbell?" I said, "Yes," and he said, "We'd like to talk to you. This is the FBI."

When I opened the door there were two men standing there and both simultaneously flashed their identifications. One was named Dodge and the other was Vern Lynch. I didn't learn until some time later that Lynch was with the Internal Revenue Service.

It was obvious from the beginning that Dodge was in command. Lynch hardly spoke. He just sat there looking very menacing and Dodge conducted the interrogation. I had quite a few of my paintings around and Dodge wanted to know if I had sold any and before I could answer, he said, "Do you know Sam Giancana?" When I replied no, he looked at me like I had lost my mind. "Do you know Sam Flood?" I nodded and he said, "Well, they're one and the same. That's Sam Giancana. Do you know what he does for a living?" I shook my head and he said, "What do you do for a living?" Again before I could answer, he said, "Has Giancana ever given you any money?"

I began to say, "I beg your—" and he said, "Does he pay your rent? Does he flash big money around? Do you know Tony Accardo?" and he reeled off a long list of names.

I felt threatened. They were not two nice men who had come in to have a conversation. Whatever was on their minds, it was not something I wanted any part of. "Just a moment," I said. "What is your interest in Sam Flood?"

"Giancana," he said. "Salvatore Momo Giancana, better known as Mooney, and he's not the kind of man a nice girl should be running around with."

"What do you mean?"

"Tell me something, how do you support yourself? Are you an heiress?"

"I don't know what you mean by an heiress, but I have inherited money from my grandmother."

"Then you are an heiress."

"Whether I am or am not, I don't see how it concerns you.

What is it that you want to know? I don't understand any of this."

Dodge said it was in regard to an organized crime investigation, and he made it sound like I might be involved in it. I didn't have anything to hide but I realized they were trying to implicate me with their questions. At this point I didn't like those two men—the one with the long grim face seated on the sofa and the other with the sarcastic questions and abrupt manner who never stopped moving. From then on I kept my answers to a simple no. When they realized they weren't going to get anywhere they finally left. Dodge's parting words were, "Think about what we told you, we'll talk to you again."

I locked the door and leaned against it. My knees were so weak I thought I would collapse before I could reach the sofa. I was shaking like a leaf. I sat as rigidly as I could, fighting to maintain control of myself. I was terribly frightened. At that moment, those two men appeared as a far greater threat to me than whatever it was Sam represented. I had gradually come to accept Sam's way of life. I was not worldly, but neither was I stupid. I had seen my share of gangster movies, and the people who bowed and scraped before Sam were not doing it for ordinary reasons.

Perhaps my reaction would have been different if the FBI had approached me when I first met Sam. The idea of associating with an underworld boss might have frightened me. But now that I *knew* Sam, they were whistling in the dark. I wouldn't have told them anything about Sam if my life depended on it. Sam was my friend, and regardless of what anybody said about him, he had my loyalty. He may have been with the underworld, but you can put me on a cross, and I'll fight you, and you still won't make me betray a friend or family. It's not anything for which I claim credit. Or something I have to work at. It's part of me, my nature, something I have no more control over than breathing.

Later after I had calmed down I called Sam, and by now I was very indignant over their gangbuster methods. How dare they do this to *me*, a free law-abiding American citizen. It shocked me that the FBI, whose public image then was that of gentlemen, would act this way. I kept thinking, "So this is how they treat innocent people." I thought of myself as innocent, which I suppose was open to debate. Still their hostile, antagonistic approach was designed to intimidate and not to induce cooperation.

When I got Sam on the line, I just blurted it out: "The FBI was here asking all kinds of questions about you." His immediate concern was whether I was all right. Other than being boiling mad, I told him I was fine and then proceeded to reconstruct the encounter. Sam was very calm. He said it was typical harassment and nothing for me to worry about. They were on a fishing expedition and the safest way to handle that was to clam up, to completely ignore them, to act like they weren't even there. That was precisely what I did from that day forward.

November 8 was judgment day. By five o'clock Pacific time, CBS had predicted Jack's victory. The polls had closed in the east when President Eisenhower came on television and pleaded with party workers in western states to "keep fighting right to the last minute." By the time the polls closed in California, the projection was that Jack would win by a margin of five million. That was not the picture the next morning. Jack squeaked by on a prayer and a few thousand stolen votes in Cook County, without which Nixon would have awakened that morning as the next President of the United States. Mayor Daley has quietly taken credit for Jack's victory, but Sam often told me, "Listen, honey, if it wasn't for me your boyfriend wouldn't even be in the White House."

AUTHOR'S NOTE: *I explored that possibility in my research for* Captive City *and concluded that the election could not have been stolen in Cook County without Giancana's approval. First of all, Daley's victory edge in 1955, the year he first became mayor, came largely from the West Side river wards, the citadel of the old Capone bloc, which later became known as the West Side Bloc. What*

194

this meant in terms of underworld control in the political hierarchy was not lost to Chicagoans who were (and still are) daily briefed on the latest intramural antics of their favorite gangsters and politicians. I went on to write the following:

"The Syndicate's trail of influence in both political parties is a well-lighted path. Its domination of politicians in at least half of the wards is a virtual dictatorship over the voters in their domain. 'The bloc's hold is so powerful,' the Daily News concluded in 1963, 'that people in its territory are afraid to vote against it—on the rare occasions when they are given a choice . . . The ease with which the West Side blocsters get elected and reelected to the Legislature is another indication of their strength. Six legislators linked to the bloc have served a total of 109 years in Springfield. Thanks to an unspoken deal between the two parties, they don't even worry about token opposition on election day.' To Cook County Sheriff Richard B. Ogilvie, a Republican, the Bloc was 'a festering sore within the body politics of this community.'

"But to Mayor Daley the Bloc is nonexistent—all politicians, that is Democrats and pseudo-Republicans, are fine, upstanding public servants, elected by the people who have the 'right to select their leaders.' At a time in history when other cities have been subjected to abrasive reforms, the results in Chicago remain dismally negative. The reasons for this opprobrious stalemate have their roots in the anachronistic power structure of ward politics vis-a-vis organized crime."

After his nationwide investigation of organized crime, Estes Kefauver had this observation to make about Chicago in his book Crime in America:

"Everywhere we went the committee found a certain amount of political immorality, but in Chicago the rawness of this sort of thing was particularly shocking. . . . There was no doubt in the minds of any of us, after the sort of testimony we heard in Chicago, that organized crime and political corruption go hand in hand, and that in fact there could be no big-time organized crime

195

without a firm and profitable alliance between those who run the rackets and those in political control."

In his book, Conversations with Kennedy, *Benjamin C. Bradlee recounts a story told by Jack Kennedy on election night: "Over dinner, he told how he had called Chicago's Mayor Richard Daley while Illinois was hanging in the balance to ask how he was doing. 'Mr. President,' Kennedy quoted Daley as saying, 'with a little bit of luck and the help of a few close friends, you're going to carry Illinois.' Later, when Nixon was being urged to contest the 1960 election, I often wondered about that statement."*

Nixon carried 93 of the state's 102 counties and lost Illinois by 8,858 votes. A switch of 4,500 votes in Cook County's 5,199 precincts would have given Nixon the state's twenty-seven electoral votes. An unofficial GOP check of only 699 paperballot precincts showed a net gain for Nixon of 4,539 votes. An official recount was not permitted by the Daley machine and the original election figures remained on the books.

However, Kennedy's narrow victory was not due alone to Illinois. Kennedy won Texas by only 28,000 votes. If the combined fifty-one electoral votes of Illinois and Texas had gone to Nixon, he would have become President with an electoral majority of two. As it was, Kennedy's margin of the entire popular vote was one-tenth of one percent.

I would smile and say, "Oh, sure," but I wouldn't pursue it any further. I didn't really want to know the details of anything. I liked being kept completely away from the seedier side of whatever his life may have been.

As the returns came in over television, the one thought that kept going through my mind was "where do we go from here? How the devil do you carry on a love affair with the President of the United States." I couldn't picture myself going to the White House for a rendezvous. I couldn't even fathom it. This troubled me but not enough to spoil the pleasure of his victory. I was so very proud of him. He had worked his heart and soul out for it. He was a very special person. There is nothing in this world that I would want that badly.

Before going to bed early that morning, I sent Jack a telegram of congratulations addressing it to Evelyn in Hyannisport. Later in the day I called her and we both reveled in his victory.

Whatever fears I had concerning the future of our relationship were dispelled the next day when Jack called to ask if I was coming to the Inauguration.

I had already given this serious thought. "I would rather not, Jack. I just wouldn't feel comfortable with your wife and family being there. I'll watch you on television."

"I wish you wouldn't feel that way. Why don't you come with Frank. The whole gang is coming. Or bring some other friends, or your family. I want you to be there."

We had a number of discussions about it. After one of his persuasive calls I weakened for a moment and called Evelyn to say that I would attend. "Jack will be very happy," she said. "I'll make all the arrangements to get your invitations out to you. Unfortunately, since you waited this long to decide, I can't send you a personally engraved invitation. I want you to know that I had you down for one but Jack told me you weren't coming. I assure you that you will have the best possible available seat and, of course, you will have tickets for all inaugural activities."

The next day I received a telegram from Robert Burkhardt, the Executive Director of the Inaugural Committee, stating that "invitations and tickets" had been set aside for me at his office. Then I received a program and various tickets in the mail. Jack was delighted that I had changed my mind, but with all that fuss I still ended up not going. The night of the inaugural ball, I went to La Scala with Travis and someone there said, "Hey, I thought you'd be in Washington tonight." For me, this justified my decision. Too many people already knew about our relationship without my flaunting it before his wife on this most important day of their life. All I said was, "It's too cold for me."

About a month after the election I finally got on Jerry's payroll. But after four weeks without a paycheck, I asked Jerry about it: "What was it you said I was getting a week?"

"Oh," he said, "I forgot all about it. I'll get a memo out on it right away."

Jerry loved memos. In the course of a day he dictated more interoffice memos than any corporation president. He had a dictating machine and his secretary was constantly transcribing his little plastic discs. Jerry turned on the machine whenever someone came into his office and surreptitiously recorded everything.

For a while, at least, working for Jerry was good therapy. It made me feel that I was pretty healthy. Jerry was fascinating to watch—if you could do it from a distance and not become personally involved. His behavior was more erratic than any of the slapstick comedy he ever dreamed up. He could be furious one minute, and the next minute be yelling for everybody to come play basketball. God forbid if he lost or anyone criticized his style of play. Jerry was convinced that he could do everything well. There were stories about his yacht and how the operators of various marinas would shudder when they saw Jerry at the wheel because Jerry thought he was an expert skipper and the result was an endless string of disasters.

Work on the picture would stop when Jerry grabbed a basketball. Afterwards he'd disappear into his dressing room and though no one knew when he'd be out, the moment he did emerge everyone had better be ready. "Come on," he would yell, "let's get to work. Don't you realize how late we are on this picture?"

Most of the people working closely with Jerry were caught in a love-hate situation. They were kept in a state of chronic anxiety. I think many ended up either with a psychiatrist or an ulcer, or perhaps with both, because very few people can function properly when they never know what to expect.

On my birthday, January 11, columnist Harrison Carroll called me at the studio with a disturbing message for Jerry. "I know you're a good friend of Jerry's," he said, "and I'm also aware that you know influential people." He paused before going on to explain that Jerry was about to be named as corespondent in a divorce action filed by a wealthy young man who was divorcing his starlet wife. Fred Otash, a keyhole type of investigator, was the one who had collected the information. "I don't know what you can do for Jerry, but I thought you should know about it, and I would appreciate your passing this on to him."

For the first time since I had met him, Jerry had a legitimate reason for being unhappy. He didn't disappoint me. His emotions ran the full gamut of his reportoire. It was a dazzling performance. He ranted and raved. He would be ruined, his wife Patty would divorce him, his audience would desert him, his friends would hold him in contempt—the dire circumstances he envisioned were infinite.

"How can I stop it?" he moaned, wringing his hands. "Do you have any idea at all? Do you know anyone who could help?"

Jerry knew of my friendship with Sam, having learned of it either from Marty Tannenbaum or Morris Levy. And because of the calls that came to the studio from Jack, he also knew about that relationship. "Well," I said, ever mindful of what he knew, "I could call Sam in Florida." I certainly wasn't going to ask the President of the United States to get a comedian out of a sticky divorce suit.

"That's great, Judy, but first let me make a few calls to check this thing out. I'll get right back to you."

It wasn't long before I was handed a memo which read:

DEAR JUDY

PLEASE PLACE A LONG DISTANCE CALL TO SAM FOR ME IN FLORIDA, FROM MY PORTABLE DRESSING ROOM ON THE SET, ANY TIME BETWEEN 2 AND 4 PM TODAY.

WHEN YOU GET HIM ON THE LINE HAVE ME CALLED AND I'LL TALK TO HIM.

JERRY

After explaining the situation to Sam, I asked if he would talk to Jerry and he said, "Sure, I'll talk to him." I went out of the room when Jerry talked to Sam and we never discussed it. Much later I did hear that John Roselli had a conversation with Otash and the evidence against Jerry was destroyed.

As I was leaving the studio that afternoon, I was summoned to Jerry's dressing room. The place was crowded with his personal staff and when I walked in Jerry stood up and said, "Happy Birthday." There was a big cake and Jerry handed me a gold bracelet. Two weeks later I had to remind him that my pay was three weeks in arrears. I don't think I was ever paid on schedule.

Jerry's close call with the starlet did not cool his ardor. Jerry was a toucher. When he walked with a man his arm automatically went around the man's shoulders. With women he never stopped experimenting, always trying to see how far he could go. I didn't mind the arm around the shoulder routine, but I constantly discouraged the other games he had in mind. He was always telling me how much he respected me as a person and how deeply he cared about me as a woman. He never stopped trying to get something going, and I would cut it off short whenever he became too suggestive in his conversation. He would use corny lines like, "All work and no play is not healthy," and would then invite me for a cruise on his yacht. I was able to fend him off for a few months, and finally he got the message and gave up on me.

Jerry's first attempt to fire me was to send his bookkeeper to tell me that they were cutting down on the staff. I immediately called Jerry, who was in Phoenix, and he apologized, saying that they were cutting down, but it certainly didn't include me.

I lasted another month. The ax fell while Jerry was appearing at the Sands in Las Vegas. I was having a drink in the Sands lounge with Jerry's secretary, Doris, when Jerry came in with his wife Patty and walked by without saying a word. A moment later Doris was paged and when she came back to the table, she said, "Let's get out of here, I have to talk to you."

"What's going on?"

"I was just given instructions not to talk to you," she said. "You tell me what's going on."

Not knowing what else to do, I called Sam. His advice

was, "Get out of there. You don't need that crap. Come on up to Chicago."

Sam was really hot under the collar when he met me at the airport. He wanted to know if I was all right and I told him that other than being upset I was fine.

"Do you want your job back?"

I looked at him and realized that I had better be careful. He was angrier than I had ever seen him. "I don't think so. I wouldn't be happy going back after the way I was treated. I'd rather forget the whole thing."

"You listen to me. All you have to do if you want your job back is say the word. If you want more money, you'll get more money."

The moment we reached the Ambassador East, Sam called someone in Las Vegas and minutes later Jerry was on the line. Sam was calm and deliberate. "Tell me, Jerry," he said, "what happened with Judy?" According to what Sam told me later, Jerry blamed his wife, saying she was jealous and wouldn't allow me on the set. "Well, listen here, you son of a bitch," Sam said, "I don't give a damn about your stupid wife. All Judy has to do is give me the okay and she's got her job back. Do you understand me?" Sam listened patiently while Jerry went into a lengthy apology. He held up the receiver so that I could hear Jerry's whining voice—he sounded like he had gone into his spastic routine. I could just picture him, jumping around and perspiring, scared out of his wits. "You better thank God she doesn't want your stinking job back, because she'd have it back and with a big raise in pay. Stop sniveling and thank your lucky stars that this lady wants nothing more from you."

I must admit that Sam's phone call made me feel pretty good. I felt Jerry had it coming. He abused people every day—and got away with it. His treatment of me was inexcusable. Now he was getting it back from someone he feared, someone he had no control over. I thought, "You're getting yours, even if I'm not the one on the phone. The person talking to you is talking for me." I wish I could have done it, but unfortunately a woman is seldom listened to. It used to bother me a great deal. The prettier you are, the less people listen. You're supposed to be decoration. This is something I've always resented.

The final blow for Jerry came from Jack Kennedy. Jerry had to be in Washington for some appearance and Doris was with him when he saw Jack. She told me that Jack said, "Hi, Jerry, how's Judy? Have you seen her lately?" Jerry was beside himself. It infuriated him that the President had asked about me instead of making Jerry the focus of his undivided attention. Jack, who knew of my falling out with Jerry, did it to needle him. Jack loved to get people off balance.

Two days later, on April 27, as we returned to the Ambassador East from the Armory, Sam said, "We're going to put on the dog tonight and really do the town."

Dressing to go out with Sam was quite a challenge. I never knew what to expect. I wore a full-skirted black lace dress with a simple high neck, the pearls I had bought in Palm Beach, and a white mink jacket. When I came out of the bedroom, Sam nodded approvingly. "You look fantastic," he said. "You're going to knock them all dead."

We then drove to Sam's house and it was my turn to wait while he went into his bedroom to change. When he came out he was holding a large emerald-cut diamond between twelve and fifteen carats, and he said, "I want you to have this." After our usual squabble, I agreed to wear it for the evening."

"If someone hits me over the head, it's your fault because I'm wearing this big rock on my finger."

He looked at me as if I had lost my mind. "Do you really think you can get in trouble with me around?"

Sam drove his little black car that evening. He never said a word about our destination. I realized it was the Villa Venice when Sam turned up a long street and I saw the large stone archway over the entrance to the parking lot. Sam slowed down and then suddenly zoomed past. When I asked him what was wrong, he said, "See all those ants out there." I looked more closely and saw that there were men sitting across the entire length of the archway, and all down the sides. They even had a couple of ladders.

"What's going on," I asked.

"We're going to a wedding reception," he said, "and those characters are Feds and newshounds, and they all have cameras. But we've got to go in there. I'm going to turn around, and you just kind of look down so they can't get a good shot of you."

He was truly enjoying it. He swung the car around and he was ho-ho-hoing all the time, and I said, "You're crazy, Sam." "Don't worry," he said, "everything is all right."

We swung through the archway and it felt like a thousand flashbulbs had gone off in one giant blinding blast. Sam was still laughing when he stopped under the canopied entrance and the parking attendants opened the doors. I must admit it was an exhilarating experience. Although I never saw it, I was told that our picture later appeared in one of the Chicago dailies.

The wedding reception was for Tony Accardo's daughter, Linda Lee, and her husband, Michael Palermo. The Accardos and the newlyweds were greeting arriving guests and collecting white envelopes like crazy. It was simply "how-do-you-do" to me, but Sam got the full treatment.

We sat at a table with Sam's two married daughters, Antoinette and Bonnie, and their husbands. The first thing Sam did was to take my left hand, as though he were being affectionate, and casually display the ring to his daughters. Antoinette nearly dropped her fork. She looked at Bonnie and they looked at him, and I quickly dropped my hand on my lap.

Sam started to laugh. "What's the matter, honey," he said to Antoinette.

"Nothing, nothing at all," she said.

Bonnie said, "May I see your ring?"

Now that I knew his game, I gave him a swift kick under the table as I raised my hand to show her the ring. "That's beautiful," she said, and it was obvious that they both recognized it. Antoinette, Sam later told me, had been

203

pestering him for her mother's jewelry, and he wasn't about to give it to her. She had gone about it in a greedy manner and now he was having the time of his life watching her squirm.

Throughout the evening an endless stream of people came to the table to pay their respects to Sam. From time to time he would introduce them, but always on a first name basis, or with just nicknames, "Judy, this is Potatoes, Crackers, Monk, Smokes, Teets, Nags, Fifi, Horse, Needles, Cowboy, Turk, Dutch—I always got the biggest kick out of those monikers. They represented more pushed-in noses and scarred faces, more dese, dem and dose sprinkled with Sicilian than all of Central Casting. They looked so tough and yet were so gentle in Sam's presence that I had the feeling that I was watching a scene from *Guys and Dolls*. There was a lot of noise and rambunctious dancing, but everybody was having a happy time.

The next day there was a pleasant surprise in the newspaper. Jack was in Chicago to attend a Democratic dinner at McCormick Place. I called Evelyn and told her that I was at the Ambassador East. She said, "Oh, Jack will be so thrilled!" She connected us and Jack said, "Can I see you?" I told him I was in suite 839-40 and I said I would wait for him if there was any chance he could make it. But I couldn't resist adding that his coming to the hotel might be too risky.

"I'll be over for sure," he said. "Don't worry about that. Everybody knows I'm in town and there's nothing unusual about my dropping over to see someone."

He made it sound so normal, but as I sat there waiting for his knock on the door I tried to envision what his visit entailed—the limousines, the motorcycle cops, the secret service, the mapping of the route, the control of traffic lights, the blocking off of streets, and Jack in his limousine discussing affairs of state, or politics, with men who would be left waiting while we kissed and talked of love.

Although we had been talking on the phone on a regular basis, I hadn't seen Jack in quite a while. I was beginning to think that our relationship might just quietly expire from neglect. I knew that Jack was impossibly busy, and though I believed him when he said he missed me and was looking forward to a time when we could be together again, I couldn't help but think it was beginning to sound like empty promises.

There was a gentle knock and I was up in a flash. A moment later we were in each other's arms and it was like we had never been apart. The way he behaved there was no doubt that he had missed me. God knows I had missed him. If the love I felt at that moment could have been preserved within my heart, I would have been blissfully happy for the rest of my life.

There was no time to luxuriate in the warmth of our love. As he was leaving he said, ''I want you to come to the White House.'' And before we reached the door it was agreed that I would come to Washington on May 4. We kissed and he was gone. The visit could not have lasted more than twenty minutes.

After Jack left I suddenly remembered I was going to Miami the next day. I was going at Sam's invitation, and I left on a late afternoon flight, traveling under the alias of Judy Norris. Sam took a later flight, arriving at one in the morning. As always, I stayed at the Fontainebleau.

The next evening, April 13, we had dinner with Skinny D'Amato at Nate and Art's, and later that evening Johnny Roselli and his girlfriend Genene Claire joined us for a drink in the lounge.

AUTHOR'S NOTE: *Born in Esteria, Italy, Filippo Sacco was six years old in 1911 when his mother brought him to the United States to be reunited with his father, who had emigrated earlier and was living in East Boston. Ten years later, Filippo was arrested as a narcotics peddler and promptly skipped bail. It was then that he changed his name to John Roselli, and would later tell the Kefauver Committee that his birthplace was Chicago.*

He served his apprenticeship in bootlegging with

Longy Zwillman's mob in New Jersey and later switched his allegiance to Al Capone, where he gained expertise in labor racketeering, extortion and gambling. By the early 1930's, he had earned a reputation as a smooth operator and he was transferred to the west coast to protect some of Frank Nitti's interests. He was given a percentage in Nationwide News, the only bookmaking wire service then in operation, and became an associate of Willie Bioff and George Browne in the International Alliance of Theatrical Stage Employees and Moving Picture Machine Operators. On the testimony of Willie Bioff, Roselli and six top Chicago hoodlums were sentenced to ten-year prison terms for extorting millions from the film industry. Nitti committed suicide to avoid prosecution and Bioff was later murdered. After serving less than four years of his sentence, Roselli came back to Hollywood as an "assistant producer" to Brian Foy, who headed Eagle Lion Studio. That was his cover while he represented Chicago interests in Jack Dragna's west coast organization.

When Dragna died of natural causes in 1957, Roselli was picked by Giancana and the Mafia's Grand Council as their top coordinator in Las Vegas and Southern California. Don Giovanni, as he was known in the brotherhood, became a man of respect. He prided himself on his ability to settle disputes without raising his voice. Slim, medium height, with sharp features, iron-gray hair and icy blue eyes that turned black whenever he had to raise his voice, Roselli had reached the peak of his profession by the time he became involved with the CIA.

As Senator Frank Church's Intelligence Committee unhappily discovered in 1975, Giancana and Roselli had been recruited by the Central Intelligence Agency to arrange for the assassination of Fidel Castro. The middle-man in the operation was Robert Maheu, a former FBI agent who later gained notoriety when he was fired as Howard Hughes's alter ego in Las Vegas. From the testimony of CIA officials, Maheu and Roselli before the Senate committee, the code name for the operation should have been Keystone. It was the greatest slapstick conspiracy ever conceived in real life.

It has been described as a plot, but Webster's says that a "plot suggests careful foresight in planning and a continuity or complexity of positive action by one or a number of persons . . ." So a plot it wasn't. Fiasco is the word. No one knows how many fiascos there were between March of 1960 and the end of 1965—they began before and ended after the Kennedy administration. The original objective was to "dispose" of Castro before the Bay of Pigs invasion.

Even the committee's report was hard pressed to describe the fiascos: "The proposed assassination devices ran the gamut from high-powered rifles to poison pills, poison pens, deadly bacterial powders, and other devices which strain the imagination."

One wild scheme was "to spray Castro's broadcasting studio with a chemical which produced effects similar to LSD, but the scheme was rejected because the chemical was unreliable. During this period, TSD [Technical Services Division] impregnated a box of cigars with a chemical which produced temporary disorientation, hoping to induce Castro to smoke one of the cigars before delivering a speech. The Inspector General also reported a plan to destroy Castro's image as 'The Beard' by dusting his shoes with thallium salts, a strong depilatory that would cause his beard to fall out. The depilatory was to be administered during a trip outside Cuba, when it was anticipated Castro would leave his shoes outside the door of his hotel room to be shined. TSD procured the chemical and tested it on animals, but apparently abandoned the scheme because Castro cancelled his trip."

Unable to destroy Castro's image, the CIA decided to go all out on destroying the person. The cigars were now impregnated with a botulinum toxin so "potent that a person would die after putting one in his mouth." The cigars were delivered to an "unidentified person" and that was the last anyone heard of them. *Various other fiascos resulted before August 1960, at which time "the CIA took steps to enlist members of the criminal underworld with gambling syndicate contacts to aid in assassinating Castro. The origin of the plot is uncertain." The committee was not noted for its use of hyperbole.*

Colonel Sheffield Edwards, Director of the Agency's Office of Security, picked Maheu for the job because he was "tough enough" to handle the assignment. Maheu picked Roselli, who in turn picked Giancana, his old boss, as the "back-up man." Maheu, who had known Roselli prior to this time, denied that he was aware of the extent of Roselli's underworld connections and activities, but recalled that "it was certainly evident to me that he was able to accomplish things in Las Vegas when nobody else seemed to get the same kind of attention."

Maheu's cover story, as outlined by the CIA, was that he would "approach Roselli as the representative of businessmen with interests in Cuba who saw the elimination of Castro as the first essential step to the recovery of their investments." Maheu was told to offer $150,000 for Castro's assassination, which made it pretty high as hit contracts go in the Mafia.

In his testimony, Roselli said that Maheu's approach was that "high government officials" needed his expertise in recruiting Cubans to knock off Castro. Following that first meeting, which was at the Beverly Hills Brown Derby restaurant on September 14, Roselli went forthwith to Miami to work out the details for the first officially approved hit of his career.

At this point, I should explain that there is nothing clear-cut in the committee's report. It is one long collection of conflicting testimony presented in glorious confusion. Any writer could take this report and arrive at any conclusion he wished without any concern for the truth and still be in the committee's ballpark. It is simply a question of multiple choice.

Roselli and Maheu were registered at Miami's Kennilworth Hotel from October 11–13. On the eighteenth,

Roselli introduced Maheu to a Sam Gold (Giancana), who would be his "back-up" or "key" man, and to Joe (Santos Trafficante), who "Gold said would serve as a courier to Cuba and make arrangements there." Trafficante, whose specialty in recent years has been the drug traffic, had been the Mob's top gun in the good old days of Batista.

Although it was Giancana's job to locate someone in Castro's entourage to make the hit, Roselli testified that none of the Cubans eventually used in the fiascos were acquired through Giancana's contacts. There is persuasive evidence that Giancana thought the whole thing was a lark. Consider what happened when Giancana talked Maheu into putting a bug into the room of comedian Dan Rowan whom he suspected was having an affair with Phyllis McGuire, who was then having an affair with Giancana.

Bear in mind that the committee presents several versions of this fiasco. In one version, we are told that Maheu took the problem to Colonel Edwards, who concluded that the CIA did not have "the capability of accomplishing this," but gave Maheu a thousand dollars to hire Arthur J. Balletti, a private detective, for the job. Instead of the requested bug, Balletti decided to install a tap on the phone. The ensuing events were described by a CIA official as a "Keystone Comedy Act."

The report states that "On October 31, 1960, Balletti, believing that the apartment would be vacant for the afternoon, left the wiretap equipment unattended. A maid discovered the equipment and notified the local sheriff, who arrested Balletti and brought him to the jail. Balletti called Maheu in Miami, tying 'Maheu into this thing up to his ear.' Balletti's bail was paid by Roselli."

Giancana thought it was hilarious when Roselli told him about Balletti's arrest. "Giancana laughed," Roselli said. "I remember his expression, smoking a cigar, he almost swallowed it laughing about it." This upset Roselli no end. "It was blowing everything," he said, "blowing every kind of cover that I had tried to arrange to keep quiet." Only then, we are asked to believe, did Roselli tell Giancana that the CIA was involved in the operation "in order to have him keep his mouth shut."

What is intriguing here is that on the very day Giancana was supposedly introduced to Maheu, October 18, J. Edgar Hoover sent a memorandum to Richard Bissell, the CIA's Deputy Director for Plans, and reported the following:

"During recent conversations with several friends, Giancana stated that Fidel Castro was to be done away with very shortly. When doubt was expressed regarding this statement, Giancana reportedly assured those present that Castro's assassination would occur in November. Moreover, he allegedly indicated that he had already met with the assassin-to-be on three occasions. . . . Giancana claimed that everything has been perfected for the killing of Castro, and that the 'assassin' had arranged with a girl, not further described, to drop a 'pill' in some drink or food of Castro's."

In another part of the committee's report, from information provided in the Inspector General's Report, we learn that the CIA's "Support Chief contacted Roselli in early September 1960, and during the week of September 25, the Chief, Maheu, and Roselli met with Giancana and Trafficante in Miami."

With the FBI on the scent, the boys started manufacturing alibis. Again the Senate committee was presented with a multiple choice situation:

—Roselli said that Maheu gave him two explanations for the tap: First, that Giancana was concerned that Phyllis was having an affair; and second that he had arranged the tap to determine whether Giancana had told Phyllis about the assassination "plot," and whether she was spreading the story. Maheu later gave the FBI the second explanation.

—In a memo to Bobby Kennedy, dated May 14, 1962, Colonel Edwards stated that "At the time of the incident neither the Agency nor the undersigned knew of the proposed technical installation."

210

—The CIA's Support Chief testified that Maheu had informed him of Giancana's concern over Phyllis and his request for the bug. Otherwise, Giancana had threatened to fly to Las Vegas himself. Because Giancana's departure "would disrupt the negotiations," Maheu "secured the Support Chief's permission to arrange for a bug to insure Giancana's presence and cooperation." Balletti's boss told FBI agents that Maheu paid him a retainer of a thousand dollars for the job, and the Support Chief confirmed that the CIA "indirectly" paid for the tap because "we paid Maheu a certain amount of money, and he just paid it out of what we were giving him."

—Joseph Shimon, an acquaintance of Giancana, testified that Giancana told him he had gone through Roselli in his request for the bug. Shimon said Giancana told him he had paid Maheu five thousand dollars for the tap, that the CIA had not known about the tap in advance, and that Maheu subsequently decided to use his connection with the CIA operation to avoid prosecution for his involvement in the tap. Maheu testified he didn't remember receiving the money.

—Edwards told Maheu that if he was "approached by the FBI, he could refer them to me to be briefed that he was engaged in an intelligence operation directed at Cuba."

—On April 18, 1961, Maheu informed the FBI that the tap involved the CIA, and suggested that Edwards be contacted.

—On April 20, 1961, the final day of the Bay of Pigs fiasco, Edwards told the FBI that the prosecution of Maheu might reveal sensitive information concerning the Bay of Pigs invasion.

—In a memorandum to the Attorney General, dated May 22, 1961, Hoover summarized Edwards' statements which spelled out Giancana's CIA link. The CIA had relied on Giancana because of his contacts with gambling figures who might have sources for use "in connection with CIA's clandestine efforts against the Castro government." Although none of Giancana's efforts had "materialized to date," there was hope that his work "may eventually pay off." Edwards had never been "furnished details of the methods used by Giancana and Maheu because this was 'dirty business' and he could not afford to know the specific actions of Maheu and Giancana in pursuit of any mission for the CIA." Hoover went on to state that Edwards had acknowledged the "attempted" use of Maheu and "hoodlum elements" by the CIA in "anti-Castro activities" but that the "purpose for placing the wiretap . . . has not been determined." There was no mention of assassination attempts in Edwards' statements, nor was there any indication that Hoover had connected Giancana's CIA link with his boast to kill Castro that Hoover had reported on October 18, 1960. See pages 5–7 for the committee's analysis of whether the President or the Attorney General ever learned from Hoover of the underworld's involvement with the CIA in assassination attempts.

—Whatever the Attorney General did or did not know, the Justice Department decided that it would not be in the "national interest" to prosecute Giancana or anyone else involved in the wiretap incident.

—After considering the above contradictions, plus many more, the committee observed that "There is some evidence, however, suggesting that the CIA itself may have instituted the tap to determine whether Giancana was leaking information about his involvement" in the fiascos.

In a way it is fitting that the report is as confused as the operation it investigated.

The Bay of Pigs invasion, April 17–20, was considered by President Kennedy to be the worst defeat of his administration. While he publicly assumed "sole responsibility" for the fiasco, he privately confided to Ted Sorenson: "How could I have been so far off base? All my life I've known better than to depend on the experts. How could I have been so stupid, to let them go ahead."

According to the Senate committee, "There is some

evidence that Giancana or Roselli originated the idea of depositing a poison pill in Castro's drink to give the [assassin] a chance to escape." Roselli wanted something "nice and clean, without getting into any kind of out and out ambushing," preferably a poison that would disappear without a trace. Giancana had ruled out any notion of ambushing Castro. At first the CIA was under the impression that Castro would be gunned down in gangland style, but Sam pointed out that although popular in Chicago, this method presented a recruitment problem in Cuba.

The first batch of pills was rejected because they would not dissolve in water. A second batch, containing botulinum toxin, "did the job expected of them" when tested on monkeys. After a "contact inside a restaurant frequented by Castro" was found, money and pills were delivered to Roselli, Trafficante, and the Cuban with the contact at the Fontainebleau. Roselli testified that "Maheu opened his briefcase and dumped a whole lot of money on his lap . . . and also came up with the capsules and he explained how they were going to be used. As far as I remember, they couldn't be used in boiling soups and things like that, but they could be used in water or otherwise, but they couldn't last forever. . . . It had to be done as quickly as possible." Maheu denied any knowledge of this incident.

Testifying to the same incident, Robert Shimon said that he was present with Giancana at the time of the delivery. He had accompanied Maheu to Miami to see the third Patterson-Johansson fight (March 12, 1961), and he shared a suite with Giancana, Roselli and Maheu at the Fontainebleau. Maheu, Shimon said, told him that he had a "contract" to kill Castro, and that the CIA had given him a "liquid" to put in Castro's food that would kill him in two or three days without leaving a trace. The Cuban was contacted outside the Fontainebleau's Boom Boom Room, and when Roselli left with the Cuban, Maheu said to Shimon that "Johnny's going to handle everything, this is Johnny's contract." Giancana later

213

told Shimon that "I am not in it, and they are asking me for the names of some guys who used to work in casinos. . . . Maheu's conning the hell out of the CIA." A few days later, Shimon received a phone call from Maheu, who said ". . . did you see the paper? Castro's ill. He's going to be sick two or three days. Wow, we got him."

The attempt to poison Castro's drink either failed because the Prime Minister stopped patronizing that particular restaurant, or because somebody forgot to give the "go signal" to the contact, who subsequently returned the cash and the poison. Maheu did not know who was responsible for giving the signal. Another prospective assassin, an official close to Castro, was fired before he received the poison.

In the fall of 1961, the CIA placed William Harvey in charge of the continuing fiascos. In April 1962, Harvey instructed Roselli to maintain his Cuban contacts but not to deal with Maheu or Giancana, who were described as "untrustworthy" and "surplus." There were more fiascos, with three-man teams being dispatched to poison Che Guevara as well as Fidel and Raoul Castro. Harvey was getting discouraged. "There's not much likelihood that this is going any place," he told Roselli, "or that it should be continued." In January 1963 Harvey terminated the underworld phase of the operation and directed Roselli to "taper off his communications with the Cubans." Roselli broke off contact but neglected to tell the Cubans that the hundred fifty thousand dollar bounty had been withdrawn.

Maheu testified that "Giancana was paid nothing at all, not even expenses, and that Mr. Roselli was given a pittance that did not even begin to cover his expenses."

Roselli, who at the time of his appearance before the committee was fighting a deportation order, told the committee that he paid his own way, paid for his own hotel and travel expenses, and never "took a nickel." "No, as long as it is for the Government of the United States," he said, "this is the least I can do, because I

214

owe it a lot." His motivation, he added was "honor and dedication."

When the FBI threatened to have him deported in 1966 unless he talked about some of his Mafia associates, Roselli did not forget those years of dedication. He contacted Edwards, who told the FBI that Roselli wanted to "keep square with the Bureau," but was afraid that his associates might kill him if he talked. Then the next year when Roselli was arrested for a million dollar card-cheating scam at the Beverly Hills Friars Club, he asked Harvey, who had left the Agency, to represent him. Harvey tried his best to have the CIA stop the prosecution, but to no avail. Roselli was convicted and sentenced to five years, with a concurrent six months on the alien-registration charge. He was released from prison in September 1973, but things were never the same again for Don Giovanni. On August 8, 1976 his body was found stuffed in a chain-wrapped oil drum floating in Biscayne Bay off Miami. The cause of death was asphyxiation and the modus operandi, said the police, clearly earmarked it as a "true gangland-style killing." But the police always say that when they don't know what else to say. Chances are we will never know the who or why of it.

But that was all in the future. Back in April 1961, Johnny Roselli was enjoying the best of both worlds.

I had met Johnny once briefly years before when Billy was at Warner's, but I had forgotten until Johnny reminded me of it that evening.

"Don't you remember," he said, acting surprised at my faulty memory, "I was standing with Briny Foy and I said you were prettier than Elizabeth Taylor."

I laughed. "How could I forget such a generous compliment. I happen to think she's a great beauty."

"Well, she's no match for you."

"What are you trying to do," Sam said, "turn her head?"

215

"A fact's a fact. Listen, I think I know something about beauty. I know Liz and I'm telling you this gal has it all over her."

"What else is new," Sam said, giving me a big wink.

At nine-thirty on the morning of May 3, I left by train for Washington. I had a drawing room and I was so tired after three days of vacationing in Miami that I slept nearly the whole way, arriving at seven the next morning. Evelyn had made my reservation at the Mayflower, room 484, and when I called her later that morning she said that "The President" would not be able to see me until the next day. Was that all right with me? I said it was and not to worry because I had friends staying at the hotel.

As it happened, Dick Elwood was at the Mayflower and that evening we went to dinner with a Colonel Jackson from the Pentagon. Dick was in electronics and did considerable business with the Pentagon. Whenever Jackson and a General Meyer came to California, both Dick and Bob Whittaker entertained them in the most lavish manner.

The next morning Evelyn called to say that "The President" would see me at four-thirty that afternoon. I don't know what happened to me, but Evelyn's emphasis on "The President" began to make me nervous. Suddenly, I didn't want to go to the White House. It was not anymore the place where Jack lived. It was an historic landmark where the President of the United States resided. What it was, in fact, was a monumental stumbling block. As I think back on it, I realize that I was intimidated by "The President" and the White House. As it got closer to the appointed time, my anticipation to see Jack became completely overtaken by my anxiety over what would happen once I got there. The anxiety gradually turned to anger. The next thing I knew I was having a tantrum.

Dick Elwood, who had come to visit with a friend, couldn't believe what was happening. "You ought to be ashamed of yourself," he said. "How many people get a chance to even go to the White House, much less be *invited by the President*."

"Don't lecture me," I said, pacing the room, "I'm not impressed."

I was growling and grumbling up to the time the cab drove up to the West Gate, which leads to the Oval Office, and I had to identify myself to the security officer. As the cab drove up to the door of the West Wing, the anger was replaced by shame. How could I have been so childish? I thought, "You really have a lot of gall pretending to be so blasé about going to the White House." I was impressed!

It was a humbling experience to walk through that door and to show my identification to the policeman seated at the desk near the entrance. I sat on a leather couch in the reception room beyond the policeman's desk and wondered what would happen next. I wondered if my hair was all right, if my lipstick was on straight, or if the skirt to my magenta Dior suit was wrinkled in the back.

A black man came out and escorted me into the Cabinet Room. I sat in one of the chairs that were lined up against one entire wall. "The President will be with you shortly," he said. I thanked him and a moment later I was alone in that big room and thinking, "What's happening?" My head was swimming. How in God's name were we ever going to be alone together?"

Then Jack walked in and I forgot all about "The President." I said, "Hello, Jack, how are you?"

"Great now that you're here," he said. "It's so good to see you!" He leaned over to kiss my cheek. He took my hand and sat down next to me. "What a way to end a day! You look ravishing."

I thanked him and we exchanged pleasantries for a few minutes. He said there was something he had to do that evening and would I please stay over until tomorrow? "I didn't want to tell you on the phone," he said, "because I was afraid you'd leave. That's why I had Evelyn arrange this meeting. Something came up that requires my immediate attention. I'm really sorry. Will you stay over?"

"Yes, I will," I said, and then I told him about my tantrum. How angry it made me having to come to the White

House and how ashamed of myself I had been when I came through the gate.

He laughed and I asked him how he was handling his job. He said, "Well, I don't know. I'm so busy I haven't had time to stop and find out."

"How do you like it, sitting up here on top of the mountain?"

"It depends. There are times when I'd prefer to be somewhere else."

It was not a serious conversation. It was just two people very pleased to see each other. I knew he was terribly busy and so after thirty or forty minutes, I stood up and he put his arms around me. "It's been a long time," he said. "Far too long. But we'll fix all that tomorrow. Can you come at one-fifteen?"

"I'll be here."

He looked at me a moment. "I had forgotten how beautiful you really are," he said.

"I hadn't forgotten how handsome you are!"

We kissed, only lightly, because Jack did not show a great deal of affection unless he was assured of privacy.

A White House car drove me back to the hotel. I called Dick Elwood the moment I walked into my room. I was so keyed up I had to talk to somebody or burst. It took hours and a little help from Jack Daniels to calm me down. I was so grateful that Dick was there. He was the perfect confidant. After all those months of depressions, I could feel myself getting really manic. I don't know how many times I went over every minute detail of that visit, and through it all Dick just sat there smiling as though he were hearing it for the first time.

At one o'clock on Saturday afternoon, a White House car picked me up at the Mayflower and brought me to the West Gate entrance. I waited in the reception room only a moment before a short stocky man came in and introduced himself. His name was Dave Powers and he would later tell me that it was his job to put The President to bed each night and to get him up each morning. He made it sound like it was a sacred trust. Whenever he intoned "The President," you had the feeling that church bells would start ringing and that people in great numbers would kneel as Dave, in his Boston ⁻Irish brogue, began with, "Our President, who art in heaven—" and not certain of the words, the people would murmur their response as they had learned to do in Church.

"The President will see you now," he said, "come with me."

As we walked down a hallway, Jack came out of the Oval Office and waited for us. There was a big smile on his face and I quickened my step.

"Finally," Jack said, putting his arm around my shoulder, "I've got you where I want you."

We went down another hallway and as Dave opened a door, Jack said, "How about a swim before lunch?"

I looked at the swimming pool and couldn't believe my eyes or my ears. "Not a chance," I said. "I didn't get all fixed up to go swimming."

"It will relax you," Jack said. "There's plenty of time. There's nothing like a swim to sharpen the appetite and loosen the old muscles."

"My old muscles are plenty loose and don't worry about my appetite. If you have to worry about something, worry about my hair."

"Dave, bring her a bathing cap."

"Don't bother, Dave."

"We have all styles of bathing caps and every size of bathing suits."

"I don't doubt it for a minute—thanks but no thanks."

Dave said, "I don't think you're going to convince her. She's not going to fall for your line."

After a little more kidding, Jack asked if I minded if he took a swim, and I said, "Please, be my guest."

"Dave, take Judy upstairs and fix her a nice drink."

"That's the first sensible suggestion I've heard today," I said.

"Let's hope it's not the last," Jack said, as Dave escorted me out of the room. We took the little elevator to the family quarters on the second floor. As we came into the living room I had a familiar feeling, for much of the furniture was from their Georgetown home. Dave handed me a drink and what happened next was also familiar. Like Kenny O'Donnell before him, Dave wanted to know everything about me and my family.

Luckily, Jack did not take a long swim. All of a sudden, he seemed to burst into the room. He looked at Dave and said, "Well, Dave, what do you think of my Judy?" Like that. Those were his exact words. Dave said, "She's a very fine lady, very fine lady, and she sure loves her family."

Jack had a daiquiri and we talked for a while before going into the dining room for lunch. Jack sat at the head of the table, with Dave on his left and I on his right. Lunch itself was most uninteresting—a cold soup and hamburgers. It struck me funny that Jack had to ask for the ketchup, which he proceeded to load on his hamburger. It doesn't matter where you live, you still have your same old basic taste.

Almost immediately Jack started pumping me for gossip, most of it directed at Frank. What was Frank doing? Was it true that he was seeing Janet Leigh? We went through the same old routine. I denied I knew any gossip and he insisted that I knew plenty. It went back and forth in a lighthearted way until Dave said, "You're not going to get anything out of her, I can see it!" Jack said, "Come on, now, Judy, just a smidgen, nothing shocking or disgraceful, just something amusing."

"As I've said before, Jack, pick up a movie magazine."

"Thanks a lot," he said, turning to Dave with a helpless gesture. "Doesn't she remind you of a career diplomat?"

When lunch was over, we went back into the living room and Dave excused himself, alluding to something or other that needed his attention. Then Jack said, "I want to show you the other rooms." He took me into their bedroom and again I noticed that the furniture was from the Georgetown house. The twin beds were on the right and we turned left, into a small alcove leading to another bedroom with a large double bed. There was a stereo in the alcove and Jack put on the music from Camelot.

220

We stood beside the bed and he put his arms around me. "What a way to spend Saturday afternoon," he said, hugging me. We were standing close to a window and I could see the Washington Monument in the distance. But directly below me was the south lawn, which is known as the President's Park, and it gave me the strangest feeling to be standing there in the arms of the man I knew as Jack, but that the whole world recognized as the thirty-fifth President of the United States.

Then he kissed me and I forgot about monuments and parks. It was not long before I went into the bathroom to undress. When I came out Jack was already in bed, lying on his back, and this was the first time that he remained completely on his back. He was having trouble with his back, but there is something about that position, if not arrived at naturally, that makes the woman feel that she is there just to satisfy the man.

At first that was not the feeling I had with Jack. Because of his back problem there were times when there was nothing else he could do. On this day, he held me, he kissed and caressed me, and gently maneuvered me into that position. By this time I was familiar enough with Jack to feel completely free and uninhibited in making love. At this point in a relationship, all positions are beautiful expressions of one's love. Whatever brings two people pleasure is beautiful. It is the only way it should be with lovers.

After making love, as I mentioned before, Jack said and did all the right things. He was so relaxed, so tranquil, so serene that he became an entirely different person. For that brief moment, I don't think Jack Kennedy had enough ambition to carry him an inch beyond that bed. The fire in the dynamo that so impressed the world had been momentarily banked and he was like any other man luxuriating in the warmth of a woman that had brought him pleasure.

We talked, we dozed, we casually caressed, but as time passed I began to feel uneasy. I felt I was not where I belonged; that when I left it would seem like it had never happened. The feeling of unreality that began then was something I was never able to shake whenever I was in the White House. It was fine when he came to see me. Then he was Jack, who had to find his own way home.

Finally, I said, "God, I have to go or I'm going to miss my plane."

"I wish you didn't have to leave," he said. "I wish you could be here in Washington all the time."

"I've thought of it," I said, "but it just wouldn't work out."

"Wouldn't you like to come to White House functions? I want to put your name on the list. You wouldn't have to come to all of them but at least you could select the ones you want. That way we would see each other a lot more often."

"Jack, I know it's an honor to be on that list, but you know I couldn't attend functions with your wife there. I've told you before, Jack, it's something that I just will not do."

"I know how you feel, but give it some thought, will you?"

"My God, Jack, I would be so uncomfortable. I couldn't survive one of those evenings."

We exhausted that subject, as we did so many others, without arriving at any real decision. By now I knew I would never make my plane to Chicago unless I got out of there in a hurry. Jack was not in the least perturbed. "Get dressed," he said, "I'll take care of everything." And, my God, did he ever.

A White House car zipped me to the Mayflower, and while I settled my account with the cashier, my bags were loaded in the car, and we made record time to National. I raced through the airport only to discover that not only were they holding the plane for me, but it had been called back to the terminal after it had started to taxi out to the runway. I have never received so many dirty looks in my life. Those were the days of bomb scares and people were terribly nervous about flying. When the plane returned to the terminal, everyone was thinking that something was wrong. Then I stepped into the plane and if looks could kill, that would have been it for me. The only amusing moment was when I noticed that Eunice Shriver was on the plane. It was the kind of irony that I could appreciate at that moment.

222

X

The plane landed in Chicago at six-forty. Actually I was on my way to Las Vegas, with an hour layover in Chicago— just enough time to have a drink with Sam and discuss the plan he had in mind. This trip was his idea. While in Miami I had told him about my experience with Jack Entratter at the Fontainebleau, and the fact that ever since then I had been *persona non grata* at the Sands. They were always sold out when I called for a reservation. But the main reason for going to the Sands was that Jerry Lewis was appearing in the Copa Room. "You're going to sit right up ringside with Joe, and if that doesn't make that little son of a bitch a nervous wreck, I'll eat my hat. This is your chance to get back at him. With you sitting there with Joe, he won't know what to expect."

As far as I was concerned, Jerry Lewis was a dead issue, but I could see that it was important for Sam to make this last gesture at squaring things for me. Also there was the matter of Jack Entratter. "I've had a little talk with Jack," Sam said, "and I don't think you'll have any more trouble at the Sands. In fact, Jack insisted on personally picking up your tab, and, listen, I don't want you disappointing him. Give him a chance to make it up to you."

Before going to the show the next morning, I had dinner at the Angus with Johnny Roselli and Joe Pignatello, who was now operating an Italian restaurant in Las Vegas.

Joe and I saw the late show and I doubt that Jerry ever had a more miserable time. Joe and I never took our eyes off him. We just stared and didn't laugh once. It was a terrible show.

Jerry doesn't function well when he's nervous. He spotted us almost immediately and from then on it was downhill all the way. He is a worrier and I am sure Sam was right. He didn't know what to expect.

After the show Joe had a good laugh. ''You really got back at him, didn't you?'' he said. ''Boy, just leave it to Sam. If you ever got a problem, just leave it to Sam. He knows how to fix things real good. You couldn't have done nothing better than that. The guy really panicked. He was sweating bullets. That was the longest show of his whole life.''

I left for Los Angeles the next day and was met at the airport by Dick Elwood. Since Travis's marriage and Dick's divorce coincided almost perfectly, Dick was now my closest male companion. Every single woman needs a Dick Elwood in her life. He is the man who is always available when you need an arm to lean on or a sympathetic ear. He is the escort who makes no demands, who loves you in his own quiet, patient way, hopefully awaiting the day when the man *you* love leaves you and he can move into the breach. It never occurs to him that you may never love him, no matter what happens to the man you love.

Knowing how Dick felt about me, I spent entirely too much time with him. I cared a great deal about him as a person, but I knew I could never love him. By remaining aloof, I think I fed that love he had for me—there was no way he was going to get over it. I was close and yet so far out of reach that I became an irresistible challenge to his male ego.

Dick was a sharp businessman, strong-willed, hard-headed, and tremendously well liked by all who knew him. I certainly enjoyed being with him. He moved in fast company. He worked hard and he played hard. Taking the lead from his wealthy friends in Palm Springs and Beverly Hills, he entertained lavishly on a regular basis.

Now that I knew Johnny Roselli, he began calling me quite regularly to inquire about my health and state of mind. I noticed that his calls were more frequent when I was not in contact with Sam, who would occasionally disappear for periods of time. Other times he would call and ask me to relay a message to Sam: "When you talk to Sam would you have him call me at such and such a place, at such and such a time." Then Sam would do the same thing. The first thing I knew I found myself relaying messages back and forth. But that was the extent of anything that I consciously did for them. Occasionally I would have dinner with Johnny and Genene, usually at Perino's. They treated Johnny like a king at Perino's. They were not as obsequious as the Singapore with Sam, but not too far removed from it.

I flew to New York with Dick on June 6. He was going to New York and from there to Washington on business. He had a reservation at the Plaza, but I couldn't get one. The hotel was booked solid for the entire summer. So I talked to Sam. "Don't worry about it," he said. "I'll make a reservation for you at the Lexington. When you get there, call Joe DiMaggio. It might take a couple of days but he'll get you into the Plaza."

I called DiMaggio and he said I could move into the Plaza on the eighth. My brother Allen was to join me on the thirteenth and I had already arranged to take him to the Bahamas as a high school graduation gift. But on the tenth, while he was entertaining friends in New York, Dick Elwood suffered a heart attack. I rushed to the hospital the moment his doctor called me. I visited him daily and after he was well enough to eat solid foods, I had the Plaza prepare a special lunch for him every day which I carried to him on those heavy silver platters.

When Allen arrived on the thirteenth, we both went to see Dick at the hospital. Allen liked Dick and he knew how I felt about helping a friend in trouble. I didn't know what to do. I didn't want to disappoint Allen because I knew how much he had looked forward to this trip. On the other hand, Dick needed to see a friendly face every day. Who else would bring him lunch from the Plaza? Allen solved my dilemma by saying that he would be just as happy staying in New York.

That evening we had dinner at the Round Table with Morris Levy and did the town until the early hours. On the fifteenth Morris gave a party at Birdland. It was Count Basie's opening, and there was a big celebration. We sat at a long table with about forty interesting characters. There were bottles of booze and mixers the whole length of the table. I was sitting between Morris and Allen, and across from Allen was a blonde in a low cut dress with a bosom that looked like it was the biggest silicone job on record. She looked like she was going to explode with every breath she took. She focused on Allen and his eyes were about ready to pop out of his head. Every time she moved I thought her plastic balloons were going to knock over the bottles sitting in the center of the table. The more nervous Allen became, the faster he drank. I didn't pay too much attention at first. I was enjoying Count Basie and Joe Williams. By the time I did realize what was going on, she was trying to get Allen up to her place, and he was falling completely apart—a six foot three bruiser turned to Jello. Suddenly I was coming on like mother hen, but every time I tried to talk to him all he'd say was, "Leave me alone." Finally I said, "Okay," and by now I was furious. "You're going to get rolled. That is, if you're lucky. Otherwise, you're going to get something a lot more painful."

"Leave me alone."

Morris kept glancing at me and shaking his head. "Will you leave the kid alone?" he said. "Let him enjoy himself, let him have a good time."

"What are you talking about," I whispered fiercely. "Have you looked at that thing?"

"That thing," he said, "happens to be a very sweet gal."

"Jesus!"

"Calm down. Everything's taken care of. It's my little graduation gift for the kid. She'll either make a man out of him or kill him trying."

After that I kept Allen's glass full. Before long he was gulping down straight Jack Daniels like it was Dr. Pepper. Around four o'clock a whole bunch of us loaded Allen into Morris's limousine, feet first. He was still saying, "leave me alone," but you had to pay close attention to make out the words. He sounded like his tongue was too big for his mouth.

While in New York I saw *Camelot* twice. It starred Richard Burton, Robert Goulet, and Julie Andrews, and I was just in love with it. Of course, the music had a special meaning for me. It was thrilling to sit in the darkness of that theater and dream my own version of *Camelot*.

Before going to New York that spring I leased a two-bedroom house in Malibu Colony for the summer. It was Dick Elwood's idea that a small group of friends spend the summer together. Dick leased a big old mansion that was right on the beach, and my house was across the street from his, so his friends used my tennis court and my friends used his beach. All the parties were held at Dick's place. Bob Whittaker was Dick's guest almost every weekend, and on many of those weekends they entertained colonels and generals from the Pentagon, with Colonel Don Jackson and General Lou Meyers frequent guests. There were a lot of pretty girls and wining and dining and extravagant presents. It was hard to say which came first, business or pleasure.

I had talked it over with Sam before taking the Malibu house.

"What do you think about it?" I asked.

"I'm not too sure," he said. "Are you going to be down there alone?"

"No. My brother Allen is spending the summer with me. He's going to take care of the place for me, sort of earn his room and board."

"I'd like for Johnny to look the place over from time to time."

"Why don't you come down and look it over yourself? It's really very nice."

"Not me," Sam said. "I'm staying out of California."

Sam had often told me that the Los Angeles police had the most relentless intelligence system in the country. It was impossible for him to come into any part of Southern California without being harassed.

Others who took houses in the Colony that summer included Albert and Joyce Linnick—everybody called him Albie, and he was a lawyer in Los Angeles; Paul and Renon Ross—he was a Hollywood publicity agent; Lionel and Louise Steinberg—I can't remember his specialty; Diane

227

Gussman and her husband who was seldom there—the house belonged to her family and she later sold it to Lana Turner.

It was a crazy drunken summer. From just the small group named above, there were two divorces and one suicide attempt. The worst tragedy was Dick Elwood. The change that came over him after his heart attack was shocking. He became a weakling overnight. He seemed to thrive on sympathy. He became a little cocker spaniel around me, sitting at my feet and whining all the time. He wanted me to love him and I couldn't stand even to look at him when he acted that way. It was pitiful the way he walked around moaning and groaning over me all the time. By the end of the summer everyone thought I was a real heel. They felt sorry for him. They didn't know about my relationship with Jack, and they would say, "She's always running off, just leaving him alone all the time." They thought we were lovers.

I became very impatient. His weakness disgusted me. I have a tendency to need strong people around me. If a man is wishy-washy with me, I will walk all over him. It's a bad trait but I can't help it. I respect strength. I don't like a bully, but if a man doesn't like what I'm doing, then let him speak up and we'll talk about it. I am not the strongest woman that ever lived but I can't stand a man who is weaker than I am.

His mooning over me was so grotesque that even my parents began referring to him as my "little puppy dog." I regret today that I treated him so badly. I wish I could have been more compassionate. But I was having my own problems that summer.

I was never at the beach for more than a week or two at a stretch, but whenever I was there the partying and drinking were constant. I think we were all drinking with a vengeance. I drank Jack Daniels until dinner and then I switched to Green Chartreuse, which is a hundred and ten proof, and drank it straight up. I gained more weight that summer than I ever had before. I wasn't fat—I could still wear a bathing suit without looking too terrible—but I wasn't Miss America either.

I remember waking up with some of the most horrendous hangovers. I could hear people on the tennis court and it sounded like a bomb going off every single time someone hit the ball. Besides the drinking, I was taking Percodan to kill the pain caused by adhesions from my operation. The day was divided into two parts—mornings and early afternoons were for sobering up, and the rest of the time was devoted to drinking.

One of Allen's eighteen-year-old school friends, who came down to spend a week with my brother while I was in Washington, ran away to San Francisco with Joyce Linnick. Joyce was thirty and had two small children—a girl and a boy who had cystic fibrosis. I was blamed for that marriage breaking up.

Johnny Roselli took Diane Gussman and me to dinner at Romanoff's one evening. After dinner we stopped at the bar for a drink and someone called out, "Hey, Campbell, what the hell are you doing here?" I nearly fell off the bar stool. I turned and it was Frank Sinatra. He was just beaming as he walked over to us.

"You look like you're in a good mood," I said.

"What do you mean by that crack, Campbell?" he said, narrowing his eyes to simulate anger. "Are you implying something nasty?"

"You better watch it, fella," Johnny said. "I don't think you realize who you're hustling here."

Frank raised his arms, executed a graceful salaam, and everybody laughed. The two men shook hands and we all went over to Frank's house for a nightcap. When we got back to the beach, Johnny asked to bunk on the sofa for the night, but not long after I was in bed, I heard him sneak out the front door and walk across the street to Diana's house. That was the second divorce.

Renon Ross was pregnant that summer and she and Paul were going through a terrible time. She was having emotional problems and Paul had no patience with her. She got drunk one night and ran into the ocean. The water was rough and it was pitch black. She was rescued two or three times before she became too exhausted to try again. There is no question in my mind that she would have drowned if someone hadn't gone in after her.

I saw Jack in the White House five times that summer but the most memorable visit was on August 8. I arrived in Washington the day before and as usual Evelyn had made my reservation at the Mayflower—room 353—and there was a "WH" notation on my bill indicating that the White House had requested the reservation. When I called her, she said Jack would see me for lunch the next day and that she would send a White House car.

The eighth was a Monday and it was hot in Washington. I wore an apple green Chanel style silk suit, with a straight skirt and a very simple square-cut jacket. Evelyn met me in the reception room and escorted me down the hallway past the Oval Office and around toward the main part of the White House. Jack and Dave Powers were standing together, near the pool area. Jack had his arms folded across his chest and watched me very intently as I walked toward him.

"Well, that's a nice quiet color to wear to the White House," he said.

He was smiling, but not enough to get away with that kind of a crack. "If you don't like it, I can always leave."

He laughed. "You look gorgeous!"

"Fine," I said, "but that's still no way to open a conversation."

"Really, Judy, I was giving you a compliment."

We kidded back and forth. He wanted to take a swim and again I refused. This time he passed it up. We went upstairs and sat around and talked for a while. He wanted to know if I was enjoying my summer at Malibu and I asked him how he was enjoying his at Hyannisport. He asked about Frank again, and although I felt that his interest in Frank was genuine, I found it a little annoying that I always seemed to remind him of Frank. Then as we walked into the dining room, he said, "Have you heard from Teddy?"

That stopped me. "You mean your brother?"

"Yes. Has Teddy called you?"

"Of course not," I said. "You should know that."

"Well, I just wondered."

Jack never forgot what Teddy had tried in Las Vegas.

Several times when we were in bed he said, "Boy, if Teddy only knew, he'd be eating his heart out." I think he got a big kick out of the fact that he had succeeded where Teddy had failed.

Just as we were finishing lunch, Jack said, "I want to ask you something that's quite serious." He paused, glanced at Dave, then looked directly at me. "Did you repeat a story to the effect that I had tried to get you into bed with another woman?"

I looked at him and almost died. The combination of being Irish and German is a disaster at such times. My temper flared instantly. It was inconceivable to me that he would approach this subject in front of Dave Powers. The way he phrased the question, his tone of voice, implied that I was lending credence to a malicious story someone had invented.

"Jack, you know damn well I would never repeat that story to anyone." Of course, I had told Dr. Sherman and Travis, and possibly Dick Elwood. It was the kind of thing I couldn't hold inside of me. I was so upset I had to talk to someone. I just couldn't stew in it alone. I have often wondered how Jack could have gotten that information. I must have discussed it on the telephone and now that I know as a fact that the FBI surveillance included wiretaps, that's another possibility.

At that moment, however, the very fact that Jack was right made me all the more furious. I said, "How dare you discuss this with me in front of *him*."

AUTHOR'S NOTE: "The only Campbell I know," Dave Powers told the press when the story broke in late 1975, "is chunky vegetable soup." Newsweek reported that Judy Campbell's name did not appear in Powers' White House logs. Yet when I interviewed Powers for my biography of J. Edgar Hoover, he had this to say about his record keeping: "Ken O'Donnell and I had the job of keeping the President on time. Every minute of the President's day in the While House is accounted for in these books. Now, when the President would leave the

I stood up, nearly knocking my chair over. "I'd really like to leave, Jack. I'm very upset about this."

"Well," he said, and seemed embarrassed, "I just wanted to talk to you about it. A story got back to me."

"Well, that's what you get when you want to hear gossip all the time. But I'm not going to discuss it with you. If you think I'm running around telling tales, then it's time we call it quits. Perhaps you should behave; you should conduct yourself in another way."

"Oh, Judy, please calm down a little."

"Listen, Jack, this stems from one place and that's you."

Jack stood up and came around the table. "Come in the other room," he said, taking my hand. "I want to talk to you."

Dave casually left the room. By now I knew what it meant when Jack said he wanted to talk to me. I let him lead me to the bedroom because I didn't know what else to do. I was fighting mad and yet I felt guilt and shame. And fear. How had the story gotten back to Jack? I had told three or four close friends in California, people I thought I could trust, and the story had gotten all the way back to the White House. It frightened me to contemplate what that involved.

We sat on the bed and he kissed me, but it was hopeless. I can't control my emotions that easily. I was in no mood for love. When he became more amorous, I said, "Jack, please, I can't—not after what just happened. I really would rather leave."

"Wait a couple of minutes, you'll feel better. I was so looking forward to this afternoon."

"You should have thought about that before embarrassing me like that in front of Dave. I just don't understand you, Jack. Why couldn't you have waited until we were alone? That would have been fine. But this way doesn't even make sense."

232

"I'm sorry, Judy, if I upset you. I feel very badly about it."

"You're damn lucky I didn't blurt out in front of Dave how I felt about your behavior that night. You made it sound like I was spreading lies about you."

"I'm really very sorry," he said.

"But I have more respect for you than to do something like that," I said, forging ahead, determined to say my piece at any cost. "And I have more respect for myself, too."

We talked it out, or I should say, I talked it out until I felt a little better about it. But I still wanted to leave. Finally, he said, "I think I'm going to take a nap. What would you like to do?"

"I'd like to leave."

"Would you let Dave show you through the White House?"

I agreed and we walked out to the living room and Dave was sitting there. Jack said he was going to take a nap and would Dave give me the grand tour. Dave said he would be delighted and he started out, all chipper like nothing had happened, rattling off historical data as we moved from room to room, but none of it was registering. We looked at portraits and at the dishes used by each president. I was not seeing or hearing anything, and finally I asked if he would get me a car because I was really tired and would he tell Jack that I would talk to him later.

"Oh, I wish you weren't so upset," he said. "Come on, walk around a little, you'll calm down. Let me show you the White House the way no tourist ever sees it."

"Thank you, but I really need to get back to my hotel and just think a little by myself."

All the way back to the hotel I kept telling myself that I was making too much out of it, but that didn't help either. I think I might have been more reasonable if I hadn't felt so guilty. If only he had gone about it more discreetly, I might have apologized because I knew I had talked out of turn. I knew I should have kept my big mouth shut. But coming out with it in front of Dave just got my back up. There was no reasoning with me after that. I was young and immature in so many ways, but even now I think it is human nature to look for ways of excusing one's own mistakes. I made a mistake and Jack made a mistake, but I forgot about mine and wouldn't let him forget about his. I wonder what Jack really thought about my tantrum. Did he realize I protested too much? If he did he never let on. But Jack, I suppose, was a pretty fair actor.

When Jack called later in the day, he seemed surprised that I hadn't come back with Dave to wait for him. I said I thought it was pretty obvious why I hadn't and he said, "The day sure didn't pan out the way I had planned it."

"Well, I'm not too impressed with your planning."

He asked if I was leaving and I said I hadn't made up my mind. "May I call you tomorrow?" I said yes and he paused a moment. "Any chance of your having dinner with me tomorrow evening?" "I don't know," I said. "Ask me again tomorrow. Maybe I will have calmed down a little."

Around eight o'clock that evening Sam knocked on my door and I nearly fainted when I saw him standing there with his son-in-law, Anthony Tisci, who was married to Bonnie—Tisci was then administrative aide to Congressman Roland Libonati. Sam was the last person in the world I ever expected to see in Washington. He had never mentioned ever going to Washington. I was pleased to see him but for the life of me I couldn't figure out what he was doing there or how he knew that I was there. Knowing what I know today, I should have been terrified.

I said hello and Sam sent Anthony on an errand before coming into the room. As soon as we were alone, I asked him what he was doing in Washington and he said he was attending to some business. When I inquired as to how he had found me, he just gave me that same little smile that said, "I've got ways of finding out." I should have been more suspicious of his actions. Instead I took it as a compliment. I was pleased at the lengths he would go to find me.

He wanted to go out to dinner but I suggested room service. He said that was fine because he couldn't stay long. I was relieved to see him after what had happened that afternoon. At that moment he was a joy to behold. He was so easy to handle: a little peck on the cheek, a little squeeze, and he was happy. The way Jack was behaving, and with Dick Elwood groveling at my feet, Sam was the only stable part of my life. I have said it before and I can't say it too often: he was there when I needed him; he solved my problems, he gave me wise counsel, he would have given me millions if I had asked for them—from what I now understand, he had the millions to give—and he never caused me any problems. Although he wanted a more intimate relationship, he didn't pressure me. When I think of it now, I realize it was all too ideal, all too studied and planned, but for me at that time Sam was winning his way into my heart.

I was in a better frame of mind when Jack called the next morning. We had a friendly chat and Jack made the right move. He said he wouldn't be able to see me that day, but could I make it on the twenty-fourth? I didn't want to be angry with him so I said I would be back on that date. By the time we hung up the relationship was back on an even keel.

I arrived back in Malibu on August 10 and two days later we had a sensational luau at Dick's place for about two hundred guests. The caterers, who also provided the entertainment, arrived early in the morning and cooked a pig in the sand. They fenced in a large area with bamboo, erected a dance floor, covered the ground with grass mats and with colored pillows to sit on, and everywhere were flowers and fresh fruit. There were sword and torch dances, and hula lessons for anyone brave enough to face the onslaught of inebriated critics. My parents came and had a great time. It was the best night of that whole summer.

On the fourteenth I was back in Chicago. I was at the Ambassador East nine days, and saw Sam every one of those days. A few days after I arrived, my mother called early one morning to say that my sister Jackie was in the hospital. She was pregnant and the doctor thought she was going to lose the baby. The whole family was frantic because she had had about five miscarriages and one in approximately the seventh month. She wanted a baby so desperately that if she lost another one I don't think that emotionally she would have been able to handle it. I wanted to come home but my mother advised against it.

Usually Sam picked me up around noon but I was beside myself after my mother hung up. So I called Sam. "I'm coming right over to get you," he said. "I don't want you to be alone." He was at the hotel within a half hour. Johnny Roselli was with him and we drove directly to the Armory. Once ensconced in Sam's booth with them on either side of me, Sam said, "I'm not going to let you think today."

The martinis started coming and Sam said, "Drink up, it's going to be a long day." We had left word with the hotel to switch my calls to the Armory. I think I talked myself out about Jackie in the first two hours. We were drinking head-to-head and after a while they were coming pretty fast. I was a pretty fair drinker but I have a good biological alarm system that slows me down when it gets a little too frantic. After a while I had three and four drinks lined up before me.

"Come on," Johnny said. "A little less talking and a lot more drinking."

By midafternoon, when we were all pretty well into our cups, Sam said, "Come on, let's get some fresh air." We piled into his little black car and the next thing I knew we were in Queen of Heaven Cemetery. Johnny and Sam started running around looking for the name Roselli on tombstones. Every time they found one, Johnny would say, "Ah, I remember him well," and would go into a long story about this uncle or that aunt, or niece or nephew, and it was a riot to see them having so much fun. "Ah, poor Uncle Giuseppe," Johnny said, waving us toward a large tombstone. "Died of lead poisoning. What a prince among men he was, my Uncle Giuseppe. Very rich, big man in olive oil and machine guns, wanted to put me through college, embalming college, but I preferred the other end of the business." That had them both going hysterical. I was laughing right along with them, but they knew something that made it much funnier. I had no idea that Johnny's real name was Filippo Sacco. It is quite possible that Johnny was trying to connect himself with fake relatives. I wonder if he tried to use some of those names when the FBI later got him on the alien registration charge.

It was a crazy day and by evening the news about Jackie was more encouraging. Although she was in the hospital several days, the baby was born later that month.

A couple of days later while I was riding with Sam, there was a show tune on the radio and he started after me to sing. He had been trying to get me to sing ever since I had mentioned that I had an operatic voice as a child.

"How do you expect me to do anything for you if you won't sing? How do I know you can carry a tune without a bucket?"

"I don't want you to do anything for me. And besides, what can you do for me?" I said, teasing him back.

"You'd be surprised what I can do for you."

"All right," I said, "I'll sing but only if you promise not to do anything—and to not mention it again. I'm sick of hearing about it."

"You've got my word."

It was a defiant type of singing. I was tired of being teased about it and I thought I'd show him once and for all. It was a light operatic show tune, and I started to sing along with the music. I hadn't sung in a long time, and I dreaded the high notes coming up. I have three separate ranges, and when I broke for a high note, Sam said, "Oh, that's falsetto." I stopped and looked at him. "What do you know?" We kidded about it, and he said, "You have a beautiful voice. Let's do something about it."

"Sam, you promised."

"Wouldn't you like to cut a record?"

"No!"

"Don't you want a career?"

"No. And must you always act the impresario?" I said this for a reason. The first time Sam saw some of my paintings at the Navarro he wanted to fill every restaurant in Chicago with them, and with outrageous price tags. They would have been sold if he had to buy them all himself. Sam wanted to create a career for me—acting, singing, painting, I could have had my choice. I think he truly felt that a career in the arts was the ultimate accomplishment.

My lack of interest puzzled him. Whatever Sam did for a living, he was a product of the work ethic. He couldn't understand a life of idle luxury. To paint was self-indulgent unless you put a price tag on it. Some people will tell you that work is good for you, but that is in the same category as exercise—it's good for *you* if *you* like it. As one comedian wisely observed, if everybody had the same taste, we'd all be killed in the rush.

When we got to Sam's house that day he took me to the basement kitchen-family room area and opened a door that was always kept locked. It led to a large room which he used as a den, and where he kept his safe. He opened it and took out a solid gold charm bracelet that had been his wife's. "You won't take diamonds," he said, "so how about a little trinket, something to remember me by."

"Thank you," I said, "it's beautiful."

"Well," he said, rubbing his hands in sheer delight, "I've finally got you to accept something without an argument."

August was my month for accepting gifts without an argument. Jack had something for me when I saw him on the twenty-fourth. The ritual was the same as before: Evelyn made the reservation at the Mayflower, arranged for the White House car, and Jack was waiting for me in the hallway near the Oval Office. This time, however, he was alone. Dave Powers was nowhere in sight. We went straight upstairs and had daiquiris which were brought out by the same black man who always waited on us. As soon as the drinks were served, Jack said, "I have something for you."

"Oh, oh," I said, "big chief has a little conscience medicine."

Jack leaned back in his chair and laughed, "God, you don't let loose very easily."

"I don't know what you're talking about."

"Just for that, I'm going to make you wait for it."

"That's not fair."

"It's something very special. I hope I can give it to you today."

"Oh, that's really cruel."

"There's not another one like it in the whole world."

"Well," I said, "why don't we have lunch and go talk this over in your private office."

"Great idea," he said, taking my arm to escort me into the dining room. I haven't the faintest notion what we had for lunch that day. Whatever it was, rest assured that it was bland and totally uninspired.

When we entered the bedroom I took a small Congressional directory from my purse and handed it to him. "Would you do me a favor," I said, "and sign this for my mother."

"Well, since you put it that way, how can I refuse? I think your mother is lovely. I have great sympathy for her. I can't understand how she ever raised such a brat."

"My God, you think my mother's lovely and feel for her. Can you imagine how I feel for your mother, who is a saint in my mother's eyes, having a son who misbehaves like you do."

We bantered back and forth while he walked over to the window and signed the book on the page opposite his picture. The signature is just a mish-mash. He could just as well have signed J. Edgar Hoover for all I know. Since then I have read that Jack's signature was never the same twice.

After he handed me the book he said, "Now, I have something for you!"

We both were in a light, happy mood, and I just looked at him, and we were standing beside the bed, and I said, "I know, Jack, you've given that to me before."

He roared with laughter. "That comes later. I really do have something for you."

He handed me a nicely wrapped box and inside was a velvet case. I took a deep breath and raised the lid. I almost fainted when I saw a large diamond and ruby brooch. The design was similar to a daisy with four rows of petals. Each petal was eighteen carat gold, and each had a cluster of nine or ten rubies in the center and about thirty full-cut diamonds set in platinum along the edge. I was speechless and confused. It was the same old problem: Where do you draw the line? I looked up and there was such a look of pride on his face that I knew there was no way in this world I could refuse it. This was his peace offering, his way of saying he was sorry, and I was touched deeply by it.

"Oh, Jack," I cried, putting my arms around his neck. "It's magnificent."

And it truly was magnificent. I have seen enough jewelry to know that it takes more than gold and precious stones to make something beautiful. Some of the most expensive jewelry can be the ugliest.

"I thought it would look beautiful on you."

"But why, Jack? You didn't have—"

"Just a minute," he said. "Things haven't gone the way I had hoped for us. It's my way of saying how much I care for you."

"But it's not necessary, Jack."

"As a rule I don't give a lot of presents," he said. "It's something I don't think about. But I wanted to do something special for you and I know how you feel about accepting gifts. Wear it and enjoy it. Let this remind you that if my intentions go astray from time to time, my heart is in the right place."

I was thrilled with it, delighted he thought this much about me. It was just a marvelous day. We lay in bed for the longest time after making love. He got the biggest kick when I jumped out of bed to get the brooch. I was just ecstatic about it and I kept opening the case and looking at it.

"Oh, I love you," he said, and it was like a wave of warmth washing over me.

Sometimes Jack would become wistful and talk about the constricting nature of his office. He seemed to yearn for the ordinary pleasures of the average mortal. He liked to walk in bare feet, to loaf around in old slacks and a sweatshirt, to go sailing, to feel the wind and sea on his face. There was a tremendous conflict going on within him. I think he had a natural desire to be just an elegant bum, to be on the sea under the sun, to play games and to make love. But there was this other drive for power and the two drives were in constant conflict. He was either running to or away from his job. The real problem came when he tried to run in both directions at the same time.

The job was keeping him away from me, and I was keeping him away from the job. I would tease him about loving his country more than me: "Well, you made your choice. I know where you stand—you love your country more than me."

"Just like a woman," he would say, "to put it in that light."

Whenever we fantasized about what he would like to show me, it was never Paris or Vienna; he was always going to take me someplace where we could be alone. I could understand that when I thought of what he had to cope with in that office. He was constantly surrounded by people, being clocked and watched all day long, until he had hardly a minute to himself. The time we spent together was not all that much in the framework of an eighteen-hour day in a seven-day week. It was a brief diversion, a momentary escape from organized bedlam. In a way, I was a refuge. He could hide from the rest of the world and have a good time doing it.

As I was leaving that day, I told Jack I would be at the Plaza until the thirty-first and he promised to see me if at all possible. He was commuting to Hyannis every weekend and he said he would drop over at the Plaza either on his way down or back from the Cape.

Dick Elwood was in Washington and that evening we went to dinner with General Lou Meyers. Throughout the summer, Dick had been forming a new company called Magnatronics—it had something to do with new transistorized military equipment. Dick had been discussing it with Jackson and Meyers, and he had been after me to become a member of the firm. He even had my name printed on business cards. As it turned out, he wanted me to present some papers about the company to Jack, and I didn't like the idea at all. I wanted to help him because I knew he was

241

having financial problems, but there was no chance that I would ever directly approach Jack. Dick indicated that it could mean quite a sum of money for me, and I told him, as I had from the very beginning, that I wanted nothing to do with his company. I did agree, however, to give the papers to Evelyn Lincoln.

Before leaving for New York the next morning, I called Evelyn. "I've got an envelope that a friend wanted me to present to Jack," I said, "but I would rather have you read it and decide whether it is something you want to give him." She said, "Fine, I'll arrange for them to expect you to come through the gate." I dropped it off on my way to the airport. I was in her office two minutes and that was the last I ever heard of it.

Suite 1529-31 at the Plaza was elegant. But instead of waiting in lonely splendor, I did what comes naturally for night people in New York. I dined late and drank until early morning. Whether it was The Colony or the Round Table, El Morocco or Birdland, the result was the same. It kept me from having to spend too much time with myself.

Even Jack was impressed with the size of the suite. "I could hide in here for a week," he said. "I must say this is an improvement on the first night I was here. There's room to breathe." He toured the whole place, inspected the kitchen, bounced on the bed, stretched out on the living room sofa and nibbled on hors d'oeuvres.

"Yes, I wish I could hide you for a month, but what about the guys in the hallway. Wouldn't you worry about them?"

"Depends on how preoccupied I am," he said, pulling me down on the sofa next to him. A moment later he picked up a magazine and began reading. I sat with my head on his shoulder. It was a comfortable intimacy. We kidded and kissed and as we grew more passionate love took its natural course—at the right moment we just naturally flowed into the bedroom.

There was nothing forced or awkward or vulgar about any of it. Time was the only enemy. He acted like he had all the time in the world. I was the one who watched the clock, always wondering how much time this busy man could spend

242

with me. Sooner or later, depending on where we were, one of us would have to leave. We would never spend a full night together. We often talked about that at the White House. "If only I could keep you right here, and have you waiting here for me when I came back. Then in the morning we could make love before breakfast, and after lunch, of course," And I'd say, "Oh, sure, and before and after dinner." It was a longing that could never be satisfied because of his other longing.

The happier the visit with Jack the greater was the emptiness afterward. My emotions were so mixed up. I felt fulfilled by his love and by my love for him and yet at the same time I was empty because that wonderful moment together was gone again until the next time—and when would that next time be? Toward the end of our relationship, even the phone calls began to irritate me. What good does it do to keep telephone contact with someone you care deeply about if you can't touch him, you can't see him? It is more emptiness.

I used to detach myself from the reality of his wife. Jackie Kennedy did not exist for me. I deceived myself into thinking that he rejected that part of his life; that he wanted to be with me but there was nothing he could do about her. That was my way of rationalizing, of being able to live with the situation. If one can live with emptiness? I wanted to love and be loved on a daily basis, but I was closing the door to that possibility. You can't find it by going with a married president, not in a million years.

XI

Throughout the fall of 1961, winter and spring of 1962, I continued to see Jack at the White House. The routine never varied except that in the evening the White House car deposited me at the East Gate, which is the one used by tourists in the daytime. Either Jack would meet me in the entrance hall near the door or an aide would escort me to the little elevator and Jack would be waiting in the family quarters. I would arrive at seven or eight, and we would have a couple of drinks before dinner, most often frozen daiquiris.

Evening was a more relaxed time for him. It seemed like his time was more his own. I don't ever remember anyone barging in with messages. The only interruption was the telephone. Nothing drastic ever happened; he never had to be called away. We would have a relaxed dinner, the usual meat-potato dish. Later we would make love and spend the rest of the time in bed. I was always the one who decided it was time to leave. I'd say, "It's getting late and I really think I should go," and he'd say, "Stay a little longer."

Some nights when he wasn't feeling too well, when his back was bothering him, you could tell it by his face. He looked haggard and worn. Gradually, over this long period of time, I began to notice a change in his attitude. I understood about the position he had to assume in lovemaking when his back was troubling him, but slowly he began excluding all other positions, until finally our lovemaking was reduced to this one position. It is impossible for me to pinpoint when I first realized it, because it was such a gradual process, but slowly I began to feel that he expected me to come into bed and just perform. There would be a moment of stillness when I came into bed and it was almost like he expected me to roll over and put my arms around him and make love to him. I knew I was through the minute I did that, which is a bad way to have to feel. Perhaps other women were that way with him, but that is against my nature.

I think that Jack's natural preference, which he had tried so hard to repress early in our relationship, was for the woman to be the aggressor in lovemaking. He wanted the woman to make love to him. I had sensed it for a long time. Sometimes I could almost feel him shake himself out of it when he felt me withdraw from him. He would look at me and reverse his action. He would roll over and kind of smile, as if to say, "I've got to meet you halfway or you're not going to make a move."

But the move that he did make was not spontaneous, and the feeling that I was there to service him began to really trouble me. I tried to excuse it. I realized that the pressures of the office were probably getting progressively more demanding. He had been sitting in that chair now for quite a while. The weight of his office was getting heavier on his shoulders, and he was changing. He wasn't as happy-go-lucky, not as relaxed and cheerful. He was somber, sometimes downright solemn. He would drift off into his own private world, and I could feel him a million miles away. He had more important things on his mind. The excuses that I invented didn't make me feel more sympathetic. I've always been overly sensitive about being rejected. I would instinctively draw back from him and he would ask me, "What's wrong?" And I would say, "If you're really not here with me, I'll leave."

Then he would come back from wherever he had been and apologize. Other times, when he was particularly tired, he would get short with me. "You're hard to please," he'd say. "You're absolutely right," I'd say. "I'm very demanding. When I'm on that plane tomorrow, I'm going to feel very guilty about having taken up so much of your time."

"Oh, Judy," he'd say, "I'm sorry. Please forgive me."

This conversation, with variations, happened several times.

By early 1962, I dreaded going to the White House. I wanted to see Jack, but not in that place.

What is strange to me is that Jack was a different person when away from the White House. For example, there was the evening in mid-November 1961 when he came to my apartment on North Flores. He had come to speak at a dinner at the Hollywood Palladium. I remember he had been in Texas the day before for the funeral of Sam Rayburn, and I think he had made a speech in Seattle just before going to Texas. He had called me in Palm Springs every day for a week to make sure that I would be in Los Angeles for his visit. He wanted me to attend the dinner and I said, "Shall I call Evelyn?" and he said, "No, I'll take care of everything."

Jerry Nathanson, who was in real estate and politics in Palm Springs, was seated next to me and Evelyn at a table that was directly in front of the speaker's dais. Whenever I caught Jack's eye, he would raise an eyebrow in recognition. After a while it became hysterically funny. I am sure Evelyn and Jerry wondered what was wrong with me. I am afraid that I don't remember a word that was spoken by anyone at that dinner. There is just something about a political dinner that trigger's some little mechanism in my ears that make the words bounce out before they can register on the brain.

For the first time since I had known Jack I did something that took him completely by surprise. Before I showed him through my apartment, I sat him down and handed him a pencil sketch of himself which I had done on canvas with the intention of later doing it in oils. He was floored by it. It seemed to shock him that I had taken the time to draw his picture. He was flattered by the compliment. That is how ingenuous he could be at times. Having painted a number of portraits, I think very few people are flattered by the image reflected by painters—or cameras, for that matter. I don't like photographs that look like me. I only like the ones that look glamorous and not like me at all. It's a natural reaction. Jack was vain in that he liked things to compliment him. So it was a compliment to me, too, that he liked the sketch. It's possible, of course, that he liked the idea that I was home thinking about him when he wasn't around. After Jack's reaction to the sketch, I just left it that way instead of going to oils.

I gave him a tour of my apartment and tried to mimic Dave Powers, describing various pieces of furniture and fixtures as though they were historical monuments. I took him into the bathroom and explained that many movie queens had sat on that throne. Jack immediately got into the act. He inspected closets and admired a hanger, a garment bag, making a great fuss over little things because it was not all that large an apartment.

Once in the bedroom, he completely ignored the bed—which was not easy. It was a massive bed with a tremendous headboard. The bedspread was a heavy beige brocade, and if not obvious in color, the bed was obvious in size. Jack walked around it like it wasn't even in his path. Then suddenly, "Hark! What have we here?" "Sire, this is a President-size bed, circa 1961, a mysterious contraption designed for the dubious pleasures of our ancient leader. As you will note, sire, it is grander than the less important king-size antique used by the limited rulers of the pre-atomic age. I beg thee not to sit on it, sire, for it is possessed of an evil spirit that makes the strongest men go ape."

Before the words were out of my mouth, Jack had me down on the bed, rolling and laughing. There was nothing wrong with his back that night. It was a joyous reunion, as though two lost lovers were meeting after a long separation. Before leaving that evening, he made me promise to come to Florida in late December.

This was my second visit to see Jack in Palm Beach. I had seen him in early spring that year, but that was before my first White House visit and at a time when he was still a neophyte at his job. Both times I was picked up in Miami and driven to the same house in Palm Beach which I have described as similar in appearance to Sam's place. It was the typical Floridian one-story-pastel-colored-upper-middle-class-subdivision-retirement-haven. The house Jack used was on a fairly flat area and near the water. There was a large green lawn, large swimming pool, and it was all enclosed by a shoulder-high wall.

I arrived around one that afternoon. Jacked opened the door and there was not another soul in sight. There may have been an army of Secret Service men hiding in the bushes and closets, but to the naked eye, we were completely alone. Jack was wearing light tan casual slacks, a yellow short sleeve sportshirt, and beige canvas shoes with no socks.

He was in great spirits as we strolled leisurely toward the water. He loved the sea. I don't think any man ever loved it more. When we came back some invisible cook had prepared a seafood salad. We sat at a glass-topped table which was almost identical to Sam's. It gave me a weird feeling.

I remember lying in bed with the windows wide open and the sun warm on our flesh. He couldn't have been more attentive and loving. It was an idyllic afternoon, one that left me with renewed hope for the future of our relationship. I was able to kid myself a little while longer about an impossible situation. The problems in my head and the emptiness in my chest would not disappear by becoming more deeply involved with a married President who could cheat on his wife but who was becoming irrevocably wedded to his job.

Again gradually, I got the feeling that he was planning for his family to be in the White House for quite some time. I think that's why he worried so about Teddy being immature. It was a concern of his that he expressed on numerous occasions. It was concern and not criticism. I can't recall specifically what it was that Teddy had done to cause this concern, but whatever it was, Teddy had failed in some areas of responsibility, and it had made a strong impression on Jack.

It was also my feeling that Jack was leaning less on the family and making more of his own decisions without the family pow-wow. His father had suffered a disabling stroke and Jack was almost totally his own man. I say this not from any political knowledge, but from the impressions I got from hundreds of casual conversations over a period of nearly two and a half years. For whatever it's worth, Jack believed in a Kennedy dynasty, and he was going to be the patriarch.

By this time, Jack was beginning to reflect the importance of the office. That was the feeling he conveyed to me. He became more impressed with the fact that he was the President. Not anybody around him, not his aides, not his advisers, not his father, not his family—*he* was the President. Whereas before it had always seemed like a joint effort. It may well be that he finally had to have that attitude because the responsibility did lie on his shoulders. When the problems came, they came to him. When something went wrong, it was his mistake. He became very sensitive about what was said about him. And sensitive about his appearance because he was unsure of himself in the way he looked and the way he dressed. This was a likeable quality. He was a handsome man and he was a charming man but still he was not a vain man.

Although he was feeling more important, he could conceal it. He could fool the best of them. He could be so humble when he didn't feel it, and he could charm the socks right out of your shoes. He had an incredible talent in that direction. He knew just what he could do with people.

I was not as aware of this talent in the beginning. That was something that started coming through after we became more comfortable with each other. It was like any other relationship. You see your mate differently after you've been intimate for a long time. You see him in good and bad moods, and when the pressures get heavy on him, you sometimes get the brunt of it at the least expected moment. I was seeing different sides of Jack. I was seeing a more real Jack. In the beginning, he was all charm and romance, just sweeping me right off my feet. When a romance is in first bloom, your total concentration is on the other person. You try to impress him; you want him to like everything about you. As you become more comfortable with each other, the concentration falters.

As he started to be more sure of me, I sensed that he was taking me for granted. He had won me over and I was going to stay won as long as he so desired. This feeling could have come from my own insecurities. There is no reason why he should have had to woo me constantly. Yet I didn't want to be a possession, someone he could command to appear in various places whenever the urge struck him.

I used to agonize over his phone calls. The tone was getting more imperious. He would call and say, "Can you be in Washington on Sunday?" Sometimes it was within a day's notice. Either I wasn't up to making a trip or I'd just gotten back from someplace, or I was in Palm Springs and I didn't want to leave. I didn't appreciate being beckoned. I realized he was probably in the middle of some world-shaking decision, and he didn't have time for polite amenities, but it didn't help my disposition. There were times when I really wanted to go, but I'd say no because his tone hit a wrong chord. He didn't have any patience with it at all. He wanted a reason and sometimes I was good at inventing excuses and other times I was very bad. I didn't think fast enough for him. He knew exactly what I was doing.

"Well," he would say, "if you don't want to come, then don't!" And hang up!

I would sit there and stew. I was angry and I was hurt. But I was becoming ambivalent about our relationship. If he called and I wasn't at my place he would call my mother, and she would call me, and sometimes I would avoid calling him back until the next day. When I did return his call, he would want to know what was wrong, and I would invent more excuses.

If I said it was too short notice, he would say, "You know what my time is. I have so little time to spare," and the attitude was that because he was the President, because he had so little time, I was supposed to jump every time he wanted to see me, and I found myself getting irritated with the situation. I would hang up after one of his calls and say to myself, "What the hell's the matter with you? What are you so tense about?" I realized that flying all the way across the country just to see him for two hours was not worth it. Being in love with him was becoming too much trouble.

After a while I began pushing the situation until I was

daring him to get mad at me and yet I didn't want it to end completely. I was so confused about everything that at certain times I felt guilty about the way I was treating Jack. I would think, "This is dumb, and what are you doing?" I'd call Jack and say I could be back at a certain time and leave the decision up to him. It never worked out on that basis, but at least I felt better about it.

Whenever Jack got short with me, my first instinct was to make him feel foolish, and a good way with a man in that position is to tell him he's acting like a child. I would say, "Don't be so childish." I'm afraid he didn't appreciate that at all.

For a long time he could still laugh at me and kid himself out of the doghouse, but by late spring 1962 he was less inclined to agree that he was being childish. I began avoiding his calls and avoided calling him back, and his calls became less frequent, but there was never any definite break-off point. I didn't know I no longer loved Jack until I realized I didn't care if I never saw him again. I didn't wake up one morning and say, "I no longer love Jack." It happened so gradually that I wasn't really aware that it was over until long after it had ended. It just dwindled away and at one point the telephone finally stopped ringing. The last conversation could have been, "Can you be here on Tuesday," and I said, "No, maybe in a couple of weeks." But that was at least three months after the March 22, 1962, White House luncheon between Jack and J. Edgar Hoover, who supposedly told the President of my relationship with Sam. The Senate committee's report states that "According to White House logs, the last telephone contact between the White House and the President's friend [me] occurred a few hours after the luncheon." The inference is that Jack immediately contacted me and said don't ever darken my door again. Nothing could be further from the truth. If what the committee says about the White House logs is in fact true, then it is pretty obvious that Hoover spoke to Jack about me. It is too much of a coincidence that it would happen on the same day. The only explanation I can offer is that our calls were either no longer recorded in the logs, or they have been deleted. The point is that Jack never mentioned any of this to me. I saw Jack in March and April and the calls did not stop until sometime in June. And they stopped, not because of any outside force, but because of natural attrition. The spectre of the White House killed the romance. Not J. Edgar Hoover.

XII

I found that I was happier with Sam. It was a more natural relationship. We spent days and weeks at a stretch together. There was that quality about Sam that made me feel that he would move mountains for me. He was a widower with a family, and in a sense I felt he was faithful. I didn't believe that any man was ever completely faithful to any woman, but whatever Sam may have been doing on his own, he managed quite well to create an illusion of fidelity.

In mid-October 1961 I leased a house in Palm Springs for three months. I kept my North Flores apartment and commuted quite regularly—that is, when I was in California. I got back to painting. That was when I did the sketch of Jack. By now there seemed to be countless people who knew about Jack. Complete strangers would come up and say, "Are *you* the Judy that's going with Jack Kennedy?" The "ladies" at the Racquet Club, particularly Gloria Cahn, who had a terrible crush on Jack, would always ask me about him. Gloria would be sitting by the pool and as I walked by, she would say in her bitchiest tone: "Been to Washington lately?" I would look directly at her and sweetly reply, "Oh yes, just returned." That was my way of turning the knife a little. The talk was going like wildfire. Even Walter Winchell got his two cents in. In his May 8, 1962, column, he wrote: "Judy Campbell of Palm Springs and Bevhills is Topic No. 1 in Romantic Political Circles."

It took such a long time to work up to an intimacy with Sam that I don't remember just when it happened. I always enjoyed being with Sam but now I was anticipating seeing him. I completely stopped thinking about Jack when I was with Sam.

I must say that Sam was entirely different in my eyes than anything reported in the press. He was so gentle with me. I have since read that he and Phyllis used to have rip-roaring battles. I never once had any kind of a battle with Sam, and I've got a pretty fair temper. I would be angry with him about one thing or another, but it never amounted to anything. He never abused me physically or mentally. If he got mad at me for any reason, or if my being upset over something annoyed him, he was silent. But it was a strong kind of no nonsense silence.

Only once did he walk out in anger. We were kissing and it became a little too passionate, which was something I had always tried to avoid, and when I refused to go any further, he walked out without saying a word. I left for New York the next morning, and no sooner had I walked into my room at the Plaza than he was on the phone apologizing. A moment later he had a piece of jewelry delivered to my room.

It was not long after this incident that we made love for the first time. He had become more difficult to restrain, but also it had reached the point where I wanted him to make love to me, and I wanted to make love to him. When it happened, it was that simple. Yet it had taken over a year and a half to get to that moment. For the first time since I had left Travis, I had my man with me when I woke up in the morning. Love with Sam was not as exciting as it had been with Jack, but it was gentle and tender and emotionally fulfilling. It left me with a comfortable feeling instead of a gnawing emptiness. I felt like I really knew how to handle Sam. Once we became intimate, Sam did not change with me, he didn't revert to some unreasonably possessive creature. If possible, he was more attentive.

Was Sam using me because I was the President's girl, as many writers have suggested? All I can say is that Sam had been after me to leave Jack for a long time. He would point out that Jack was married and try to make me understand the futility of the situation. Sam couldn't have been more delighted when I finally stopped seeing Jack. As I said, I had a hard time letting go of Jack. I liked the feeling that he was there and still wanted to see me. That's the way it was. I don't understand it when I look back on it. I guess Jack represented a form of emotional security.

Sam was not too thrilled the few times I saw Jack in 1962. Before we were intimate he would kid me about Jack, but now it wasn't funny anymore. I could tell by his silence that he didn't like it. But he listened when I explained that I was confused, that I needed time to work it out. He promised to be patient, but I knew it was eating away at him.

Sam wanted to show me Europe, but I was sensitive about traveling with a man who wasn't my husband. I didn't like the way it looked. I've always been overly concerned about appearances. Having been exposed to people in show business, I've seen what reporters can do to the most innocent situation, and I've seen what is done to situations that are not so innocent. It is shocking to see the lies the press can get away with. I could imagine what would have been written about my traveling in Europe with Sam Giancana. I think I was on a plane with Sam only twice the whole time I knew him. And that was twice too often as far as I was concerned. We never shared the same hotel suite. In New York we didn't even share the same hotels—mine was the Plaza, his was the Hampshire House. When he stayed the night, it was in my bed, and not I in his. I may have been involved with public figures, but I have always been a private person.

For example, several times Jack suggested that I fly with him on Air Force One. I could have met him at a certain point and we would have flown the rest of the way together. He had no qualms about asking me. It wasn't maybe it could be done this way or that way—he had it all worked out. But I knew I wouldn't be walking out with him. I would be hiding back there in the plane until the excitement of his exit had died down. That was so far out of character for me that instead of being flattered by the offer, I was insulted and told him so in no uncertain terms. But Jack could laugh at me at times like that. I think he just loved intrigue.

Whatever Sam's intentions may have been in the beginning, he fell in love with me. In a nice way he did become possessive. He wanted me to live in Chicago but I refused because I still wanted my independence. Whenever I was with him whether it was in Chicago, New York or Miami, and I talked of returning to California, his mood would change to one of displeasure. But instead of arguing about it he would say he had to leave for a while. A few hours later he would be back with some extravagant gift. "This is for the birthday I missed in 1958," he would say, or it was for prior Christmases, Easters, Valentine's Days—he would always have an excuse for the presents.

I could understand the pleasure Sam derived from giving me lovely presents. As I said, it makes me happy to give someone a present. But what do you give someone like Jack or Sam? They can go out and buy the world. One day I got this brainstorm. They both smoked Schimmilpenninck cigars, which are imported from Holland, and are quite thin and short. I went to a jeweler in Beverly Hills and had two solid gold cigar cases made and gave them each one.

In March 1962, I moved into a new apartment at 8401 Fountain Avenue. It was in a new four-story building with four large apartments on each floor. Johnny Roselli considered moving into the building himself. "Christ, with the both of us living here," he said, "this has got to be the safest place in town." He was referring to the FBI surveillance which intensified until they were watching our every move. "With the FBI watching it all the time," he said, "you don't have to worry about anybody breaking into your apartment." As it turned out, every apartment except mine was broken into during the time I lived there. The only burglars who ever broke into mine were FBI agents, and I caught them in the act.

I had left for lunch with Johnny at the Beverly Hills Brown Derby, when I realized that I had forgotten a piece of jewelry I wanted to have repaired. I drove back to my building and when I walked into my apartment, there were two men standing in the middle of my living room. I took a step back, ready to scream, as they both fumbled around for their

256

identification folders. When I saw they were FBI agents, I completely lost control over the situation. Instead of writing down their names and calling the Beverly Hills police, I screamed for them to leave. They were out of there so fast it took me a moment to realize that I was screaming in an empty room. When I told Johnny about it at lunch, his first question was whether I had recognized the agents. He advised me not to do anything about it until he had a chance to talk it over with someone. That evening, when I talked to Sam, his advice was to let Johnny handle it.

By the end of September that year I was again experiencing abdominal pain. I had been planning on going to Chicago for a long visit, and since I needed an extensive diagnostic examination, my doctor suggested Billings Hospital at the University of Chicago. I felt a little better when I arrived in Chicago and I postponed the examination.

Sam had to be in Florida on business and I went to join him at the Eden Roc. The day after I arrived Sam said, "Come on, I have to go somewhere." I had long since stopped asking where we were going. Whatever answer he gave me we would end up somewhere else. So I'd grab onto his arm and we would be off.

We came to a beautiful residential area and Sam stopped in front of a new house. It was a huge place, very modern, with lots of glass and stonework, and a swimming pool that was half indoors and half outdoors. It was very plush but not my cup of tea. I prefer older houses. I like warmth in a home. This was a Miami house, too cold, too stark.

"What do you think of it?" Sam asked.

"I think a lot could be done with it," I said, not know ng what he had in mind.

"Pretty swanky, don't you think?"

"Are you thinking of buying it?"

"I'll tell you something," he said. "I'll buy it if you decorate it for me."

I just jumped at that. I love interior decorating. I have done it for many friends. At one time I had checks printed up that said "Judith Campbell Interiors," so I could shop in wholesale houses. I even had my license. "That's something

I'd love to do," I said, and from the look on his face, I knew he thought he had me hooked.

He had a couple of aces up his sleeve. He played the first one when we got back to the hotel. We were having a drink and I said, "Are you really going to buy it?"

"Like I said, if you decorate it."

"You really know how to get to me."

"Yep, I figured that would please you," he said. "But there is one other condition—"

"I just knew it. What is it?"

"Well, if I buy it and you decorate it, you have to live in it."

"Sam, for God's sake, I don't want to live in Florida."

"No, wait, I want to give you the house. You only have to live in it when you want to, like in the winter when the weather's great here. Whatever you do, it'll be yours. I'll see that all the papers are in your name and I'll even pay the gift tax."

"Oh, no, the deal's off," I said.

"But why can't I give you something like this," he said, and I could see he was getting frustrated. "You can't buy it yourself."

He was getting frustrated and I was getting irritable. I would reach a point in a discussion where I didn't know how to handle it. It went around in circles until finally Sam gave up and said he had to go somewhere.

I took a hot bath and tried to calm down. I knew I hadn't heard the last of it. Sam was persistent. Sure enough, it came up again at dinner that evening. We covered the same ground, with the same result.

When we got back to my suite after dinner and a few drinks in a couple of bars, Sam said, "I want to talk to you seriously about this house."

I was exhausted. "Oh Sam, no more, please."

"No, I mean in another way," he said. "Would you live in it if we were married? Would you accept it as a wedding gift?"

That just about knocked me right off my feet. "That's not a fair question," I said, and I know my voice was shaking.

258

"Well, honey, I am asking you, and I know it's a stupid way of saying it, but will you marry me?"

To this day I don't know exactly what I said at that moment. I know I told him I needed time to think about it. I mentioned my disastrous marriage and my fears of getting married again. I know I brought up the fact that he had to be away so much of the time. I didn't think I could sit somewhere and wait for him. To me that was a lonely way of life.

Sam agreed that I should think about it. "You don't have to tell me now, you don't have to tell me tomorrow. I want you to think about it until you're sure of your decision."

After Sam left that night, that called for another hot tub. Deep down I knew I wasn't ready to get married. I didn't believe in marriage, not with the people I was seeing—there had to be something very wrong with it. I wished that Sam hadn't forced the situation. As things were we had a marvelous relationship. There was, for me I know, a total kind of fulfillment. I recalled how it had been before we were intimate. I was like a child going out to play; there was something shallow about it that I realized only after we became closer. There was a different feeling between us. The anxieties vanished. I knew I had been right in the choice I had made. Sam was the better man for me.

The way he treated me, the way he talked about his feelings for me, I knew that Sam loved me. He told me often enough. Sometimes I could feel him watching me for the longest time and then he would say, "You are really beautiful. Would you believe it, I really love you." Other times he would say, "What is this you think you've got? Who do you think you are? Why should I love you?" With Sam, "I love you," came out very often and in many different ways.

Feeling the way I did made my decision that much more difficult. Sam called around noontime and I invited him to my room for brunch.

"I'm not going to press you," he said, the moment I opened the door.

"Am I glad to hear that," I said, "because I've been thinking about it all night and it's troubling me."

"Okay," he said, and he was in a good mood, "not another word about it."

After we had eaten, he said, "Come on, I have to go somewhere." He headed straight for a jewelry store. "See anything you like?" he asked. I selected a pearl brooch and a pearl ring, and Sam picked a diamond watch for me, and all of a sudden I thought, "Oh, oh, what's going on?" He wasn't going to pressure me and here we are in a jewelry store. I felt like I was being set up for the slaughter. At any moment I expected him to buy an engagement ring. Sam excused himself and went in back with the owner. When he came out there was that little mischievous grin on his face.

He was up to something all right, as I discovered that evening when he picked me up for dinner.

"Ah, I see you're wearing your ring and brooch," he said, casually reaching into his pocket and handing me something wrapped in the jeweler's tissue paper. "Well, wear this too."

It was a diamond bracelet over forty carats, with the center diamond about two carats, and a circle of baguettes perfectly graduated in size all the way around it. It was the most delicate, the most exquisite bracelet I had ever seen.

I just about died. "Sam, you didn't—"

"No, I didn't. I just asked you to wear it, just wear it. Is that asking too much after what you've put me through?"

So I didn't say anything more about it. I didn't even thank him. I thought to myself, "Okay, but you're getting it back tonight." But I couldn't take my eyes off it all evening. When we returned to my room after dinner, I took it off and said, "You take it, Sam. I don't want to keep this in here all night."

"You're not supposed to give that back to me."

I started to say something and he stopped me. "Don't, it's too late, I'm too tired, and I can't argue with you. You be a good girl and accept it." And I did.

I wish I could have postponed my decision forever. But I knew that wasn't possible with a man like Sam. So when he called me the next day about going out to lunch, I invited him to my suite. "Oh, that doesn't sound good," he said.

Over lunch I told him that I had made a decision and in

light of it, I didn't know how I could keep the bracelet. "My God," he said, "you're not going to start in on that again."

"I love you, I know I love you," I said, "but I just can't see myself getting married right now."

"Okay, but why don't you think about it a little while longer."

"That wouldn't be fair, Sam, because I don't know when I can ever face the prospect of marriage. I don't like saying this because I don't know what's going to happen. I love seeing you and I love being with you, but marriage is out of the question. I just couldn't cope with it."

He was quiet for a while and he just looked at me—he would get a look on his face sometimes that I couldn't figure out. I couldn't tell whether he was angry or just thinking. It was a subtle, deceiving look that was a little unnerving. After a long silence, I said, "I'm sorry, Sam. I truly am."

"You don't have to be sorry," he said. "I'm sorry, but that's the way it goes."

No more was said about it, but I could tell that he felt rejected, and terribly disappointed. I didn't know what to do. His mood changed and he said he had to go out. When he called later in the day to make plans for dinner, I asked, "Are you all right?" "Yeah, I'm fine," he said, and he sounded like he had been drinking. Nothing more was ever said about it again. As I look back on it now, I can see that our relationship started on the road to dissolution on that day.

At the time I went into Billings, on October 10, Sam said he would be away but that John and Maryann Matassa would look after me. In the hospital it was discovered that I had a chronic kidney condition. After I was released, I moved into the Oak Park Arms to be closer to Sam, but I didn't see him for several days. Then one night I went out to dinner with the Matassas and two minutes after we sat down Sam walked in, a big smile on his face, and I thought that everything would be fine, but it was never again the same. He would take me to his home and to dinner, but the marvelous times of being together all day every day had stopped.

It was around that time that I first heard about his relationship with Phyllis McGuire. I read something in the paper and mentioned it to John Matassa. "Oh, I was hoping you wouldn't see that," he said. I pressed for more information and he said, "You mean to say you don't know anything about it." When I shook my head, he said, "Well, everybody else does."

That was as far as he would go and I didn't want to pursue it further. I didn't like the idea. It was a blow to my ego. To be honest, I felt I had Sam right in my pocket. He wanted to marry me and I had rejected him. This gave me a feeling of power, of being one up on him. But the minute I heard about Phyllis I felt that little twinge of jealousy. It bothered me but I was vain enough to think that Sam was purposely making me jealous, that it was just part of his plan to bring me around to marrying him. What I didn't realize was that Sam's vanity and ego were far superior to mine. For a long time I had the feeling that he was trying to teach me a lesson: "You're the one that's going to be sorry!" Rejection is hard for anyone to accept gracefully, but a man like Sam, with his money and power, had to find some way of maneuvering around it.

When we went out in the evening it was usually to the Villa Venice. That was when some of the top acts in the country were appearing there. It was there that Sam introduced me to Eddie Fisher. Sam and I were sitting in a small banquet room when Eddie came in to see Sam, who was in one of his aloof moods. The more Eddie talked the more apparent it became that Sam didn't like him. It got downright embarrassing. On the other hand it was equally apparent that Eddie had come to pay homage to Sam. Throughout dinner Eddie kept looking at me and finally he said, "You look like my wife Elizabeth." He said his wife, but at that time they were either separated or divorced.

"Careful," Sam said, "her head is big enough now."

"No, really, I mean it. She has the same kind of beauty as my wife Elizabeth."

Sam clanked his fork on his plate and gave Eddie a look that is impossible to describe. "Shut up, kid," he said, "too many people tell her things like that."

I couldn't believe my ears. It was not the words as much as the look and tone of voice that surprised me. Eddie just froze in his chair and I could feel my pulse throbbing in my temple. Then Sam laughed and Eddie was very quick on the upbeat. A moment later we were all laughing.

I saw Eddie's closing show with the Matassas. It was very schmaltzy with heart tugging songs. He brought the house down. Between shows that evening Eddie sat with us, and it came up in the conversation that I was going to New York for a few days. Eddie asked if he could contact me there and I said it was fine, but after he left I asked the Matassas about it. "That's okay," John said, "Sam won't mind."

I left for New York on November 28 and at Sam's suggestion I stayed at the Essex House. The first thing Eddie wanted to know when he called was whether Sam was in town and the next was if Sam would mind if we had dinner together. I said no to both questions and that evening I went with Eddie and Dr. Max Jacobson to the Plaza's Persian Room to see Robert Goulet.

Max Jacobson didn't lose any time telling me that he knew about my relationship with Jack. "The Secret Service really have their hands full tonight," he laughed. "They're not only following Jackie, who's in town to see me, but they're following Jack's girl who just happens to be with me."

That kind of talk hadn't surprised me in a long time. What did arouse my curiosity was his comment that Jackie was coming to see him. Then he proudly explained that he gave her shots, which he described as vitamins and enzymes. I have since read somewhere that Max also gave the shots to Jack and was with Jack in Russia during his historic meeting with Khrushchev.

My first experience with one of Max's shots came two nights later. Eddie and I went nearly two days straight without sleep. We talked our problems out, letting our hair down, and poor Eddie was torching for Elizabeth in the worst way—he had an ache for her that just wouldn't quit. In the process, we consumed an unhealthy quantity of alcohol and very little food. It hit me when Eddie was taking me back to the Essex House. Suddenly, I thought I was going to faint. "My God," I cried, "I don't know what's happening to me."

"Hold on," Eddie said, "I'm taking you right over to Max."

Max looked me over and said, "Don't worry about it, you're all right. It's just a combination of the medication for your kidneys, no sleep and the drinking. This will fix you right up."

He gave me the shot and I instantly felt fine. He never mentioned that it contained amphetamine. Eddie had left for the airport to catch a plane for Los Angeles, and I took a cab back to the hotel. There was a mixup about my messages—I had called earlier and had been told that I had about fifteen messages, but now there were none. For all I knew, Sam or the FBI had stolen them. I was upset about the messages and then suddenly I could feel myself beginning to panic. I was on the thirty-fifth floor and got this irresistible impulse to jump out. I suffer from acrophobia, but now all I could think of was running across the room and leaping through the window. I could visualize myself tumbling through the air screaming, and splashing on the street. I sat on the floor of the bathroom, which was the farthest point from the window, and I was shaking so hard my teeth were chattering.

The phone rang and I nearly jumped out of my skin. I crawled to the nightstand and picked up the receiver. It was Uncle Armand calling from the airport. "You'll probably think I'm crazy," I cried, "but I feel like I'm going to jump out the window." And I was holding onto the phone as though it were my last hope on earth. "Oh, you're going to be all right," Uncle Armand said. "Now don't worry about it, you're going to be just fine." He couldn't get off the phone fast enough.

Finally I called Max and he was there with a psychiatrist like a shot. When Max realized that it wasn't a psychological problem, he gave me a shot to counteract the other one. I calmed right down. He made me swallow one sleeping pill, left another one on the nightstand, and confiscated the rest. I must have slept fourteen hours.

I went back to Max's office the next day for an examination and he gave me another shot. I started feeling better, stronger, more active, really alive. I thought it was the vitamins and enzymes, but it really was amphetamine. Whenever I felt low, I got one of Max's shots. Sometimes it was once a day; at other times it was once a week, depending on my state of mind.

I was in good company. Besides Jackie and Jack Kennedy, some of his other patients included Jay Lerner, Johnny Mathis, Margaret Leighton, Andy Williams—a veritable Who's Who of the entertainment world.

Max tried to teach me how to administer my own shots—made me practice on an orange so I could get the feel of the pressure needed to stick the needle in my buttock—but I never could do it. So when I was in Chicago, Max would mail the medication to a Dr. Yacullo. In California, I would see Max's son, Tommy, who was a doctor in Canoga Park.

In the meantime I was in contact with Sam, and he was after me to return to Chicago. I went back on December 8 and moved into the Sahara. Instead of a suite I asked Sam to get me a single room, and he couldn't believe it. I didn't realize it then, but the shots were making me jumpy. I felt more secure in one room. I didn't have to worry about a second room. As a child I was always frightened by darkness, and now I could feel myself becoming more insecure at night. Whenever I went out with Sam I always had him search the room when we came back. After my experience at the Essex House, I wanted something small and close to the ground.

I have always been fascinated by the way the press labels restaurants and hotels owned by the underworld. It can be the finest place in town, but, as far as the press is concerned, it's always a syndicate joint. The Sahara was a new garish multimillion-dollar hotel on Mannheim Road, which was described in publicity brochures as a "little bit of Broadway, a little bit of Hollywood, and a whole lot of Miami Beach and Las Vegas."

Whatever it may have cost, or imitated, the Sahara was

strictly a joint because the man who operated it, Manny Skar, was the typical joint operator. Manny belonged in a sleazy carnival. He was a crude, coarse, vulgar, loud, fast-talking, boorish simpleton who made the criminals who stayed and dined at the hotel look classy by comparison.

During the two months I stayed at the Sahara I became very fond of his wife, Bea—we spent a good deal of time together, enough for me to know that she was a lovely woman. But I never could understand how she could love that ridiculous clown, this *mamzer*, who took sadistic pleasure in humiliating her in public. He had a mistress by the same name whom he called Bea One and he referred to his wife as Bea Two, and this was quite a funny joke to Manny. He took delight in showing their wedding picture to point out the size of Bea's nose before her plastic surgery. Bea took it all to heart and still she loved that little worm. Even after his enemies gunned him down in his car one night only moments after he had let Bea out in front of their apartment building, she mourned him for years.

It was a cold winter, with leaden skies and wind-driven snow. I spent days on end in my room.

Except for Sam and Bea, the only other person who was able to penetrate beyond the blankness of my mind was Tony Bennett. We had much in common. We are both shy, reserved people, not at all outgoing. His awkwardness, his discomfort, his not knowing what to do with his hands on stage has become part of his personality, his style as a performer. Once you know him, he is a very gentle, warm, sensitive, unpretentious human being.

While he was appearing at the Sahara, his room wasn't too far from mine and we got together a few times and talked about art. I remember one time I had a greeting card from Sam sitting up against the mirror. It was one of those silly little cards and Tony sketched it in a couple of seconds. He is a fine artist and he tried to encourage me to paint again. "The thing to do," he said, "is to sketch everything you see. Take your phone over there. Sit down and sketch it from every possible angle. You'll be amazed at how many differ-

266

ent shapes it presents. There's a hundred things in this room you could sketch, and all of them would present different problems depending on the time of day, on light and shadow, angle, perspective, and it's all fascinating once you really get into it." It was inspiring to think about, but I just couldn't muster the energy.

In a way, I was trying to make up my mind about whether to continue seeing Sam. I wasn't ready to go home. I wasn't ready to put all this behind me. I had to stay there to see what was going to happen. I suppose I wanted the decision to be made for me.

Sam and I were still intimate, but he never stayed the night anymore. He was pleasant enough when he was with me but it wasn't the same as before. I thought he was still playing the game of teaching me a lesson and that eventually things would work out.

At times I was convinced that there were other games being played. Ugly, frightening games. My room had been part of a suite but the connecting door was locked and Sam had promised me that the other room would not be rented. But some nights when my light was out, I could see a light coming from underneath the door. I would watch that light for hours, and sometimes a shadow would flicker across it and I was convinced there was someone in that room. Other times there would be a little tap or a bump on the wall, almost like an accidental sound, and I would have to talk to myself: "Stay calm, everything's all right, don't let your imagination run away with you."

When I couldn't stand my imagination any longer, I would call the manager and complain that someone was in the other room. "That's not possible," he would say, "we're not renting that room." "That's funny," I would say, "because the light's on in that room and I just saw a shadow underneath the door." "Oh, well, maybe someone just went in to check it." "At two in the morning?" "The room is checked periodically." I never got any other explanation.

I left for California on February 4, 1963, and on that day at least, Sam was his old self. My plane was leaving at

267

six-fifteen that evening, but John Matassa picked me up at the hotel early in the afternoon and brought me to a coffee shop where Sam was waiting for me. There was another man sitting with Sam in a booth, but the moment I sat down, two men walked in and sat at the counter.

"It's the Boy Scouts," Sam said, shaking his head in disgust. He pulled out a miniature camera that was hidden in a Zippo-type lighter. He winked at me, lifted the top of the lighter and sighted through a tiny viewer. Aiming it at the two men, Sam snapped their picture and lighted his cigar at the same time.

By this time, of course, the FBI were all over Sam. There were carloads of agents parked near his house, the Armory, the Villa Venice, the Fresh Meadows Golf Club, the Sahara, the Fontainebleau, even St. Bernadine's Church—wherever Sam went, the FBI was sure to go, en masse. And they did the same thing to me.

AUTHOR'S NOTE: *In June 1963, Giancana petitioned the federal court in Chicago for relief. He charged the FBI with harassing him by keeping his house under constant surveillance and by dogging his footsteps even on the golf course. "How would you like it," his attorney told the judge, "if you were on the eighteenth hole trying to line up a putt, and there were six FBI agents watching you?" Because of the surveillance, Sam's score often soared to 115, some twenty-odd strokes above his normal score.*

Federal Judge Richard D. Austin granted an injunction limiting surveillance to a single FBI automobile, parked at least a block away from Giancana's home, or a block behind when following his car. He further stipulated that a disinterested foursome must play between him and the agents whenever he went to a golf course. "I know there are some not interested in civil rights and not concerned with privacy who will in the future approve of this type of harassment," Austin stated in his opinion. "I cannot give my sanction."

The U.S. Circuit Court of Apeals thought otherwise: "Defendants in this case [FBI] are part of the executive department of the United States and they are not subject to supervision or direction by the courts as to how they shall perform the duties imposed by law upon them. . . . This would be an unwarranted interference and intrusion upon the discretion vested in this case. . . . For these reasons the preliminary injunction . . . shall be stayed pending further review thereof by this court." A year later, the appeals court vacated the injunction.

"If those two characters are in here," Sam said, "there's a bunch more around outside. "Come on," he said, "let's have some fun." Sam exchanged car keys with Matassa, and the plan was that John and the other man would take off in Sam's car. We went out and the two agents remained seated at the counter. The cars were in a huge parking lot, jam-packed with cars and people, which made it easier to switch them.

John and the other man roared out of there, tires screeching, and an FBI car was hell bent after them.

"We pulled a fast one," Sam laughed. But no sooner were we out of the parking lot than there was another FBI car after us. The chase that ensued was something out of *The French Connection*. We went around corners on two wheels, even up on the sidewalk a couple of times, and all the time Sam was yelling and whooping it up like a wild man. I think he was reliving the days when he was the fastest wheelman on the West Side.

"You're not scared, are you?"

"No," I cried, "it's great. Go faster!"

Dr. Yacullo had given me a shot that morning so I was in great spirits. (Unfortunately, it was not until years later that I discovered the shots contained amphetamine—naive me, I thought it was done with vitamins and enzymes.)

Suddenly, we came to a tire skidding stop behind a motel and Sam said, "We've lost the dummies!" We sat there for only a moment before Sam pulled out again. "The hell with

269

it," he said. "They know we're going to the airport, so let's give them a ride for their money."

And we were off again, with Sam whooping and slapping the steering wheel, and I whooping right along with him. After being cooped up for two months, I felt as frisky as a cub coming out of hibernation. That was probably the best time the FBI ever made going to O'Hare. There must have been four or five carloads of them at the airport. They were angry enough at this point to show themselves. They don't enjoy it when the prey plays games with them.

We got out of the car and Sam had his arm around me, smiling like he was having the time of his life. Although my legs were a little wobbly, I was smiling, determined never to let the FBI think that I was upset or afraid of anything, because that was giving them an edge they would use against me. I don't know about the rest of the Bureau, but I can tell you that I have no respect for the ones that hounded me to the very edge of my grave. Their behavior and tactics were ruthless. If they had suspected the smallest chink in my armor, they would have destroyed me on the spot. My motto was to keep my chin up and my upper lip stiff, but in the end it didn't work out quite that way.

We arrived at least an hour before my flight and naturally gravitated to the cocktail lounge. "I don't want you to worry," Sam said, "but they'll be on the plane with you. Is someone meeting you?" I said that my father would meet me, but that wasn't good enough for Sam. "Call him now and ask him to come right out to the plane. Have him tell them you're not feeling well and they'll let him meet you right at the door."

While I made my phone call, Sam went to talk to someone. When I came back he had another plan. We waited until almost flight time. Sam let me start down the ramp and then suddenly he was right behind me as I boarded the plane. I had never seen grown men scurry around like that before. Credentials were being flashed all over the place. Sam sat next to me and calmly carried on a conversation in a tone loud enough for at least six pairs of flapping ears to hear him.

270

"I just can't wait to get there," he said. "Now it's your turn to show me around."

"My mother will just love meeting you. She certainly has enjoyed you on the telephone."

Split seconds before the stewardess closed the door, Sam gave me a kiss on the cheek and darted out of the plane. It is impossible to describe the pandemonium that ensued—men frantically unbuckling seat belts, leaping out into the aisle, grabbing coats and briefcases, tripping and bumping into each other as they raced out of the plane.

Sam probably laughed all the way home. But for me, now alone on that plane, the harassment that would eventually lead me to a desperate suicide attempt was moving into its final stage.

XIII

I was followed, hounded, harassed, accosted, spied upon, intimidated, burglarized, embarrassed, humiliated, denigrated and, as I said, finally driven to the brink of death by the Federal Bureau of Investigation. Those were the days when special agents were thought of as Simon-pure guardians of our liberties. They followed me in cars with license plates that couldn't be traced through the Department of Motor Vehicles. They wiretapped my phone, my parents' phone, and only God and J. Edgar Hoover know who else's. They probably bugged every room I was ever in for more than two minutes. It was a cruel and relentless invasion of my person and privacy that kept scores of men illegally employed as burglars and eavesdroppers in an effort that must have cost millions and produced nothing of any value to anyone. They must have accumulated tons of reports and transcripts, all signifying nothing, and no doubt most of it long ago shredded. The only ones incriminated by the ''evidence'' were them.

My first reaction was, ''Who do they think they are? What do they think they are going to find out from me?'' I made up my mind that I would never talk to them. My other reaction was, ''Okay, Sam, I'm with you. If you have to fight them, I'll fight them, too.'' I remember once telling Sam about the FBI following my mother and me one day while we were shopping in Beverly Hills. They used three or four cars and you could see them talking over their little microphones.

''My mother really held up,'' I said, and I was so proud of

272

her. "She was just an old trouper. You have a strong supporter in my mother." That's the way I felt about the whole thing. If that made me a criminal, then so be it.

Sam laughed, getting a real kick out of it, because he just loved my mother. He reached into his wallet and handed me a business card. "Whenever anybody gets too nosey, show them this card," he said.

I looked at it and burst out laughing. In the center of the card was the word RETIRED, and at the four corners it read: NO ADDRESS . . . NO PHONE . . . NO MONEY . . . NO BUSINESS. On the back were these words: "Under the Fifth Amendment to the Constitution of the United States, I respectfully decline to answer, on the grounds that my answer may tend to incriminate me." I have kept that little card all these years because it was exactly the way I felt.

The FBI not only questioned all my friends, but I think they questioned anyone who had the misfortune of riding in an elevator with me. And they were such hypocrites. Special Agent Dodge questioned Betsy Duncan, who was one of Johnny's many girlfriends, and she said, "If you want to know anything about Judy Campbell, I know she just came back from the White House. Why don't you go ask the President." Dodge let it go right over his head, acting like he hadn't heard a word she said. That was early in 1962, when Hoover ordered that top priority investigation of me. When Betsy told Johnny, he thought it was the greatest thing he'd ever heard. He's the one who told me about it, and his comment was, "Good for her."

I became very clever on the phone with Sam and Johnny, having a conversation about nothing and yet telling them what was on my mind. In a way, I was like a citizen in Orwell's *1984*. I was living in a dictatorship where your every word and movement were monitored and filed away for future condemnation. Hoover was God and the special agents were his avenging angels, recording everything in that big ledger up in the sky so that some day St. Peter could consign me to the fires of hell for all eternity.

There came a time when I was convinced that Jack knew everything about me and that he knew about Sam and

Johnny, because I couldn't picture the FBI doing all this to me without his knowing about it. The more I thought about it, the more it bothered me that Jack had never once asked me for the names of any of the people I was seeing in Chicago, New York, Florida, or any of the other places I told him about. All he ever asked me about was Frank, and all he seemed to care about was Hollywood gossip. Didn't the Secret Service want to know if I was safe?

Believe me, it is easy to get paranoid when you are being watched day and night, and the watchers make sure you know you are being watched. It makes you suspicious of the most innocent gesture or remark, and it calls for a lot of breast beating and soul searching.

Returning to California after my stay at the Sahara, I went to the Racquet Club in Palm Springs to soak in the sun and think things over. I wasn't sure about Sam any more. I wasn't even sure I wanted to see him again. I knew I didn't want to go back to Chicago. That was an abnormal way to live. I was seeing only the people Sam knew. They treated me as Sam's girl, and if I just blinked an eye at someone, everybody had better stand up and shout. These thoughts were an indication of the way I was beginning to feel not only about Sam, but about my way of life. I was so tired of being hounded, but I didn't know what to do. How to stop it!

I left Palm Springs on March 6 to visit Tommy Jacobson. I was getting depressed and I needed a shot. I stayed overnight with my parents and the next morning I drove my mother's Thunderbird to Canoga Park, which is at the extreme western end of the San Fernando Valley, a good twenty miles from Beverly Hills. Guess who was waiting for me in the parking lot? I came out the front entrance and had to walk around to the parking lot behind the building. I was about halfway to my car when I heard someone yell, "Judy!" Since I knew so many of the people who visited Dr. Jacobson, I immediately turned to acknowledge the greeting. God, it was Dodge and his buddy coming at me from either side and they were about on top of me. "We'd like to talk to you about Sam Giancana and John Roselli." And they were waving their little folders with their badges and credentials in front of my face. I turned, got in my car and drove out of there without saying a word. Before now I had been accosted in familiar places—restaurants and stores I frequented—but here in this unexpected Godforsaken spot, it scared me more than ever.

All the way back home I tried to figure out how they knew I was there. I knew I hadn't been followed from my mother's home. FBI surveillance is not all that difficult to spot once you've been through it a couple of times. The only answer was that my parents' phone was tapped. Either that or Jacobson's.

I called Sam from a pay phone and he wanted to know if I was returning to Palm Springs. When I replied yes, he said, "Okay, someone will be in touch with you."

Back in Palm Springs I was immediately swept into the swing of it. The next evening I had dinner with Charles and Judy Offer—Charles was a wealthy banker—the Sontags, and Bo Bolinsky, who was then one of the Angels' hottest pitchers. In those days the Angels had their spring training camp in Palm Springs. Bo was a character. He should have been an actor instead of a ball player. He was tall and had this dark tan, but he was not the typical handsome man. He looked more like a good-looking boy. His problem was that his education had been neglected and he spoke with "dese, dose and dem" pretty much like some of the characters I had met at the Armory. But Bo had a flair; he was fun and charming, and pining something awful for Mamie Van Doren—he and Ray Anthony.

My life has either been woven in a blanket of coincidences, or it has been one monumental conspiracy. Frank Sinatra called on March 11 to invite me for dinner at his home. He said that Ruby and Connie (they owned Ruby's Dunes, the most fashionable restaurant in Palm Springs) would be there and asked if he could send his houseboy George to pick me up. I accepted the invitation but said I would drive my own car. An hour later, Sam called to ask if I would have Frank call him. When I told Frank about it that evening, he said, "Okay," and not another word. Although

275

Frank never mentioned Sam to me, Sam talked about Frank. Sam respected Frank and he liked the atmosphere around Frank. He knew Frank liked tough guys, and I've heard Sam say on numerous occasions that Frank was a frustrated gangster. Anyway, on that evening in Palm Springs, Frank was in his Dr. Jekyll mood which meant we had a pleasant relaxed evening.

The next evening I dined with Travis and his wife Carolyn, and Harry Gould, who was an executive with PepsiCola. Carolyn and I had worked out a momentary truce. The next night it was the Chi-Chi club with Jerry Nathanson, and so it went from night to night.

On the seventeenth I had dinner at Ruby's Dunes with Johnny Roselli and Peanuts Danolfo.

AUTHOR'S NOTE: *A former dealer in some of Moe Dalitz's old midwest illegal gambling operations, Nick "Peanuts" Danolfo's career at the Desert Inn improved considerably following a conclave of fourteen Mafia bosses, including Giancana, at the Jackpot Motel in 1960. Danolfo went from "host," a meaningless title, to general manager in one giant leap.*

To avoid being noticed leaving Las Vegas they had driven to Palm Springs in an old dilapidated car. Sam had sent them to tell me that Jimmy Cantillon would be handling my problem with the FBI. Jimmy Cantillon was Johnny's attorney in Los Angeles.

Jimmy is a good Irish Catholic boy with a taste for whiskey, a roving eye, and the face of an altar boy. But appearances can be deceiving. Jimmy can win you over in two seconds flat, yet he can be ruthless, cold, calculating and cruel at the time you need him most. Depending on some kind of reading on the meter in his head, Jimmy would either hum with enthusiasm when I needed him, or he just tried to fluff it off. The same set of circumstances on different days would receive opposite reactions. Jimmy was only available when it suited his purpose, whatever that may have been, from hour to hour. The reason I inherited his services, as I later discovered, was not because of my own problem with the FBI, but because a federal grand jury in Los Angeles was looking into organized crime.

Exactly eleven days after I gave Sam's message to Frank, I got the surprise of my life. That evening I went to see Bo pitch against the Cubs and then went on to the Key Club. They had pool tables and Bo, who was quite a pool player, had to sharpen his game for a charity match. We had a drink in the lounge and headed for the tables in the back. But as we walked past a closed door I heard voices, very faintly, and instantly knew that Sam was in that room. I got this terrible sinking feeling, but as Bo practiced, I kept telling myself that I was imagining it. It was nerves.

When Bo finished practicing we went back to the lounge and a moment later the door to the room opened and out came Frank, and right behind him was Sam, and some other men. My heart stopped beating when Sam looked directly at me and just walked past without a sign of recognition. The one thing that kept going through my head was that Sam knew I was seeing a lot of Bo and was not happy about it. It took a lot of Jack Daniels before I dropped off to sleep that night.

Sam worked in mysterious ways. He was on the phone the next day, acting like nothing had happened. I figured if he wasn't going to bring it up, I certainly wasn't. After the usual amenities, Sam said, "A friend will be in touch with you tomorrow about that business. He, and that other guy, should be able to take care of things for you. Any more problems just give me a call."

The friend turned out to be Sid Korshak, whom I had previously met with Sam in Chicago.

AUTHOR'S NOTE: *The underworld ties of Sidney R. Korshak are in every way as mysterious as those of Meyer Lansky. Born in 1907 and admitted to the practice of law in Illinois in 1930, his early background is pretty much a blank, except that he grew up on Chicago's West Side in the days when Al Capone ran the show in that town. As a young attorney, Korshak got to know a number of the Mob's captains and lieutenants, earning a reputation as a shrewd legal adviser, but there is no record of his ever being arrested. His close link to the gang was first revealed in 1943 during the celebrated movie extortion trial that sent John Roselli and six of his cohorts to prison. Willie Bioff, the stool pigeon in the melodrama (later murdered by a bomb), testified that he had been introduced to Sidney Korshak by Charles "Cherry Nose" Gioe, one of the defendants, as "our man." "Pay attention to him [Korshak]," Gioe had warned Bioff. "Remember, any message he may deliver to you is a message from us."*

Chicago columnist Irv Kupcinet, another good friend of Korshak, asserted that Korshak was undoubtedly the highest-paid attorney in the United States. This is especially impressive considering that Korshak does not practice law. He calls himself a labor-relations man, but the two most descriptive words would be "finder" and "fixer." Korshak has been involved in more "deals" than there is space in this book to recount. Somehow, whenever Korshak gets involved in any negotiation, his group usually comes out on top. His influence over the Teamsters' pension fund, over racetracks, Las Vegas hotels and casinos, the liquor industry, and the entertainment world, to name a few interests, are as mysterious as his ties to underworld bosses. The question today is not whether he has ties to them, but whether they have ties to him. It is quite possible that the tail is now wagging the dog.

I had seen Sid around the Racquet Club for years. He and his wife Bernice were very friendly with the Hollywood crowd.

We met at six for a drink in the bar at the Racquet Club and went on to Ruby's Dunes for dinner. Sid is tall, with a long face, large soft nose, and small eyes that never seem to blink. Everything about him is slow, deliberate, relentless. I had the feeling that he was just sitting back and watching and listening, and if it didn't go the way he wanted it to, he would just take his time and he would do something about it. No hurry. It can always be done—that kind of attitude. No one was going to stop him. No one was going to say anything unpleasant. No one was going to change his mind.

I was never afraid with Sam, but Sid frightened me. I could feel the power he wielded as he sat there watching me. This was not my first impression. It evolved over a series of meetings in Palm Springs, Las Vegas, and Beverly Hills.

That first night, after I had told him of my grievances against the FBI, he calmly informed me not to worry about it. It would be taken care of.

I was reaching a point where I didn't want much more to do with the situation. I would be loyal to Sam and Johnny because I had more feelings for them than I did for the FBI. I would have stuck up for them to my dying day. After what the FBI had done to me, I had no use for them. I wouldn't have talked to them even if Sam had been out to kill me.

At one point in our conversation I told Sid I knew Sam was in Palm Springs. "I don't like the idea that he came here without telling me," I said, "when he was on the phone with me just the day before."

Sid didn't even move his head. I had the feeling that my words were going into his little eyes instead of his ears. I had about as much chance of staring him down as I would have had with a lizard. "I don't like it at all," I repeated. I didn't say I was uneasy about it because that would be the last thing I would ever want Sid to think about me.

One day, Sid called and asked me to fly to Las Vegas so that we could talk. He had made all arrangements at the Riviera Hotel, with my suite down the hall from his. Vince Edwards was making his singing debut that evening, and I went with Sid, Stella Stevens, Betty Mahoney (one of Johnny's girlfriends), Tony Martin, and Allard Roen, an executive at the Desert Inn. I stayed three days and probably talked business with Sid three minutes.

Eddie Fisher started calling; we dated a few times and became good friends. Eddie was a great one with the phone when he got lonesome. I have a precious image of Eddie. It happened at his home one day when he was playing gin with Yul Brynner. Yul was smoking a huge black cigar and Eddie decided he'd light one. God bless him, he was such a little man, that cigar just overpowered him. He looked like a little kid smoking his daddy's cigar. Whenever I think of Eddie, I can see that cigar stuck in his face and I just have to smile.

On April 15, Eddie gave a cocktail party at Au Petit John in Beverly Hills. He had taken the place over completely and it was jampacked with people—even when he was having financial troubles, Eddie did things in a big way. After the cocktail party, he and I got into his limousine with Angie Dickinson and Alain Delon—we were going to Paramount Studios to see a private showing of *Come Blow Your Horn* which Eddie had arranged for his guests.

As soon as I was introduced to Angie, she let out a shriek: "You're Judy Campbell?" I told her I was and she said, "John has told me so much about you!" All I could say was, "Oh, really." At first I thought she meant John Roselli, but then I realized that she meant John Kennedy. She kept saying, "Oh, I'm so glad to meet you. I've heard so much about you."

After the movie the four of us went to LaScala with Bette Davis and her daughter, and again Angie started out on how much John had told her about me. I couldn't figure it out. Why would Jack Kennedy discuss me with Angie Dickinson? I had a lot of questions I would have liked answered, but there wasn't a chance I would discuss them with her.

I met Sid at his Beverly Hills office on the nineteenth—he had a small office on the second floor of a building that served as the reservation office for the Riviera Hotel. I said something to Sid that day that I will never forget. I was sick of the intrigue, of not knowing what was going on, fed up with men cheating on their wives—every husband I knew was making his grab at me if he got a chance. I was sick of conversations with Sam where I wasn't able to say anything on the phone. I couldn't blurt out something that was bothering me, everything had to be said in a roundabout way.

I looked at Sid and said, "You know what I want?" And

before he could answer, as if he would, I said, "I want some man to keep me!" I think he blinked. For a moment, I think I saw the wheels turning as he studied me with those little eyes. I did it deliberately just to see his reaction. It was the last thing in the world I wanted, but I was tired of all the shenanigans, of being kept in the dark. I wanted to throw a curve at somebody. I didn't know anything about any of them and they knew all about me, and it was bothering me. I felt like I was in a giant maze and they were watching me running around in circles.

Sid's reaction was to continue the conference for later in the afternoon. We would have cocktails in the Polo Lounge of the Beverly Hills Hotel. I kicked myself all the way to the hotel. I knew it would be repeated, but it is hard to explain the feeling I had when I said it. What I had wanted to say was, "Okay, all of you think I'm this way, let me throw a little shocker at you and see what you do." It was so totally out of character that I will never forget saying it.

I began spending more time at home, painting and ruminating about my situation. I was concerned about getting involved with other people. Some people, I realized, were afraid to be around me because of Sam. Others were avoiding me because the FBI had questioned them about me. I didn't like what was happening to me. My depressions became more frequent.

I developed female trouble and had a D&C on the morning of June 6. The next morning two FBI agents walked into my hospital room and accused me of having had an abortion. "A what?" I yelled, speaking to them for the first time since the day they had broken into my apartment. "An abortion," they repeated in unison. "You people are insane! I didn't have an abortion. How dare you walk in here and accuse me of that?" "Well," one of them said, "we think you did." They came at me from both sides of the bed, and they looked so menacing that I screamed out, "You get out of this room, right now!" "Take it easy, you're only helping yourself if you name the doctor who performed the abortion."

I think any female kind of operation does something to a woman's nervous system—there's a certain depression, a

281

helplessness, and I got hysterical. I started screaming for help.

They turned and walked slowly to the door. Before leaving one of them said, "I wonder if the little guy, Jacobson, did it?" He turned and there was the most hideous leer on his face. If I could have killed that man, I would have on the spot. There is nothing heinous about an abortion today, but in 1963, my God, it was the sin of the century. They knew precisely what they were doing when they falsely accused me of something like that. As far as I know, they never talked to Dr. Jacobson or to my gynecologist. It was just another ploy in their vicious cat-and-mouse game.

The surveillance intensified that summer. I went to visit my sister Jackie in Cardiff-by-the-Sea, which is near San Diego, and a friend of her husband, Dick Taylor, rented a car for me. In no time flat, the FBI were at the rental agency wanting to know who had rented the car they had seen me in. The men at the agency told Dick, "Jesus Christ, what's going on? Do you know the FBI have been here several times asking about you and about the car you rented for the girl, causing me as much a hassle as possible."

Dick drove me to Pasadena and I hid out at the Arroyo Inn. Jimmy Cantillon took a sudden interest in my case. I would either go to his office or he would come to Pasadena. I went back to Cardiff for a couple of days and then back to Pasadena. To put it bluntly, they had me trying to hide from the FBI wherever I went.

As I later discovered in a front page newspaper story, this was happening at a time when Sam and Phyllis were vacationing at Frank's Cal-Neva Lodge up in Lake Tahoe. The incident not only caused a big commotion in the press, but because of it Frank was forced to sell out his interests in Cal-Neva and the Sands. It seems that Sam's name was in a "black book" in Nevada and that meant he was *persona non grata* in any of the state's gambling places.

It gave me something to think about. I was still talking to Sam on the phone, but except for that brief glimpse of him at the Key Club, I had not seen him since February 4. As far as I was concerned, the romance had vanished as completely as

282

that winter's snow. For weeks, literally, I agonized over that damn diamond bracelet. I didn't want to send it back in the mail, nor did I want a confrontation with Sam, but suddenly, returning it to him seemed the most important thing in the world to me.

As it happened, I had left some jewelry in Chicago to be repaired, and so on September 29, I flew to Chicago and stayed with the Matassas overnight. The next morning I picked up my jewelry and John drove me to O'Hare. Just before boarding the plane I handed him the bracelet, which was gift wrapped, and asked him to give it to Sam. I was taking the coward's way out, but I didn't want any more meaningless arguments.

It was two or three days before Sam called, and I figured it probably had taken him that long to cool down. "You didn't have to do that," he said. "I know what you're thinking about, but none of it has anything to do with the bracelet. It was a gift and I know how much you love it. Would you keep it if I sent it back?"

"No, I don't want it back, Sam," I said. "It's not the kind of gift that I can keep. Our relationship was different when I accepted it. The less said about it now, the better."

For me, at that moment Sam sounded too reasonable. I guess I was getting cynical. After all, I would either be questioned by the grand jury or the FBI. No matter how interested he was in Phyllis, he wanted to keep me on his string. Perhaps my returning the bracelet made him think I was severing that connection.

I hastened to reassure him that I considered him a wonderful friend, that there would always be a warm place in my heart for him, and that whenever I had any problems he was the one I would call, because I valued his advice.

I continued hiding. Jimmy Cantillon moved me into the Airport Marina Hotel. Not only were the FBI looking for me to serve me with a summons to appear before the grand jury, but Jimmy and Johnny were keeping very close tabs on me. I was sick to death of it all, all those lonely nights in hotel rooms, and it began to dawn on me that I could go to jail. If the grand jury gave me immunity, and I took the Fifth

Amendment, as I knew I would, I could be imprisoned for contempt for the term of that grand jury. Jimmy didn't tell me that, but I was reading everything I could find on it; on the other hand, I didn't mention it to Jimmy, either. That was precisely what happened to Sam in Chicago two years later. They gave him immunity and he ended up serving a year in the Cook County Jail.

Someone worked a miracle. I didn't have to appear before the grand jury. As I look back on it now, I should have realized that there was no way the Justice Department would bring me before a grand jury and risk the possibility that my relationship with Jack would be revealed. I was never before a grand jury. Not in Chicago when Sam was jailed for contempt, not during Johnny's two trials in Los Angeles. I didn't know it then, but I had diplomatic immunity.

The questioning by the IRS and the FBI amounted to nothing. They never asked me anything about myself. The line of questioning was, "Do you know so-and-so?" One long list of meaningless names. "Did you ever see John Roselli and this so-and-so together?" "Do you know where John Roselli was on such and such a date?" They never asked me where I was on any date. Of course, I wouldn't have told them. I gave my name and took the Fifth Amendment on everything else, without a single objection from them. The interrogation, like the surveillance, was just another exercise in harassment. The questions were innocuous. They knew where Sam and Johnny were on the dates in question. They had been on top of them day and night. So I sat there with Jimmy and declined to answer silly questions from clerks, really, who were taking their orders from Washington. They didn't ask me about my income, my associates, my travels, my family, or my way of life. They treated me as though I had no existence of my own. The way I feel about it now, I think if I had volunteered to go before the grand jury they would have disbanded it—post haste.

AUTHOR'S NOTE: *At this point I would like to quote from an FBI document that has been in my files many years. It is dated October 23, 1963, and it is a report by Special*

Agents Andrew V. Furfaro and Clarence A. Turner. The subject of the report is Sidney R. Korshak. The opening paragraph reads:

"On this date, the witness appeared in the office of Assistant U.S. Attorney Thomas R. Sheridan to testify before the above agents, in lieu of appearing before the Federal Grand Jury which had subpoenaed him to appear on October 29, 1963. The interview was quite cordial and informal, and in most instances Mr. Korshak volunteered information without being asked."

If the report, which is five pages long, is a fair summary of the interrogation, then the information "volunteered" by Korshak was as innocuous as the questions propounded to Judy. Korshak talked about Jake Arvey's son, Irwin, whom he described as "presently a paranoid." Jake was "very ill" and had lost "¾ of his stomach," but Jake was still alive and kicking political asses at this writing.

Korshak was the "first person to be subpoenaed by the Kefauver committee to testify from Chicago," but "he was not asked to testify."

He admitted "he is a member of the Friars Club, but that he is not proud of, nor does he go near the place. That the Friars Club is a 'cesspool.' That the members are not a social and charitable fraternity but a collection of gamblers who wager on anything if the odds are right. That he suggested that they seal up the Friars."

In reference to the McClellan committee, "Robert Kennedy and Pierre Salinger appeared in his [Korshak's] office, and questioned him about sweetheart contracts between unions and management. He appeared before the committee for one hour, and Kennedy questioned him again, and then thanked him for appearing."

Korshak said "he represents racetracks in the Chicago area. Mervyn LeRoy called him one day before the expected employee strike at Hollywood Park and asked him to help. He went to Hollywood Park, and met *with twenty-eight attorneys from other racetracks, and union officials for the employees. The other attorneys resented his presence, but he was able to settle the strike for which he received a three year contract. He maintained that this wasn't a sweetheart contract but that he merely brought union and management into accord through some of his contacts."*

Korshak said he "was the legal counsel for the Duncan Parking Meter Company." He named some of his close friends (Dinah Shore, Cyd Charisse, Kirk Douglas, Debbie Reynolds, Harry Karl, etc.) and said "he uses his influence to get employment for his friends at the Riviera Hotel in Las Vegas. That he would rather not say anymore about Las Vegas."

Finally, when asked about one of the principal subjects of the investigation, he said he didn't "personally know" John Roselli, but that he knew about him. Not a word was said in the report about Sam Giancana or Judy Campbell.

On November 19 there was a confrontation with Dodge in Jimmy's office. Jimmy had told the FBI about the two special agents who had broken into my apartment and Dodge wanted me to identify them. They threatened to subpoena me if I didn't consent to the interview, and Jimmy said, "All right, but she will not answer a single question." Dodge looked directly at me and said, "Will you identify the two men you found in your apartment?" I looked at Jimmy and he said, "She will not." I didn't open my mouth once—Jimmy had given me strict instructions not to say a word. He never explained his reasoning, but I think he and Johnny wanted something to hold over their heads.

Johnny reserved a room for me at the Beverly Crest Hotel on November 20, two days before Jack was assassinated. I was sleeping when my mother called to tell me to turn on the television. I couldn't believe it. I buried myself in that room for days, and all I could think of was "My God, Jack is dead!"

My escape when I couldn't handle an emotional problem

286

was to stop eating and drink myself to sleep. It took very little liquor to keep me in a stupor when I didn't eat. I would wake up, take half a drink and go right back to sleep again. It was the only way I could blot it out of my consciousness. Otherwise the horror would start happening all over again. By staying in a stupor, I wasn't bothered by dreams. In a natural sleep I would have been dreaming, aware subconsciously that something was terribly wrong. Every time I woke up from my stupor, the shock was there, the horror repeated again, and I couldn't get past the fact that he was dead, and all that death implies—the awesome finality of it.

I couldn't think of myself in relation to him. All I could think about was him. And her! God my heart ached for her. That woman handled herself so magnificently—I think I ached as much for her as I did for him. She may have had the best possible medical attention, but there is just so much anybody else can do for you. The rest of it has to come from inside and her strength was indomitable.

It was years before I could get it out of my system. I would be doing well and suddenly I would fall apart. I would force myself out of it, acting as if nothing had happened, and again the grief would take over. It would overcome me at odd moments and I would stay home for days on end. The problem was that I never let myself go completely. I stopped myself from crying it out. I knew it was best to get a hurt out of your system, but I never allowed myself to do that. I think I was afraid of what might happen. Instead of purging myself, when my insides were just wrenched, I would put music on that fed that terrible sadness aching inside of me.

After five days went by without my answering the phone, Johnny became so concerned that he had the management admit him to my room. I didn't want to see him, but he patiently resisted me, until finally I agreed to have dinner with him. Except for what I had nibbled on from room service, this was my first meal in all that time.

The next day we drove to Palm Springs and stayed at Paul Ross's place, where Johnny's girl, Dorothy Towne, joined us. The only memorable moment about that trip was the day we went to the Canyon Country Club. Frank, Dean, and

287

about ten others were seated at a long table, and there was not one greeting from any of them. It gave me the weirdest feeling. I was with Johnny, Dorothy, and another couple, and it was as though the two groups were complete strangers. Whenever our paths crossed thereafter, I never again spoke to Frank or Dean.

Around mid-December I rented a house at 2314 San Ysidro, off Benedict Canyon, in Beverly Hills. It was a new house in a subdivision built going up a hill, on tiered lots, with the street curving at the top where it leveled off. Construction on the level part was just beginning, and that was where the FBI stationed themselves around the clock— they could look right down on me.

It was a two story house with the master bedroom upstairs, and the staircase was completely enclosed in glass on three sides. It was an impossible situation once the FBI zeroed in on me. If what the FBI did to me at that time was not a crime, then we live in a lawless land.

I became, quite literally, the victim in a Hitchcock melodrama. They were always there during the day but it was at night that they really became sinister. They made me a prisoner in my own house. Every time I went out I was accosted by agents in private and public places, intimidated and humiliated, until I was afraid to leave the house. There was always at least one car on top of the hill, and others would drive back and forth all night long, and blow their horns every time they passed my house. Others would park on the street near my house and they would turn their lights on whenever I was on the staircase. They became so aggressive that I began to fear for my life.

My brother Allen moved in with me for a while and I slept with a loaded gun on my bed. I had my mind made up. If anybody walked through that door I would fire point blank and ask questions later. Allen finally got so nervous he moved out, leaving me completely alone. After Allen left I stayed awake at night and watched the activity up and down the hill.

I became convinced they were deliberately trying to break

288

me down. From listening to my phone calls, and perhaps from electronic devices planted in my house, they knew that I was doing badly at this point. They were giving it that extra push to drive me over the edge. Jimmy Cantillon became very elusive, Sam was seldom available, and Johnny had vanished somewhere. (The intensity of their surveillance became apparent during Johnny's Friars trial. It came out in testimony that they knew where I was every minute of the day and night.)

Out of the blue, Johnny called to invite me to a New Year's Eve party at the Desert Inn. I jumped at the opportunity. I felt like a drowning woman being offered a life raft. The party was at the Desert Inn Country Club. I sat next to Johnny and his girlfriend—it was either Betty Mahoney or Dorothy Towne—and across from Moe Dalitz, who was introduced to me as the president of the hotel. Moe kept trying to get Johnny to tell him my name, and Johnny would laugh and not answer. I danced with Moe a couple of times and learning my name seemed to be his main preoccupation. Every time he asked me I smiled and pointed to Johnny, and it became quite a game.

The drinking was pretty heavy and it was a long noisy evening. As we were walking back to the hotel, with Johnny and his girlfriend ahead of Moe and me, I began arguing with Johnny, nothing serious, mainly taunting him about something. Moe turned me around and gently kissed me on the cheek, saying, "Come on, now, don't get so mad."

God, I hauled off and whacked him right across the face with all my might. Everybody froze as though a shot had been fired. Johnny looked at me and shook his head. "You know something," he said, "you must be crazy."

I was just as stunned as any of them. I had never done that before in my life.

Around noon the next day Johnny started banging on the connecting door to my room. When I opened it he was standing there with a big grin on his face. "Do you know who you smacked across the face last night?" I said, "I don't care who he is." Johnny doubled over laughing. "You're really crazy. Nobody smacks Moe Dalitz across the face. Christ, don't you know anything yet? Haven't you learned anything?'' He was preaching but laughing at the same time. He flopped into a chair. ''I couldn't believe it when I heard that crack,'' he howled. ''I was afraid to look. I thought he had smacked you and I would have to start picking up the pieces all over the place. Do you realize how hard you hit him? Jesus!'' He couldn't go on for a while. ''You should have seen the look on his face. You nearly knocked him flat on his ass. You pack a mean wallop, sweetheart!''

The next day I was back in my glass cage. Between January 2 and March 21 something happened to me that is almost impossible to explain. I became obsessed with the idea that the FBI would wait a certain length of time for me to commit suicide, but if I failed them, they would devise some diabolical means to kill me and make it look like suicide or an accident. I felt that any group of men capable of torturing me that way were capable of the most evil acts imaginable.

Gradually I began having difficulty going up the stairs. In the morning, after a night's vigil, I could barely lift my legs. I had to pick each leg up and place it on the next step. Later in the day I would be looser and could walk around without too much pain. My ankles swelled and turned fiery red, almost purple, and I sat and looked at them in total amazement, as though they belonged to someone else.

The periods of immobility began to last longer. Sometimes I felt so bad when I went to Dr. Jacobson's office that I couldn't lift my feet and had to take short, shuffling steps. After the shot I could move a little better, but after a while they made no difference at all.

One day I tried to brush my hair and realized I couldn't get my arm up. Another day I struggled to get my arm up but I couldn't close my fingers around the brush handle. If I gritted my teeth and really tried, the pain became excruciating. All my joints—ankles, knees, hips, shoulders, elbows, wrists, fingers—felt as though they had rusted shut. One afternoon I woke up—I had been up all night watching the activity on the hill, with the doors locked and the gun at my side—and discovered that I couldn't get out of bed. I was lying perfectly rigid. Luckily the phone was on my bed and after an enormous effort I managed to call my mother. I explained what was happening and I said, "Mom, the doors are locked but I will try to make it over to the balcony and drop the keys." It must have taken me over an hour to crawl the ten or so feet from my bed to the balcony. My mother and Allen were waiting below, their faces ashen as they watched me struggle the last few feet.

An ambulance took me to Valley Presbyterian. They recognized the symptoms right away—I had a high fever— and they put ice in my mouth, gave me a tremendous shot of Demerol, placed a cradle at the end of the bed and put a blanket over it. I couldn't stand even the weight of a blanket over me. They gave me Demerol every four hours at first, and then every three hours, which knocked me right out each time. Every so often they would change my position. The only time I was able to move by myself was during that brief moment between shots. I weighed barely a hundred pounds when I went into the hospital. For my height and bone structure, it meant that I looked like death warmed over. My normal weight then was one hundred twenty.

A neurosurgeon was called in to join a team of several doctors, and they gave me a series of tests. They found calcium deposits in all my joints, but the deposits in my ankles were so heavy that there was the possibility that I would never walk properly again.

My parents were blaming Dr. Jacobson's shots for my condition, and though I was afraid they were right, I didn't want to admit it to them. Besides I was in too much pain to think about it. After I told the doctors what I had gone through, they explained about the relationship between emotional stress and arthritis. If a person has a tendency toward arthritis, great emotional stress can sometimes trigger it.

It took five weeks for the swelling to go down, and during this entire period I was on Demerol. The day they released me my father said, "She's coming home and we're going to take care of her." He was furious at what he felt I had allowed to happen. When I left the hospital they gave me cortisone and twenty-six other kinds of pills, but no pain killers.

I began having withdrawal pains that evening and I called my doctor. "My God, do something for me, please! I'm going out of my mind." What he lacked in sympathy he made up in firmness. He said it was time for me to stop taking the pain killer. In other words, it was all right for me to scream my head off at home; in the hospital they like to keep things nice and quiet, even if it means discharging you from the hospital with a dependency created by the doctor.

For nearly two days I went through hell. Monsters came out of the walls. Cold sweat and nightmares in living color: men chasing me with daggers and guns, weird, grotesque images dancing and laughing, horror movies dredging up all the distorted fears buried in the darkest recesses of my feverish brain.

It took months for me to feel strong enough, mentally and physically, to venture out on my own. I was in pain but the unhappiness was the deepest hurt. Much of it stemmed from my inability to organize my life, to find a niche with meaning and stability. It wasn't that I wanted to relive the past. Jack was dead and Sam was out of my life. My problem was that I didn't know what or where I wanted to be. I was beginning to think that I was never going to fall in love deeply enough to ever risk marriage again. I didn't trust men. I wasn't a career woman. My most peaceful moments were when I was painting, but it takes more than peaceful moments to fulfill ones's life.

XIV

Early in January 1965, Dr. Krohn told me I was pregnant. My first thought was that it couldn't be possible, that somebody had made a terrible mistake. When it finally sank in, I thought seriously of an abortion. Friends suggested reputable doctors in Sweden and Japan. I even got my passport, but at the decisive moment I couldn't go through with it.

I went to Encinitas to stay with my sister Joan, who had recently been divorced, and I took long solitary walks on the beach, trying to gather the courage to tell my parents. Finally, I called my mother and both she and my father were unbelievable. She said, "We're coming right down to get you."

They moved me into their home and told me not to worry. They would be with me when I had my baby and they would take care of me. Despite all their concern I still became withdrawn, closing myself off in my room, not wanting to see or talk to anyone. I even stopped seeing Dr. Krohn because of the fear of running into someone I knew in his office. I became a recluse in my own home. I spent my days lying on the bed, staring up at the ceiling, my head buzzing in paralyzing turmoil. I couldn't think straight. Every thought was confused by five others. My only salvation was total blankness, which in a way is a form of self-hypnosis. I would stare at the light fixture, concentrating on one aspect of its configuration, blanking out everything else, and hours would vanish without a trace, day would turn into night. For sleep I would take Tuinal and continue that journey through my empty world.

One day when my father was out of town on business voices intruded into my blankness. It was an ominous and discordant sound. A moment later my mother opened the door and said, "Judy, two FBI men are here to see you."

My mother left the room and as I put on my robe I could feel the tightness in my chest, the trembling in my legs, that these confrontations always caused. As I came into the room, Dodge was showing my mother a picture of Johnny and the other agent was waiting to show her a picture of Sam. I went absolutely berserk. I screamed for them to leave and they just stood there. Dodge said, "All we want to do is talk to you and your mother about these men."

"Get out of here," I cried, "and if you ever bother my mother again, I'll kill you!"

My mother grabbed me before I could lunge at them. "Please, will you leave," she said, and still they stood there, with the pictures in their hands, mumbling, "But all we want to do is talk to you . . . "

I was hysterical by the time my mother got me back into my room. There is no way I can measure time for that moment. It may have been one or two days before I arrived at the crucial decision that my life was impossible. That the FBI would never leave me alone; that I could not bring up a child with the FBI hounding me; that it wasn't fair to the child to have him come into this kind of world— what would that child think of me; that I couldn't give him up. My situation had become so oppressive that I was completely irrational.

I sat on my bed, emptied a full bottle of Tuinal capsules into my hand and gulped them down. Just as I was sinking into that warm peaceful glow, my mother came into the room to say that Joan wanted to speak to me on the phone. I grinned and fumbled for the phone, my head so heavy I could barely lift it. The moment I spoke Joan knew something was wrong. That telephone call saved two lives.

I was taken to the hospital by ambulance and I remember vaguely waking up when the ambulance was backing into the hospital entry. Then I remember, again vaguely, being on a table with a huge light overhead and masked faces looking down at me. After that I was out for a day and a half.

Two months later, on May 28, 1965, my baby was born. He was a seven-month baby, but for the reasons stated in the Prologue to this book, I had made up my mind to find a good home for my son, a home where he would be protected from the hounding and persecution of the FBI.

It was a year before I could force myself to sign the adoption papers. I placed myself under the care of a psychiatrist, trying to find someone to give me the strength that would make it possible for me to give my child his chance in life. My whole family wanted to adopt him, but I knew that was no solution. I saw him only once in my whole life. One night I came to visit my mother, not knowing that he was with her, and I couldn't resist holding him. It made the final separation that much more painful, but now at least I knew that he was a sound, healthy boy, and that my suicide attempt had not harmed him in any way. That thought had tormented me for a year. My parents had told me he was fine, but I was so convinced that he was deformed I hadn't believed them.

The next day I signed the papers. My God, the terrible things my mother said to the women from the adoption agency. She wanted to kill those two women—but she was my mother and reacting as the child's grandmother.

I made my decision and I have had to live with it. I hope and pray that the sacrifice was not in vain, and that his identity will never be revealed. I have not forgotten him. I am forever longing to call the adoption agency to ask if anything has happened to him? Is he all right? Does he need anything? Can I do anything for him? Is he still alive? The anxiety is everpresent—it never leaves me. Yet I can honestly say that there are three things I know I did right in my lifetime: what I did for my child, what I did for my mother when she had cancer, and what I did for myself when I married Dan Exner.

XV

For seven months I was able to conceal from my mother the medical verdict that she was dying from cancer of the pancreas. Because her mother had died of cancer, also of the pancreas, my mother had been convinced she was going to die the same horrible death. If she had known she had cancer she would have lost her will to live. During all those agonizing months I was able to convince her that she was having trouble recuperating from a bladder operation. I never left the house. I was at her bedside every waking moment. Every morning I would find her crying and I would begin all over again to convince her that she was not dying, that she was going to be fine. Toward the end she started to vomit blood in the middle of the night. I would hold her through the convulsions and sit with her the rest of the night holding her hand. She died on April 7, 1971.

My father, who had been so strong all those years, could not accept the fact that she was dying. After she died he never forgave himself for his weakness. He would play her favorite music and collapse in tears. Not long after my mother's death, Dad was operated on for cancer of the prostate. We moved to Cardiff and I took care of him for the two years before he died. The two illnesses ruined him financially. I used all my funds and sold most of my jewelry and possessions to help defray the medical expenses.

It was in Cardiff that I met Dan. Until I met him I was a lost soul. If I could have gone to another planet to be away from all the people I had known in my lifetime, I would have gladly boarded that rocket ship. By then Dick Elwood was dead, Johnny was in prison, and Sam was living in exile in Mexico. I was alone, adrift in self-pity. I was still a night person, sleeping fitfully in the morning, and roaming the beach at night. More than once I was tempted to walk into the waves the way Renon Ross had done that night in Malibu. I would have succeeded because there was no one around to save me.

When I met Dan in the spring of 1973, he was playing golf every day, preparing to join the professional tour.

All the years of mistrust and indecision fell away when I got to know Dan. I fell in love so completely that I couldn't bear to be separated from him for a single moment. All the love that had been suppressed for so many years came pouring forth and it overwhelmed me. I had never known that love could heal aches and wounds and make you whole again.

We lived together nearly two years before we were married on May 20, 1975. He played golf every day from six in the morning until dark. Dan was accepted for the Florida minitour beginning in November. We purchased a motor home, put all of our furnishings and clothing into storage, and bought new golf wardrobes.

Dan drove the motor home to the golf course every morning, and I would sleep a little longer as he teed off at first light, long before the club was open. He would come back to the motor home around ten and I would fix something for him to eat, and then we would both go out and spend the day in the sun together. Because of the way we are with each other, it was an ideal life for the two of us. I loved every minute of it.

We were, to use a corny but apt phrase, in seventh heaven until the Senate committee issued its subpoena on September 12. There is not much sense in going over all the aggravation of the committee's intrusion into our lives, the arbitrary and belligerent attitude of their investigators and attorneys, which was equal in every way to that of the FBI and CIA agents they were supposedly investigating. As I said in the Prologue, they intimidated my sister and threatened to drag her forcefully to Washington unless she disclosed our whereabouts, creating the impression that we were in hiding when all the time were at my father-in-law's home, completely unaware of their interest in me. My name was now Exner, but that was hardly an alias.

My first awareness of the committee's existence was on June 19 when Sam was murdered in the basement kitchen of his Oak Park home. That was when I heard of his and Johnny's connection with the CIA, and the fact that Sam was killed a few days before he was to testify. I felt sorry for Sam but I never even dreamed that it could involve me.

Everything was so confused, so incredibly absurd. It would take another book to describe the sequence of events that finally resulted in our going to Washington on September 18. The next day Dan and I were ushered into a glass cubicle the size of a closet and introduced to Chief Counsel Frederick A. O. Schwarz, Jr., and Minority Counsel Curtis R. Smothers, who did most of the talking. He explained that he could not tell me exactly what it was they were going to discuss, but that it had something to do with President Kennedy, John Roselli and Sam Giancana.

After this briefing we were taken to another building and introduced to our committee-appointed attorney. Although Senator Towers had promised Dan we would have our choice of one of five prominent attorneys, there stood Henry A. Hupschman, barely out of law school, who served us well, but neglected at that moment to mention that he was with Sargent Shriver's law firm. When I told him I had a suitcase full of records and diaries covering those years, he asked if there was anything in my records relating to CIA assassination plots. I said, "Absolutely not," and he replied, "Well, then it's immaterial, and don't say anything about it." His position was that all questions should be answered with a yes or no, and nothing should be volunteered.

The next session was in Senator Towers' inner office, but Towers was not present. Schwarz, Smothers, and about six other staffers were there, but we never saw any member of the committee. I was so upset that I was sick inside. Dan held my hand and I was so grateful he was there with me. I couldn't have handled it without him.

The entire line of questioning, as best I could figure out, was directed at whether I had affairs with the men on their list. At one point, they asked Dan to leave the room because some of the questions would relate to classified documents. I could see the words TOP SECRET stamped across the papers, but the questions were the same as before. Every time they asked me about someone, the questioner would say, "Was he also a *friend?*" and the manner in which it was said left no doubt of the inference—*friend* was their euphemism for lover. I wanted to explain, but I had been warned not to volunteer information. So I answered yes or no but I knew what was going on in their heads and probably going down for the record.

That is another reason, along with those stated in the Prologue, why this book had to be written. For me, after all the years of harassment, the Senate committee was more than just another intrusion into my privacy. If they didn't start out to destroy the life we were building for each other, the result was nonetheless the same.

The notoriety that followed the committee's leaking of distorted and out of context information not only made the golf tour impossible, but it placed our very lives in jeopardy. No one really knows why Sam was murdered, or Jack, for that matter, and now Johnny. Life in the underworld of crime and the netherworld of politics is cheap. From what I have observed, it is impossible to tell the good men from the bad; all I can say is that some people are deadly serious about the games they play.

If my life has taught me anything, it is that I am a survivor. After what has happened to me, I am fortunate that I can still trust people, that I can still feel friendship and love for others. I thank God for Dan. Because of him I am stronger. The heartaches for my son, for my mother, for my father, are still there. But they are more bearable with Dan at my side. He gives me strength and hope for the future.

Bibliography

Books and Movies Actually Cited

BOOKS

Andersen, Christopher, "*Jack and Jackie, Portrait of an American Marriage*", (1996), ISBN 0380730316

Bradford, Sarah, "*America's Queen: The Life of Jacqueline Kennedy Onassis*" (2000) ISBN 0141002204

Bryant, Traphes, "*Dog Days in the White House*"

Exner, Judith, "*My Story*"

Fratianno, Jimmy "The Weasel", "*The Last Mafioso*", as told to Ovid Demaris

Giancana, Antoinette, "*JFK And Sam: The Connection Between the Giancana And Kennedy Assassinations*"

Giancana, Antoinette, *Mafia Princess: Growing Up in Sam Giancana's Family* (1984)

Hersh, Seymour M., "*The Dark Side of Camelot*"

Jacobs, George, "*Mr. S: My Life with Frank Sinatra*" (2003)

Kelley, Kitty, "*His Way: The Unauthorized Biography of Frank Sinatra*"

Lawrence, D. H., "*Lady Chatterley's Lover*"

Leamer, Laurence, "*The Kennedy Women*" ISBN 0449911713

Mailer, Norman, "*Harlot's Ghost*" (1962) ISBN 0345379659

Miller, Henry, "*Tropic of Cancer*", Grove Press

O'Brien, Michael, "*John F. Kennedy, A Biography*"

Parks, Lillian Rogers, "*My Thirty Years Backstairs at the White House*" with journalist Frances Spatz Leighton.

Russo, Gus, "*Supermob: How Sidney Korshak and His Criminal Associates Became America's Hidden Power Brokers*"

Safire, William, December 16, 1975 in *The New York Times*

Safire, William, *The New York Times* in article entitled *"The President's Friend"*

Sinatra, Tina, *"My Father's Daughter: A Memoir"*

Summers, Anthony and Robbyn Swan, *"Sinatra: The Life"*, a chapter in this book entitled *"The Candidate and the Courtesan"*

Newspapers and Magazines

Anderson, Jack, columns in the Washington Post dated January 18, 1970 entitled *"6 Attempts to Kill Castro Laid to CIA"* and in the subsequent column dated February 23, 1971 entitled *"Castro Stalker worked for the CIA"*

Los Angeles Times, December 18, 1975, *"John Kennedy's Mystery Woman Tells Her Story"*

"Movie Stars Parade" magazine, August, 1955

Kelley, Kitty, *People* magazine, February 29, 1988

Time Magazine, December 29, 1975, *"Scandals: J.F.K. And the Mobsters' Moll"*. Companion article entitled *"Jack Kennedy's Other Women"*

Washington Post on November 16, 1975 on page 6A, *"Probers Doubt Kennedy Knew of Poison Plot Against Castro"*

Court Decisions

Giancana v. United States, 352 F.2d 921 (C. A. 7th Cir.), *cert. denied*, 382 US 959 (1965), cited in *Shillitani v. United States*, 384 U.S. 364 (1966)

Furman vs. Georgia, 408 U.S. 238 (1972)

Loving vs. Virginia, 388 U.S. 1 (1967)

MOVIES

"Backstairs at the White House" (1979) starring Olivia Cole and Leslie Uggams

"Bob & Carol & Ted & Alice" (1969) starring Natalie Wood and Elliott Gould

"Camelot" Lerner and Loewe Musical (1960)

"Can-Can" (1960) starring Frank Sinatra, Shirley MacLaine, Maurice Chevalier, Louis Jourdan and Juliet Prowse

"Cell 2455, Death Row" (1955) starring William Campbell and Marian Carr

"Forrest Gump" (1994) starring Tom Hanks

"The Front" (1976) starring Woody Allen

"The Ladies Man" (1961) starring Jerry Lewis

"Love Me Tender" (1956) starring Richard Egan, Debra Paget, Elvis Presley, William Campbell

"The Manchurian Candidate" (2004) starring Denzel Washington, Liev Schreiber and Meryl Streep

"The Naked and the Dead" (1958) starring Aldo Ray, Cliff Robinson and William Campbell

"Ocean's Eleven" (1960) starring Frank Sinatra, Dean Martin, Sammy Davis, Peter Lawford, Joey Bishop, Angie Dickinson, Shirley MacLaine and Cesar Romero

"Power and Beauty" (2002) starring Natasha Henstridge, Kevin Anderson and Peter Friedman

"The Rat Pack" (1998) starring Ray Liotta, Joe Mantegna, Don Cheadle, Angus Macfadyen and William Petersen

"Rebel Without a Cause" (1955) starring Natalie Wood, James Dean

"Rio Bravo" (1959) starring John Wayne, Dean Martin, Ricky Nelson and Angie Dickinson

"Sailor Beware" (1952) starring Dean Martin and Jerry Lewis

"The Seven Little Foys" (1955) starring Bob Hope

"Star Trek" series, with William Campbell as Klingon Captain Koloth

"Sugartime" (1995) starring John Turturro and Mary-Louise Parker

"West Side Story" (1961) starring Natalie Wood and Rita Moreno